Backstage Pass
SEPT 10 1972
LAS VEGAS CONVENTION CENTER

AGE PASS

ROBIN TROWER
&
HUMBLE

HUMBLE PIE

Tourin'

STAGE

BACKSTAGE

HUMBLE PIE
J.GILES BAND

WATER

OUT
AMPHITHE
8 JULY

SPECIAL GUES

APPROVED BY

BEST SEAT IN THE HOUSE

DRUMMING IN THE '70s
WITH MARRIOTT, FRAMPTON, AND HUMBLE PIE

BY JERRY SHIRLEY

EDITED BY TIM COHAN

© 2011 by Jerry Shirley

ISBN 978-1-888408-13-3

REBEATS PUBLICATIONS
219 Prospect, Alma, Michigan 48801
www.Rebeats.com

Printed in the United States of America

Dedication

A Life in Three Acts

Act One

When I was 17 and brand new to living in the public eye, I used to really worry about what people were saying about me.

Act Two

Then, when I got to 23, I decided that I didn't give a fuck what people were saying about me.

Act Three

Now that I am in my late 50s, I've come to the realization that they weren't talking about me in the first place!

These pearls of wisdom were given to me by my dearly departed friend who showed me how to stay sober. He was the only one to succeed in seeing me through my first year of sobriety. It took me 10 years to get that first one. He held my hand through what must have been at least 400 12-step meetings in one year, and all he would say about it was how I was helping him much more than he was helping me. His name was Tommy Cusick. He died at the age of 73, having just seen his 43rd anniversary of sobriety.

This book is dedicated to my departed family—Mum, Dad, Angus, Jane, Marjorie, Ernest, Tommy, Steve, and Greg. I miss you all on a daily basis.

The "life in three" acts concept—

The first act of naïveté and wonder,

The second act of jaded ambivalence,

The final act of recovery success with my children
and victory over my demons.

Table of Contents

Testimonials and Love Letters

I loved their grooves and sleaziness. Jerry was always solid, and Steve Marriot's voice was amazing. It sailed over the heavy groove. They were a great hard rock band!
Carmine Appice DRUMMER FOR **VANILLA FUDGE**, **CACTUS**, AND **BECK, BOGERT & APPICE**

Back in the late Eighties, I asked Steve Marriott who was his favourite drummer ever. He told me that Jerry Shirley was his man! He said Jerry stuck by him through good and bad. I'll never forget that conversation.
Steve Arthurs WRITER, LONGTIME FRIEND OF STEVE MARRIOTT AND HUMBLE PIE

My love affair with all things Humble Pie started many years ago with the album Eat It *and the song "Black Coffee." The swagger and power of the band was incredible. My brother John was a big fan of the band, and especially of Jerry Shirley's drumming. Many years later I sang lead on three songs at a Steve Marriott tribute. The biggest honour was that I was also asked to sing background vocals with the remaining members of Humble Pie, who were getting together for the first time in 30 years. I will always remember that concert as one of the highlights of my life. Jerry later joined my band and we spent many years together touring, finally recording my last album,* Duchess. *It was an honour to play with him, one of music's most inspiring drummers and, I'm so very fortunate to be able to now say, a very great friend of mine.*
Debbie Bonham VOCALIST AND SONGWRITER

Humble Pie was one of the greatest rock bands in the history of music! Due to their love of R&B and the blues, they forged their own unique sound. Jerry Shirley's rock-solid and swinging drumming, coupled with the soulful and powerhouse vocals of Steve Marriott, were a force to be reckoned with! Their live shows were legendary! In a world of mediocrity in music, Humble Pie is "one of a kind!"
Bobby Caldwell DRUMMER FOR **JOHNNY WINTER**, **CAPTAIN BEYOND**, AND **RICK DERRINGER**

Jerry's playing was the glue that held Humble Pie together; his personality is the glue that few people have, but all wish they did… God blessed him.
Mark Clarke BASSIST FOR **URIAH HEEP**, **RAINBOW**, AND **MOUNTAIN**

Jerry Shirley assaulted his drums with power, precision, soul, and an uncanny sense of controlled abandon. He oozed teenage angst, yet he played with the balls of a man. He was the perfect role model for countless young, aspiring rock drummers in the early Seventies—and that includes me!
Dennis Diken DRUMMER FOR **THE SMITHEREENS**

Wow, it's like having two Jimmy Pages in one band, and a baby-making rhythm section that just don't quit!
Ahmet Ertegun FOUNDER OF ATLANTIC RECORDS

Jerry personified the way I thought a great rock drummer should play and sound. He just drove that band!
Jimmy Fox DRUMMER FOR **THE JAMES GANG**

A jolly entertaining read, and it brought back a good few memories.
David Gilmour GUITARIST AND VOCALIST FOR **PINK FLOYD**

All those years in Montrose, standing on the side of the stage watching Steve Marriott do his thing, had a profound influence on how I perform and sing to this day.
Sammy Hagar VOCALIST AND GUITARIST FOR **MONTROSE**, **VAN HALEN**, AND **CHICKENFOOT**

I saw them play at Wolverhampton Civic Hall, and went backstage and met them. They had an edge onstage, they were tight, and, most of all, they had swagger. They spoke to me, in a big way—they were the business. I've seen all the greats throughout my career, and the Pie, with both Peter and later my friend Clem, were untouchable. I will always have in my consciousness the love, vibe, and spirit that the Pie had, which helped me as a lad to become a live performer. I urge every young rocker to dig into Humble Pie. You will not be disappointed.
Glenn Hughes BASSIST AND VOCALIST FOR **DEEP PURPLE** AND **BLACK COUNTRY COMMUNION**

I remember the first time I met Jerry—at one of our gigs. His dad asked me to take a look at his son, the drummer, in the act supporting us. I went over to watch him, and remember thinking to myself that he was great, which led me to get Steve Marriott and have him watch Jerry play. We were both, of course, impressed, and joked that if I ever got sick, he could be my stand-in. Thank God I never got sick, or I could have been out of a job! I am still great friends with Jerry to this day, and I will never forget the meeting between myself, Jerry, and Steve. Little did I know that the meeting between the two of them would be the beginning of a great new band of the future—and the rest, as they say, "is history."
Kenney Jones DRUMMER FOR **THE SMALL FACES**, **FACES**, AND **WHO**

When I first heard them play, I thought, "These guys sound like they come from Texas"—until they opened their mouths!
Bobby Keys SUPERSTAR SESSION SAXOPHONIST

Humble Pie is my favorite band of all time. The albums were great, but the live performances were brilliant. Steve Marriott, for my money, is the greatest rock 'n' roll frontman ever, period, end of story. He was a powerhouse, and nobody could touch him, not Elvis, not Little Richard, not anybody. Steve's signature guitar hooks set up the thunder and funk that Greg and Jerry laid down. Those live shows are forever burnt in my soul and fuel me when I perform.
Glenn Letsch BASSIST FOR **ROBIN TROWER**

I got into the band from digging Performance—Rockin' the Fillmore. That album ranks as my all-time favourite live recording, and I feel blessed to have caught the band live. The brutal force of Humble Pie blew me away. Marriott strutting his stuff, accompanied by Frampton looking every inch the rock star while the band rocked out, was a sight and sound to be savoured.

Glen Matlock BASSIST FOR **THE SEX PISTOLS**, **RICH KIDS**, AND **SLINKY VAGABOND**

Playing with Jerry was a highlight for me. What a drummer, and what a great bandmate as well. We played, laughed, wrote songs, shot pool, and of course had a couple of pints along the way. There was a lot more to it, but that's another book.

Joey Molland GUITARIST FOR **BADFINGER** AND **NATURAL GAS**

Two groups changed my life: the Rolling Stones and Humble Pie. The Stones and I had parted ways in 1967. When Steve Marriott left the Small Faces and formed Humble Pie, I thought that God had decided I deserved a second run. I never considered the Small Faces my second run—they were a recording group, not a band. Humble Pie amazed and rearranged me. They still do. I have two favourite drummers that blessed my life: Charlie Watts is one, and the other is Jerry Shirley.

Andrew Loog Oldham PRODUCER AND MANAGER

In the 1970s, Bad Company were rehearsing at Pirate Sound in Los Angeles, and Humble Pie were in the adjoining studio. During a break, Steve Marriot came in and chatted to us. Next thing I knew, Paul Rodgers and Steve were singing with us, and the atmosphere was electric. They both went the extra mile in a mind-blowing vocal performance. To be playing with two of the all-time great blues-rock singers was amazing. I will never forget it—even the roadies applauded! Praise indeed!

Mick Ralphs GUITARIST FOR **MOTT THE HOOPLE** AND **BAD COMPANY**

I saw Humble Pie when I was around 15 years old; they were awesomely good. My band idolized them, and I thought Steve Marriott, with his guitar slung so low, was the best frontman I had ever seen. I even got to meet Steve backstage as he was getting into his limo after the show. I'm still high from that brief encounter!

Joe Satriani GUITARIST FOR **CHICKENFOOT** AND EXTENSIVE SOLO CAREER

Humble Pie was, and continues to be, an inspiration. The riffs. The guitars. The vibe. More relevant today than ever. Humble Pie Forever.

Gene Simmons BASSIST AND VOCALIST FOR **KISS**

Jerry represents possibly the greatest era of rock music and the defining role of the rock drummer. Humble Pie was notorious as the best band to see live, and their performances inspired me to play drums. And Jerry made it cool to add some artwork on the front head of a kick drum. He not only played loud, he looked fucking loud! Long live the Pie, and God bless Jerry's hands, feet, and heart.

Chad Smith DRUMMER FOR **RED HOT CHILI PEPPERS** AND **CHICKENFOOT**

Drink, drugs, fights, failure, success, hit records, failed relationships, proud moments, loud moments, satisfied moments, humble moments. That is the life of Jerry Shirley in a nutshell. The stories contained here are entertaining, endearing, and downright gut wrenching. But that is who Jerry Shirley is… besides being a drummer, that is.

David Spero DJ FOR WMMS AND OTHER CLEVELAND STATIONS

I was a fan of Stevie Marriott from the days of the Small Faces. That whole British Invasion sound was a huge influence on me and on KISS. So when Humble Pie got together, I was in from the start. What I loved so much about Humble Pie was that it was no-frills rock 'n' roll. And the way Marriott connected with an audience was something that really inspired me. He was almost like a preacher—it was evangelical! And that was totally what I wanted to be. For me, Humble Pie were heroes.

Paul Stanley GUITARIST AND VOCALIST FOR **KISS**

My first memory of seeing Jerry Shirley was at the Domino Club in the Lion Yard, Cambridge, in 1968. The first thing that hit me was how loud his bass drum was. It was power mixed with a great ability. Early on, I was lucky enough to see Humble Pie rehearse and work in the studio. The combination of the four guys involved was pure magic, and I knew that they were destined for great things. Over the years, our friendship has grown as life has taken us along its many paths. Jerry's daft sense of humour and ability to see what is good and bad has always been there for me if I needed a word of encouragement or advice, so thank you, mate. Rock on!

Rick Wills BASSIST FOR **FRAMPTON'S CAMEL**, **FOREIGNER**, AND **BAD COMPANY**

I remember my brother bringing home Humble Pie's Performance—Rockin' the Fillmore. *Holding the cover, looking at Jerry Shirley's drums while listening to "C'mon Everybody," it was like I was standing right behind him. Jerry laid the law down on what a rock drummer should sound and look like. His sound was as real and raw as any I've ever heard.*

Fred Young DRUMMER FOR **THE KENTUCKY HEADHUNTERS**

Humble Pie gave every gritty rock 'n' roll club band a realistic hope that rock was very alive in the clubs. Jerry Shirley was the working-class rock star, and I worshipped Steve Marriott as a frontman and vocalist. Even though the country folks don't know, Humble Pie helped make the Kentucky Headhunters a reality… and at the heartbeat is one of the greats—Jerry Shirley.

Richard Young GUITARIST AND VOCALIST FOR **THE KENTUCKY HEADHUNTERS**

Foreword by Peter Frampton

When Humble Pie first started touring, I used to share a hotel room with Jerry. I had a girlfriend, later to become my wife, but Jerry was still testing out prospective "future ex-wives." So I used to feel a bit like Jack Lemmon in the film, *The Apartment.* I think I spent more time waiting outside our room than actually in it!

Listening to Frampton Comes Alive *mixes, 1975.*

Jerry has always been a wonderful and uniquely talented drummer, but more than that, he's a charmer! He is, as we say in England, "the salt of the earth," and he's one of the very few true friends I have had in my life.

Being a part of such a unique band as Humble Pie will always be one of the best times in my life. Steve Marriott coaxing me to form my own band, later to become Humble Pie, then introducing me to Jerry, was just the beginning of a period of five albums' worth of fiery creativity.

My dream had always been to join the Small Faces. Steve exuded such soul-dripping talent. And as I was to find out, there is nothing more "adrenalizing" than singing on the same microphone as Steve. Nothing!

The day after Steve left the Faces and we had already started planning the Pie, Ronnie, Mac, and Kenney came over to my dingy basement flat in Hammersmith and asked me to join the Small Faces. I thought, "How could anyone 'replace' Steve?!?" I was very flattered, but it was too late.

Peter onstage with Performance *t-shirt, 2010.*

Our first rehearsal in Jerry's parents' front room, jamming on songs from the Band's *Music From Big Pink,* was truly a "eureka" moment for me! It was the best possible band I could ever have been in, to this day!

We were young and infallible, and nothing could stop us doing what we were about to do. Jerry has a way of telling his story with the same excitement as when he lived it!

This is the way it happened—faults and all! Hey, I was there… Thanks, Jerry, for putting it straight, once and for all. Love you, brother.

—Peter Frampton

Acknowledgements

I would like to dedicate the book to these people for being the force that drove me to write it and for helping me in my life, both personally and professionally.

Daughters Sarah and Isobel and granddaughter Sofia (the loves of my life), son-in-law Emiliano, Mum and Dad R.I.P., brother Angus R.I.P., Ernest and Marjorie Tipson R.I.P., Jane Tipson R.I.P., Barbara Tipson, Steve Marriott R.I.P., Greg Ridley R.I.P., Tommy Cusick R.I.P., Tom Shikner, Bill Brucken, Jim Buccigross, John Price, Mark Butcher, Bill Anthony, John Doumanian, Audrey Zelaney, Alex King, Bill Graham R.I.P., Frank Barsalona, Mike Walsh, Mick and Maggie Young, Lou Lerer, Ruth Cleveland AA, Pete and Nancy Loynes, Warwick McCredie R.I.P., Alan "Dreamy" Lee, Cynthia Campbell, Aaron Campbell, Lottie Shirley, Cheryl Shirley, Linda Peterson (née Azios), Sanford Radinsky R.I.P., Jeff Dunham, Dupuy Bateman, Dave Clark, Mick Brigden, Bill Ludwig III and Ludwig Drums, Paiste Cymbals, John Hammel, Sir Paul McCartney, Bill Harrison, Ted Sellen, Rick Wills, Lynny Wills, Willie Wilson, Jenny Field, Eddie Wilkinson, Pete Bullick, Ian Rowley, Gerard Louis, Bobby and Nancy Barnard, Billy Jeansonne, Paul and Sharon Mellers, Joan Bonham R.I.P., Steve Herman R.I.P., Bobby Tench, Anthony Jones R.I.P., John Skinner, Craig and Pam Christie, Tony Rybka, Antoinette Moore, Jerry Levine, Rodney Eckerman, Ronnie Eckerman, Jane Garaghty, Randy Burton, Barbara Skydel, Tony Catalano, Alan Greene, Jerry Moss, Herb Alpert, Ahmet Ertegun R.I.P., Gil Friesen, Charlie Huhn, Wally Stocker, Peter Wood R.I.P., Tim Renwick, Bob Argent, nephew Robert Shirley, sister-in-law Leona Shirley, Lenny Gannon, Steve Gannon, Roger Peters, Gala Pinion, Lindsey Korner, Elizabeth Robinson, Francesca Overman, Pete Townshend, Buddy Rich R.I.P., Gene Krupa R.I.P., Cecil Shirley R.I.P., Al Jackson R.I.P., Sonny Payne R.I.P., Keith Moon R.I.P., John Entwistle R.I.P., Syd Barrett R.I.P., Rick Wright R.I.P., Fred Astaire and Ginger Rogers R.I.P., and David Niven. R.I.P.

*I would also like to thank these people for their
direct help in producing the book.*

This list has to start with the dream team of people who helped me find a level of excellence that far exceeded my expectations. They were motivated by a labour of love, and I cannot thank them enough for their absolute dedication to this project. The best team money can't buy.

Jill Anterio, Rob Cook, Brad Smith, Tim Cohan, Jon Cohan, Linda Nelson, Nicole Julius, Chad Smith, Billy Amendola, Dan Muise, and Greg Vick.

*Plus the rest of these kind friends and associates
who helped me put these memoirs together.*

Peter Frampton, Clem Clempson, David Gilmour, Jenny Dearden, Michele Anthony, Andrew Loog Oldham, Kenney Jones, Kay Marriott (Steve's mum), Kay Marriott (Steve's sister), Debbie Bonham, Billy Jeansonne, Scott Rowley, Max Bell, Fin Costello, and Dave Carlson.

*And all the additional people who wrote
testimonials and are not mentioned above.*

Carmine Appice, Steve Arthurs, Bobby Caldwell, Mark Clarke, Dennis Diken, Jimmy Fox, Sammy Hagar, Glenn Hughes, Bobby Keys, Glenn Letsch, Glen Matlock, Joey Molland, Mick Ralphs, Joe Satriani, Gene Simmons, David Spero, Paul Stanley, Fred Young, and Richard Young.

Photo credits

All materials were supplied from the archives of the author, with these acknowledgements: Tony Gale, "Pictorial Press" www.pictorialpress.com (p. 50), Jenny Dearden (pp. 54, 197), John Kelly (p. 68), Keith Morris (p. 124), Clive Arrowsmith (p. 190), Mick Brigden (pp. 201, 236), Chuck Pulin (pp. 204, 271), John Bellissimo (p. 206), Fin Costello (pp. 242, 246, 248), Ted Sellen (p. 252), Peter Wood (p. 303). Thank you for your cooperation.

Preface

We were due to play one of our favourite gigs near the end of the '75 farewell tour—the Warehouse in New Orleans. It was the biggest, sweatiest, hottest, greatest rock 'n' roll club in the entire Deep South. Not only was the gig the greatest, but partying in the French Quarter afterwards was also always fun, if somewhat dangerous. We had progressed to playing the larger Municipal Auditorium on previous tours, but for the farewell tour, it had to be the Warehouse—two shows, 8:00 P.M. and 11:00 P.M. It was the only place in the country other than the Fillmore East that playing two shows in one night was enjoyable. What we did not know was that the road crew had conspired to give us the most incredible surprise anybody could have conjured up to take with us into our breakup.

At the last minute, our tour manager was informed that there were some surprise VIPs coming to the late show, and that he needed to make sure there were adequate seats in the wings on each side of the stage to accommodate these visitors: a band that were big fans of Steve and Humble Pie. We knew nothing of this, and went on for the late show to a steaming reception, literally—it must have been 100 degrees and 100% humidity. A real hardcore rock 'n' roll club, packed to the rafters with nearly 2,000 dedicated Pie fans going absolutely nuts. We were pleased to see the place packed, because Led Zeppelin were playing that night down the road in Baton Rouge, and it hadn't seemed to affect our attendance at all.

As we started the second song—"C'mon Everybody" from *Smokin'*—I got into the groove, and the audience were swaying back and forth so much that it looked like the safety barriers at the front might give in. When we got to the second verse, I looked to my right and then to my left, and I couldn't believe my eyes. To the right were Jimmy Page and Robert Plant, and to the left was John Bonham! I almost fell off my drum stool. I had to do a double take or two before I realized that this wasn't some kind of dream. Apparently they had moved their start time in Baton Rouge up a little so that they could get to our late show.

You could not have come up with any more exciting tour bonus for me than to have John Bonham taking the time to come and see our band on our farewell tour. It doesn't get any better than that, unless, of course, Jimmy Page and Robert Plant happen to come with him. What a buzz! It still gives me goosebumps thinking about it now.

There aren't many in my generation of musicians who can say that Led Zeppelin came to check them out. Plus, I found out 30 years later from John's sister, singer Debbie Bonham, that we were one of Bonzo's favourite bands and that he loved my playing. Money cannot buy that little lot, and to hear that extra added bonus all these years later made me realize that maybe I was doing something right after all.

It is amazing to think that, a little over six years earlier, I had got a call from Steve Marriott asking if he could join the group that Peter Frampton and I were forming when I was still only 16 years old. I've often said how that one phone call changed my life forever. What started with some secret little rehearsals in my parents' living room, learning songs from the Band's *Music From Big Pink* to see if we could in fact play together, soon developed into the British press hailing us as one of rock's first supergroups. We had a big hit with our first single in Europe, but were unknown in America and failed to light that place up until we had toured countless times and turned into the toughest and tightest band in the world. We took no prisoners and helped to mould what was to become known as stadium rock. We signed one of the first multimillion-dollar record deals and helped write the blueprint of what became the standard party-central routine that all self-respecting rock 'n' rollers followed for years to come. We earned a fortune, we spent a fortune. We didn't sell our t-shirts, we gave them away. And we ended up with some brilliant memories of the greatest times of our lives.

While it wasn't all pretty, it was never, ever boring. This is the story of the ups and downs of those magnificent times—from station wagons to Learjets to tour buses, we did it all. Not bad for a young lad from Waltham Cross.

Chapter 1
Every Mother's Son
February 1952 to November 1961

In which the awkward bugger's dad meets his mum;
a notorious progenitor meets the gallows; I give my first
performance—drunk—at the age of two; and I am relieved
of the only appendix you will encounter in this tome.

At the beginning of 1971, I had a Rolls-Royce in the drive of my 400-year-old Elizabethan farmhouse. The house was snugly nestled in its own three acres, along with a host of outbuildings that included a three-bedroom cottage and a huge Essex barn. When I stepped outside through my front door, I walked on a red-brick bridge over a pond edged by quietly majestic weeping willows. It was heaven on earth, and I was only 18.

Just over a year earlier, I'd joined a new band called Humble Pie, which the British press had immediately dubbed a supergroup, comprising as it did mega-pop-star Steve Marriott and the nearly-as-famous Peter Frampton, along with Greg Ridley from the highly successful rock band Spooky Tooth… and me, whose previous band's output consisted of precisely one single, which had promptly and spectacularly flopped. The next several years were a heady joyride of incredible proportions: recording eight studio albums and a classic live double album, touring the world and basking in the adulation of countless fans, meeting and playing with some of the most legendary names in rock music, and generally having more fun than should rightfully be allowed by law.

But by 1975, the party would wind down almost as quickly as it had started.

How did all this happen to a shy little short-arse kid from Waltham Cross who miserably failed his 11+ school exam? It's a good question. I suppose I am a product of both my family and the golden era of rock music. But before I get to the music, I think it's best to start, just as those weeping willows did, from the roots…

Margaret Shirley came home from work, having been to the doctor's on the way. It was the early spring of 1949. Her world had just come apart at the seams, and she was desolate, inconsolable. According to the doctor, the tests said that she was unable to have children—no ifs, no ands, no buts or even maybes. Just no babies. As she waited for her husband, Robert, to come home, she wondered how he would receive this dreadful news, knowing how desperately he wanted kids. She prayed he wouldn't take it too badly.

She shouldn't have worried. This indomitable man—who had survived Dunkirk, El Alamein, and everything else World War II and Adolf Hitler could throw at him—looked at his distraught wife, smiled gently, and said, "We'll see about that, my dear." Nine months later, my older brother, Angus Robert Tipson Shirley, was born. Dad wanted to call him Frederick Angus Robert Tipson Shirley, but Mum put her foot down, so A.R.T.S. he would proudly remain. Being a primary-school teacher, Mum knew the school-yard piss-taking that would have ensued. Fred Farts, Flatulent Freddie, etc., etc.—all of which was precisely why the old man thought it was a good idea!

Angus was born on January 30, 1950. Little did my parents know then that on the same date, just three years earlier, a certain Stephen Peter Marriott was born in the East End of London, but more on the significance of that little fella later.

Just over two years later, on March 21, 1952, across the Atlantic in Cleveland, Ohio, the Moondog Coronation Ball was held at the Cleveland Arena. This gathering has since been considered the first that was officially called a "rock 'n' roll" concert. Six weeks prior to this, on February 4, Robert and Margaret welcomed their kicking and screaming second son, Jeremy Duncan Tipson Shirley, into the world. Mine was a breech birth that took 36 hours to complete. Poor old Mum, it must have made her eyes water—and it set the tone of my character for years to come. "You always were an awkward bugger, coming out arse

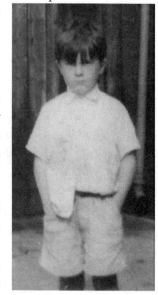

At the start of my image-conscious ways. Check out the attitude and the hairstyle—years ahead of my time!

2

backwards as you did" was Dad's colourful way of summing up my argumentative tendencies.

When I decided to write this book, I realised early on that this part of it would have to be as much about the two sides of my family and their history as it would be about me, for two reasons. One, out of respect; they were truly wonderful people. And two, their stories are fascinating in their own right.

My father was half-English and half-Irish, whilst my mother was half-English and half-Scottish. I once wrote a song to sum up that little nest of vipers, the title of which was "Part of Me Is Irish and Part of Me a Scot, the Rest of Me Is English, I Fight With Me a Lot!" I didn't need to finish the song, as the title said it all, really.

Ladies first…

Mum was born in 1914 in Kuala Lumpur in Malaya, as it was then known. Her missionary father was a linguist who had astonishing knowledge and talent; while he was in a Japanese concentration camp, he wrote a Chinese-English dictionary, no mean feat when you consider the limited resources available. Being the devout man of God that he was, when he needed pen and paper, he would do what came naturally—he would pray for his needs—and lo and behold, they would appear. Apparently, a sympathetic guard who overheard Grandpa's heaven-addressed wishes would kindly oblige by leaving the supplies under his pillow.

Mum's sister Ethel had been born in China in 1912, and her brother Ernest was born in Australia in 1917—all of this continent hopping happened before commercial flight existed. In fact, the three children circumnavigated the globe no less than three times, all before my mother's 20th birthday.

As a fully fledged member of a very devout Plymouth Brethren family, Mum only started to question the religion's belief system when she fell madly in love with a young Indian boy on the boat home from India, where she had attended grammar school. Her parents barred her from seeing him, simply because he was of a different colour. This broke her heart and made her furious at the same time, and the hypocrisy, along with the plain and simple bigotry of it all, formed within her a vehement anti-prejudice attitude that lasted the rest of her life.

Once home, Mum went on to attend teacher-training college at Homerton College in Cambridge, where she officially severed her ties with the Plymouth Brethren.

Dad, although a very clever man indeed, was born to earthier pursuits. He came into this world in North London in 1910, the son of a pig farmer. His mother was from an Irish horse-breeding family. Dad played the drums in the Casino Dance Band alongside his brother Cecil, who played piano exquisitely. (Some things never change—this pattern was to be repeated years later by my brother, Angus, and me. Our band was called the Apostolic Intervention; Angus and I preferred the Casino Dance Band as a name.)

Dad met his first wife backstage at a dance where his band were performing. A couple of months later, she turned up with some interesting news: she was pregnant. So Dad did the honourable thing and married "Aunty" Gladys, and, pretty soon thereafter, my half-brother, Barry, was born.

Dad (Major Robert) in his David Niven lookalike period just after the war.

Grandpa Shirley was the first man on his street to buy an automobile. Not long after it arrived, Dad decided that, in order to fully understand the workings of the combustion engine, he would have to totally dismantle it and then put it back together, which he promptly did. From then on, there was nothing he couldn't do in the area of mechanical engineering, and those skills would serve him well for the rest of his life, proving particularly helpful when he was an officer in World War II, serving in the desert under Field Marshal Montgomery.

On September 3, 1939, my father went to sign up for the Army and soon found himself on his way to France as part of the British Expeditionary Force. It wasn't long before he realised that life as a private in the British Army didn't really appeal to him. He was told about the Officer Training Corps and resolved to take the entrance exam when he got back home.

Dad managed to survive Dunkirk, and, after a brief period of R & R, he was sent off to his new barracks in Aldershot to get re-kitted. Like most of the men who lived through Dunkirk, he had left all of his kit on the beaches. On arrival at the barracks, he walked into his Nissan hut and chose the bed in the far corner from the 12 in the hut. On each bed, there was a basic kit that included a British Army standard-issue helmet, or tin hat, as they were called. When he had received his first tin hat, he had scratched his initials inside it and covered them with a blob of black sealing wax; he subsequently lost that helmet on the beaches of Dunkirk. Now, as he looked over his new kit in Aldershot, he saw that the tin hat looked strangely familiar. He turned it over and, to his utter astonishment and disbelief, there was the blob of black wax. Just to be positive, he scraped the wax off, and, sure enough, there were his initials, R.S.

Thanks to this more-than-simple twist of fate, Dad somehow knew deep down that he would survive the horrors of war that were about to ensue. I, for one, am most grateful that he did. Soon afterwards, he took the Officer Training Corps exam and passed with flying colours. He spent most of the rest of the war as Captain Robert Shirley, becoming Major Robert Shirley (Acting) by the end.

Dad would always tell me with immense pride how our ancestor Laurence Shirley, the fourth Earl of Ferrers, was the last man to be tried by a jury of fellow Lords and the first to be hung by the trap-door method. As proud as he and Grandpa were of this, they withheld, with foolish reticence, the vital information as to why the fourth Earl was hung up like a kipper. So I went with my two daughters and looked it up at the library, and, sure enough, the *Doomsday Book* revealed all. It turns out that Laurence was a pisshead, who, in a drunken rage, accused his rent collector of favouring his estranged wife in rental disbursement, then shot him. How you do.

Does alcoholism run in families? I think there's a strong possibility. At least today you can get help in rehab, a slightly better solution than the gallows, assuming, of course, that you haven't topped anybody. Grandpa Fred Shirley liked a tipple, as did my father. Grandpa's drinking career came to a crashing halt when he came home a bit worse for wear one too many times for Grandma Shirley's liking. She was a formidable woman who you did not want to piss off, and nobody knew that better than Grandpa Fred. So when she gave him an ultimatum—"It's me and the children [all seven of them], or the booze"—that was that; he never drank again. My father never entirely stopped drinking, but eventually slowed down. Booze certainly adversely affected his life over the years, but he did survive its ravages for the most part, bless his heart.

After graduating from Homerton with honours (Mum was a very smart lady who later became a member of Mensa), Mum started teaching in Luton. While she was there, she met and fell in love with a man, a butcher by trade, and after seeing him for a while, she got engaged. Fortunately for me, she did not marry him. Thank God she didn't; otherwise I might have ended up as a butcher who supported Luton Town Football Club. That would have been ugly. I don't have anything in particular against butchery or Luton Town FC, but it would have meant that I'd have missed out on being a drummer in a great rock 'n' roll band and a devout Tottenham Hotspur FC supporter.

Mum trying her best to look like Ava Gardner. My parents loved the movies and took us all the time.

After the war broke out, Mum found herself teaching very large classes (40 plus) of children in and around the outskirts of North London. She shared a flat with two girlfriends. One was Aunty Marjorie (who went on to marry Mum's brother Ernest); the other was a lady called Mary Iola Hewitt, better known as Iola, a name I've never otherwise heard, before or since. Iola met an American brigadier general called Henry Lee Badham, who she promptly married. Mum, not to be outdone, also had a whirlwind romance that resulted in marriage, but that's where the similarity ended. Iola's marriage lasted until she died. They had two remarkable children. The daughter, Mary, starred opposite Gregory Peck in *To Kill a Mockingbird* at the tender age of 10. Her brother Johnny went on to become a very successful movie director whose films have included *Saturday Night Fever* and *War Games*. On the other hand, Mum's marriage lasted less than a week, which I would imagine is some kind of record. That's all we ever knew about the marriage. She never spoke about it, other than to chuckle over it from time to time.

Once my father had earned his commission, he was sent off to North Africa as part of the British Eighth Army, Field Marshal Montgomery's infamous Desert Rats. Starting as lieutenant, he quickly moved up to captain and stayed at that rank until late in the war, when, as part of the peacekeeping role that the British Army were given, he served as Acting Major Robert Shirley. He would have probably become a full-blown major, but, unfortunately, a couple of hell-raising incidents prevented that from happening. One involved fishing with hand grenades, which was spectacularly effective and fed lots of hungry troops, but was against all regulations, to say the least. A large net would have sufficed.

As the war came to an end, so did Mum and Dad's respective marriages: Mum's one-week wonder and Dad's to "Aunty" Gladys, his backstage babe. Soon thereafter, my parents met through my Uncle Cecil, who had dated my mother briefly and introduced her to his brother Robert. After Mum and Cecil stopped seeing each other, Dad stepped in and asked Mum out. They got on famously and soon realised that they were meant for each other. With the war finally over, they, like most people, were at a loss as to what to do with the rest of their lives. As horrific as the war was, it was also all consuming and, in a way, very exciting. A lot of people just wanted to get away from it all and went in pursuit of happiness and the quiet life. This included the Shirley family. Dad, his sister Vivian and her husband Len, and Dad's parents all went down to Cornwall to renovate an old mill house that Uncle Len had somehow managed to buy. It was in dire need of repair, so my father was in his element. When it came to fixing things, whether it was a car or a house, he could do it all.

So off our intrepid band of wandering property developers went. The deal was simple: Len bought the mill and Dad fixed it up. My mother went along and found a job teaching, which she had become very good at.

Just before moving down to Cornwall, Dad had proposed in a somewhat unusual way. Apparently, back in those days, you had to go to Tottenham High Road to pick up your marriage licence so that you could get married there or anywhere else. The marriage licence office was even open on Saturdays to accommodate working people. So, when Dad called Mum out of the blue and asked her to meet him at Tottenham High Road on a Saturday afternoon, she knew it could only mean one thing, as she wasn't a football fan and as Tottenham weren't playing at home that weekend anyway—he must be about to propose. That, of course, was precisely what he did.

With all the necessary paperwork filled out, off they went to their new life in Cornwall. After the wedding and reception in Newquay, Dad immediately tackled the first job at hand: fixing up Trewerry Mill. He did a beautiful job on both the house and the grounds, and they still look good to this day. In fact, when I took a friend and my daughters to have a look at it many, many years later, the present owner told us with great pride that an eccentric ex-army brigadier, whose horse (when the soldier was a bit worse for the wear) would bring him home from the pub, fixed the place up to look just the way it looks today. Once we told him that it was Dad and that the only thing he got wrong was Dad's rank, he was so ecstatic that we got a free round of Cornish cream tea out of it.

After Dad completed work on the mill, it was time to move on to more buying, fixing up, and selling of houses and cottages. Unfortunately, Uncle Len's lack of commitment was causing problems. My father was a very generous man who would literally give you his last fiver if he thought you needed it more than he did. The problem was that, as he was not a rich man, his giving nature often left him in the shite, which would piss Mum off no end. After he went to great lengths to help out his sister and her husband, Mum finally put her foot down and insisted that he started getting his fair share of the business or they would have to move on and do something else to make a living.

Not long after being told that she could not have children, Mum got pregnant with Angus. This prevented her and Dad from having to get tough with Len about not being paid properly; all they had to do now was say that, with a child on the way, Dad needed to find a job sooner than later. Then another bit of good fortune came their way in the form of a good job offer up in the North London area. So, they moved back to Cheshunt, less than 10 miles north of Tottenham, which suited Dad immensely, and Mum found a job close by in Waltham Cross. Dad's job came with a nice flat right next door to his place of work. The flat was in a house called Ivy House, which was located in Crossbrook Street, halfway between Cheshunt and Waltham Cross.

I have a few vague memories of the place, but we moved out by the time I was four years old. There was one particular incident there that I am not surprised I didn't remember, even after Mum and Dad told me about it later in life…

From time to time, our parents would have dinner parties or go to the theatre with friends and invite them back after the show for a nightcap. Angus and I would be well and truly asleep by the time the party started—or so my parents thought. What they didn't know was that we used to spy on the revelry from a walkthrough closet that had one door to the living room and another that opened into our bedroom. The living room door had a small hole in it, so we could see all the people having a really good time.

One fine evening, when I was about two and Angus four, he noticed that the partygoers were all drinking an amber-coloured liquid that came in a strange bottle with big dimples on its three sides. He also noticed that the more they drank, the more fun they seemed to be having; in fact, some of them had so much fun that they would have to sit down and take a nap. Sometimes Mum and Dad couldn't wake them up and would let them sleep on the couch. They must have been *really* tired.

The idea that this magical potion could make a whole roomful of people feel so good made Angus determined to try it out himself. Not wanting his little brother to miss out on any kind of fun—and, I suspect, needing a guinea pig—he got me up one morning and put me in my high chair, then put some of the amber liquid in a saucer and started to spoon-feed it to me. The taste was so foul that I refused to drink it, so he laced the whiskey with copious amounts of sugar. We went on to become as drunk as skunks and waddled into Mum and Dad's bedroom, very unsteady on our feet and singing, "My old man's a dustman / He wears a dustman's hat." Our parents' giggles quickly disappeared and were replaced by deep concern when I managed to fall flat on my face.

Angus was my hero, and I worshipped him. I was also intimidated by his intelligence. We both attended the primary school where Mum taught. My mother usually showed sound judgement about us kids, especially on matters to do with our education in this very rough-and-tumble part of North London. But, for some unknown reason, she completely lost the plot when it came to choosing our school clothes: the Scot in her saw nothing wrong in sending me to school wearing a kilt. In theory, there is nothing wrong with wearing a kilt; however, in my case—being sent to school on your first day when your name is Shirley, you have wavy brown hair and bright blue eyes, and you're wearing a skirt—it did not go down well at all. "A Boy Named Sue" comes to mind. It did, however, teach me how to run fast and how to fight when necessary, which is not something I'm very proud of now, but, back then, in a North London school, you either learned how to look after yourself or you would get bullied relentlessly. You might think that having your mother teaching in the same school you were attending would be an advantage. Wrong. It just made a bad situation worse.

After a little time had passed, Mum stopped putting out the dreaded kilt for me and replaced it with normal clothes. I had no idea why she suddenly stopped until recently, when I found out that it was because of my brother. He had gone to her and pleaded my case for me, and that was that—no more kilt. God bless his cotton socks, he had suffered the dreaded kilt himself and didn't want his little bruv to endure the same bullying he had been subjected to. That's what I call brotherly love.

With older bruv, Angus (left).

We moved a lot during my early years: eight different houses by the time I was 14. Most of these moves were very exciting for my brother and me, with one exception. When Angus took his 11+ and passed with flying colours, it happened to coincide with Mum and Dad's decision to buy a pub. Geographically speaking, this threw my warm and cosy existence into complete chaos; we had moved just too far for me to stay at my old school. Angus was now in grammar school, Mum had quit teaching to look after the pub, and I was left to fend for myself at a new school, with no big brother to protect me.

At this point in the story, things start to get out of control. The first and biggest problem that I had to come to terms with was getting acclimatised to my new school. To this day, I have absolutely no idea why I had such a hard time settling in. Prior to this, I was a pretty honest kid, but I'm afraid "Thou shalt not bear false witness" soon became "Thou shalt lie through thou's teeth."

The list of imaginary ailments I suddenly developed was pretty lame and extremely transparent. They were designed to prevent me from having to attend school; however, having a mum who taught, and therefore could spot a lame excuse from a thousand yards away, meant I was never able to get out of going to school as a result of any of these lies—until my final attempt at it. This last dodge was not only successful, it was also spectacular in its consequences.

At my old school, a friend of mine had taken six weeks off as a result of appendicitis; I remembered the symptoms reasonably well, so I decided to give it a go. I must have done a good job because the next thing I know, I'm in an ambulance being rushed to East Herts Hospital.

Having never before been successful at the art of skiving, I was at a loss as to what to do next, so I decided to just go with the flow, have a few days off school, make a miraculous recovery, and Bob's your uncle—or, in my case, your dad. But it didn't turn out to be quite that simple. On the morning of the third day, the nurse started to serve breakfast, as she did every morning. The food was excellent, so when the trolley got to my bed, I said, "Egg and bacon, please." The nurse turned to me and said in a very stern tone, "No breakfast for you today, my boy. They are operating on you this morning."

I went into complete nervous meltdown. "No, no, no! It's all a huge mistake! I was just pretending to be ill so that I wouldn't have to go to school! *Please* don't operate! I was lying about the whole thing! Honest, I was!"

This outburst put the hospital and my parents into a serious quandary. Should they believe what I was saying now and give me a serious telling off, or should they go ahead with the surgery, believing that I was now lying about my previous lying and so there really was a need for the operation?

The end result is that I no longer have an appendix. Apparently, when they removed it, it was a bit swollen. As that organ is of no use to the human anatomy, it is better off gone because if it bursts in later life, it can kill you by poisoning the bloodstream, a condition called peritonitis.

The boy in the bed next to me was very proud of the fact that his father had bought him a complete football kit as a coming-out present. Not just any old kit; to make matters worse, it was a Tottenham kit. Mind you, I have to say this lad deserved everything he got because, at the grand old age of 14, he was in hospital to be circumcised. Being the cheeky little sod that I was back then, when Dad came to visit me after my operation, I told him about this boy and then said, "I want a drum kit for my coming-out present." Bless his heart, Dad found me a Bitzar drum kit (bitsa this, bitsa that), and, soon thereafter in our house, the rock began to roll.

Chapter 2
Ready Steady Go!
November 1961 to December 1966

In which I start playing in the pub (at nine years old); discover rock 'n' roll; see two dynamic duos and two fantastic foursomes on telly; and dodge jelly babies at a very Fab Christmas show.

My "Bitzar" drum kit consisted of a Gigstar bass drum, a Broadway snare drum (which may also have been made by Gigstar), an Olympic hanging tom, a strange pair of bongos that attached to the bass drum, a pair of hi-hat cymbals, and a ride cymbal. The Olympic hanging tom was an add-on that I got about a year after the original kit, and a floor tom came later, too.

We set the kit up in the public bar so that Dad could recruit various musicians, who would have anything-goes music nights every Friday. The "band" would usually consist of a pianist and a drummer, who would make use of my kit. On the really happening nights, Dad would hire an actual entire band, who would bring their own equipment. These were the nights I loved the most because it meant I could watch a drummer who invariably had a kit far superior to mine.

I would practice when I got home from school, and sometimes get to play along with one of the pianists, before the pub opened its doors.

It was at about this time that I discovered rock 'n' roll music. Angus and I had become huge fans of Buddy Holly just before he died, which was not long before I got my drum kit. Also around this time, a certain local boy came to everybody's attention. His real name was Harry Webb, and his band was originally called the Drifters, but he had changed his name to Cliff Richard, and his band had become the Shadows because they had to: there was already an American vocal group called the Drifters. The Shadows is a much cooler name anyway, as is Cliff Richard.

The appendix scam ended up being extremely fortuitous for a number of reasons, but it also had its dark side, and that pattern has stayed with me my whole life. Just when things seem to be going great, something comes along and gives me a huge beating. On the plus side, I did get six weeks off school, I no longer had an appendix to threaten my life, I was the proud owner of a drum kit, and I now had a six-inch scar to prove what a tough guy I was. On the minus side, I had missed all that school at a very important time: the entrance exam to grammar school was looming large.

Soon after we moved into the pub, I discovered two double acts who would profoundly affect my entire being. I saw them on television, which had by now become huge in its own right, and at that time, I learned so much from it.

The first duo were Fred Astaire and Ginger Rogers. Rock 'n' roll it wasn't, but swing it did. I soon became a walking encyclopaedia of all things Fred and Ginger. The fact that Fred played drums like a pro came as no surprise; after all, tap dancing and drumming are cut from the same cloth, rhythmically speaking. But as natural as it was for Fred Astaire to be a good drummer, that doesn't mean that a drummer—yours truly, for instance—will be a natural dancer. Far from it,

A good little schoolboy desperately trying to make the grade to be admitted to grammar school. I eventually succeeded.

I'm afraid: I couldn't dance my way out of a paper bag. Still, I certainly became a huge fan of anything to do with the Swing era of my father's youth, right the way through to Count Basie and Ray Charles. To this day, my personal musical ethos is, "If it don't swing, it don't mean a thing," simply because swing can be applied to just about any rhythm pattern; it's the human element in a rhythm section.

Speaking of swing, the other duo I saw on television back then were the two greatest American drummers ever: Gene Krupa and Buddy Rich. One night, some show on the telly featured one of the now-famous drum battles between the two masters. It came on out of the blue, and when my father yelled at the top of his voice, "Come here quick!" I ran to see what all the fuss was about. I was mesmerized. I have to say that I'm not a fan of big, flashy, drum-solo-type drummers, but this was different. First of all, Krupa and Rich swung like a big pair of tits, plus they used syncopation as if they had invented it—and for me, at this early stage in my musical education, they may as well have.

The year spent living in the pub had both pros and cons to it. On the plus side, there was my discovery of drums, Fred and Ginger, Krupa and Rich, rock 'n' roll, dancing girls, blues, and big band swing, As if that lot wasn't enough to keep me occupied, there was my introduction to the musical genius of Ray Charles and Peggy Lee, both of whom came to me by way of my mother.

Back then, for your parents to steer you in the right direction, musically speaking, was a real bonus, and I consider myself incredibly lucky in that regard. It was a fantastic kick-start in the right direction, which was summed up years later by none other than (this is where the name dropping officially starts, folks) Sir Paul McCartney, while I nervously interviewed him for a radio station I was working for (98.5 WNCX, "Cleveland's Classic Rock"). He was talking about his discovery of Ray Charles through the records being brought into Liverpool from the USA by the merchant seamen. As he told me this, I said, in a matter of fact way, "Yeah, my mum turned me on to him when I was about nine years old," to which he replied, with wide-eyed surprise, "Boy, you were really lucky!" Not that I needed reminding how lucky I was to have a mother with such impeccable taste, but to be reminded of it by a fellow musician who embarked on his voyage of musical discovery a few years before I did, and whose name was Sir Paul McCartney, was fan-fuckin'-tastic!

Mum also had a tremendous outlook about music in general, and was typically non-judgemental. When asked what type of music she liked, she would reply, "I like any type of music, so long as it's good" or "All types of music, so long as it's well played."

The strange thing about living in the pub was that, even though we were, in theory, spending more time together, what with living and working under the same roof, we actually saw very little of each other. Mum, too busy to make me lunch, gave me lunch money to spend at the local café instead, and that's when the first signs of my addictive nature appeared. As is always the case with me, however, even the deadly serious sides of life come with an equally strong sense of humour attached. A prime example is my first addiction: Spam. That's right folks: Spam, egg, and chips, to be precise, every day for lunch at the café, for a whole year. I can recall being told about a kid at my previous school who would eat nothing but beans on toast! His bean consumption wasn't the slightest bit hazardous to himself or anyone else, other than the perils of sitting downwind of him in class.

At school, I had befriended a chap who was a great footballer and happened to be the head boy. His name was Eddie Wilkinson, and we became inseparable. Being Eddie's best mate ensured my place in the hierarchy of our class and on the playground. Plus, he played a pretty decent clarinet. This helped our position in school because, if asked, we could perform a mean version of Acker Bilk's "Stranger on the Shore."

I'll never forget my first school report from Abel Smith Primary School. I got a C average, with marks from B- to C- in every subject, except one: I received an A in Music, accompanied by the prophetic note, "Rhythmic work excellent."

Missing a lot of school for various reasons, along with changing schools so close to the 11+, was always going to be a recipe for disaster. Sure enough, when the letter came through the letterbox, it informed me that I had failed the exam and therefore would not be eligible to attend the grammar school that Angus did. I would have to wait another two years and take the 13+, but to do that, I would have to go to a paid school.

	School Report for the year ending July '62

NAME SHIRLEY   JEREMY   CLASS H

Grading : A—Very Good ; B—Good ; C—Average ; D—Weak ; E—Very Weak.

		GRADE	REMARKS
ENGLISH	READING	C+	Needs more confidence in oral work
	WRITING	C-	Must practise
	SPELLING	C	
	COMPOSITION	C+	Quite good, but must improve presentation.
	COMPREHENSION	C	Has tried hard
MATHS	MENTAL	C	Jeremy appears to be over-
	MECHANICAL	C	anxious in these subjects.
	PROBLEM	C	
	PHYSICAL EDUCATION	B-	Keen
	MUSIC	A	Rhythmic work excellent
	HAND/NEEDLEWORK	B-	

FINAL GRADING REACHED IN THE   Third   YEAR   GRADE C

OBSERVATIONS. Jeremy has made quite good progress this year but I feel that he could do even better if he made a little more effort. He needs more confidence in himself.

Signature of Parent/or Guardian.   JShirley

Date 17th July 1962.   AJ Richards   Class Teacher.   Head Teacher.

Report card foreshadowing future occupation.

In the early 1960s, if you did not pass the 11+, the only way you could get the all-important grammar school education was to pay for it. At the time, there was a network of schools in and around London and the Home Counties called Clark's College. The one nearest to us was in Enfield Chase. Unlike my experience at Abel Smith Primary, I settled in at Clark's immediately. There were several reasons why: I was a little older; getting there was a public-transport adventure every day; they played football, not rugby; the football coach was a recently retired Spurs player called Terry Medwin; and the girls were gorgeous.

The only problems were not being in the same school as Angus, and the huge sense of guilt I had developed because Mum and Dad had to pay for me to attend Clark's. Every night, without fail, I said the same prayer as I got into bed: "Dear God, please help me become a successful musician so that I can pay Mum and Dad back for what Clark's College has cost them." I literally did this every night, not because I had to, nor because I had found some newfangled religious cult. It was a simple feeling from the heart that I had to pay them back because I felt so bad about letting them down. And, of course, I was hoping that what they say was right: "Be careful what you pray for, as it may come true."

In the Valkyrie with my first decent semi-pro kit, a Premier set bought brand-new with a little help from Dad.

I dedicated the next two years to studying for the dreaded 13+, with improving my drumming skills a close second. Practising drum rudiments was never my strong suit, but I was able to keep my hand in by doing gigs locally with the band Angus and I had put together. Our band was a legend in our own lunch break, rehearsing in our living room, dressed in our band uniform of sleeveless black suedette V-neck pullover vest, white shirt, blue tie, and black trousers. This snappily dressed little outfit comprised Peter Smith (aka Wag) on lead vocals, Angus on guitar, Martin something-or-other on bass, and me on drums.

We went through several names, none of which stuck for more than a couple of weeks. In fact, I don't remember ever doing a gig as a member of the Cementones (for solid rock, get it? Hey, it was Dad's idea!); the Other Name Band, featuring Sue Denim (my idea); or Dick Hampton and the Weapons (Angus's gem).

The old man, through his chain of old friends in the local business community, had secured a gig for us—a charity show for a local disabled children's home—which was announced in a feature article in the big local newspaper. Dad was tailor made for the role of manager/agent/publicist, as he was a natural salesman. He also had a range of friends and associates from having been a Freemason all his adult life and a Grand Master of at least two Masonic lodges. So, there we were with a big gig, a feature in the local rag, and… no name. As a stopgap, we finally settled on the Valkyrie, for no reason whatsoever, changing it immediately *after* the show, which clearly illustrates our lack of common business sense.

The wait to find out the results of the 13+ seemed to go on forever, but was actually only about six weeks. By the time I got the results, I'd forgotten they were coming. In fact, my brother was able to play a little game with them. He intercepted the letter and casually read it to me, with Mum present, as a "Fail," just to see the look of horror on my face. I'm not sure whose devastated reaction seemed worse—mine or Mum's—but, judging by the haste with which Angus told her he was "just kidding," she must have shot him a look that only he and I could translate into "DEATH SOON TO FOLLOW!" In any case, the truth was… I had passed with distinction!

The great shame about my achievement in passing the exam and getting into grammar school was that the 13+ itself was probably the last stroke of work that I did as part of my formal education. Once I got into grammar school, that was it. I just stopped. It was as if I had been there all along, and now I was just coasting and allowing outside interests to take over.

Everybody says they will never forget the first time they had sex, got drunk, got high, or attended their first rock concert. (If, however, they all happened on the same day, chances are you wouldn't remember any of it!) There wasn't a lot to remember about the first time I got high, for one simple reason: absolutely fuck-all happened. And the "crowd went mild," if you know what I mean. Then, on the third attempt, ahhh, yes, there it was—all of a sudden I was laughing my arse off for no apparent reason, and I wanted to eat a pile of chocolate bars the size of a house.

But that first experience smoking hash was not the first time I'd taken a drug. Like many others during those early Mod days, my introduction to drugs came through speed—in my case, French blues—and I loved it. Within half an hour, I was telling anybody who would listen how much I loved them. I soon found out they weren't, in fact, listening—mainly because, like me, they were speeding and therefore too busy telling me how much they cared about me to be listening. Believe me, two speeding Mods having a conversation was a sight, or should I say sound, to behold. Instead of conversing back and forth, everybody spoke at the same time. Yet it was all so deep and meaningful, man. "Love ya, man, I really do. What was your name?" And so it would go on and on and on and on… until the pills wore off. Then came the scourge of being a Mod: *the dreaded comedown.* The only cure for a comedown from speed in those days was to drink fairly heavily, but that was a pretty crude remedy that had its own drawbacks, like a hangover. Now the only cure for all of this is, of course, more of the hair of the dog that bit you. It took years of educating myself about addiction to realise that the insanity of the disease of alcoholism is that, once you have done something that is Clearly Very Bad for You, you go and do it all over again!

During the spring and summer of 1965, two bands appeared on *Ready Steady Go!*—the best show ever broadcast on British television—that forever changed my life. The first were the Who, performing "I Can't Explain," pound for pound the greatest debut single ever by a British rock band. Then, not to be outdone, Small Faces performed "Whatcha Gonna Do About It" that summer. (Although, it has to be said, it was the Kinks, with "You Really Got Me" in 1964, who really got it all goin' on, and apparently inspired Pete Townshend to write "I Can't Explain.")

There have been a number of books and various album liner notes that tell the story about how my brother and I were complete Small Faces freaks, and that our band did nothing but try to copy Small Faces. Whilst it was true that we did that to a certain extent, we were also a Who copy band—and in that period between the early spring of 1965 and the end of 1966, just about every band in England was doing the same. That's how much influence those two bands had on everybody. A lot has been made of the fact that our band's name was Little People, which seemed a pretty blatant rip of Small Faces—but we had changed our name to Little People a full two months before we first saw Small Faces on *RSG*. The thing that struck us, and me in particular, was the incredible likeness among Kenney Jones, Keith Moon, and I. With Kenney and I, it was like looking in the mirror; it was freaky.

Bearing in mind that we were all still kids, you can just imagine how it bowled us over to see Small Faces, a band of really cool-looking midgets who played great, sounded huge, and were on TV. They showed us that almost anything's possible and that we did have a chance, so long as we played our cards right. There were other similarities as well, although if you tried to guess who influenced whom, you might be surprised when you learned

the truth. For example, I had just bought a new Ludwig Silver Sparkle Super Classic drum kit, so when I first saw Kenney on *RSG* shortly thereafter and noticed he was using the exact same kit, all I could say was, "Far out, man," in the ver-

The only surviving photo of me playing my first set of Ludwigs.

nacular of the time. It had actually been Keith Moon who influenced me to get the silver kit, as he had one when I saw the Who on *RSG*. That's probably why Kenney had one, too. Kenney loved Keith's playing at the time, which is understandable: Keith was on fire back then. You could go to see the Who and not take your eyes off Keith the whole night—he was that good. Townshend was the same; you couldn't take your eyes off him either. Thank God that, in those days, bands played two, sometimes three or four, sets in one night, so you got a chance to focus on Keith and Pete, one set at a time.

By now we were living in Broxbourne, in a house near the river. The house was perfectly situated for a couple of young rock musicians, largely due to its close proximity to several great local venues. We were literally surrounded by great live rock 'n' roll: Wolsey Hall in Cheshunt, the Rhodes Centre in Bishop's Stortford, the Corn Exchange in Hertford, and the Locarno in Stevenage, to name but a few. All were within a 20-mile radius of home, and two were less than five miles away.

The list of performers we saw or supported at one or more of these venues, mostly in 1965 and '66, and often multiple times, reads like a Who's Who of British popular music of the time: Who, Small Faces, Spencer Davis Group, Zoot Money's Big Roll Band, Animals, Them (featuring Van Morrison), Moody Blues, Merseybeats, Fruit Eating Bears, Nashville Teens, Pretty Things, Creation, Mirage, Birds, Kinks, Action, John Mayall & the Bluesbreakers, Cream, Geno Washington & the Ram Jam Band, Screaming Lord Sutch, Steampacket (whose ranks included Long John Baldry, Rod Stewart, Julie Driscoll, and Brian Auger), Shotgun Express (Beryl Marsden, Rod Stewart, Peter Green, and Mick Fleetwood, among others), Undertakers (featuring Jackie Lomax), Georgie Fame and the Blue Flames, Gary Farr and the T-Bones… and several others lost to the vagaries of my memory.

On top of that little lot, Angus and I also saw, just before and during this period, many other acts elsewhere in England, including the Beatles, Rolling Stones, Yardbirds (with Eric Clapton), Muddy Waters, Jimmy Reed, and Brian Poole & the Tremeloes. (Later, in '67, we supported Pink Floyd, then still led by Syd Barrett, whose two classic, fractured solo albums I would eventually play on.)

All this before my 15th birthday! Looking back, it's enough to make your head spin, but you have to remember that going to see live bands was then the only form of affordable entertainment that existed for teenagers, other than the cinema and football.

As sad as it was to see the abrupt end of my formal education, I was absorbing massive amounts of musical information that would serve me extremely well in the not-too-distant future, although I didn't realize it at the time. I became a human sponge. But the real benefits of absorbing all this live performance were all the *non*-musical lessons to be learned: how to handle an audience, the importance of dynamics (light and shade), what to wear, and, more important, the way to wear it. Then there was the one-word descriptive, "style": that which makes you stand out from the next guy. That word was particularly important to drummers, as it was used to describe the way a drummer played, whether he sat low or high, used the modern grip or the traditional one, sat very still or moved his body around a lot, twirled his sticks or not. "So-and-so had a great *style*." The closest word today would be "technique," although it's not quite the same.

Other obsessions included the record collection and music on the telly. One friend in particular had an astonishing record collection. His name was John Price, and he is still a friend to this day, as are, I'm proud to say, the large majority of people I have mentioned in these pages so far—the ones who are still breathing, anyway. John ran the local record shop, which was more like a head shop in its atmosphere—and because all we did there was smoke dope. I soon came to realise how good things sounded when I was stoned. The great TV shows of the time—some of the finest ever broadcast—included the aforementioned *RSG, Thank Your Lucky Stars*, and *Top of the Pops* (which, curiously, was the least liked, cheesiest, and most uncool of them all—who knew?), plus any number of one-offs.

It has to be said that not everything you heard back then was good. Even considering how young and impressionable I was, I could always tell good from bad because I had started to play at such a young age that it gave me a different perspective than those who were music fans only, and not players as well. Although everyone starts out as fans, musicians are the biggest fans of all—so long as they don't get too jaded along the way to admit it.

Watching the good teaches you what to do, and watching the bad teaches you what *not* to do. I'm not here, however, to lambast those who suck; I'm here to celebrate the true giants of the Sixties music scene who I was privileged to learn so much from. They were huge talents who I owe such a massive debt of gratitude that it's hard to know where to start.

The one element of the Beatles that is sorely overlooked and understated is how good they were live. Back then, it all started and finished with live performance, which is a truism that's lasted to this day. If you haven't got it live, you may as well forget it, because you'll *never* become huge. Oh, you can make a great record that might sell zillions, but if you can't back it up live, you won't be staying at the party very long—in fact, I highly doubt whether you'll even make it to the encores!

In December 1964, Angus and I were lucky enough to get our hands on two tickets for one of the famous Christmas shows that the Beatles put on each year at the Hammersmith Odeon. The bill was outstanding: you saw not only the Fabs, but also the Yardbirds with Eric Clapton, Elkie Brooks backed by Sounds Incorporated, Freddie and the Dreamers, and more.

But Angus came to see and hear one thing only: Eric Clapton... and Clapton was sensational. The Eric Clapton we know and love today was very different back then. He moved! Not as extremely as Pete Townshend, but that kind of thing; there was even a windmill or two thrown in for good measure. It has to be said, though, that Eric arrived on the scene at least a year before the Who, and at the time, the word was that he intentionally put a stop to the stage-mover part of his performing style—and started standing in one place and using his guitar to emote for him—because others around him had taken to the mover-and-groover approach. Let's face it: the only thing Eric ever needed to show his emotions onstage was his guitar.

I also had reasons other than the Fabs to want to see the show. Tony Newman, the drummer with Sounds Incorporated, was out of this world; he too was a show all by himself. Plus, the band were as tight as a duck's bum, and Elkie Brooks sang her arse off. The show just kept getting better and better, and The Beatles hadn't even played yet. But they had appeared in short theatrical comedic skits a la Morecambe and Wise, which I thought was incredibly inventive for the time, but it sent the Beatles fans into distraction. Even Freddie and the Dreamers were entertaining, if you like that sort of thing.

And then the Beatles played. By that stage, they could have gone on and whistled "Dixie," and it wouldn't have mattered; they were that big. And the audiences were, in general, too busy peeing themselves and chucking jelly babies every which way to mind what was coming off the stage at them. The atmosphere was electric. It's often been said that you couldn't hear the Beatles when they played live and, equally, that they could not hear themselves. Well, I don't know about other gigs, but that night at Hammersmith they were *steamin'*. John and George's combined guitar sound was a great example of how rhythm guitars should be played. The bass sound was huge; Paul was playing lovely pedal bass through a lot of the tunes, which suited them perfectly. Ringo swung from the hip. And the vocals were outstanding. Not bad for a bunch of lads who couldn't hear themselves!

It was a wonderful time to be a young man in pursuit of his dreams.

Chapter 3
"Is Madame Garcia With You?"
December 1965 to December 1966

*In which the mighty Valkyrie become Little People;
my impossible dream comes true; Syd Banger takes us under
his wing; Andrew Loog Oldham doesn't want us to be Nice;
and Jimi likes me, but Ginger... not so much.*

With the extreme luxury of being surrounded by all this live music and having parents who were, as always, incredibly supportive, and who had become surprisingly lenient and liberal, we started to get the machinery of a working band whipped into shape. The first casualty in the line-up of the Valkyrie was Martin, the bass player, who had to go for personal reasons—getting engaged, or going to university, or some such circumstance. That was fine by us, as we were by now fully fledged stoners, and Martin didn't get high. He was a nice guy and a good player, and as we had not got it in us to fire him for abstinence, we were quietly thrilled that Mick Simms, the new bass player we recruited, loved to get high—*and* had a Morris Minor Van that fast became our mobile clubhouse. Park up, roll up, and laugh and eat for hours. As soon as Mick joined, we went into a small studio in the West End to record our first demo. The session went really well. We did one original and a Mose Allison cover, "Parchman Farm."

Around this time, we started to get heavily into blues music. It was one thing to be a seriously devoted listener of the blues, but it was a whole different ballgame to play it well. True feeling is so much a part of the form that you can't fake it—not if you're trying to do it for real—or you'll soon get found out. "It ain't what you do, it's the way that you do it" has never been more true than when it comes to the blues.

In and around the Hertford area, there lived an inordinate number of truly great blues players. Some, like Mick Taylor and little Jimmy McCulloch, went on to become world-renowned players—both of them with

John Mayall & the Bluesbreakers, then, of course, Mick with the Stones and Jim with Wings. But there were others from that area who were equally as good—and some who were, arguably, better—who never got past the local club and pub scene.

One of these bands was called Snook's Blues. The quality of each player was as good as it gets. In particular, the harmonica player and the guitarist—Bob Argent and Dick Wall, respectively—were the best in the country, or equal to the best, at that time. Snook's Blues are a perfect example of how the music business resembles a huge lottery, where having the talent is equivalent to buying the ticket. You have to be in it to win it—although there have been, sad to say, plenty of examples of huge success on the back of very little talent indeed. Snook's Blues were in it, but, unfortunately, while they had the talent, they had no luck at all. In most cases, *damn hard work* is the final and most important ingredient in a band's success if they are talented and lucky enough to become huge *and* want to stay there for a good while. But, as David Niven once said about acting, it sure beats working for a living.

Snook's Blues broke up prematurely, and we had the good fortune to be there when they did, so we swooped down like musical birds of prey and pinched their harp player, Bob Argent (and, later, their bass player, Dino Dines). With Bob on harmonica and rhythm guitar, we changed our name to the Little People, and soon were off and running.

><

Little People played hundreds of gigs all over the country, supporting dozens of great bands, including the Who, many times over. By the time we had supported the Who on several shows, we had seen the Small Faces a few times, but had never appeared on the same bill with them. Not long after we first saw them, I had a

THESE ARE THE LITTLE PEOPLE

MICK
bass

JERRY
drums

ANGUS
lead

BOB
rhythm

PETER
vocal

The band that Kenney Jones and Steve Marriott first saw me in.

dream that we opened for them, and while we were playing, they watched me from the wings and afterwards offered me the job of standing in for Kenney Jones should he ever get sick. They say to be careful what you pray for, as it might come true—and although this was a dream, not a prayer, it did indeed come true.

Dad had befriended a local promoter at a previous show we had done for the guy, and they had become partners on the shows the promoter put on at Wolsey Hall in Cheshunt. The promoter had been experiencing problems with the local authorities, so Dad told him that he could almost certainly make his problems go away, and that's precisely what happened. Getting his sons' band on this promoter's shows from then on was a shoe-in. Sure enough, it was only a matter of time before the promoter booked the Faces and hired us to support them. Because we were playing some of the same soul covers as the Faces, we had to alter our set list a bit. "Shake," "Ooh Poo Pa Doo," and other soul classics had to go, simply because the Faces were already well known for their unique renditions of them. Lots of bands did these tunes, but the Faces had made them their own.

Many bands at that time were either managed or road managed by the father of a band member. Some of these guys were looked upon as a pain-in-the-arse male equivalent of a pushy stage mum, but not Dad. His approach was practical: he would help us buy the equipment by acting as a guarantor for finance agreements, then we would make the payments out of gig money.

During our first set on the night of the Faces show, I looked to my left and, sure enough, there was Kenney Jones watching me play. I did my best to keep my cool and, most important, not screw up. He immediately dispelled my fears by giving me a huge smile and a big thumbs-up. What a nice guy. To this day, Kenney remains one of rock 'n' roll's true gentlemen and, I'm proud to say, a dear friend. That thumbs-up alone made my night, but when I looked over again, Kenney had Steve Marriott with him, and Steve was sporting an equally big smile and giving me another thumbs-up! After our show, they came and found me, gave me lots of encouragement, and asked, "Would you like to be Kenney's stand-in if he ever gets sick?" I couldn't believe what I was hearing; I remembered the dream, and it felt like déjà vu. So what started out as a childhood dream come true ended up becoming a friendship and working relationship with Steve Marriott that lasted for 25 years until his tragic death in a house fire in 1991, and a friendship with Kenney that has, as I said before, lasted to this day.

This incredible night of nights eventually changed my life forever, but in the immediate future, absolutely nothing happened. I never did act as Kenney's stand-in, not as a member of the Small Faces anyway (I did sub for him on some Immediate sessions). In fact, we completely lost touch with the Faces for quite a while, so I just put it down to a great night to remember and a great example of what a smashing bunch of lads they were back then.

They were very aware of how lucky they were, and were always keen to spot other young musicians who they could somehow encourage or give a helping hand.

The list of bands that the Small Faces befriended is long and impressive. You see, they just couldn't believe their luck: they'd had so much success, while others, who in their opinion were much more talented, did not. This drove them to help their fellow musos, which set them apart from many others in their position, who did not do nearly as much to help others. Still, I must say that the genuine sense of brotherhood that existed between bands in the mid-Sixties was one the defining and most endearing qualities of the music scene of that outstanding era. I, for one, am extremely proud to have been part—even though it was a very small part—of arguably the most creative decade of the twentieth century. I, as they say, am not worthy!

Little People carried on with our routine of playing lots of gigs, getting stoned, and listening to some of the greatest music ever to be produced. Stax were on a roll, as were Tamla Motown. Chicago blues was on fire; Muddy Waters was especially hot. Small Faces were at Number One with "All or Nothing." And, oh yeah, England won the World Cup!

Unfortunately, playing lots of gigs didn't peacefully coexist with school for me and Angus. We were simultaneously expelled when the headmaster finally got sick and tired of us showing up for school too sick and tired to do any work, because we had played a gig the night before and had not got in until four in the morning. We were often found asleep at our desks when we bothered to show up at all, which was not that often towards the end of our time there.

At around the same time, we were playing as the backing band for the Dixie Cups, a black American girl group best known for their smash hit, "Chapel of Love." At one show, at the Twisted Wheel in Manchester, the local Mods preferred us to the girls and let them know it in no uncertain terms. When we were fired for blowing them offstage, we were at a loss as to what to do.

It was early November 1966. By now, Little People's line-up had evolved even further. We had lost bassist Mick Simms to university, so Bob Argent moved over to bass, and we added ex-Snook's Blues bassist Dino Dines on Hammond organ.

We were on Shaftesbury Avenue, and I was looking in the window of Drum City, when somebody in the shop caught my eye. It was Steve Marriott, looking every bit the star, charisma just flowing out of him. He was dressed immaculately in a suit he designed and had made by Dougie Mill-ings, the famous bespoke tailor who had made all the suits for the Beatles. Steve's attire was very subtle—a miniature black-and-white dogtooth check for the jacket, a matching double-breasted waistcoat, black silk-mohair trou-sers, and a pair of white trainers—plus, he smelled like a million bucks. Dino walked straight up to him and asked if he would write and produce a single for us! I couldn't believe how much front Dino had to do this. Steve was taken aback, but soon recovered his composure and said, "Okay, here's my address and phone number. Give me a call, and we'll figure it out."

We couldn't believe our luck. One of the biggest rock stars in the British music industry at that time was offering us a song, the facility to produce it, and the record label to release it. We called him the next day and arranged to see him that night.

Steve in the same outfit he wore the first night we went up to see him in William Mews.

We all piled into the group van and headed to William Mews in Knightsbridge, the trendiest area of London. Steve had recently moved out of the group house and into a swank, ever so la-di-da mews house. It had a small living room, a tiny kitchen that seldom got used, and a bedroom and bathroom upstairs that you got to by way of a spiral staircase. (We didn't know it at the time, but, the year before, George Harrison and Ringo Starr had also lived in William Mews.)

I'll be the first to admit that I was pretty star-struck back then, although, in my defence, I was only 14. Steve was, as usual, immaculately dressed. He had on a golf-shirt-style sweater and a pair of mohair pants that were the bottom half of yet another Dougie Millings suit. He could not have been a more gracious host. We soon established the basis of all musicians' friendships in the mid-Sixties, which was that we were all stone-heads—dope smokers mainly, who made the occasional foray into liquid methedrine. LSD was yet to appear, and heroin and cocaine were around, but not yet on our agenda. This first night was all about getting to know each other, which back then meant get-ting *really* stoned. We had arrived armed with a lump of black hashish as a sort of "thanks for the invitation" present. It was a much appreciated gift, and also helped a great deal to break the ice.

Once we were settled in and had smoked a few spliffs, everybody, Steve included, started to relax, with one painful exception: Wagger. He chose to behave like a complete and utter twat, taking the piss out of everything

Steve said or did, for reasons known only to himself; maybe he was jealous. That aside, we had a tremendous evening, with Steve playing his favourite role of teacher. He loved nothing more than playing music he had recently discovered to a willing student who was keen to learn. I, for one, probably learned more that night than I had since I started playing five years before. So, while Steve was performing his party trick, I was egged on to perform mine, which was to roll a joint using nine cigarette papers, or "skins" as they're known. Steve was suitably impressed—so much so that from then on, he always introduced me as "a great little drummer who's only 14 and rolls a great nine-skinner."

As the evening wore on, it was painfully clear that either Wagger had to get rid of his attitude or we had to get rid of him. As Dino could sing every bit as good as he, it was a simple case of firing Wag and continuing as a four-piece. The sacking was helped along by a short phone conversation I had with Steve soon after the night at his house, in which he said something like, "I'd be glad to help you guys. You're all really nice lads, but the singer's got to go." A few days later, we were due to play a gig. We stopped at Wag's house, but instead of picking him up, we fired him right there on the pavement outside his house. He took it quite hard, which surprised us, and actually got tearful about it. But from our point of view, his bad attitude toward Steve, along with a fairly long list of other indiscretions, meant it had to be done. From what I understand, he didn't have to cry for too long, as he inherited his father's business and eventually became filthy rich.

Now that the dirty deed was done, it was time to get serious about playing as a four-piece with a Hammond organ, which allowed us to pursue all sorts of musical roads that had previously been out of bounds. Dad found a rehearsal room in a local school that we could use pretty much whenever we chose to without it costing us a penny. At this juncture, the band were showing great potential: we had good equipment that the gigs were paying for, and the friendship with Steve was developing nicely. In fact, it wasn't long before Steve made good on his agreement to record a single for us. He called one afternoon, asked if we could meet him at IBC Studios in Portland Place, and, almost as an afterthought, said, "Could you bring your equipment?"

Angus and I rounded up the troops and we headed for IBC, which Steve knew because the Small Faces had recorded their hit "Sha-La-La-La-Lee" and some other tracks there; the Stones, Who, and Kinks had also graced its hallowed halls. On arrival, we set up our gear and were ready to go. Steve got there soon after we did, and started to get a drum sound with the engineer in the control room as I bashed away on my kit in the studio.

When Steve's voice came through the talkback speaker—"'Ere, Jel, come and 'ave a listen"—I thought to my naïve, 14-year-old self, a listen to what? So, I dutifully walked upstairs to the control room and stood there in utter amazement as the huge speakers played the biggest drum sound I had ever heard. "Wow, that's great! Who is it?" I asked. "You, yer fool," Steve replied. Unbeknownst to me, they had been recording while we were doing the drum check.

We then got the rest of the sounds and started to learn the song, a Marriott/Lane composition called "Tell Me (Have You Ever Seen Me)." Ronnie Lane was also there, but he left in a bit of a huff. He had not seen eye to eye with Steve over the issue of other people recording their songs. From what I could gather, Ronnie didn't regard us as worthy proponents of his works, which is fair enough—we didn't exactly represent a nice little earner, did we? Steve didn't care about all of that; he just wanted to do a favour for a bunch of well-meaning youngsters who had become his mates, and there's nothing wrong with that in my book.

Everything went along very smoothly until we started to try to tape some of it. For no apparent reason, Bob Argent, our bass player, lost his nerve and froze. In very short order, I saw this chance of a lifetime disappearing before my eyes. But instead of saying, "Sorry, lads. My partner doesn't fancy it, and your bass player's fallen apart. See ya," Steve just carried on by picking up the bass and playing it as if he were our bass player—and we got it in the first take!

After adding some overdubs, including Steve on harpsichord and me on tympani, Dino did a fine job on the lead vocal. Steve and the engineer mixed it… and our very first single was done and dusted. There were a few minor details to sort out before we could release it. We had to play the song to Andrew Loog Oldham, the head of Immediate Records, to get his approval (to our great relief, he loved it); our name had to go; and we had to come up with a B-side.

Steve wanted to call us the Nice, but Andrew said no to that idea: he wanted to call us the Apostolic Intervention—and as he was the boss, we had to go along with it. We all hated it with a passion, but what are ya gonna do? It did hurt a bit when he turned around almost the next day and called P.P. Arnold's backing band the Nice. But it didn't really matter that much; we were just overwhelmed with gratitude that we had a single coming out that was written and produced by our hero, Steve Marriott.

The next hurdle was coming up with a B-side. In keeping with a Small Faces tradition, we chose to do an instrumental, which we recorded at Regent Sound on Denmark Street in the West End. We came up with a pseudo

Booker T. & the MG's rip-off that we called "Madame Garcia" after our euphemism for hashish. At that time, there were some huge drug busts in the music industry by a particularly zealous Scotland Yard detective, Sergeant Pilcher. So, to be safe, we developed code for telephone conversations: "Is Madame Garcia with you?" and so on. It sounds ever so hokey now, but back then it was better to at least try to be safe, so as not to be sorry.

Modern-day music historians who have studied the Small Faces have come to believe that "Madame Garcia" was in fact a Small Faces outtake, but that's not true. It was written by my brother Angus and Dino Dines, and performed by the Apostolic Intervention. But a Small Face, Steve, did appear on it, in addition to producing it: he played some lead guitar and sang a couple of backing vocals.

For a while, Steve would quite often call me and a few other of his musician mates to do sessions for him—recording whatever he or we fancied at the time—at Olympic Studios in Barnes. It was *the* hot place to record. There were two studios in the complex, with No. 1 being the most sought-after studio in England, and No. 2 a close second. All Steve wanted to do back then was work, work, and work. The man possessed limitless natural energy, and when he added abundant amounts of liquid methedrine to that, there was no stopping him. He had the luxury of an open-ended tab at Olympic No. 2, which made life extremely interesting, as the list of acts that recorded in the neighbouring No.1 during that time included the Rolling Stones, Jimi Hendrix Experience, Traffic, Chris Farlowe, and, on a couple of occasions, the Beatles.

To coax Glyn Johns to the session, Steve would tell him it was for the Small Faces—and then spike Glyn's tea with methedrine. So, even as Glyn was throwing his usual hissy fit about being conned into working with a bunch of unknown reprobates like us, he would inexplicably start to see the absolute sense in it! After all, who wouldn't want to work with the soon-to-be fabulous Syd Banger's Wally-Smashing Big Roll Band? One of Steve's finer band-name inventions, Syd and His Wally-Smashers was used for just about any set of players he had corralled for the evening's fun and games. I've been told that these Syd tracks would occasionally surface as part of recordings by the Andrew Oldham Orchestra, but I've never seen or heard any officially released evidence of such shenanigans, and Andrew recently confirmed to me that they were never released under the orchestra's name.

During these sessions, while I played my drums so Glyn could get a sound, Steve, bless his heart, would bring in some of his famous mates from No. 1 next door to listen to his little 14-year-old prodigy slap the crap out of his kit. At the time, I had the habit of playing with my head down, so the first I knew of it was when I looked up to see the likes of Jimi Hendrix, Mick Jagger, or Charlie Watts standing there, watching me with big smiles on their faces. Hendrix was great—he just said, "Yeah, man, that's cool, that's really cool"—whilst Charlie said, "Cor blimey, that's enough ta make me wanna cut me wrists orff." They were all such gentlemen, and I can never thank them enough for the encouragement they gave me. You see, I was shot through with insecurities about my playing—I didn't think I was any good. Plus, I was almost painfully shy at times, which is probably a big part of why I liked speed so much.

As if to make sure that none of this would go to my head, I got knocked down a peg a few months later when I was playing a gig at the Speakeasy. I could see Ginger Baker in the crowd—by the bar, of course. Although I hadn't played that well, it certainly wasn't a dreadful show. As we finished, I realized I would have to walk right past Ginger to get to our dressing room, and, bolstered by those kind words of encouragement just a few months back, I braved it. Just as I got to within hearing range of him, he looked straight at me and said, "Fucking shit!" No kind words of encouragement from Ginger, no big smile—just a scowl and "Fucking Shit!" So, just in case I was getting a bit too puffed up about my abilities or generally making a complete prat of myself, the Almighty (with a little help from Ginger Baker) slapped me down—and for that I am most grateful!

We now had a new name and our very own single with a cool B-side, and it was being released on Immediate, the hippest label of the time. Immediate was started by Andrew Oldham and his partner Tony Calder in July 1965. Andrew formed the company to accommodate all of his projects outside of the Rolling Stones' affairs. (He had discovered the Stones in 1963, going on to manage them until he sold his share to Allen Klein in 1966, and to produce all of their records until 1967's *Their Satanic Majesties Request*.) Immediate was also a vehicle for the Stones' extracurricular projects. It was literally a music factory where just about every top session musician, producer, arranger, and happening new band would work in some capacity or other. The label's first release was the McCoys'

The Apostolic Intervention's single (in both senses of the word) release, written and produced by Steve Marriott.

"Hang On Sloopy," a huge Number One hit, and in the first three years of its existence, Immediate seemingly couldn't put a foot wrong, and Andrew certainly had the Midas touch. Immediate was an exciting place to be back then; it simply oozed talent, charisma, star quality, originality, and plain old showbiz chutzpah—and we were sat smack dab in the middle of it.

Our introduction to Andrew was the stuff of "legend in his own lunch break"—literally. We arrived at Immediate's office on New Oxford Street promptly at 11:00 a.m., and were ushered into Tony Calder's office. Tony was the straight guy, the paperwork guy; Andrew was the creator. While Tony gave us the business talk, we played him our freshly produced single. He didn't comment on its quality, its content, or anything else—all he did was look at his watch and time it. So long as it was less than three minutes long, it was fine by Tony, and as the A-side and B-side were each barely two minutes, we were golden as far as Tony was concerned.

Suddenly, in burst Andrew through the adjoining door to his office. He didn't have star quality, he *was* Star Quality. He was dressed immaculately in a three piece handmade silk-mohair suit and smelled like a million bucks. (I was starting to see who Steve was stealing some of his licks from.) He was carrying a huge pile of records, both singles and albums. The very first thing he said to us was astonishing, profound, and *very true*. It went like this…

"In order for you to be successful in the music industry, you have got to learn how to write your own music. In order to do that, you have got to learn how to steal *without anybody realizing you've done so*. So here, I want you to take these, and steal, steal, steal, without getting caught!"

He then handed us a perfectly rolled joint to take into the demo studio for inspiration, and disappeared as quickly as he'd arrived. So that, ladies and gentlemen, was our introduction to the wonderful world of plagiarized rock 'n' roll—and Noel Gallagher wasn't even born yet!

We would spend untold hours at Immediate, either writing in the demo studio—nothing more than a small room with a piano and a reel-to-reel tape recorder—or hanging out in Andrew's office, smoking hash with his chauffeur, Eddie Reed, who could roll the most perfect joints. They looked exactly like cigarettes, so they could be smoked just about anywhere without being spotted as joints. The smell of the hash could be a bit of a giveaway, but, with enough front and plenteous amounts of strong cologne, Andrew could get away with smoking Eddie's hash joints anywhere he chose.

Don't get me wrong. I do not mean to imply that we had the run of the place; we didn't. In fact, in the world of Immediate Records, we were as far down the food chain as you could get. Still, we were treated with respect, and, as we were one of Steve Marriott's projects, it gave us a certain amount of leverage, I suppose—especially as Immediate were, technically, still in the throes of signing the Faces. It wouldn't be good business to piss off the lead singer at this juncture, now would it?

All of this was happening in the last few weeks of 1966. It was too late to release a single by an unknown band before Christmas, so Andrew rightfully decided to hold back our release date until the spring. In any case, we still needed photos taken and artwork designed. Andrew did everything first class; even a lowly band like us were sent to the best photographer, and at that time the best was Gered Mankowitz. He had just done the cover for the Stones' latest album, *Between the Buttons*, and his next big assignment was… us! What a charmed life we were leading, and I'm proud to say we were very thankful—because, I believe, of the way Mum and Dad raised us to be grateful for what we were given and to show that gratitude.

Chapter 4
Happy to Be a Part of the Industry of Human Happiness
August 1966 to July 1968

In which the Intervention's debut fails to bother the charts;
we get a taste of peace, love, and thievery at Ally Pally;
we storm Prickwillow with a little help from our friend Steve;
I am schooled in the fine art of fornication;
and four Little Women open for Hendrix.

As 1967 drew near, Steve was having trouble with his neighbours at William Mews, so he moved to Devonshire Place, off the Marylebone Road near Harley Street. This relocation was a mixed blessing. The good news was that Steve was now near the Immediate offices, IBC Studios, and one Dr. Robertson, who was renowned in musical circles for freely distributing all manner of pills and potions to his "patients." The bad news was the neighbours—well, it was bad news for Cilla Black anyway; bless her heart, she just was not ready for Charlie Mingus, Ray Charles, Jimi Hendrix, Lord Buckley, and Booker T. & the MG's at full volume all night long.

At about the same time, three things happened that sent the music scene into the stratosphere, and then some. The first was the Beatles coming off the road and concentrating on studio work. Their first post-touring outing was *Revolver*, which cemented their role as musical trendsetters and got everybody's attention as a sign of tremendous things to come. (One of the album's tracks was "Doctor Robert," which some say was the band's thinly disguised tribute to the aforementioned Dr. Robertson.) The Beatles had single-handedly raised the bar of excellence to such an extreme height that just trying to keep up was not an endeavour for the musically faint hearted. The second event was the arrival of a real gentleman called Jimi Hendrix, who took everybody by storm. And the third was the appearance of a substance that had been experimented with by the CIA in the 1950s as a means to make spies more talkative—whilst gently sending them completely bonkers—LSD.

And consider this: in the 12 months from October 1966 to October 1967, you heard, for the first time ever, "Strawberry Fields Forever" and "Penny Lane" (a double A-side single) by the Beatles; "Hey Joe," "Stone Free," and "Purple Haze" by Hendrix; "I Feel Free" and "Strange Brew" by Cream; "I Can See for Miles" by the Who; and "Good Vibrations" by the Beach Boys!

With the release of the Beatles' single and the sudden appearance of the Jimi Hendrix Experience, it felt like the entire music business had been given a warning shot across its bow that something *huge* was about to happen. There was a palpable excitement in the air that made it clear that things were never going to be the same, that any and all previously set boundaries or limitations were being blown out of the water, and that *absolutely anything* was possible now.

It isn't easy to try to recreate the excitement of that time on these pages, but it's important to remember that the way Hendrix played had *never* been done before, and the way the Beatles were experimenting in the studio had *never* been done before either. So, if you can imagine hearing, for the very first time, the music those two artists produced at the start of 1967, you might just about be able to get an idea of what the musical atmosphere was like back then.

When Eric Clapton and Pete Townshend first went to see Hendrix in London, they came away completely done in, as if they had seen and heard something that was not of this earth. They felt as if they may as well give up, as he was already doing everything they were still trying to do. Thankfully, their reticence to continue was short lived. It does, however, give a powerful illustration of Jimi's mind-blowing effect on everybody.

So this, dear reader, was the atmosphere that surrounded us—four little lads from North London—as we were about to launch our recording career. We were fully aware of our place in the grand scheme of things, which was as far down the pecking order as you could possibly be without not actually pecking at all. But we weren't inspired to give up; we were just "Happy to Be a Part of the Industry of Human Happiness," to quote Andrew's utterly daft Immediate slogan.

I'm not sure what was responsible, but something unusual was happening to our little band: we were starting to get pretty good. We had begun to get a grip on improvising, and it was great fun. It suited us, as we were not the most structured set of people you were likely to meet—plus, it was fast becoming the thing to do. It had even been given a new name: jamming.

Jazz musicians had been doing it for years, and we were listening to a certain amount of jazz back then: Charlie Mingus, Jimmy Smith, Jimmy McGriff, Ray Charles with Count Basie (my personal favourite). Also, a lot of hash was being smoked, and LSD was starting to be consumed. All this added up to a much more free-form approach to playing rock.

Improvisation also covered a myriad of sins. If you were a bit short on new material or finding it hard to come up with a lot of original tunes, it was an easy way to pad out your show. You could take a song with a simple three-minute format, leave an opening in the middle for jamming, and very quickly end up with a 20-minute epic. Now your previously short show could easily become as long as you liked.

It was only weeks before the famous Summer of Love would begin, and our debut single was about to be released. Did we feel intimidated? Nah. Scared to death? Yeah! Still, things started to noticeably improve for the Apostolic Intervention. With the release of "Tell Me (Have You Ever Seen Me)" set for the beginning of April, we started to get a better class of bookings, particularly in and around London. We somehow managed to blag a residency at the Electric Garden, a new, happening club in Covent Garden. It was one of the first clubs that catered to the up-and-coming psychedelic movement and, along with UFO, was the Mecca for partakers of mind-altering drugs like LSD. Pot and hash were smoked openly at these places, but, although alcohol was served as far as I remember, it wasn't on the agenda of the fledgling hippie scene (or the underground scene, as it was then known).

When the release of our long-awaited (by us) single finally arrived, it created, sad to say, as much excitement as watching paint dry. It got a few lukewarm reviews (including a half-decent one from Alan Price of the Animals, who was reviewing celebrity singles that week in *Melody Maker*) and failed to make any impression on the charts whatsoever. When we inquired about its progress, we got the standard industry reply, which, roughly speaking, went: "It's too early… it's too early… it's too early… It's too late." At least it flopped in outstanding, never-to-be-repeated fashion. Now that I possess over 40 years of experience in such matters, I can easily see why it stiffed: it simply wasn't good enough. Not that it was bad by any means; it just wasn't a strong enough tune to stand out amongst the other releases of that time. I can also see now that it lacked the required amount of promotion a single needed to succeed.

Gered Mankowitz's publicity shots of the band turned out to be excellent, as you would expect, and the flurry of good gigs we booked were getting even better. We managed to get a spot on the "Alexandra Palace International Love-in Festival," which was described as a "happening," whatever that was supposed to mean (the opposite of a non-event, perhaps?). We were thrilled to be on the bill because there were lots of big names there, including Pink Floyd and the Crazy World of Arthur Brown. (Three months earlier, Ally Pally had hosted the "14 Hour Technicolor Dream," which featured some of the same acts—plus Yoko Ono, who invited the audience to come up one at a time and cut her clothes off with a pair of scissors, as you would.)

Somehow, we managed to secure the most curious spot on the bill at the Love-in Festival, one that clearly illustrated just how far down the food chain we in fact were. They wanted us to open the show before the bulk of the audience arrived (no surprise there) and then close the show—or, should I say, be the last to play. Bearing in mind that the event was around 12 hours long, that meant going back on the next morning—not a pretty sight.

The whole show was pretty shambolic, as were most of the early hippie festivals. We went on in the evening to start the show… and the crowd went mild. Until, that is, Angus, while holding his guitar, also grabbed his microphone, which, unbeknown to him, was live. He got the biggest shock of his life—an electric one, that is—and was literally thrown clean across the stage. At this point, the audience finally came to and, thinking it was part of the show, gave us, or at least our levitating guitarist, a standing ovation—before going back to sleep when he couldn't repeat it.

As we weren't due on again until the following morning, we put our equipment at the back of the stage in readiness for that second set. As if to prove to us that the peace-and-love ethos of the new hippie movement was in fact a load of bollocks, when the time came to go on again, our PA system had been stolen. (So maybe a "happening" was an event where they "happen" to steal your equipment?) Thankfully, we had put the guitars and drums back in the van, and the Hammond organ was too heavy to pinch. We never did play our second set, due to lack of equipment on our part and lack of interest on the audience's part.

Through all this, Steve, bless his heart, went way beyond the call of duty, trying to help us. One example was when he asked a friend to put us on a gig supporting Screaming Lord Sutch in Newmarket. Another was when he showed up unannounced at a gig in a faraway place out in the fens called Prickwillow—and that tale is the stuff of real Steve Marriott legend.

At the time of the story I'm about to tell, Steve was at the absolute zenith of his powers as a member of the biggest band in the land. Everybody loved the Small Faces. Even the people who, for one reason or another, didn't like them, secretly did. They were, as Paul Weller has put it, the perfect band. They even played their one shortcoming—the fact that they were short—to their advantage. After all, they weren't just a bunch of short-ass midgets, they were an extremely talented, funny, original, great-looking, fantastic-live bunch of short-ass midgets.

Small Faces publicity photo.

To compare how big they were from late '67 into early '68 to Michael Jackson in the mid-Eighties, or the Beatles and Stones in the early Sixties, would not be exaggerating at all. (It is a great shame for them that their financial fortunes could not also compare so favourably, but that was the Small Faces for ya. More on that later...)

Out of Steve's growing hunger to get away from the whole pop-star pin-up shtick that had been haunting him and the band for some time, he looked for any opportunity he could find to cut loose, get away from it all, and just play the blues with his mates somewhere—anywhere, frankly. But his life had been lived in the proverbial fishbowl since the Faces found success, so that was a lot easier said than done.

Steve was dating yet another stunner, a blond from Sweden called Eve. He had just moved into the house in Chiswick where he famously "sat on the karsi while he sussed out the moon" on any "Lazy Sunday" he might choose. (For you non-Brits who don't know, "karsi" is slang for "toilet.") Only on this particular Sunday, he also chose to call a limo (one of the luxuries that came with the Faces signing to Immediate) and, with the Swedish stunner in tow, was driven down to Mum and Dad Shirley's house in Nazeing, Essex, so that he could follow us lot to Prickwillow. Eve is over from Sweden for a visit—does he take her to Tramp or the Speakeasy or some trendy restaurant in Mayfair? If he had, he would have caused a huge stir, the paparazzi would have done their thing, and Eve might have preferred that as a night out—but no, he takes her to Prickwillow so he can play the blues with his mates. You gotta love him.

So this huge black limo pulls up outside our folks' house, and out jumps *Steve Marriott*. The neighbours could not believe their eyes; they were gobsmacked, to use the modern speak.

Steve absolutely adored our parents, especially Mum. He got on particularly well with her—the two of them made each other laugh a lot, and Steve loved that she treated him like a completely normal person.

After tea and sandwiches, it was time to hit the road to Prickwillow. What a sight we were: the group's van—our clubhouse on wheels—followed by a great big black limousine carrying one of the most famous rock stars in England and his Svenulan beauty ("Svenulan" being Steve-speak for "Swedish"). By now, the neighbours had given up all pretence of subtlety and were lined up outside their houses, waving as we drove past, as if to a member of the Royal Family on the way to cut a ribbon somewhere.

We arrived at the gig and formulated a plan, deciding to say nothing whatsoever about Steve's presence. Our luck was in; the hall had an old-fashioned stage with a curtain that actually opened and closed. So, we decided that when we started our second set, Steve would already be onstage with us and would start to play and sing right from the start—before anyone could see him—while the curtain was mysteriously taking its sweet time to open.

We started the second set with Steve's favourite slow blues, "Five Long Years" by Eddie Boyd, which Muddy Waters had made his own. The hall was packed to the rafters, simply because it was a Sunday night in Prickwillow, and back then, nothing else ever happened on a Sunday night in that neck of the woods. As the curtain slowly opened and the penny started to drop, the collective look of disbelief on the audience's faces was remarkable. As soon as they heard that voice, they knew immediately who it was; they just couldn't quite believe it. Quite frankly, neither could I. The sheer power of Steve's voice completely bowled me over. Even though I was only 15, I had been playing either semi-pro or professionally since I was nine, and in all that time, I had *never* heard anything quite that powerful. In those days, we didn't have monitor systems for the band to hear the vocals through; the PA system was there solely to amplify the vocals for the audience. We had, by the standards of the time, a pretty decent PA, and I was used to just barely being able to hear the lead vocalist through it. But I could hear Steve loud and clear.

Four hundred jaws dropped simultaneously, and everyone tried to get closer to the stage en masse, so that by the end of that first song, all hell broke loose. All I remember about the rest of the evening is how much better everybody played, especially yours truly. It was the first of many huge musical eye-openers that were in store for me. I realised that, given the opportunity to play with extremely high-class musicians, I could rise to the occasion, above the standards I was used to—and maybe, one day, go on a hell of a journey. Again, be careful what you pray for.

We played and played, and then, when we were done playing, we played some more, and all the time the crowd was going absolutely nuts. They just could not believe that there they were, deep in the heart of Prickwillow, and there he was—none other than Steve Marriott—singing and playing his arse off. We were told afterwards that a number of them thought at first that it was someone doing an incredible impersonation of Steve; but, believe me, by the end, everybody knew full well that it was the man himself.

Considering the number of times Steve was asked, "Are you really Steve Marriott? You are, aren't you?" that night, he handled it all really well. To be honest, I think he got quite a kick out of it, simply because we had pulled off the surprise so perfectly. On the way home, when we stopped at a big transport café for a bite to eat, the guy next to Steve in the queue, waiting to order his food, suddenly realised who he was standing next to and said, "It's not, is it? You're him, aren't you? Can I get your autograph?" Steve was still being nice, but by now he was playing up to the centre-of-attention rock star role a bit. He asked the chap who he wanted the autograph made out to, and as he started to write, the guy turned to the whole room and announced at the top of his voice, "I can't believe I'm talking to Rick Nelson! Thanks, Rick! I've got all your records!" Apparently, this bloke had readily spotted that Steve was a star (it was hard not to)—so he had the right persona, but the wrong person. True story.

This was a truly magical time for Angus and me. In fact, it was a truly magical time, full stop. Something was about to happen that was going to change, yet again, the standard of how things were recorded and push the bar higher forever. This something was called *Sgt. Pepper's Lonely Hearts Club Band*, and it changed the world through music. The Beatles had pulled off a master stroke, and everybody knew it. They had made the perfect record, and no one could get near it, not for a while anyway. Part of what made it so perfect was its many imperfections, which made the music human, but made the Beatles appear, to us mere mortals, as if they were of another world. Thank God for those imperfections. The out-of-tune guitars, the comb-and-paper brass sections, and the slightly behind-the-beat way that Ringo, bless him, plays the grooves—they made young working musicians such as ourselves realise that great rock 'n' roll does not need to *be* perfect, it just has to *feel* perfect.

Although I had effectively finished my formal education as early as September 1966, I was supposed to have continued at home through a correspondence course, which, because my mother was a teacher, satisfied the authorities. Once February 4, 1967, came round, I legally didn't have to pick up pen and paper anymore. So it was that, at the grand old age of 15, I was officially a fully professional working musician, although in real terms I had already been so for nearly three years.

Once I turned 15, I did make a couple of attempts at working in the real world, mainly because that was the legal age to start work if you left school. But there was another reason why I had to have a look at finding "real" work: the band was falling apart at the seams. After the single flopped and a few other ill winds blew through our camp, the whole thing just wasn't paying the bills anymore. Back then, a young man who was not bringing in any money did not just go and sign on for the dole, as they seem to be able to do today—he *had* to go and find work.

I had for some time been working as a painter's mate, helping a friend of Dad's called Mick Young, better known to all and sundry as Mick the Brick. Mick was (and still is) quite a character (and has, by the way, remained a lifelong friend, although I rarely see him since he moved to Australia many years ago), who later achieved global notoriety by getting into the Guinness Book of World Records for being the planet's fastest wallpaperer. Dad recruited him to roadie for us at night, and I would help him paint houses by day. I am forever grateful to Mick for this, as he taught me a lot about life in general, way beyond how to paint a house. Being at least 10 years my senior, and quite the expert himself, he gave me invaluable knowledge on the all-important subject of What Women Want.

In the late Fifties, there was a TV show called *Six-Five Special.* It was one of the first rock 'n' roll shows aired on British television. Every week, they had a troupe of professional dancers on the show; I suppose they were the original Pan's People (the featured dancers on *Top of the Pops* some years later). One of them was an old friend of Mick's, and, once he and I had become firm friends, he decided it was time for me to receive some practical sex education. Today, I suppose, you could call it "on the job" training. I will forever remain grateful to this fine young lady for helping me along the way to at least a basic working knowledge of what makes the fairer sex happy.

I am going to openly admit to stealing a few words from my favourite autobiographer, David Niven, simply because the words his Pimlico hooker used in her bedroom tutelage were exactly the same as the first line Mick's beloved dancer friend, Sheila, said to me: "Use yer elbows, dear. That's right. Now slower, slower." She continued with, "See, I told you, young lad: it's not a sprint, it's a fuckin' marathon, innit. Now, sprint at the end if you must. That's right, youngster. Go on now, go, go, go... YEAHHH! Cor blimey, love, you sure you haven't done this much before? Oh, that's right, yer a drummer, ain't yer? It's all that natural fuckin' rivvem, innit." Ah, bless her heart, Sheila had such a way with words. She also had a machine gun, rat-a-tat-tat laugh, which caused an interesting expand-and-contract effect in her nether regions and left Air Vice-Marshal Sir Harold Pilferington-Spludgebucket (aka my bits and pieces) wondering whether he was getting a congratulatory pat on the head or a severe throttling. In fits of laughter on the way home, Mick the Brick and I could be heard singing (to the tune of "Fascinating Rhythm") "Paradiddle pussy is Sheila's M.O.!"

As sad as it was, it was inevitable that Angus and I would eventually break our musical ties. It wasn't easy by any means. We had been inseparable since the beginning of our musical journey, with rare exception. Angus had grown tired of all the bullshit the music business wears like a bad suit that it never takes off. He did not care for Dino, and, frankly, neither did I. Angus had been going out with a very pretty local black girl, Denise, and he wanted to do more than just see her every now and then. So, he decided to quit the band and try settling down with her for a while, thus making our parting of the ways, musically speaking, a lot easier, since I didn't have to leave him in order to go forward myself. Still, it was very strange not being with my bruv at all times.

I had, however, seen it coming for a while. As incredibly talented as Angus was in so many different ways, the one thing he was not that great at was playing the guitar. There were a couple of practical reasons why his guitar skills didn't exactly flourish. Angus was left handed, yet, for some reason, his first guitar tutor insisted that he learn to play right handed. Also, as a teenager, Angus had had an accident that cost him the tips of his left-hand fingers (which a right-handed player uses on the fretboard), and once that had happened, he really struggled to improve. I was always very proud of how my older brother tried to continue in spite of this obvious setback, which was nothing to do with his decision to call it a day—he'd just simply had enough.

The last gig the Apostolic Intervention played was at the De Montfort Hall in Leicester, opening up for Family. Angus decided to mark the occasion by going onstage wearing nothing but his guitar, laying his soul—well, his arse, anyway—bare for the sake of his art.

A few days later, I saw an ad in a music paper that a band called the Wages of Sin wanted a drummer and a Hammond organist. I called and spoke to their manager, who sounded keen to give Dino and me an audition. (It's amazing what youthful ambition will do to influence your decisions; even though I didn't like Dino, I had no problem moving on to another band with him.) So off we drove in the cold, early January night to Royston, just south of Cambridge, to audition at the house of the lead singer and bandleader, Colin Freeman.

The lead guitarist was an extremely gifted player called Tim Renwick. Vic the bass player was also good, and Colin was at least adequate. They were obviously concerned about my age, which was understandable. They had no problem with Dino, who did his best to alleviate their concerns about me: "Wait until you hear him; he'll blow you away." With that, we chose a song that everybody knew—"Come on Up" by the Young Rascals—and went for it. We picked that tune because it *cooked*—you just can't sit down to it. The smiles all round on the faces of the band showed that they'd never heard anything quite like it. Their manager, Barry, had the biggest smile. He was so happy, he may as well have done a jig around the room, singing, "We're in the money!" "When can you start?" was his less-than-subtle response. Sensing the band were onto a winner, he didn't see the point in playing those "We'll let you know" games. This gave the band a chance to cut to the chase and get rehearsing, so that, with a little luck, they would not have to cancel any of the gigs that were already booked.

I played well with Vic (it's always a plus when I connect with a bass player), and soon realised what a privilege it was to play with such an incredibly talented musician as Tim Renwick. Tim has gone on to become one of the most successful session guitarists in the business, having played on more than a thousand albums and toured with some of the biggest names in the world of live music, including Elton John, Pink Floyd, Roger Waters, and Eric Clapton, to name but a few. He also spent a long time playing guitar for the Sutherland Brothers & Quiver, with Willie Wilson, one of my best friends, on drums.

What a lucky boy I was back then. I seemed to keep landing on my feet, continuing to be fortunate enough to find myself playing with the best of the best, and I'm glad and proud to say that this was to be the case for some time to come.

I must say, though, that the band was not completely shot through with talent: Colin, the lead singer, was as charismatic as a used paintbrush. He also wasn't the best-looking lad I'd ever met; he was your basic nose on legs, with hair and a pulse. Still, he could sing—if you like Engelbert Humperdinck, which, of course, none of us did. On top of that, the rest of us had one big thing in common that Colin didn't share: we were stoners. Smoking hash was a religion to us, and anybody who did not partake was considered weird or, as we used to say, a straight, a Norman normal, or just plain uncool. So the first order of business, once Dino and I got established within the ranks, was to engineer the expulsion of the lead singer from his own band. Ah, what wonderful, morally sound people youthful ambition had made us. In truth, though, it would be a necessary move for the band so that it could progress in the climate of the times. Show business is a cold, cold world, with the moral fortitude of a kleptomaniac prostitute.

We agonised over the impending firing of Colin for some time. Finally, we decided to take the high ground and do the right thing: we just didn't bother to pick him up on the way to the next gig. What a fine, upstanding set of self-serving assholes we were—we never wrote, we never called.

Once the dirty deed was done, we had to change our name from the Wages of Sin, as that belonged to Colin. We chose Little Women. Don't ask me why, 'cos I have no idea; it simply seemed like a good idea at the time. Anyway, I blame Tim Renwick, as he thought of it—that's my story, and I'm sticking to it.

Now that we'd changed lead vocalists, with Tim and Dino sharing those duties, we also had to change the entire repertoire, and that cemented the strong bond between us because it was such fun figuring out in which direction we wanted to go. Much great music was being produced in 1968, so as a cover band desperately striving to find our own feet, we had a veritable mountain of choices to pick from. With Colin at the helm, the band had been a fairly lucrative pseudo-soul outfit. The fact that he had no soul, vocally speaking, had its drawbacks but, remarkably, did not seem to prevent the band from getting booked. With that background, and because of our personal preferences, we naturally gravitated to progressive soul like Traffic and Joe Cocker, even the Doors and Buffalo Springfield, but most of all Hendrix and Cream.

In the late spring of 1968, a huge amount of wonderful music had recently been released, all of which would have a powerfully influential effect on us, as it did on everybody. There were *Mr. Fantasy* and *Traffic* by Traffic; the Stones' *Beggars Banquet*, arguably their finest hour; the Beatles' "White Album"; Taj Mahal's first album; and Jimi Hendrix's *Axis: Bold as Love* (to be followed in the fall by *Electric Ladyland*). Bernard "Pretty" Purdie had come to the fore and introduced the world to funky drumming, which was soon shortened to just Funk; Aretha Franklin was blowing everybody out of the water; and as if that lot wasn't enough, the Who had just wound up one of the finest runs of singles ever released, by any band, with "I Can See for Miles," the best four minutes and 18 seconds they have ever recorded. Not to be outdone, the Small Faces came up with "Tin Soldier," which was their equivalent. Those two bands had recently toured Australia together, and they tore the place up—I don't mean musically, although I'm sure they did that, too; I mean they *tore the place up.*

By this time, the Who were becoming truly remarkable live. They were always great, but they were now becoming un-fuckin'-believable. The Small Faces, though, were starting to lose their edge a bit onstage. The simple difference was that the Who had been touring the States a lot, whereas the

The Ogdens' Nut Gone Flake *album, with its revolutionary cover.*

Faces had never been to America. It was painfully clear to the Faces that they desperately needed to do something so they wouldn't get left behind. The something they came up with not only helped them catch up on any ground they may have lost to bands like the Who, it shot them ahead of the entire pack. It was their masterpiece, their coup de théâtre: *Ogdens' Nut Gone Flake.*

Our band house was in Great Shelford, a small village four miles south of Cambridge. Steve and his new wife, Jenny, had just moved into Beehive Cottage, a house in Essex that they shared with Ronnie Lane and his wife, Sue. He invited us down on a number of occasions, and on one of the first visits, he gave us a pre-release copy of *Ogdens'* to take home and enjoy, which is exactly what we did—over and over and over again—and we *never* tired of it. I truly believe that Small Faces were the only British band to attempt their own answer to *Sgt. Pepper* and pull it off. Of course, you could argue that I am somewhat biased, and you would be right—but I am also a working musician with almost 50 years of experience, and if there was another record released at the time that deserves that accolade more than *Ogdens',* I'm still waiting to hear it.

Once *Ogdens'* came out, it became a huge hit, climbing to Number One in five weeks, and staying there for six. The single, "Lazy Sunday," was also a huge hit that got to Number Two and stayed there for a good while. I was so proud of, and happy for, the Faces because they had done the undoable, and it certainly seemed, judging by sales, that the whole country agreed. It was a great time to be a huge Small Faces fan and an honour to be a friend of theirs, albeit a small one!

There have been many musical highlights in my life, but only a handful are in the same league as seeing the Jimi Hendrix Experience live in the summer of 1968 at an open-air festival on the grounds of stately Woburn Abbey in Bedfordshire. (And I not only saw them, I got to play on the same bill.) Jimi was at his very best, at the absolute pinnacle of his strengths and influence, palpable omnipotence at its finest, or, as they might say in Waltham Cross, "Unbe-fuckin'-lievable!"

Little Women had the daunting task of opening the show, which included, amongst others, Tyrannosaurus Rex (the pre-T. Rex two-piece, with Marc Bolan, sitting cross-legged playing acoustic guitar, and a bongo player), Family, and, of course, Hendrix. We went down quite well, I have to say, and were well chuffed with ourselves, especially as the second band on were a sort of white soul band that had recently released a fairly weak cover of a Sly & the Family Stone song. They died a death and came close to being booed off, which encouraged us even more as that could have been us, but we had survived with actual *applause*. After Family had played, rightfully going down a storm and nearly stealing the show, anybody other than Hendrix who had to follow them would not have risen to the task at hand.

I remember highlights like the debut of "Voodoo Chile," a new song from Jimi's soon-to-be-released album, *Electric Ladyland*, plus a five-minute intro to "Purple Haze" and a great reworking of the slow blues "Red House." I also remember how amazing he looked. He was a bit more tailored looking than before, and his hair was a bit shorter; he just looked *in charge*. My girlfriend at the time, Sally, who was stood next to me in the enclosure in front of the stage, right in front of Jimi, epitomized the entire audience by standing with her mouth wide open in disbelief at what she was witnessing. When the Experience came to the end of each song, the audience response was surprisingly subdued, not because they didn't like what they were hearing and seeing, but because they were in complete shock. Gobsmacked doesn't even come close to describing it accurately, unless you can imagine 50,000 gobs simultaneously smacked. After speaking to some of Jimi's crew then and later in life, I found out that this was the normal reaction at a Hendrix concert. Sitting here 40 years later, I can tell you that this was the one and only time I have ever witnessed such a response to any band.

By now, I had developed a pretty strong sense of what type of drummer I wanted to be. I had my clear favourites, the three main ones being Kenney Jones, Mitch Mitchell, and Keith Moon, all of whom represented everything, in my opinion, that was good and great about British drummers. Although, as Charlie Watts got older, he kept getting better and better, so that by the time "Jumpin' Jack Flash" and *Beggars Banquet* were released, every time he went into the studio, what came out was a master class in everything that is important about what to play as a rock 'n' roll drummer. In fact, with Charlie it is more about what *not* to play. He is, and always has been, the absolute master of the keep-it-simple approach to playing, and I've learned more from him over all these years than from all the others put together.

On the American side, there was Al Jackson of Booker T. & the MG's; Levon Helm from the Band, the greatest non-drummer drummer God ever had the good sense to create; and Sonny Payne from Count Basie's band. "But that's not rock 'n' roll!" I hear you protest, to which I reply, "Bollocks," simply because Sonny Payne and Count Basie are probably more responsible for all that is rock 'n' roll (certainly the roll part) than even the Stones. If, perchance, you question my judgement, just ask Charlie. He'll tell ya!

The reason I have made such a strong point about this is that it is at the absolute core of everything I have tried to achieve as a drummer. "If it don't swing, it don't mean a thing" has been my lifelong mantra regarding my approach to rock 'n' roll drumming. It has to make your hips move, or it ain't rock 'n' roll. After all, the term itself started life as a Black American euphemism for fucking. I therefore rest my case. I have always felt that it is the drummer's responsibility to physically move his bandmates and, as a result of that, move the audience. He very much needs the powerful and complete assistance of his partner in crime, a great bass player, to achieve this. The rhythm section is the engine room of any band, but this is particularly true in rock 'n' roll.

There is nothing in the world that equals the incredible feeling of strength when you are up there on stage, smacking the shit out of a big old kit of drums while both the bass player and rhythm guitarist are stuck so tightly to what you are playing that you can look out and see the audience swaying and dancing in time with it all. The drum throne really is the best seat in the house, especially if you see a gorgeous lady in the audience, dancing in time to your playing. That you cannot beat.

Chapter 5
"'Ello, Mate, It's Steve."
July to December 1968

In which one Pete takes me to meet another;
Steve Marriott says no thanks to some dodgy new band,
but asks to join another; "The Universal" proves to be
something less than that; and I have a serious Tooth ache.

I had not seen or spoken to Steve Marriott for some time; in fact, Angus had seen more of him recently than I had. The two of them were concerned about the amount of LSD I was taking. I had dyed my hair with streaks of silver grey, which went wrong and turned into the colours of the rainbow, with a predominance of pink and dirty yellow blond, and that had given them cause for concern. I can't imagine why.

And then, in the late summer of 1968, I received a phone call from Steve that was to change my life forever. In fact it changed *all* of our lives forever, in one way or another.

"'Ello, mate, it's Steve. How are ya? Long time, no see. How's that dodgy hairstyle of yours? Grown out yet, has it, you silly bugger? Anyway, listen. You've heard of Peter Frampton, haven't ya? That's right, the fella wiv the Herd. Well, Townshend turned me on to him, and let me tell ya, he's brilliant. He wants to form his own band; I've told him all about you. Can you get down here tomorrow?"

The potential from this one phone call was mind boggling.

The next morning, I had a problem with transport to get me down to Beehive Cottage: I didn't have any. Charlie Weedon, our new roadie, was a bit of an unreliable character, and I didn't know him well enough to feel comfortable with taking him into Steve and Jenny's house, which was a sound decision on my part. I chose instead to ask a lifelong friend called Pete Loynes, who I knew had no axe to grind. For one thing, Pete, at the tender age of 21, was already financially independent due to a one-armed

Jenny and Steve at Beehive Cottage.

bandit and pinball machine business that he and his brother had started with their father soon after leaving school, and Steve was a pinball fanatic who wanted a machine at home. For another, Pete was a fan of rock music. He was immensely well mannered and diplomatic, and got on with Steve and Jenny immediately.

Meeting Peter Frampton was a breath of fresh air. He was very down to earth and, like me, worshipped the ground Steve walked on, so the two of us hit it off right away. He loved Kenney's style of drumming, and, as Ken and I played so similarly, it was highly likely that he would like my playing; I was just praying that he would like the whole band.

Pete Loynes had often called by the band house at lunch time. As I was always the only one up, he would take me to the local pub and treat me to a hearty meal, knowing how hungry I was. We would wash all our food down with ample amounts of gin and tonic (with ice and lemon, of course), and Pete would order lots of extra food to put in a doggy bag for the others. So, on the way back from Beehive, I promised him that, if and when I made it as a big rock star, I would take him on a bachelor's holiday to Ibiza as a thank-you for all his kindnesses. Be careful what you pray for.

Once I got back from meeting Peter Frampton, I was completely honest with the band, telling them of his interest in recruiting me for a new band he was putting together. I also told them that, as the band were to play at the student union at Jesus College in Cambridge in a few days, it would be the perfect place for Peter to come to see us. Who knows, he might just like the whole band.

When the big day came, Peter and his girlfriend, Mary Lovett, drove up to Cambridge to see Little Women play. After the show, he offered to drive me back to the band house so we could talk along the way. He was super-nice and said he would love to use me, and that everything Steve had told him about me was true and then some. So, would I like to form a band with him? "Absolutely" was my reply—and, by the way, what about using the rest of the band?

Peter was very tactful about it, but said no. I think he respected my loyalty to my friends and, had the band sounded better than we did that night, I think he might have considered it. The quality of the musicians involved certainly couldn't be bettered; however, we just weren't knocking them dead as a band yet. And, to be fair, Peter was only looking to fill the drum seat at the moment, and he certainly was offering *me* the job. I was thrilled. We agreed to keep in touch and, in the meantime, to keep our eyes open for a keyboard player and a bass player who could at least sing strong background vocals, if not lead vocals as well. The hunt was on. Telling the guys was not going to be easy, but, when I did, they completely understood and, I have to say, were really sweet about it.

Herd publicity photo, with Peter Frampton (third from left).

For a long time, nothing happened on the Peter front, and I started to wonder whether the possibility of being in a band with him might end up being a storm in a teacup. Little Women kept on keeping on and also kept on changing, which at least made it interesting. Rick Wills, who had joined the band as second bassist (playing alongside Bob) briefly that summer, was now well and truly in love with his new girlfriend, Lynny Parfitt. So he decided to quit and go back to his job with the Soul Committee, the big local soul band, because with them, he at least got a paycheck. Lynny, in the meantime, was getting a crash course on how financially insecure the music business was, for the most part, proving to be. So then there were three again, although we did have our eye on another bassist, Dave Wilkinson, who was a great player, looked great, and was keen to get involved.

Whilst home in Cambridge visiting family after his first tour of the States with Pink Floyd, Dave Gilmour stopped by the house in Shelford to visit Rick, who he had previously worked with in the Flowers (yes, 1967 has got a lot to answer for!), which was the name that Dave's band Jokers Wild took when they were working in the south of France. That was the beginning of a friendship between Dave and I that has lasted all these years. We asked Dave if he would help us by overseeing the production of a demo we were putting together. The old man had recruited an old army buddy of his who had some money he wanted to invest in the music business. So it was that a certain Major Morgan came to fund the making of our demo, which nothing came of, unfortunately, other than the fact that it taught Major Morgan a very important lesson in what not to do in the music business—invest in it.

If you had told anybody that the Small Faces' reaction to the success of *Ogdens' Nut Gone Flake* would be to break up, they would have told you that *your* nut was gone, and rightfully so. But, in fact, they did break up, not right away, but shockingly soon after the album's release. There were many, many extenuating circumstances that caused the split, and I will do my level best in these pages to explain, as honestly and as carefully as I can, exactly what happened. I will also do my best to be respectful to the two most important figures in the story, bearing in mind that they are no longer with us and that all of us involved miss them both tremendously on a daily basis. Simply put, Steve Marriott and Ronnie Lane were without a doubt the greatest songwriting team to come out of England in the Sixties after only Lennon/McCartney and Jagger/Richards, and it was a horrible, horrible thing to witness their breakup first hand, as I did.

Once *Ogdens'* had got to Number One and stayed there for six weeks (it was the big hit of the summer of '68), the Faces started to face up to a few home truths. First of all, their live show had started to fall behind that of their most immediate competitors, the Who. As they had toured with the Who in Australia very recently, they came away from that experience having watched a master class in great live performance every night. Steve spoke about it at length, and I'm sure all four of them knew deep down that something had to give. They had known for a considerable time that they were becoming stuck in a rut from a live point of view. All the Australian trip did was to confirm their worst fears and make them see just how far behind they had fallen.

To make matters worse, in those days it was nearly impossible to reproduce something like *Ogdens'* live. Steve had become very insecure about his lead guitar playing and wanted to add another guitarist to the band. Enter Peter Frampton… Steve was even toying with the idea of a brass section and backing singers, although I'm not sure if those little gems made it much past the drawing board. They did play a gig where I believe they used a brass section (although it might have been overdubbed afterwards), which was recorded live in Newcastle City Hall.

They'd had another failure that was, perhaps, an omen of things to come that no one grasped. Steve and Ronnie wrote a single for P.P. Arnold called "If You Think You're Groovy," and the Faces backed her on it. It should have been a smash and, to this day, I've no idea why it wasn't, other than perhaps they should have done it themselves instead of giving it to Pat Arnold. Who knows. I do know that it was the best three minutes of Kenney Jones drumming ever recorded.

The Faces had a short respite from the problem of what to do next in the form of some sessions in Paris with the French superstar Johnny Hallyday, the French Elvis Presley. The sessions had been arranged by Glyn Johns, the Faces' engineer extraordinaire who was engineering and/or producing just about every major act on the planet. He also had a knack for picking the best up-and-coming bands around; his ear was faultless.

Glyn had just finished recording a new album at Olympic in a very short time; it was by Jimmy Page's new, as yet unknown, band. At one time, Jimmy had approached Steve about being the lead singer for this outfit. Steve was immensely flattered, but gracefully declined and suggested in his place an old friend of his called Terry Reid. Due to prior commitments, Terry was also unable to get involved, and in turn suggested an old friend of his from Birmingham called Robert Plant. I wonder whatever happened to that band... I heard they were calling themselves the New Yardbirds; they'll never make it with a daft name like that. Apparently, the forerunner of all of this was a band that was formed one drunken night at the Speakeasy, which consisted of Jimmy Page on lead guitar, John Entwistle on bass, Keith Moon on drums, and Steve Marriott on lead vocals and rhythm guitar. Aside from the musical cacophony that may well have ensued had this line-up survived, they would have engulfed and devoured every hotel available, leaving none for the rest of the music business to stay in!

The sojourn to Paris apparently went really well. Peter Frampton did in fact join the band for the trip, but the band said no to the idea of him joining permanently. Everybody got along and enjoyed the diversion from the problems that were raising their ugly heads back home. Peter has always referred to the trip as his way of joining the Small Faces for a week. Johnny Hallyday recorded some Marriott/Lane songs, and a good time was had by all. However, the Faces' problems didn't evaporate in their absence, so when they got back it was, in Small Faces-speak, own-up time.

The immediate problem they had to face was one of huge consequence, in Steve's life anyway: the failure of their new single, "The Universal." Steve was extremely proud of this record, probably more so than anything he had done thus far. They'd had one of the longest runs of successful singles of any band at that time. Almost everything they touched had turned to gold, from "Sha-La-La-La-Lee" in 1966 right through till *Ogdens'* in 1968, so the relative chart failure of "The Universal" (especially after they'd scored three consecutive Top 10 singles with "Itchycoo Park," "Tin Soldier," and "Lazy Sunday") well and truly rattled their confidence cage, Steve's in particular. It also got panned in the press, fickle buggers that they are. Up until then, the Faces had enjoyed a reputation as the darlings of Swinging Sixties London and the journalists who chronicled it. Now, all of a sudden, they were no longer flavour of the month, and Steve's previously unflappable self-assurance was shaken to the core.

Steve Marriott's muse and wife, Jenny.
Check out the late Sixties eye makeup.

I also think he felt the band had let their resentment of his position as frontman and the inevitable attention it drew to him get the better of them. It seemed to me, as an onlooker, that they had become embittered towards him and his newfound happiness in his marriage to Jenny, who was herself at the height of her game as a top model (as they were known back then), the predecessor of today's supermodel but without the paycheck—sadly for Jenny, whose face was all over London as one of the Harp Lager Girls.

You couldn't go more than 10 minutes in London without a huge mugshot of Jenny's beautiful eyes floating past you on the side of a bus or staring down at you from a huge billboard on the side of the road or a poster in the underground. It was an amazing photo campaign in that men all over England lusted after the Harp Lager girl, even though all you could really see was her huge, great big beautiful pair of… eyes. I kid you not. She was lovely, Jenny, and still is. She was like a big sister to me, and remains so, God bless her cotton socks.

Steve was an intense person and could be exhausting to be around. Mac (Ian McLagan, the Small Faces' keyboard player) wrote in his book that when Steve left the band after spending three-and-a-half years with him, almost 24/7, the only thing Mac felt initially was pure exhaustion, and he slept like a baby for the first time since the band began. The word "overwhelming" was often used by others to describe Steve's nature, but Steve himself never understood that. *"I'm not overwhelming, am I? HUH, AM I?!?"* would be his response. Everything was his way or no way, and the infuriating thing about this side of him was that he *was* right most of the time.

What was happening to the Small Faces was not that different from what was happening to the Beatles. The Faces had all recently married, they had virtually quit the road to concentrate on studio work and were very successful at it, and, much like the Fabs, they had lived in each other's back pockets for several years, without a break. But they, unlike the Beatles, were skint. They had little or nothing to show for all their hard work, and, believe me, they had worked their arses off. It was soul destroying.

I still hadn't heard anything from Peter Frampton, so I thought, "Oh well, maybe some other time"; at least it was nice to be asked. I then decided to tell the band that I would commit myself to it for the foreseeable future. We had gone through one final change, which made us a three-piece yet again, when Bob Argent left to go back to being an electrician and Dave Wilkinson replaced him after playing in tandem with him for a short time. We had moved out of the band house and temporarily set up shop in my parents' house to rehearse for some upcoming gigs and to generally regroup.

It was getting to the end of 1968. We had been booked for New Year's Eve at a pub in Tottenham, and for some reason Dino had called to say he was coming to check out the new line-up. This had inspired us to try to do our best, as we were still a bit resentful towards him and desperately wanted to impress his cocky, arrogant, "Ooh, look at me now, I'm a rock star" self. (Amazing what playing keyboards for Keef Hartley will do for you.) Feeling full of band commitment—one for all and all that—on the way to the gig I told the band that I was going to tell Peter Frampton that I had decided to stick with them, wish him well, thank him for his interest in me, and say, "Let's stay friends."

The band were overjoyed with this show of solidarity, and we went into our gig with high hopes for the evening. Unfortunately, we played like a bunch of amateurs and were not together at all. I don't know if Dino held a jinx on us, or what. After the show I went over to him and asked what he thought, apart from it being a bit untogether. "A bit untogether?" was his smartarse reply. Off he went, and all I could think of was how I desperately wanted to do something one day to really shove it to him. Be careful what you…

That same night, unbeknown to us, Small Faces were appearing at Alexandria Palace in North London, no more than five minutes from where we were performing. On the bill with them were Spooky Tooth and Alexis Korner. After our show, we went back to my parents' house and were just sitting around chatting about our next plan of attack, when the phone rang. Angus answered it. I didn't think twice about it until five minutes later when Angus came in and said the phone call was for me. It was Steve.

"'Ello, mate. Listen, I've left the Small Faces, and I was wondering if I could join your and Peter's band. I've asked Peter, and he said he had to think about it and was gonna call you and talk to you about it. He tried to talk me out of leaving the Faces; I told him it was too late, that it was a done deal. What do you think about it? By the way, I've also got Greg Ridley, the bass player with Spooky Tooth, who wants to come along with me. What do you think?"

Greg Ridley (standing, second from right) in Spooky Tooth.

To say I was gobsmacked doesn't come close to getting it. Completely dumbfounded is a bit closer. Speechless, certainly, for a brief moment. Once I'd regained my composure, I started to try to talk him out of quitting the Faces; they were, after all, the greatest band in England and, without a doubt, my personal favourite. But Steve was adamant—he was leaving, and that was it. So, after failing to change his mind, I was ecstatic.

As a drummer, the huge defining factor for me was the inclusion of Greg Ridley on bass. He was, at that time, the most respected bass player in the business as far as American funk-style playing was concerned. The idea alone of playing with Greg was so exciting it gave me goose bumps, let alone having Pete and Steve along for good measure. I couldn't stop thinking of the musical consequences. The *vocals*! My God, the vocal possibilities were incredible, but I had to get myself together and go back into the living room to tell the guys what had just happened.

Before I could do that, the phone rang again. Sure enough, it was Peter. What did I think? We talked about it at length, and we both felt pretty much the same—so long as we behaved in a dignified manner about the whole affair and were not seen as instigators in Steve's decision, we would be able to move forward with a clear conscience. We both felt we had just formed potentially the greatest band in the world as the result of one phone call from Steve. Not a bad New Year's resolution.

What had happened at Alexandria Palace depends on who you talk to, but the end result was that Steve stormed off the stage in the middle of a jam that Alexis Korner had joined the Faces for, and it was proving to be calamitous. Storming off and leaving your bandmates stranded is extremely bad form in anybody's book—it is definitely transgressing one of the unwritten laws—but, back then, Steve, when he felt like it, was at his height of showbiz petulance, and this had been brewing for a while. Sadly, it all came to a head that night. I've since heard it said that Steve concocted this disastrous affair, but, I'm sorry, I doubt that very much. Steve was many things. Devious—yes. A *huge* pain in the arse—definitely and often. But to be that calculating—no, not enough to do something like that anyway. He was obviously capable of leaving his mates in the lurch like that, but to plan it ahead of time? No way, simply because that would mean he planned to embarrass himself as well as his mates in front of a huge crowd, and that was definitely not on the agenda in Steveworld.

I went back into the sitting room and told the lads what had transpired. They were the epitome of class and immediately said, "You have to do this without any question of a doubt. If it were any of us, we would jump at something like this straight away, so *go for it, my son*." With that out of the way, everybody just cheered and hoopla'ed around the house, going crazy 'cos one of us had finally got something going on. As so very sad as it was that the Faces were splitting, it was also the greatest night in my young life so far, and the beginning of the most incredible journey I have ever been on before or since. So fasten your seatbelts, and enjoy the ride. I know I did!

Chapter 6
Natural Born Bugie
January to April 1969

*In which the Pie gets baked and cooks at our first rehearsals;
we shop for a manager and a record company, incognito;
and I narrowly avoid becoming a notch on a
famous impresario's bedpost.*

The first few days of 1969 had a dreamlike quality attached to them 24/7. I wasn't to know then, but it turned out to be the longest dream I've ever had. It started on January 1, 1969, and didn't stop until the last week in April 1975, with a few "déjà vus all over again" on and off until 1986.

We had to organise a rehearsal sooner than later just to make sure that it did in fact work. This had to be done in top secret to avoid the press finding out, as there were all kinds of contractual bits and pieces to sort out before we could officially announce our intentions. Finding a place to rehearse away from the eagle eye of the press wasn't going to be easy—but as in all things back then, when it really mattered, a call to the cavalry (my parents) fixed the problem. A few days after Steve called me, we got together for our first rehearsal, in Mum and Dad's living room.

We chose to start off with small amplifiers and a small kit, consumed as we were with admiration for the Band after hearing their debut album, *Music From Big Pink*. Pete Townshend had brought a copy over from the States for Steve and Ronnie Lane to listen to, and it gave us a lot to think about, musically speaking. We decided to pick one of our favourite songs from the record—"We Can Talk," the first track on side two—and see what came out. It sounded wonderful, just incredible! The feel, all the instrumental parts, the lead and background vocals—all learned, played, done and dusted in no more than 10 or 15 minutes. Such a shame that we didn't tape it. Oh well, it was only used as an indicator of what we had or had not got—and boy, had we *got*.

So with that done, Steve, Peter, and Greg left the house, putting on their long trench coats and pulling their hats down over their faces to avoid any possibility of being seen by the paparazzi or some nosey neighbour who might sell the info to the papers. We only cared about all this because of all the contractual complexities that still had to be sorted out before we could legally play a note together. Thank God that back then the whole paparazzi thing wasn't anything like it is today; if it were, our life together as a new band would have already been made very difficult indeed. It might have even been prevented from happening at all, as there were a couple of managers on Peter's side that would have demanded large lumps of cash that we did not yet have.

The next step was to start the discreet hunt for the right management team and record company. At the end of the Sixties, the managers in London could be divided into two groups: the old-school guys who, for the most part, weren't to be trusted; and the younger, hipper guys who liked to position themselves as at least honest—and some of them were indeed pretty much upstanding chaps.

We put together a short list of all the guys we thought would at least be able to do a good job, then set up clandestine meetings with them in various small, dark, off-the-beaten-track watering holes in and around the West End of London to see who was interested and who was not. The list was eventually whittled down to three people: Chris Blackwell, who ran Island Records and managed Traffic; Kit Lambert, who ran Track Records and managed (with Chris Stamp) and produced the Who; and Andrew Oldham, who ran Immediate Records and had managed the Small Faces and—until 1967, when he sold his contract share to the notorious Allen Klein—the Rolling Stones.

Chris Blackwell would have been a good choice, as Island was probably the most successful label in the "music to be taken seriously" department. That was important to us because Steve and Peter were determined to avoid the teenybopper side of the business, and Greg was already with Chris as a member of Spooky Tooth. Chris, however, declined the invitation. He felt that, as a manager, he could only do his best when he concentrated all his energies on one act, and, as he had long been Steve Winwood's manager, he didn't wish to take on anything that could jeopardise his relationship with Steve and his band, Traffic. He was a complete gentleman about it, wished us well, and assured us that we were going to be huge, which was very sweet of him.

Next up was Kit Lambert. While our meeting with Chris Blackwell was, if memory serves, in his office, our meeting with Kit was a classic film noir, back alley, smoky bar affair. This time I joined the others in wearing velvet fedoras and long trench coats with the collars pulled up. I've no idea who *I* was hiding from, as no one knew who the fuck I was—still, when in Rome…

I got particular satisfaction out of our meeting with Kit Lambert, having first met him back in the Little Women days. You see, Kit, being as bent as a nine-bob note, often spent his evenings at the Speakeasy trying to pick up young boys. Little Women were playing at the Speak one night when Kit was there on the prowl. He was very charming and complimentary about our group, and chose to concentrate his conversation on me. Kit was way ahead of the times in his view of things to come in the music business. The statement he made to me that was furthest ahead of the curve was, "The future of rock 'n' roll is in video." He said this in 1968, a full 13 years before MTV, which clearly shows how much of a visionary the man was… or how creative his pick-up lines were! He invited me back to his place to discuss the future of the group. When I told the rest of the band, they all said, "Great! Go for it!"—but for some unknown reason declined to accompany me. I wonder why? The rotten buggers!

When Kit and I arrived at his flat on Half Moon Street, I sat there in extreme apprehension as he disappeared into his bedroom. He soon reappeared, dressed in a silk smoking jacket and carrying a large, old-fashioned spray bottle of perfume. He then proceeded to spray exuberant amounts of strong-smelling Chanel No. 9-Bob Note onto the electric bar heater, which set alight with a loud (and appropriate) *poof*! Seemingly pleased with his gay pyrotechnics, and without being asked, he performed several encores, then offered me some cocaine. At that point, I knew it was time for me to leave, so with the deepest voice I could muster I said, "I'd like to get a cab, if that's okay." At least he was good enough not to argue; he just called a cab, looking somewhat dejected. Apparently, I was in high-class company as, according to Steve, Kit had done the same thing to Ronnie Lane a few years before—except in Ronnie's case, Kit literally chased him around the flat before Ron, like me, got out with his dignity intact.

So, less than a half-year after my ill-fated solo encounter with Kit, meeting with him again, this time as a member of Humble Pie, had a certain *je ne sais quoi* attached to it. Not knowing exactly how he would react, I at least had the extreme satisfaction of knowing I was there as a member of a band that he had a more than passing interest in signing—and that I didn't have to lose my aforementioned dignity to be signed. To his credit, he behaved with complete decency; even though the flaming Chanel incident had happened only a few months earlier, he gave no indication of it ever happening at all. But then again, what would he have said? After all, nothing untoward occurred, and, truth be known, he probably didn't even remember me—why would he? All I represented was a failed attempt at getting laid and the relief of not having to get out of all the promises of instant stardom that I'm sure he made to a long line of pretty boys in exchange for a bit of rumpy bumpy.

At the meeting, Kit was his high-camp, creative self, politely trying to explain why he thought he wasn't the right man for the job, as a result of his intensive involvement in an all-consuming Who project. He waxed in lyrical verbosity about this thing they were working on called a "rock opera." "I mean, really, have you ever heard of such a ludicrous concept?" was our reaction in the car on the way home. "Thank God we didn't pick such a lunatic as our manager!" We learned only a few months later, when "Pinball Wizard" and *Tommy* were near the top of the charts on both sides of the Atlantic, that perhaps he wasn't such a lunatic after all. As we Who fans would say back then, "God bless the 'Oo!"

This brings me to the last but not, by any means, least of our choices: Andrew Oldham. Andrew was so important to the formative years of the Stones; insisting that they learn how to write songs for themselves and others was just one of his several injections of foresight, creative genius, and business acumen. He taught them early on that "business" was not a dirty word, being a good businessman was important, and a huge catalogue of songs was a musician's pension—all pretty farsighted thinking for a kid who was only 19 when he took on the Stones in 1963. Keith and Charlie have long since buried the hatchet with Andrew, and I can only hope that, as I write this, Mick has done the same. I know from personal experience that a feud left unresolved can get really painful should one of the parties pass away unexpectedly prior to making amends. So, if you have not already done so, kiss and make up, girls, sooner than later. We are not, any of us, getting any younger, as you both know only too well. After all, chaps, it wasn't so long ago that I was the precocious 14-year-old who you gave such generous help and encouragement, and, not to put too fine a point on it, I will be 60 in less than a year if the good Lord's willing and the creek don't rise.

Andrew wanted Humble Pie so bad he could taste it. You'll notice I said "wanted," not "needed"—although his label did need a winner, what really appealed to him was the challenge of putting together a band with such incredible potential, and who required his PR expertise. We definitely needed that, as a new phenomenon had recently reared its ugly head in the press: the so-called "supergroup," whereby various members of successful groups would leave them to form new and exciting line-ups. It all sounded great on paper, but did not always work out as well as it might have, thus giving the press a field day, with endless possibilities to jerk off to—metaphorically speaking, of course.

Once it was agreed that the band would be handled by Andrew and would record for Immediate, we were pretty much off and running—but we couldn't tell anybody. In fact, we had to keep the whole thing under wraps for some time for a number of reasons, not least of which was Andrew very wisely insisting that we not announce anything until we were well rehearsed and at least ready to record. This meant that most of the initial rehearsing and recording was done in secret; we were becoming short-arse secret agent men, 003.5. Again, I wasn't entirely sure what I was being so tight lipped about, as nobody knew me from Adam. Mind you, as they say in Cleveland, Ohio, if you don't like the weather, stick around for a minute, as it *will* change. It wouldn't be long before I too would understand what being instantly recognisable was like.

Whilst all of this was going on, we still had to come up with a name, which was proving to be extremely difficult, as it always is. We finally decided to each come up with two favourite choices and put them into a hat, shake it up, pull them out one at a time, discuss the pros and cons of each, and make a decision. Finally, a name got pulled that made instant sense. It was one of Steve's choices, and as soon as it was read out, I shouted, "That's it!" It was Humble Pie, the perfect way to respond to the supergroup handle that was being tagged on to the leaks that were starting to slip out in the press. Humble Pie… it just felt so right. Of course, there were going to be cynics out there who would beat on us whatever we called ourselves. We did not want to be thought of or referred to as a supergroup; we were genuinely horrified at the idea, especially me. After all, no bugger had any idea at all who Jerry Shirley was. And now, here I am all these years later, a veteran of more than 80 tours of the USA, writing my memoirs—and still no one knows who the fuck I am. Ain't life great!

As it turned out, when we were eventually announced to the world, the press were very welcoming and not at all cynical, generally speaking. The one cheap shot we got was actually a backhanded compliment. It came from John Gorman, a member of the Scaffold, which also included Mike McGear and Roger McGough. Gorman and McGough were beat poets and comedy writers for TV and highbrow newspapers; McGear was Paul McCartney's brother and an accomplished photographer. In his weekly review column, Gorman, in describing our grand entrance into the music business, pointed out that our name would be more appropriate if it were Arrogant Casserole. We all thought this was hysterical and definitely a compliment, coming from John.

Even though I was a complete unknown, the other three were big stars, and them forming a band, and the potential break-ups of the bands they left, was Big News (although, in fact, none of the bands involved broke up, to their collective credit). In a way, my absolute unknown status was a newsworthy plus: "On drums they have *who*? Jerry *who*? Jerry Shirley from *where*? Waltham Cross, where's *that*? He's *how* old? *16*?" The greatest thing about this is that the band could have asked just about any drummer in the country, and any drummer would have said yes—but they didn't; they chose me. That is what's commonly known as a right result where I come from. I simply could not believe my luck; I still can't, to tell you the truth.

Once we started to rehearse full time, we sounded fantastic, and all four of us were thrilled with the way it was coming together. The other three treated me with such class; I have remained forever grateful for their kindness. They made me feel their equal in every way, and it wasn't long before we became a really tight band and a close band of brothers. It was like having three big brothers looking after me, each fulfilling a different role. They truly were the greatest bunch of lads this young man could ever have the privilege of working with and being a friend of.

I will never forget coming home at the end of the first week of rehearsals, finding Angus there, and saying to him, "Well, bruv, it's official. I have definitely joined the greatest band in the world!" It was sounding that good: so good it was frightening. Sen-fuckin'-sational, in fact. Please forgive my use of poetic licence, but that is simply the most accurate descriptive I can use to conjure up a precise picture of how things were sounding.

We were already supremely tight. Although we were still using relatively small amplifiers, we had a huge, ballsy rhythm section that swung like a stripper's tits. The guitar players were two of the best in England (although no one knew it yet), plus they both played excellent keyboards. Steve was also a phenomenal blues harp player. And, as if that lot were not enough, there were the *vocals*. It was like having Ray Charles, Little Richard, Otis Redding, and Tina Turner all wrapped up in three white, blue-eyed soul singers. Absolutely remarkable. The Tina Turner comparison is a reference to Steve's astonishing range: he could hit inhumanly high, seriously nuts-crushing notes in full voice, not falsetto, which must have hurt like hell.

The variety of styles we were capable of pursuing was equally exhilarating. We were all such big fans of anything and everything that could be regarded as soulful, whether it was rock, jazz, country, or, obviously, soul and blues. This meant that our first minor problem, although we didn't see it as such back then, was deciding which direction to follow. The answer was simple: do all of them! It never occurred to us to do things any other way.

We were having so much fun as a combination of musicians who seemed able to tackle any form of music that pulled our collective chain, so that's exactly what we did. When we formed, our credo was "Don't be tied down to any one form," and, right or wrong, we stuck to it, like crap to a blanket, for a long time.

The one form we avoided like the plague was pop. It's not that we didn't want our music to be popular, but we shied away from anything that appeared to be blatantly pop. We tried to appeal to the albums market, not the obvious singles market, which had become so associated with the teenyboppers that bands had gone to the extreme of not releasing singles at all. Led Zeppelin, for instance, categorically refused to release singles, at least in the UK. Pink Floyd, once Dave Gilmour took Syd Barrett's place, also said no to going down that road. Not everybody became that precious (including us, as you will soon see), but we started from the "albums only, man" standpoint, trying to be as underground as possible. The hippies referred to their music as "underground, man"—at the time, everything had "man" attached to it. "Hello, man. How are you?" "I'm fine, man. You?"

In those early days, our enthusiasm for the job at hand was admirable, and our work ethic, as it's now called, was superb. We rehearsed five days a week, approximately eight hours a day; we never drank anything stronger than our precious cups of tea; and the only drug we indulged in was our beloved hashish, which we most certainly did partake of, in no small measure, I might add. Once we got into the routine and discipline of those first rehearsals, there was nothing that could stop us. Steve and Peter had lots of songs, and both Greg and I were encouraged to write, which we did, with some decent results, I'm proud to say. We also drew material from two other sources: group-written songs, which usually came out of one of our many jams in Magdalen Laver, and the occasional cover if it felt right.

Like kids in a candy store, we went about each and every task with renewed vigour. The task I personally enjoyed most was going to Drum City in the West End to buy some additions to my kit. But, truly, every aspect of this period was sheer, unadulterated fun.

Chapter 7
POP GIANTS' SUPERGROUP
May to November 1969

*In which we cannily cut the Calcutta chorus,
then charge our batteries in Spain; David Bailey shoots me,
but I'm the one who lands in the Old Bailey (no relation);
we pull the old switcheroo on the BBC;
and the music press sends me a Penny for my thoughts.*

By now we were well and truly into our routine of rehearse all week, go to the Immediate office on Friday afternoon to pick up our wages, and take care of the coming week's essentials. In our case, that did not include buying groceries, paying bills, or any other such mundane non-essentials—it meant going to Chelsea Antique Market for clothes, then around the corner to our dealer's house for an ounce or two of the best hashish money could buy.

Our wages were fantastic. We were receiving £60 pounds a week (the equivalent of about £600 pounds or more in today's money), which wasn't bad for a 16-year-old lad, plus every expense imaginable was taken care of for us. This was before the record deals that were soon to be commonplace, whereby the record company advanced the band an enormous amount of spondoolies, and the band took the dosh and spend it on cars and houses because they were not yet required to use it to finance the making of the record, as the record company paid the recording costs separately. Ahhh, those were the days indeed!

I alluded to our obsession with avoiding pop music like the plague, due to Steve and Peter's experiences as perceived pop stars. What with Peter having been voted the "Face of '68" and Steve the "Face of '66," they were both very gun-shy of anything that would cause them to be typecast again as pop stars. So, once we started recording, everything we did was done as a part of an album and not as a potential single. We were so well rehearsed for the first album that we could play it from start to finish in our sleep, so much so that, as we were finishing it, we were already fully prepared to start the second.

The recording of the first album, as it fits into this story, could be left with not much more mention than I've already given it, if it were not the first album ever recorded by Humble Pie. But, as such, it has a place in the history of rock 'n' roll, so it requires me to go into more detail. It's times like this when I find this endeavour a little difficult. Again, I have to remember to tell it like it was and not as a blasé pro who's been doing this for nearly 50 years and to whom making a record is like putting on a pair of shoes—preferably a nice pair that fit and do not hurt your feet when you wear them. But, as extremely ordered and routine as the process is, you hope that it will be fun and still inspire a certain sense of wonder, 'cos once that's gone, I firmly believe you should stop doing it. So, my task at this juncture is to tell you kind folks, the readers, what an *incredible* experience, for me anyway, the making of the first Humble Pie album (and, later, its follow-up) was.

The bulk of the material for the first record was original, mostly Steve's compositions that he had demoed before we formed or while we were forming. Then came Peter, who had fewer songs, but they were just as strong. The two collaborated on the title track, "As Safe as Yesterday Is," and we did one cover, Steppenwolf's "Desperation." This song holds a special place in my heart because it was the first one we did when we started proper rehearsals. It was a big, moody, slow waltz that had a great arrangement with loads of dynamics, it had a terrific lyric, and it set the pattern of which direction we were trying to head in.

It was just after we put the finishing touches to "Desperation" in rehearsal that I went home and declared to my brother that I had just joined the greatest band in the world, and believe me, I had. Trouble was, unbeknownst to me, so had a number of other musicians, in both England and America. The bands that had just formed, released their first record in 1969, and became our immediate competition included Led Zeppelin; Crosby, Stills & Nash; Santana; Blind Faith; and King Crimson. It was enough to make any self-respecting midget throw in the

Early Humble Pie press photo.

towel right there and then—but not us. No sirree, it just made us grab that bull by the nuts and *squeeze*—and continue to do so for the next seven years.

We had the luxury of being able to block-book Olympic Studio No. 1 for the first three weeks of May 1969, with a hold on the fourth week, if we needed it. That's the way we worked all those years ago: fast. This was not, in our case, out of necessity; studios were still relatively cheap in 1969, and Andrew didn't believe in rushing to save money. He did, however, believe in getting on with the job as part and parcel of being a pro, but then so did we. That's how we did things, as young Turks who were proud of the way they went about their business.

I recently watched a documentary about Tina Turner. Her record producer was talking about how she bowled him over when they first started working together in the early 1980s as part of her enormously successful comeback. He described how she blew him away because she came in and did her first lead vocal note- and word-perfect in the first take. He explained that this was the one and only time he had ever seen this done before or since, and that, normally, lead vocals are recorded many times over, with the best parts from each compiled to make one good take. This put a melancholy smile on my face because it immediately made me think of Steve, who, in all the years that we worked together, rarely took more than one take to record *anything*, let alone his lead vocals, which he was famous for doing in one take. This approach was also applied to every Humble Pie backing track that was ever recorded. A vast majority of the instrumental backing tracks we cut were done, if not in the first take, then certainly within the first two or three. If it got to take five and we felt that we hadn't got it yet, we would move on and come back to it later.

This way of doing things was not unique to us by any means. It was just the way our generation were brought up to do things for a number of reasons, not least of all financial (time is money), but there were other reasons that directly affected drummers in particular, which had roots in Phil Spector's "Wall of Sound" productions of the early to mid-Sixties. Spector believed in keeping his drummers fresh so that he could get their performance in the first take or two. He accomplished this by having the rest of the band do their run-throughs without the drummer (or drummers—he often used more than one), so that when the drummer did his thing, it was as fresh as it could possibly be. I personally believe that all the best drum tracks are done in the first take or two, and that everything after that loses something special—a certain sparkle that is very hard to reproduce. So, as long as you, the drummer, have come to the party fully prepared, you should be able to take advantage of that special certain something that is part and parcel of the first take.

The guys were unbelievably good at working together vocally, in both harmonizing and sharing leads. They shared the lead line as equally as humanly possible, usually in an extremely dynamic round-robin pattern that would go from Greg to Pete to Steve, so you would get Greg and Pete with a one-two combination, then Steve with a knockout punch every third line. They would also take a song and divide it up by singing one verse each, then one together, either in harmony or unison. Plus there was more soulful call and response going on between them than you could shake a stick at. It was an absolute delight and one hell of an education.

Glyn Johns was busy with the Stones *and* the Beatles—nothing big, but he couldn't break his commitments to those youngsters, now could he?—so we got his younger brother Andy to produce the first album, which was fine by us because he was a great engineer, just like Glyn. As an extra added bonus, Andrew was, unlike his brother, a stoner, which suited us lot down to the ground. I found him to be very easy to get on with. He and I became firm friends immediately, which was great for me, as it helped me relax and get over my initial nerves simply because we were both, to a certain extent, the new kids on the block.

The first song to go on tape was "Desperation." We got it on the first or second take, and it sounded wonderful. Everybody was thrilled, but I knew the drum sound could have been better. Not that it was bad; it's just that I had a clear vision of what the drums should sound like, and we weren't there yet. Considering, however, how young I was and how aware of the fact that I was damn lucky just to be there, I didn't think it was appropriate to complain or kick up a fuss. Anyway, the band's performance was sensational, and I did play it really well, so I figured that the drum sound would improve as time went on, and that is exactly what happened.

We had a system that we stuck to in a fairly stringent fashion, wavering occasionally but not that often. We would do all the back tracks, then the instrumental overdubs, then the vocals, then the mixing. Sometimes we did the back track with a rough vocal, which was often so good that some or all of it would be used. This way of doing things was pretty much the industry norm of the day, with the 8-track tape machine, by then standard in all the big studios, making the overdubbing process a whole lot easier than its 4-track predecessor.

One of Peter's songs, "I'll Go Alone," started life as a demo that Peter and I recorded in my parents' living room on a Revox 2-track machine, and I have to say it sounded almost as good as the final version that went on the album. Peter and Steve were wizards with 2-track homegrown recording. We became very good very quickly at arranging, playing, and singing the songs. We had become a well-oiled machine, efficiency personified.

The whole of the first album was finished in just over three weeks, so instead of stopping, we just kept on recording. The one thing we hadn't got yet, mainly because we weren't trying, was a single. We had run out of available time at Olympic, so Andy suggested we move our base of operations to Morgan Studios in Willesden, which had just opened. Andy had been using it to record two other acts—Blind Faith and Jack Bruce doing his first solo album—at the same time we were at Olympic. This little set of pleasant circumstances meant that we got to hear samples of what the competition was up to, which was great fun, but also kept us well and truly on our toes.

By now, we were recording material that ended up on the second album, *Town and Country*, except for Peter's song "Stick Shift," which went on the first. We were also working in a more random fashion, in that we would come into the studio and record whatever came to mind. We didn't need to be so rehearsed, simply because we had developed an amazing sense of musical telepathy; all we had to do was run the song through once or twice while Andy got his sounds in the control room, press play, and record. Before you knew it, we would have our back track.

Steve and Peter were determined to make the band as equal as possible in every way, especially in the songwriting. As recording progressed for what was to become the second album, they wanted each of the first four songs on side one to be written by a different one of us.

My little ditty was "Cold Lady," written late one night at my parents' house. It was about a young lad who had been introduced to a beautiful lady on a blind date. She was a little older than he and came from a much more sophisticated background. He desperately wanted to get through to her, but didn't have a clue how to go about it. The song was autobiographical: Jenny Marriott had introduced me to one of her model friends, who, unfortunately, was rather stuck up, and I had no idea how to break the ice with her.

My mother, bless her, had written songs many years before. As she also taught piano, it was part of her learning curve when she was studying musical composition. As I worked on "Cold Lady," I tried to make as little noise as possible, so as not to wake the house up, but, sure enough, halfway through the task, I heard footsteps coming down the stairs. It was Mum. I immediately froze, expecting a "Keep the noise down!" bollocking, but she just smiled sweetly and said, "That sounded really lovely. What is it?" She then gave me some tips, which was great because I had got stuck and was about to give up until her intervention gave me the encouragement I needed to get the job done.

The next step was to play it to Steve: a daunting task for anybody, but for me to have to sing in front of the greatest singer in the business was something I did not think I would be able to pull off. My vocal abilities can be easily described in one short sentence: I can't sing! It really is that simple. For some reason, when my voice broke, so did my ability to sing. The best I can manage is a horrible little falsetto that makes Neil Young sound like a baritone. It sucks *really badly*.

The day after I'd written "Cold Lady," I went to Beehive Cottage and played it to Steve and Jenny. I must have been beetroot-red with embarrassment, but, fortunately, the song was pretty decent, and I somehow soldiered through. Once I had finished, I was too shy to even look up, so I stared at the ground between my shoes, hoping it would swallow me whole. Steve and Jenny were kindness itself. They told me how good it was, and Steve said he wanted to record it right away and that it should definitely be included on the second album. I realized then, more than ever, what a wonderful human being he could be. I thought it was remarkable of him to sit through the pain of having to listen to his little mate making an absolute tit of himself, and not run and hide from the ordeal or take the piss something rotten—especially considering what a wicked, unrelenting piss-taker he was.

We recorded the song the next day, with me playing Wurlitzer electric piano, Steve on acoustic guitar, Greg on bass, and Pete on drums. Then Steve sang a rough vocal that blew everybody away, and his final vocal was so moving it put goosebumps up me; he had turned a nice little ditty into an incredibly moving ballad.

As we were about to play the final mix at the end of the day, Jenny showed up with an old friend of hers. It was none other than Julie Driscoll, a big star who, along with Brian Auger and the Trinity, had recently been to Number Five with a cover of "Wheel's on Fire," a song by Bob Dylan and the Band's Rick Danko. I had a huge crush on Julie at the time, as did 90% of the male populace, and Jenny knew it. Also, as a musician, I had huge respect for her. So when she came in with Jenny, I wanted to die with embarrassment, as shy as I was. The first thing Steve said to them was, "'Ere, listen to this," and then he played "Cold Lady." When it was finished, Julie said, "That was fantastic. Who wrote it?" to which Steve replied, pointing to me, "He did." Julie (and Jenny) showered me with praise, for which I was extremely grateful, albeit a little embarrassed. It gave my confidence a huge boost, although I've often wondered whether it might have been a bit of a set-up. But it doesn't really matter whether it was or was not, does it, because it was an incredibly nice thing to do for a young lad who was desperately trying to keep up with all the remarkable talent he was surrounded by.

Soon after we became ensconced in Morgan, Steve came in with a little Chuck Berry nick called "Natural Born Bugie" (although the punch line was, in fact, "natural born woman") and a haunting ballad called "Wrist Job," based around the dirty sound of the studio's Hammond organ. Steve's idea was to record "Natural Born Bugie" as a comedy song, with a bunch of Indian and Pakistani guys singing the "natural born woman" chorus in their heavy accents. He even went so far as to go out onto the streets of Willesden and recruit a cross-section of the local Asian community—including traffic wardens, a shopkeeper, and his family—and have them come to the studio to record the repeat chorus.

Once the back track and lead guitar overdubs were recorded and we had put the lead vocals on, however, it was obvious that this was far from a novelty song, and that idea was abandoned. The groove was wonderfully tight and felt great, and the drum track had a couple of great fills on it. The lead vocal was divided among Steve, Peter, and Greg, and the planned Calcutta chorus was replaced with a three-part harmony sung by the lads, after which Steve added some Wurlitzer. No sooner had we finished than Andrew Oldham stopped by unannounced to check up on our progress. He was knocked out by what he heard and immediately announced that we had found our first single, which, considering that we were not looking for it at that particular moment, I thought was quite an achievement. "Wrist Job" was chosen to be our first B-side.

The "one song from each writer to open side one" concept was accomplished with Peter's "Take Me Back," done primarily with acoustic guitars and Moroccan percussion; Steve's "The Sad Bag of Shaky Jake," a cowboy's lament that had the best snare drum sound we had got to date; Greg's "The Light of Love," with Steve playing sitar; and "Cold Lady." We rounded out the side with a song of Steve's called "Down Home Again" and the group-"written" bit of silliness, "Ollie Ollie."

By now we had well and truly fixed any reservations I had regarding the drum sounds, and were getting some of the best I had ever heard. Andy had worked a lot with me to improve the way we recorded the kit, and, with his help, I had got a lot better at tuning it.

So it was that with the first album under our belt, I went on a three-week break in Ibiza, knowing full well that once the onslaught of touring and more recording started, it most likely wouldn't stop for a good long while. The break was at Steve's insistence, as he knew from experience that it was a good idea to charge up the batteries *before* going on tour. He was 100% right, of course, and, after all, who was likely to disagree with him? "We need to go on a three-week break in Ibiza, lads. What do you think?" "What a terrible idea, Steve. Don't be so bloody silly!"

Here was the perfect opportunity for me to pay back an old friend. As I had promised Pete Loynes a holiday in Ibiza a year or so before, unaware that I would in fact get the chance to do so as soon as this, it was a great feeling to be able to keep my promise. Unlike the other guys in the band, I was not married, nor did I have a girlfriend I felt like taking with me. As a single lad of 17, taking a mate with me and, I hoped, savouring the local crumpet was far more the order of the day.

The other three lads in the band chose their own destinations. Steve and Jenny went to Portugal, while Greg, Mandy, Peter, and Mary travelled to Majorca and stayed in a condo that I think Mandy's wealthy parents owned. At the same time, my brother Angus and Roger Peters, our best friend from early schooldays, were doing the late Sixties / early Seventies hippie trail that usually took in Morocco, India, and all points between.

Once Pete Loynes and I got to Ibiza, we located the local hashish dealer through some hippie connections that Jenny Marriott had given us the phone number for, and went ahead and bought *all* the available hash on the island, two ounces of especially strong black Nepalese. This, of course, made us extremely happy chappies and also enhanced our popularity no end.

After we had been on Ibiza for almost a week, Steve called to ask how things were there, as he and Jenny were not thrilled with Portugal. Once we told him what a fabulous time we were having, not least of all due to the Nepalese hash, he and Jenny were on the next plane to Ibiza. That same day, Pete and I were walking down the main street looking for a place to have a liquid lunch, when we spotted, in the distance coming towards us, Angus, Roger, and Larry, an American friend of theirs. We couldn't believe our eyes and knew that, from then on, a jolly good time was going to be had by all. After huge amounts of hugging and general jumping up and down in the middle of the high street, we went back to the apartment we were renting to get Angus, Roger, and Larry settled in and to smoke several large ones so that we could be in the right frame of mind to go out and face the rest of the day.

As we were about to step out, the phone rang. It was Peter Frampton asking us how Ibiza was because the condo sharing with Greg and Mandy wasn't going so well; the couple apparently did nothing but argue, and it was getting a bit tough for Pete and Mary to handle. So now we had Steve, Jenny, Peter, and Mary all on their way to join us in Ibiza.

Back then, Ibiza was not what it is today. It wasn't a big tourist destination, and it certainly wasn't the famous Party Central place that it is now. It was a sleepy little laidback hangout for hippies and a few renowned British bohemian exiles who lived up in the interior hills. Pete and I had been staying in the harbour town of San Antonio for the first few days, but, right before Angus, Roger, and Larry showed up, we decided to move to the beach and rent the condo that became home for the rest of our stay. This turned out to be a fortuitous move, as the place was big enough to house our unexpected guests.

Once Steve, Jenny, Peter, and Mary arrived, the fun became a little less boisterous, but it was still fun all the same. Looking back, it is remarkable to think that Steve's presence would have a calming effect on the proceedings, but it did—that's how different his makeup was when he was with Jenny. Steve was at his absolute best during that period in his life. I've always felt bad for anybody who only knew him in the later part of his life, because they didn't really know him at all; they completely missed his golden period, as you will see as the story unfolds.

After returning from Ibiza, we continued to record at both Morgan and Olympic, and also rented some mobile recording equipment and set it up at Magdalen Laver Village Hall. Some of the material recorded on that mobile turned out to be the best we ever did, including a version of Steve's (and my) favourite Ray Charles song, written by Henry Glover, called "Drown in My Own Tears." Our arrangement was authentic and identical to Ray's version from his live-in-Atlanta *In Person* album, recorded in 1959. Derek Wadsworth did the brass arrangement as per Ray's, and we all played on our best form. As always, the guys did a superlative job on the vocals, with Steve taking the bulk of the lead and the rest divided up in what was by now their trademark fashion, and with backing vocals that sounded like a black gospel chorus. Just as we finished putting the magnificent brass section on it, I brought Dave Gilmour to the studio to hear the results. During the drive home afterwards, he turned to me and said, unsolicited, that he thought it was the best thing we had ever done.

Sadly though, and for reasons I cannot remember, this small masterpiece of Steve's didn't make the final cut of either of our first two albums. It got left on the shelf and wasn't released until 2001, 32 years after we recorded it, on a best-of album, where it was heard by only a tiny fraction of the number of fans who would have heard it in our heyday. The one bonus, personally speaking, to it finally being released was that I got to mix it. I made sure that it was done by the best studio and engineer money could buy, thanks to Dave Gilmour letting me use his Astoria studio (located in a houseboat moored on the Thames) and his house engineer, Andy Jackson.

At some point during this period, the formation of the band was officially announced. By then it had become the worst-kept secret in rock 'n' roll. The announcement was made in a flurry of activity that included meetings about the album cover; meetings with our accountants, solicitors, and road managers; and planning the upcoming tour. I was mighty glad we had already made lots of music together; if we hadn't, I could have been forgiven for thinking that being in a top-flight band consisted of nothing but having meetings.

As I've mentioned, Steve and Peter were desperate to avoid two things with the launch of the band: being referred to as a pop group and being referred to as a supergroup. As we still had to prove ourselves, they thought the supergroup tag could be the kiss of death, and in many ways they were dead right—the potential for disaster was obvious. Being the rookie in the band, though, I didn't care, because, as I've already said, in my opinion we had formed the greatest band in the world. As shy and insecure as I still was about myself, I was full of confidence in the band.

When *Melody Maker* finally carried the story on the front page, the headline read, "POP GIANTS' SUPERGROUP." As much as the content might have made Steve and Pete cringe, they had enough public relations savvy to realise that getting the front page was

Melody Maker *front page, announcing Humble Pie.*

huge. The story got just as much coverage in the other music papers of the time: *NME*, *Disc and Music Echo*, and *Record Mirror*.

The single and album were to be released simultaneously a month hence. In the meantime, we continued to rehearse and endlessly have our photos taken, or so it seemed. The good thing about the photos was who Andrew chose to shoot them.

This part of my story is a perfect example of exactly how bizarre my life had become, bearing in mind that I had only just turned 17. Andrew always used the very best photographers, which meant that the very first photo of yours truly in the top flight was taken by none other than the legendary David Bailey. (The second set of photos were taken by Gered Mankowitz, who was to rock 'n' roll what Bailey was to fashion, thanks to Andrew's patronage while managing the Stones.) For me, the advantage of being photographed by Bailey was the quality of the scenery in his studio: there was wall-to-wall delectable crumpet, and I, for one, enjoyed it immensely. The other lads were used to it, but not this young kid. No sir, it was all new to me, and very nice it was, too.

Immediate were dragging their feet over the album cover, which was understandable, as this would be the first new album released by Steve since *Ogdens'*. Trying to follow that record—including its innovative round cover—was next to impossible. After a number of lame suggestions, Steve finally lost his rag, as only he could, and said, "Look, just put it out in a brown paper bag if you have to, but get it done!" And that's precisely what Immediate  did, although, not content with just any old brown paper bag, they produced their own by taking a picture of a brown paper parcel, sticking the Bailey photos in one corner to look like postage stamps, and writing the album title as if it were the address on the parcel. They even wrapped it with string to make it look like a real parcel. That little episode sums up a certain area of the record business: only they could make a production out of a brown paper bag.

The single was set for release in late April. The album was to follow it almost immediately, but the main cut and thrust of the promotional plans was centred around that all-important single—the one we swore we would never release. It was time for Andrew Oldham's promotional genius to kick into overdrive, and I sat back in wonder and watched a master at work. He organised a one-off performance by us at Ronnie Scott's club in the West End of London. It was the perfect choice: the sound was fabulous, it was a small venue that seated just the right number of people, and no matter where you sat, you had a great view of the stage. Andrew arranged the show for a late afternoon so that all the hardcore Fleet Street drinkers would relish the idea of a free piss-up without having to worry about going back to work. Ronnie's had an enclosure in front of the stage that accommodated the best tables, which Andrew earmarked for the most important press people and a smattering of celebs to make the press guys feel important.

The biggest stroke of genius was the menu. Andrew had the club serve these dipsomaniacs fried chicken breast with a batter that was laced with plentiful amounts of salt and hot sauce, which accelerated the already thirsty bunch into overdrive—and the only thing they could get to drink was an unlimited supply of the finest ice-cold Dom Perignon. Even the weather was on our side: it was an unusually hot spring, and the club was told not to turn on the air conditioning. We were the only entertainment, and we had an intentionally short set rehearsed up to coincide with the champagne kicking in. Suffice to say we went down a storm, and I must admit we were on top form. It was one of those moments when everything not only went according to plan, but was much, much greater than we could ever have wished. I clearly remember thinking afterwards that we sounded much better live than anything we had put on tape thus far, but, at the time, I put it down to the excitement of the moment. I certainly didn't realise what an unintentionally profound overview of our future that thought would prove to be.

Disc and Music Echo *article breaking the band after a Ronnie Scott's gig.*

The use of a short, hit-'em-and-run type of showcase certainly paid off in spades—large spades, I might add. The crowd didn't simply give us a good reception; they went absolutely berserk. From my viewpoint behind the kit, I watched the usually reserved English gentleman David Gilmour going nuts—clapping, cheering, and whistling as if his football team (regrettably, Arsenal) had just won the Cup.

So there we were having reduced the toughest audience in the world to putty in our hands. While the other guys had experienced this kind of reception before, it was a first for me, and to this day remains in the top five of our receptions anywhere in the world. That kind of reaction becomes a drug—the greatest of them all. The sensation of pure adrenalin flowing around your bloodstream for hours afterwards is indescribable and very difficult to turn off, hence the sometimes overwhelming desire to imbibe after the gig that develops into the classic after-show party syndrome. Ah, what a tough life. All this enormous fun every night of the week, plus they insist on paying you handsomely for the privilege. It definitely beats working for a living. I get irritated beyond belief at those people who have the unmitigated gall to moan about their lot in life when they are in such a position of privilege.

Once the single was out, all hell broke loose, and I started to taste first-hand what it was like to be a bona fide rock star, with all the trappings that come with it, except I couldn't see a lot of it because it was not my nature to change or take on the façade of a big shot. I still saw myself as a working musician who was incredibly lucky to be in the position I was in. Like all young budding rock 'n' rollers, I had done my fair share of fantasizing about being interviewed by the music press, being on *Top of the Pops*, being recognised on the street, or being asked for an autograph. But I always focused on the musicianship and improving my playing—plus, considering how long I had already been a working musician, the desire to indulge in those things had, for the most part, been and gone. That said, I now found myself smack dab in the middle of all that, and it had some interesting byproducts, as you will soon see.

There are very few things as exciting as waiting to hear what the new chart position of your single is, particularly if, as in my case, it's your first time up to bat. Although I had experienced it to some extent with the Apostolic Intervention, that record's monumental failure only showed me that, if it went horribly wrong, the disappointment was not unlike waiting for your lottery numbers to come up, when of course they never do. But when a single does show signs of life, there are all kinds of subtle pointers as to how well it is going to do. Airplay reports are the best indicator of what is about to happen. Reviews are always nice to get if they are affirmative, but bad ones just serve to depress everybody. Mind you, bad reviews can sometimes act as a compass to point out where you have gone wrong and, possibly, what you should do about it.

In our case, the single was given a tremendous boost when it got radio Luxembourg's Power Play, which meant they played it once an hour, every hour, for a week. Even better, *Top of the Pops* agreed to let us appear before the single got into the Top 20, which was unusual for the show. Back then, *TOTP* was broadcast live every Thursday. The show required you to mime to your pre-recorded backing track while your singers sang live. All this fed into my insecurities and plain old nerves, as I had never appeared on TV or mimed before. Fortunately, the back track for "Natural Born Bugie" was simplicity itself, and I could not have wished for an easier introduction to miming. I was also blessed that the other members of the band were old hats at such malarkey.

We arrived at the BBC's Shepherds Bush studios with our tape of the backing track, which we had been required to re-record in the BBC's little studio off the Bayswater Road. After going through the motions of re-recording, we proceeded to switch the tape with a copy of the original without the vocals so we could ensure that the sound quality was as good as it could be. This daft little song-and dance was apparently commonplace, and everybody involved knew it was going on but chose to turn a blind eye to it. Steve, by far the most experienced in television, and in filming in general, was extremely helpful with little tips, such as not to stare at the monitor screen above the audience's heads. He also said that I shouldn't allow them to put makeup on me, as, back then, TV was mainly still black and white, so that the only person to benefit from applying cosmetics to the face of a young rock star was the extremely camp makeup artist.

Andrew booked us on a short European tour to get our feet wet and to prepare us for a full-blown UK tour in the fall that would, in turn, ready us for the States. The European tour was the first in a long line of firsts that were about to hit me, as I had never been abroad to play—but it almost didn't happen, thanks to a stupid little annoyance called the Labour Law.

Many years ago, some bright spark decided to enact a law to protect underage children from being put to work. This, of course, was a fine, upstanding law to have on the books, but it was a huge pain in the ass for our little band of midgets. Needless to say, in all the excitement of becoming big rock stars, everybody, including me, forgot that I was still only just 17 years old. The only one who hadn't forgotten was the old man. Bless his heart, he had been harping on about it since he heard we were making plans to tour abroad.

We needed to get a judge to give me a special dispensation. This was by no means a fait accompli; they apparently said no most of the time. You had to have lots of good reasons why you should be given special dispensation to work abroad, let alone if you were underage.

Andrew's chauffeur, Eddie Reed, was dispatched to round up all the relevant parties and necessary paperwork, then head to the chambers of a very stuffy old judge in the Old Bailey in London. Dad's presence was apparently not essential, although his signature was, but when Eddie came to pick up me and Steve (who'd been elected to be my legal guardian whilst abroad), it was decided that Dad should come with us. We were running late and sweating it a bit because this judge had a reputation for being a cantankerous old bugger, but Dad knew all the back roads and shortcuts to get us there on time.

Our names were called out, and in we marched as if we were in the army. The judge was a sight to behold, sitting on his throne wearing the robe and the wig and the what have you. His pew was slightly elevated, which meant he was automatically looking down on us—and he had the attitude to match. He was a big man with a large handlebar moustache and a very deep, loud voice. He obviously did not suffer fools lightly and took an immediate dislike to the lawyer who was there to represent us, which did not bode well for our case.

As our case was presented, things were going so badly that the lawyer started to visibly sweat. Steve and I were standing up front with him, while Dad and Eddie stood a few paces behind us. Just when things were going from bad to much worse, the judge inquired as to the whereabouts of my parents. "I'm here, your honour," said Dad, and with that he was asked to step forward. As soon as he stood next to me, the judge seemed to soften, and after he exchanged a few niceties with the old man, I was granted my work visa and we were sent on our way. The judge even wished us well on our tour of Europe and insisted on shaking the old man's hand before we left his chambers.

The very first gig of the European mini-tour was outdoors at a shopping mall in Hilversum, the Netherlands. It was wall-to-wall people, and there was only us on the bill. As soon as we arrived at the site and got out of the car near the back of the stage, an almighty shrill scream bellowed out from all 10,000 female fans who were there, and it continued as we played. This would have worried Steve and Pete a great deal, if it were not for the fact that the men were also showing their appreciation, stomping and cheering as loudly as they could, and that we were playing really well.

The tour continued on to Bilzen, Belgium, where they held a festival called, coincidently, the Bilzen Jazz and Pop Festival. The grounds held about 40,000 people, and we were booked as the headliner, which was daunting to say the least, especially as this was to be only our second big gig. It was raining in the open air, so the stage was one big electrical shock just waiting to happen. Deep Purple and Marsha Hunt were also on the bill; both were extremely good and very hard to follow, especially Deep Purple. So guess who we had to follow?

Deep Purple were red hot, and their reputation was fierce. They had been touring America consistently, and the good old USA had worked its wonders on them. I had already started to see that America seemed to be the perfect proving ground for any touring band, and I couldn't wait for it to work its magic on us. But for now, its magic was working against us because trying to follow Deep Purple was a fucking nightmare.

As we were about to go on, the heavens opened and it began to piss down. We were using keyboards that did not like change of any kind, and they went completely out of tune. To add insult to injury, the power went off no less than *four* times during the first song.

Musicians all suffer from the same kind of bad dreams from time to time, usually along the lines of walking onstage having forgotten to put your trousers on. Or your drumsticks turn into rubber. Or your kit only has a snare drum set up. Or your lead singer turns out to be Engelbert Humperdinck instead of Steve, which really *would* be a nightmare! This gig was right up there with the worst onstage nightmare you could ever imagine, except it was actually happening. The entire evening was such an unmitigated disaster that the other bands on the bill actually felt sorry for us. That kind of sympathy is unheard of, as bands are usually a cruel lot and tend to wallow in other people's misery—and, as we had been showered with all this supergroup nonsense, we were especially fair game.

We learned an awful lot that night. The first and most valuable lesson was to never go on last at a festival. Even though that position is acknowledged as the top of the bill, things *always* go into overtime at festivals, and you can end up playing to an exhausted, half-empty crowd—and the ones who are left are either asleep or well on their way to being so. But if you acquiesce to another band on the bill and let them go on last, your seemingly noble act not only gives them the chance to headline, you also ensure that the audience is still awake and enjoying themselves immensely while you're on.

I forged some friendships that night that are still in place today. Aynsley Dunbar, whose band also played the festival, took me under his wing and gave me some invaluable tips about fine-tuning the kit. Jon Lord showed a genuine interest in the group's development and gave me some much-needed encouragement that I especially appreciated in light of the Bilzen debacle. He went out of his way to reassure me that everything was going to be all right and that I shouldn't be discouraged by that bump in the road. He didn't have to do that, and I am forever grateful to him. For someone to take the moral high ground like that in this business is always a welcome breath of fresh air.

We were booked to appear the following two nights at the world-famous Paradiso in Amsterdam, only this time we were opening for Deep Purple, not the other way round, and that was a great help to the group's demeanour. We were able to relax and make sure all the instruments were in tune, which certainly helps matters go much more according to plan. In those early days, we were experimenting with acoustic guitars at the start of the show, so that each one of us did a little acoustic unplugged deal before we strapped on the electric guitars and cut loose. This, by the way, was a full 20 years before some bright spark at MTV would come up with the unplugged idea. It also helped that the audience's frame of mind was exactly where we needed it to be. You see, in the Paradiso they can legally sell hashish and grass, as they can in all of Amsterdam—well, at least in the properly designated coffee shops, or pot shops as we used to call them.

From Amsterdam we went on to Bremen, Germany, to tape an appearance on the *Beat Club* TV show, which helped push the single to Number One in Germany. *Beat Club* was light years ahead of the rest—everybody who appeared on it had to play live, so if you didn't know your onions, you were in big trouble. To this day, our *Beat Club* appearances are still being regularly aired on the classic-rock shows on VH1 and MTV.

Once the taping was in the can, we were on our way back home—but not before I was given a guided tour of Bremen's red-light district. The road crew took charge of my initiation into the wonderful world of Germanic ladies of the night, and a sight to behold they were. I managed to get us thrown out of the district, even though we went on a slow night and the ladies were looking to "hook" any and all catches they could. When I saw them all sitting in their little bay windows dressed to kill, but with an average age of our grannies, it was not a pretty sight—"mutton dressed as lamb" does not even come close. So I broke into a rousing version of "(How Much Is) That Doggie in the Window?" and quickly received a red card, sent off from my début in the premier league of brothels. Unbeknownst to me, the one thing they would not tolerate is the clientèle making fun of the goods that are on display. Laughing at the tarts is not on; in fact; it's right out, on your ear.

It was now midsummer 1969, and to illustrate exactly how wrapped up we were in what we were doing, I didn't even notice that a certain Mr. Neil Armstrong had not only landed and walked on the Moon, he had also managed to fly himself and his very grateful crew all the way home to safety.

That summer was a rare thing in England—hot and sunny for a long period through July and August—and we were on a seemingly endless cycle of interviews and photo sessions. The interview that most sticks in my mind was one done by a lady called Penny Valentine for *Disc and Music Echo*, one of the big music papers, along with *Melody Maker, New Musical Express, Record Mirror,* and *Sounds.* In 1969, these publications were all-important. There was no MTV or VH1, or any other way of promoting your latest effort, whether it be a single, an album, or a tour. You had to rely on the good graces of all of these papers, which, in truth, were no better than the tabloid press we know today. To be fair, the writers weren't all bad; in fact, some of them were fine journalists who went on to be credible authors in their own right. But they often had their hands tied by editors who turned their well-written pieces into mindless dribble by adding a crass headline or simply twisting the original copy.

Journalists like Penny were a priceless breath of fresh air. They were on your side for all the right reasons: they were music lovers who were genuinely interested in what you were doing *and* what you had to say. Others who were top writers and, generally speaking, good eggs included Chris Welch at the *Melody Maker*, Keith Altham at the *NME,* and Pete Erskine at *Sounds.* They were friends who you could count on to at least use discretion when necessary. Don't get me wrong; they wouldn't pull any punches if they felt you needed to be told you were off base about something, or had put on a bad show or released a substandard record—believe me, through their columns, you would be, in no uncertain terms, the first to know! We had a certain advantage in Keith Altham, in that he happened to be our publicist. You would think that would be a conflict of interest, but apparently not, as he performed the same function for, amongst others, the Who.

Being interviewed by Penny was a distinct pleasure, as she was very sympathetic when she realised this was my first major interview of any sort, let alone with one of the big nationals. She was a sweet lady with a very pleasant, reassuring manner that made me relax as if I'd known her all my life.

Andrew had also done his bit to try and make me calm down. Before the interview, he had given me a pill that he called a "charmer": a Doriden, which is a mild sedative like Valium. This didn't have any ill effect on the proceedings, except I let it slip almost as an afterthought that Mum did occasionally worry about me, what with all the travelling and whatnot. It was such an off-the-cuff statement that I didn't think anything of it—until the article came out the next week.

So, on September 6, 1969, the readers of *Disc and Music Echo* learned that "Jerry Shirley is 17 years old and lives with his mother, father and elder brother near Cambridge" and that the self-same "'new boy' with Humble Pie" said that "[h]is mother is always worrying about him."

If the ground could have swallowed me up, this would have been a fortuitous time for it to have done so. Of course, it did not oblige, and I'm afraid I suffered the mandatory piss-taking that any young working musician would encounter given the circumstances. Mind you, it did teach me an early lesson in what not to say to the press, even if it's a journalist you think you can trust. (In fairness to Penny, she certainly didn't write the piece with any malice aforethought; she simply saw a sweet little 17-year-old boy whose mum worried about him.) Needless to say, Mum loved it, so, for that reason alone, it was more than worth it.

Selling out our UK tour was a foregone conclusion, but Andrew still put a fairly strong support bill on with us as insurance, including David Bowie and Love Sculpture, a Welsh band featuring Dave Edmunds that had recently had a Top 10 hit with a cover of the classical piece "Sabre Dance." Graham Bell was also on the bill with a band called Bell & Arc, whose drummer, Alan White, went on to play with the Plastic Ono Band and Yes.

We had developed this idea of starting our show with an unplugged set that featured each one of us doing a solo spot, starting with Peter, followed by me, then Greg, then Steve. On paper, this looked like a workable plan, the idea being that we come in like a lamb and go out like a lion. Well, we certainly came in like a lamb, but it was the audience that became the lions, who, by the end of our acoustic set, were ready to treat us as if we were Christians. It was horrible, a noble experiment that went woefully wrong. Suffice to say, the acoustic set had to go or at least be severely modified. We dropped my bit, which I was thankful for, as I thought it was an embarrassing waste of time. Greg's bit also got the chop, which left Pete and Steve to air their wares, and a fine job they did of it too, I might add. Peter did his song "Take Me Back" from our soon-to-be-released second album, *Town and*

Country, and Steve performed a show-stopping version of "I Worship the Ground You Walk On," an old Dan Penn-Spooner Oldham country-blues song made famous by Etta James. It never failed to amaze me how that man—with nothing more than an acoustic guitar and his voice—could hold an entire audience in the palm of his hand, often without the aid of the PA system; his voice was that powerful.

The tour went well, generally speaking; it did great business, and a lot of fun was had by all. Shooting water pistols at Dave Bowie from the orchestra pit was a regular source of entertainment, and I have to say he took it all in good humour. Andrew contributed the pièce de résistance by having his old friend Sean Kenny design a huge Styrofoam white elephant that blew smoke out of its arse. When I say huge, I mean *HUGE*: it was approximately the size of a movie screen and took up the entire back of the stage. Steve scored the best bit of witty repartee when, from the stage of the Queen Elizabeth Hall in London, his opening line to the audience was, "You'll have to forgive us tonight; we're somewhat relaxed. In fact, we're as relaxed as a newt."

The UK tour wound down, and before you could say, "Up the Spurs," we were on our way to New York City. Before we left, Immediate released our second album, but, unfortunately, that coincided with their collapse as a company. There was one small consolation, though: they released "Shaky Jake" as a single in Europe, with my song "Cold Lady" as the B-side. Apparently, it got to Number One in Scandinavia. Shame I didn't get paid.

Chapter 8

Rock-Band Boot Camp, SAS Style
November to December 1969

In which we have our first breakfast in America (with Winnie the winning Ruthie); the Fillmore East crowd doesn't instruct us to consume excretory product and expire; Steve rewrites a Moody Blues classic; I get blamed for everything but Altamont; and it's a small world with a Small Face, after all.

As Andrew Oldham likes to see, think of, and generally describe life in a series of movie metaphors, I'll say that the next few months of my life (and the group's) can only be described as *The Good, the Bad and the Ugly*. That Andrew was able to keep from us the travesty of justice that was about to engulf his business life, or at least not let it overtly interfere with the day-to-day running of our launch in general, was nothing short of miraculous. Not only did he manage to keep our career in forward motion, he was able to achieve this at the most critical time: our launch in America.

So, in this atmosphere of financial uncertainty that we were only partly aware of, we got busy with what we needed to do to go away to the USA: taking care of work visas, certain jabs that you still needed to travel to the States back then, and a variety of equipment needs (transformers, etc.). Most of all, we had to recruit an additional roadie, as our forever trustworthy head roadie Dave Clark would need an assistant. This was the perfect opportunity for me to pay back a favour to my old friend Chalky, the ever-reliable road warrior we had in Cambridge, who came with the added bonus of having already been to the States earlier that year with the Bonzo Dog Doo Dah Band. Chalky got on famously with Dave and all of us in the band, so hiring him was a done deal.

About a year before Humble Pie formed, Mum had a health scare when she found a lump on one of her breasts. Fortunately, it turned out to be a benign, non-life-threatening cyst, which was dissipated by way of a simple injection, and that was the end of that. As I was about to get ready to go on this first trip to the States, Mum found out that the would soon have to go into hospital to have a precautionary set of tests, just to make sure she still had a clean bill of health.

My initial reaction was abject fear and horror, but Dad assured me that it was just routine and just him taking advantage of his Masonic membership. Back then, Masons had access to the facilities at the Royal Masonic Hospital in Hammersmith, which was the best hospital in the country, so their families could receive a quality of health care they otherwise would not get without spending small fortunes, which they didn't have, on private health care.

Fortunately, Mum's hospital stay was only a precautionary look-see, nothing to worry about. Thank God. I was greatly relieved.

The majority of the shows on the UK tour had gone reasonably well, but we were in for a rude awakening once we got to the US. The standard of performance by all the groups we would encounter in just the first couple of weeks was truly astonishing. It was also going to be a huge culture shock to play in a country that did not have any idea of who we were and what we were about. We were actually looking forward to this aspect of playing the States—none of this supergroup nonsense, a fresh start without any preconceived notion of what we were supposed to be. So long as we were good, we hoped the Americans would be generous with their response. At that time, American audiences had a superb reputation for outstanding participation, and we were soon to find out that it was well deserved. The audiences in certain places were stronger than others, but at that time, generally speaking, they were all every musician's dream.

Coming to America was nice for me for a number of reasons: to begin with, I was on equal footing with the other lads in the band for the first time, as they had not been to the US before either, except for Greg, who had been there the year before as a member of Spooky Tooth.

We landed in New York at the beginning of November 1969. The most striking view I have ever seen at night was the NYC skyline. Millions of tiny Christmas tree lights—which were, in fact, the windows of skyscrapers and apartment blocks all over the city—added to the steady movement of the headlights of countless cars that caused the whole thing to be in a state of perpetual motion, albeit slow. It struck me that behind every window was another person's story, and the iridescent light show I was being suspended over, courtesy of British Overseas Airways Corporation, made the pure adrenalin that was flowing through me even more palpable.

We were picked up by the biggest black Cadillac limousine we had ever seen, and driven directly to the Holiday Inn on West 57th Street between Ninth and Tenth Avenues.

Like every band from the UK when they first put their feet on American soil, we headed straight for the nearest English pub we could find. Why Englishmen do that I'll never know, but I know why this particular set of Brits did—in a word, crumpet! We ended up at the Haymarket, which is now a gay bar, but back then was as heterosexual and British as Henry Cooper. All the rock 'n' roll Ruthies used to hang out there simply because it was the place where all the musicians hung out. (Steve and I wrote a song, which never saw the light of day, about certain young women who, shall we say, were rather eager to befriend musicians. The punch line of that unreleased ditty was "Ruthie takes her clothes off for anyone who plays a guitar.") As certain as death and taxes, where there are rock 'n' rollers, there's crumpet.

As we approached the Haymarket, we noticed a tall, imposing-looking black man leaving the place with two drop-dead gorgeous black ladies, one on each arm. I recognised him as Taj Mahal, one of our most recent musical heroes, who had taken the English music scene by storm the year before. All the serious blues players and lovers were taken off guard by his brilliant first album. His band was a dream four-piece with a knockout drummer who had this little trademark groove that involved a new way of approaching an old groove. (I was able to score some heavy-duty brownie points with the rest of the band because I could emulate it perfectly. In fact, we eventually used it in a remake of a Willie Dixon-written Muddy Waters tune called "I'm Ready.")

"What class! Attaboy!" I thought as we passed Taj and headed for the door of the bar. As we turned to go in, I noticed the two ladies do a one-eighty to follow us inside, leaving Taj to his own devices. No sooner had we walked through the door and found a table than they joined us as if they had known us all our lives. Their names were Winona and Devon, and they were stunning. They summoned the waiter tout de suite, ordered for all of us, and told him that *we* would be running a tab.

After we had been there for a while, the number of ladies that started to accumulate at our table was almost alarming, but who's going to complain at this stage—in for a penny and all that. The final head count of knockouts who ended up at or around our table was 12. They came in all shapes, sizes, and colours, and they all helped us consume a luxuriant amount of booze. When it came time to pay the bill, we, of course, were left holding the baby, but we were not left alone. Whilst they may have been using us to drink for free, they were quite happy to accompany us back to our hotel and start the party all over again.

By now, my attentions were being vied for by two of the better-looking girls. One was Devon, who was black as coal and just as shiny, and the other was a gorgeous girl called Jeanette, who was a big contrast to Devon: bright white, with an even brighter shock of red hair. Devon was a heroin addict who turned tricks to help subsidise her habit, while Jeanette was a barbiturate freak who kept nodding off between her attempts to get into my trousers.

Quite frankly, I was not particularly enamoured with this beauty trying to have her evil way with me, not because I didn't want to get laid, but because I was still very young and had never before experienced such a forthright approach from a woman. (It would take a few more attempts at handling such overtures before I would perfect the appropriate comeback. Thankfully, I'm a fast learner when it comes to the rhythmic use of the hips, and I soon decided that the polite gentleman's one-liner should be, "So I suppose a blowjob's out of the question?") At one point, Jeanette's inability to succeed with her advances finally got through her inebriated state. She had clearly been around Englishmen before and knew that we called cigarettes "fags," so, taking a cheap shot at my lack of interest in her amorous endeavours, she turned to me and said, "Would you like a fag? I could arrange both!"

Once the stragglers finally left the room Steve and I were sharing, we were faced with a motley collection of the girls' personal belongings: address books, lighters, handbags, etc. Winona stayed the night, not for any rumpy-bumpy reasons, although I'm sure neither Steve nor I would have said no, but because it was too late to get a cab that she could afford—or that we could pay for, as we didn't have the necessary spondoolies until management awoke to give us our per diem.

We were jolted awake the next morning by the horrendously loud trucks rumbling across Manhattan on 57th Street, having had very little sleep, due to the rock-hard beds that were standard fare in all Holiday Inns in 1969. The three of us went downstairs to the coffee shop for breakfast, where Winona explained some of the finer points of the way things worked in Rock 'n' Roll USA, including the pitfalls of life on the road.

Apparently, it was common practice for the girls to leave something behind as an excuse to call and come back—possibly to steal from you. Several girls had developed impressive collections of room keys that they had pinched from unsuspecting musicians. So far as you knew, all you had done was mislay the bugger, when, in fact, it had been added to some girl's room-key collection so that she could use it to her heart's content. Winnie was a godsend. She told us how the girls had a network across the country, and that they called each other to establish bragging rights and discuss their conquests: this guy's too small, that guy's too big; this guy's nice, that guy's not; this guy likes heroin, that guy likes opium; and so on.

Winnie painted a pretty unsavoury picture of these ladies, who were soon to be pegged with the collective title "groupies"—unfairly, in my opinion. They preferred their own title: "band aid." (This was, by the way, a full 15 years before Bob Geldof used that moniker for his magnificent charity efforts in 1984.) I thought that term was much more appropriate for these girls than "groupies," which had already developed a bad connotation: women who hung around bands with the sole intent of sleeping with them. While this part of their "service" was quite true, it was also true that they took care of just about every need we may have had.

A band-aid girl was willing to be seamstress, cook, nurse, tour guide, shrink, drug dealer, chauffeur, confidant, lover, and last, but by no means least, a bloody good friend. Needless to say, they weren't all good at all of these things, but you'd be surprised how many of them all across the US were fabulous at making you feel at home. And when you are barely 17 and this is your first trip away from England for any length of time, you become extremely grateful for all the help, particularly when you are not yet a headline act with all the bells and whistles of assistance that come with that.

Some of these girls went on to marry some of the biggest stars of my generation, and others ended up marrying doctors and lawyers. Some of them died as casualties of the Sixties, much like some of the stars they strived so well to look after. They were, generally speaking, a wonderful lot, and that is why I often rail against people using the term "groupie" to describe them. It has long been another word for "slut" or "slag," which they certainly were not. "Band aid" was certainly much better. They only hung out with you for as long as you wanted them to and did their best to please whilst in your company. At the time, there was an American advert for Band-Aid adhesive bandages that described the girls perfectly. It went something like this: "Band-Aid: it helps to heal while you need it and doesn't go *ouch* when it comes off!"

Winnie also filled us in on all the dos and don'ts of the Fillmore East, where we were to open for Santana for our American début. She told us that there was a strict backstage pecking order for the bands that played there. The opening act had the dressing room up on the third floor, the act that was second on the bill was on the second floor, and the headliner got the coveted first floor. Winnie warned us that the food backstage was often spiked with a variety of hallucinogens. This was entirely dependant upon who was headlining that particular night. For instance, if it happened to be the Grateful Dead, it was a racing certainty, whereas with Blue Cheer, it was a definite maybe—and if it was Seals and Crofts, it was definitely not.

After our first American breakfast—the most tasteless eggs and bacon I had ever been served—we went for a look at the music shops on 48th Street. The two main ones, Manny's and Sam Ash, were surrounded by several smaller ones, so that the whole area was an Aladdin's cave full of vintage guitars at reasonable prices. This gave us our first reason to become successful in the US as soon as possible: so that we could afford to buy some of these great guitars that seemed to be sprouting up all along 48th Street like weeds.

Next, we walked along Fifth Avenue, heading north to Central Park South. After having a look around Central Park, we walked back to the hotel. I was completely dumbstruck by the immense energy that literally vibrated through the streets of the great city. The number of people pushing and shoving their way through life on the streets never fails to amaze me; it is so different to anything I have ever experienced before or since. Without realising it, I was forming a love-hate relationship with New York City that would last for the next 30 years.

At lunch in the coffee shop, I learned a lesson that would last forever. I sat there politely trying to get the busy waitress's attention with, "Excuse me, miss" and "Please, could I have…" and "Would you mind terribly if…"—and all this was just to procure a menu. After about 20 minutes, I finally cottoned on by paying attention to those around me who were succeeding where I had failed. "*Gimme* two eggs over easy with bacon, coffee, and toast!" "*Gimme* a cheeseburger with fries, and make it snappy!" And so on. This was America: land of the free, home of the rude. In NYC, you don't politely ask the waitress for what you want. You *tell* her. It's not called an order for nothing. The waitresses were used to being yelled at, and unless your order was prefaced with *"Gimme,"* it didn't register.

*The fabled Fillmore East, site of Humble Pie's first US shows.
We would play there 20 times.*

It was time to go to the famous Fillmore East for the first gig on the tour. We had heard so much about it that we were already impressed before we ever stepped foot in the place. It didn't disappoint. Everything about it was better than we expected. The thing that struck us the most was the sound of the place; it was superb. Also, the venue was run with a level of professionalism that was way above anything we had experienced before, and the PA and lights were literally the best in the world at that time. We were bowled over by the whole experience, and we hadn't yet played a note.

When we started touring, there were many truly great venues all across the USA. They were gigs to die for, as the acoustics in most were sensational, not to mention the fact that they were beautiful to look at. Most of them were either turn-of-the-century Art Nouveau or mid-Thirties Art Deco, and, as time wore on, they were such perfect venues for rock 'n' roll that they would often get complete restorations. One case in point is the Fox chain of theatres, many of which were restored to their original condition.

That first show at the Fillmore East was to lead to dozens more—we ended up playing more gigs there than did any other band. It was also to be the scene of our greatest triumph just two short years down the road, with the recording of our multi-million-selling live album, *Performance—Rockin' the Fillmore*, but that would have seemed light years ahead at the time. We still had many miles to travel before that magnificent weekend in May 1971 would be upon us.

We got a very rude awakening that night as to how good bands had to be to succeed in front of a New York City audience. We were first on the bill, and we were still trying to start with an acoustic bit and then move to electric. This was not a complete disaster, but we weren't doing ourselves any favours. In fact, the audience were remarkably patient with us in the early days, as if they knew things were going to get a whole lot better before too long, and, of course, they did. But that was all in the future; for now, our lessons were there to be learned, and there were plenty of them. We had a lot of listening and watching to do, starting that very night with the headliners, Santana.

Our show went reasonably well, considering how unprepared we really were for an American audience; at least we didn't get booed off. The middle act was the Paul Butterfield Blues Band, with Mike Bloomfield on guitar, and they did great. But I was not at all prepared for what I was about to witness.

I could tell by the packed house and the sense of anticipation in the air that something special was about to happen, and I was not wrong. Santana blew the roof off the place. They were, and still remain, pound for pound, the best band I have ever seen. Their musical abilities were second to none, their songs were of a style that was entirely new to me, and the rhythm section cooked like none I'd ever heard. And then, of course, Carlos Santana himself was one of the most exciting guitar players I had heard in years. He was also an extreme gentleman. The band literally rocked the house: the balcony was moving, and bits of plaster were falling off the ceiling. The crowd's reaction was every musician's dream; they went nuts. They were standing on the top edges of the backs of their chairs—how they did that without falling off, I'll never know—and the noise they made was ear splitting. At the end of their show, Santana came back on for *seven* encores—and this was back when encores were genuine, not the contrived part of the show they have since become.

We realised then what a long, long way we had to go before we were to get anywhere near those heady heights of sheer brilliance, but it also acted as a red flag to a very determined bull. We knew just how high the bar of excellence, musically speaking, had been raised by Santana and others we were soon to see in America. We absolutely relished the challenge, and it is my personal opinion that it woke a sleeping giant in the other three guys in our band, who had, due to their past successes in England, been lulled into a false sense of security regarding what was expected of them in a live show. That first experience at the Fillmore East got their professional goals stirred up a treat, and for the next two years, all we did was concentrate on getting better and better by paying very close attention to the headline acts we worked with. With many of them, we also started friendships that have survived to this day. In fact, Michael Shrieve, Santana's drummer, became a good friend of mine, although, sadly, I haven't seen him in years.

The Fillmore East audience, while kind to us that first night, were generally not so forgiving; in fact, they were positively brutal when it came to letting an act know exactly what they thought of them. "You suck!" and "Your momma is a cocksucker!" and "Fuck off, you fucking faggot!" and "Eat shit and die, motherfucker!" were some of the well-intended constructive criticisms they were often heard to expound upon your efforts to entertain. Sometimes, it was like taking lambs to slaughter. I witnessed many an act that was big in England getting booed off the Fillmore East stage, the most notable being T. Rex. So, all things considered, we got off to a mercifully forgiving start to our American career.

The way things worked at the Fillmore East was pretty straightforward. Each engagement lasted two days, and you did two shows a day. The evening started at eight o'clock, with the opening act playing for approximately 30 minutes, the second on the bill for roughly 45, and the headliner for as long as they wished, which partly depended on how many encores they got. The "normal" shows wouldn't turn out until four or five in the morning. Some headliners, though, chose to play *all fucking night*, so that the late show would often not turn out until seven in the morning. The Grateful Dead were the most notorious for such self-indulgence, but there were others, including the Allman Brothers and Jimi Hendrix's Band of Gypsys.

The Fillmore's stage was designed to carry sound. It was built like a bass bin, which helped the music resonate and carried it to the audience in a crystal-clear fashion, so that in the quiet passages, you could hear a pin drop. Our Steve, having come from a theatrical upbringing, took complete and absolute advantage of this characteristic. Without being told, he instantly recognised the place as an old vaudevillian music hall that had probably been converted into a cinema later on.

Steve became famous for pushing his microphone away, walking to the front of the stage, and singing to the people at the back of the hall, "Are you ready?" and winding them up until he was sure they were ready. Then, and only then, would I get the signal from him—a shake of his bum or a twist of his hips—to start the song. It still puts goosebumps up me after all these years to think of him in action. He was such a master at what he did, and I was the one who had the privilege of playing drums behind him more than any other drummer, including my dear old mate Kenney Jones of the Small

Faces. Between the two of us, we hold the record of playing many, many more shows with Steve than did any other player. Jim Leverton, the bass player in Steve's latter-day bands (with whom I had the extreme privilege of playing in Steve's three-piece blues outfit, Packet of Three), is the only player who even comes close.

Many of the methods Steve used to communicate with his audience have since become commonplace with frontmen in rock bands: the call and response, encouraging the audience to sing along or clap (preferably in time) with the band, and using the band's natural dynamics to get even more audience participation. While I'm not suggesting for a minute that he singlehandedly invented these techniques, he was one of the first to turn them into an art form all its own, and was copied by just about every frontman that came along at the same time and immediately after.

He, of course, had himself borrowed heavily from the people that influenced him. Otis Redding, James Brown, and Mick Jagger were probably his biggest influences as a frontman, but there were many, many more who I'll get into later. The short list of guitar players who influenced the way he performed would include Chuck Berry, Keith Richards, Joe Brown, Eddie Cochran, and Mick Green of the Pirates, but his all-time superhero of guitar players was Steve Cropper: the way he played, the way he looked, the way he held his guitar—the whole package. If Steve Marriott could have been anybody other than himself, it would have been Steve Cropper, although I think the package he already had did quite nicely, thank you very much.

The first tour lasted six weeks. The majority of it was concentrated on the East Coast and the Midwest. We went from NYC to Philadelphia, from there to Washington D.C., then on to Pittsburgh. During this leg, we saw the band Chicago, who were then known as Chicago Transit Authority. They were stunning. All the American bands we opened for on that first trip were in a class of their own, whereas a number of the British acts we worked with then were, at best, only fair to average, with only two exceptions: the Kinks and the Moody Blues.

We did a show in Toledo, Ohio, with the Kinks, and what I remember most is everybody backstage waiting for the now-famous, almost nightly fistfight between the Davies brothers to break out. The road crew would often open a book and take bets on how many songs the show would last fightfree. That aside, the band sounded great. I had a personal interest in seeing a local lad made good in the form of John "Nobby" Dalton, the bass player who had recently replaced original Kinks bassist Pete Quaife. John was from

Waltham Cross and used to play in a local band called the Mark Four, who Angus and I had opened for and seen many times, and it was lovely to see him make it to the major leagues.

After Toledo, we hooked up with the Moody Blues for a string of dates that started in Buffalo, before we went by private coach across Niagara Falls to Toronto, Canada. That trip was fun all by itself. It was a relief not to have to fly for a few days; Steve hated flying, so he was in a much more relaxed mood, which was always good. It was our first experience taking in, while travelling by road, some of the stunning natural beauty that the USA has to offer. Niagara Falls is astonishing. The problem was, we couldn't see it. It was November, and the weather was so bad that the spray caused by the enormous amount of water zooming over the falls at 20 miles per hour had turned into a very heavy mist. I had to wait until subsequent trips years later to actually see the falls. For now, we had to take everybody's word for it.

The gigs with the Moody Blues went well, and they treated us with tremendous respect and decency. Their show had become very slick and polished compared to when Angus and I saw them years before in Bishop's Stortford. At that time, Denny Laine was their lead singer, they had just had a Number One hit with "Go Now," and they were a knockout. With Denny gone and a whole new musical approach, they were quite possibly a better band and certainly had built their popularity to a great degree. I personally preferred the way they were with Denny: a lot more gritty and bluesy; hence the name, I suppose. They had become very popular with their album *Days of Future Passed*, which they recorded with the London Festival Orchestra, and which contained a big hit called "Nights in White Satin"—or, as Steve renamed it, "Tights That I've Shat In." It's actually quite a good song unless you apply Steve's rewrite; then, I can assure you, it will never seem the same again.

Woodstock had just happened a few months before, and, as a consequence, the two-fingered peace sign had become very popular. Graeme Edge, the Moodys' drummer, had taken to standing behind his kit at the end of their show and giving the peace sign to the audience in an exaggerated fashion, with his right hand above his head. Today I can finally admit that he inspired me to start doing it too, which just goes to show I was capable of being just as pretentious as the next man back then.

As a player, the one thing I got from Graeme, when I saw him early on, was the preference for a loud bass drum. In the "Go Now" days, he had one of the loudest I had ever heard, and that was something I always strived to emulate. I told him so on these dates, though I doubt if he remembers.

That was the way I was whenever we played with a band whose drummer was my senior (which almost everybody was back then) and, as such, far more experienced. I would be very respectful towards them because of my upbringing: "Respect your elders" or, in the music business version, "Respect those who have trod the boards" (walked onstage) many, many more times than you. As I saw myself very much as a rookie, I wouldn't dream of acting like a hot-shot towards these guys who had been at it for a long time, but behaved like utter gentlemen. I decided there and then that I'd always strive for that classy gentleman's approach to this remarkable hoo-hah of a thing that was my job and loosely termed as show business. All I knew was that it beat working for a living, and for that I was very grateful indeed.

After Canada, we got to play in the famous Tea Party club in Boston. Don Law, who owned the club and promoted shows there, went on to become the biggest promoter in the Boston area, and we subsequently worked with him countless times. At that time, there were a number of great rock 'n' roll clubs across America that were custom built for live bands. You would usually play in one of them for two, three, or four nights, with at least two shows per night. This meant you got to know each city and its musical community quite well, and that, in turn, helped you deal with homesickness. In each major city, you could develop friends who would take you out to see things you would not normally see, take you to parties, or show you around the great pawn shops to look for vintage-guitar bargains.

In Boston, Chalky somehow got us invited to a party by some people at the gig. I can only describe it as a fairly typical hippie gathering, American style. Lots of people dressed like Hiawatha, wearing headbands and feathers in their long hair, sitting in circles, smoking 1969's version of a peace pipe. We were invited to join one circle and partake in the pipe, which was very nice of them. But when the pipe got a little closer to us, I noticed that it was in fact a large cock and a set of balls painted bright blue. I immediately saw the funny side of this—to me it was a "blue-veined flute" that you were supposed to suck on while a nice pile of grass glowed bright yellow in the bowl, which was, of course, cut into the balls at the other end.

I suddenly realised that we were being set up as the dumb rock musician and roadie: they were waiting to see us suck a big one. Not my cup of tea, I'm afraid, although Chalky hadn't noticed. Being a roadie, his mind was definitely elsewhere, so that while he was trying to chat elsewhere up, he didn't realise he wasn't getting anywhere, because. at the same time, he was enthusiastically sucking on a bright blue, eight-inch cock. Maybe it was his enthusiasm that put her off. I'm not sure what was funnier: watching him sucking on this thing for all it was worth whilst trying to pull the young lady or listening to him try to explain himself once he finally cottoned on to what he was doing.

At one point, the host suddenly decided to show us his pride and joy. Not realising I was an animal lover, he took us into his bedroom and opened the closet. Sitting in the corner of the top shelf, violently hissing at us, was a baby leopard or cheetah that was obviously scared out of its wits. After coming close to a bowel movement myself, I left in disgust, but not before telling the host exactly what I thought of him. I reported him to the authorities as soon as I got back to the hotel. Not that I'm a killjoy, but I hope he got in all kinds of shit, the mindless asshole.

Something else happened at that party before it went south on me that was a huge wakeup call and, at the same time, a personal call to arms. The second Led Zeppelin album had just been released, and it was enormous. The lead-off track, "Whole Lotta Love," was being played at the party on a huge sound system. The album sounded truly out of this world. It was everything I wanted us to be doing. I don't mean I wanted us to copy Zeppelin or anything like that; I just mean that they had a fullness of sound and a cohesive direction that was simply bursting with energy. I knew that huge-sounding energy from the early Humble Pie rehearsals, where the pressure was off and we were just having a blast—and I realised we had somehow lost our way, trying to please everybody, and in the process pleasing no one. It was not because we were not capable of having that again, we just needed to get busy and find ourselves, musically speaking.

The trouble was, I was in no position to tell the other guys how to run our railroad. After all, I was very much the new kid on the block and, as such, was so grateful just to be there that it would not be appropriate for me to start calling the shots, not yet anyway. I began to develop a passionate determination to do all I could to put some fire in the belly of this band of ours that I loved and respected so much. They had shown faith in me by giving me the job when there were so many other drummers they could have chosen, who I thought were so much better than me, and I was determined to give the band's engine room everything I could to pay back their belief in me. I was soon to find, in the most obvious place, a willing partner who also felt we had lost our way with the overemphasis on the unplugged approach, and that we could be so much more exciting—Greg Ridley.

I did not take into consideration the fact that we were currently doing the very thing that was the catalyst in Zeppelin's development: touring America. It was like rock-band boot camp, SAS style. (For American readers: Special Air Service is a regiment of the British Army renowned for its incredibly rigorous selection and training process.) Any band—as I mentioned before regarding the Who—that toured the States a lot got real good, real quick.

Deep down, Peter and Steve knew we needed to shift up a gear or two if we were to become a big, all-conquering band in the States, or anywhere else for that matter. What also needed to happen was for those two to sort out their respective roles in the band. The problem with that was that Steve was very reluctant to take a pure frontman role, as he felt it was, after all, Peter's band that he had joined. And, after nearly four years with the Small Faces of being the frontman to beat all frontmen, he really did want to take a back seat and just play a little rhythm guitar to back up Peter. His commitment to Peter was commendable, but an awful waste of the best frontman in the business. Of course, Peter was no slouch as a frontman himself. The answer to this problem came very soon: so long as we had two of the best frontmen in the business, why not use them *both* as frontmen?

Following Boston, the tour continued on through the Midwest, taking in Cleveland, Detroit, Grand Rapids, and Chicago, and then we were to head to the West Coast. This was a time in the history of American music when the West Coast had become the new Mecca for all things cool and hip. As a place for the rich hippies and musicians to live, Laurel Canyon had become the new Beverly Hills, and the Sunset Strip was still the site of every happening club, shop, and restaurant. The bands in California had been heavily in the ascension for the last two or three years: Buffalo Springfield, the Byrds, Jefferson Airplane, Love, Mothers of Invention with Frank Zappa, Captain Beefheart, and the entire psychedelic movement in San Francisco. The latest supergroup to take America, and the rest of the world, by storm was Crosby, Stills & Nash, who soon added Neil Young to make them Crosby, Stills, Nash & Young. They were phenomenal, but, as with all truly great things, there was a downside. With them, it was their name. In and by itself it's fine, but, unfortunately, it led to a rash of bands that all sounded like law firms, with Emerson, Lake & Palmer being the best of several examples.

Even the hotels where we were to stay in California had carved out a place in the history of rock 'n' roll. Shortly before we stayed at the Continental on Van Ness Avenue in San Francisco, Keith Moon, according to hotel staff, drove a Lincoln Continental into the swimming pool, We soon found out that Keith had apparently driven a Bentley or a Rolls or a Cadillac or a Lincoln into several swimming pools across the States, according to the front-desk staff in most Holiday Inns and Ramadas from Des Moines, Iowa, to New Haven, Connecticut, from Albuquerque, New Mexico, to Portland, Oregon, and all points between. Keith himself claimed it was a Lincoln at a Holiday Inn in Flint, Michigan, but others say the incident never happened at all.

Then there was the now-infamous Hyatt House in LA, which became lovingly known as the Riot House. We were the very first rock band to stay there, but more on that later…

We couldn't wait to get to "The Coast," as it was called. It was the last leg of the tour, which was great; it was coming up to Christmas, which was even better; and the rest of the band were in fine fettle as they had persuaded Andrew to fly out the two remaining wives, Jenny and Mary, to be with Steve and Peter for the duration of the West Coast leg. (Greg's wife Mandy had been on the entire tour, which had caused more than a little consternation within the troops.)

There was this ridiculous game that had been playing out between Steve and Peter and their spouses at home. It was called "Why are you sharing a room with *him*?"—with "him," of course, being me. As I was the only bachelor in the band, it was naturally assumed by home base that my room was where all the action was. I can't think why; I was such a good little boy whose mother worried about him! The married lads asked their wives how I could be a threat to their completely puritanical behaviour. After all, it was *their* collective duty to keep their eyes on *me*. They both *had* to share the role of my surrogate big brother, didn't they? "No" was the girls' usual reply to this altruistic line of reasoning, and, from then on, a pattern started to develop: I was blamed by Steve and Peter for *everything*.

Jenny: "Who's that girl I hear in the background?"

Steve: "Oh, that was Jerry's new friend."

Jenny: "But I just got off from Peter's room—they put me through to him by mistake—and he said that was Jerry and his new friend *there*."

Steve: "I know, two at a time. Sent one to my room for cigarettes. Dirty little toe rag, isn't he!"

Ah, yes. Halcyon days indeed!

To be fair, in those early days, Steve and Peter were actually very well behaved. Whilst they might have done a lot of window shopping, they weren't buying at all, God bless 'em, they were both so very much in love with their wives that buying just wasn't on their agendas.

The main reason the "Who's rooming with who?" question kept coming up was actually at the root of what was wrong with Steve and Pete's friendship. They respected each other enormously as musicians, but as friends they could not have been more unlike each other if they had planned it; they were complete chalk and cheese. I, on the other hand, got on great with both of them, so, in a way, it was good that they had a neutral room to go back and forth to and from. We were on such a tight budget at the time that we couldn't afford individual rooms, so we had to double up in some formation or other. The wives at home saw it as a natural fit for those two to room together and for me to have the single room. In any case, that was all put to one side when they joined us, and the whole thing went back to the happy families scenario of just a few short months before in Ibiza.

The first West Coast gigs were in San Francisco at the famous Fillmore West. The reputation of this place was that, by comparison, playing at its hard-to-please East Coast cousin was like giving candy to kindergarten kids. The Fillmore West audiences were notoriously difficult to satisfy, and we soon found out why—they were so stoned that you could easily mistake the real culprit, barbiturates mixed with cheap red wine, for total lack of interest. The Ripple-and-reds crowd, as they were affectionately known, became our latest challenge. We were determined to leave our mark, and in this case the goal was simple: if we woke 'em up, we had scored. With this lot, the last thing in the world you wanted to do was knock 'em out!

Bill Graham ran this Fillmore with the same military efficiency he was famous for at the Fillmore East. One of the subtle differences was the approach to backstage hospitality. There was a short list of extremely efficient helpers who would be assigned to each group as a social director, if you like, who would act as tour guide, nurse, and procurer of stuff. And by that, I mean *any* stuff, not just the obvious. If you wanted to find antique-clothing stores, good pawn shops for old guitars, classic old American cars (for the richer rock star), or a day trip to Sausalito, they would take care of it for you. They were great people, and some of them became lifelong friends. They were also closely connected to the network of band-aid girls—which was an extra added bonus for yours truly, as you can well imagine—and were more than happy to help me in the ongoing search for my future ex-wife. In fact, they were quite happy to help me find all three of them!

Chris O'Conner was a large ball of crushed-velvet womanhood with a huge shock of dark brown, fuzzy hair. She was a fellow short-arse, but she was not small in any way, shape, or form. Chris had been assigned to us—

specifically, Jenny, Steve, and me—to act as our Mrs. Fix-It, which she did with resounding efficiency. You name it, she did it for us. She was an absolute sweetheart who made sure we trod through the potential minefield—better known as the backstage at the Fillmore West—with impunity. This was where we were strongly reminded of the dangers of backstage food and drink, with good cause, as the headliner was going to be the Grateful Dead.

Chris was also a photographer and occasional writer for *Rolling Stone*, back when it was still a fledgling music rag that also dealt in social commentary. It was run out of San Francisco and had very recently done a front-page story on our good friends in band aid. The girl they used for the front cover shot was a 19-year-old called Karen. Thanks to Chris and her mother-hen instincts, Karen was added to my list of future ex-wives. Pretty soon, Karen was looking after my every need with faultless efficiency. She was gorgeous and smelled of patchouli oil. She had been the girlfriend of Jack Casady, the bass player with Jefferson Airplane and Hot Tuna, and had borne him a son when she was quite young; the little fella was already a toddler around two or three years old. On the first night that Karen took me under her wing, she made me a home-cooked meal at her apartment and had me stay the night.

The following morning I was awoken by someone standing over me, pulling on my nose. The bed was just a mattress atop a box-spring on the floor, and when I opened my eyes, I got quite a start—standing there, looking right at me, eye to eye, was a three-year-old carbon copy of Jack Casady. I was being taken care of by the woman on the cover of the latest *Rolling Stone*, who was also the mother of a famous rock star's son. (That edition of *Rolling Stone* became known as the "groupie issue," and was soon quite famous in its own right.) I had definitely arrived, and I was not even going to be 18 for another two months. Life was very good indeed.

It was around then that the "just when things are looking good, a pile of shite lands on the hood" pattern in my life started, and it's still with me 40 years later. At least now I know when to duck.

I had been speaking to Dad as often as money would allow. The last time we talked, he told me that Mum was to be discharged from hospital, after undergoing her precautionary tests, on the day I was due home. So Dad could pick me up at the airport in my newly re-sprayed white Daimler Majestic, and then we could go on to the Royal Masonic to pick up Mum. In the event, that's exactly what happened. But little did I know that there would turn out to be more to it than I could ever have imagined.

><

At the beginning of December 1969, a lot was happening in America, both musically and socially. The Charles Manson murders had occurred only months earlier, and the Stones were getting ready to play a huge free concert at Altamont, that now-famous racetrack just outside San Francisco. There was talk that the size of the crowd would outdo Woodstock (although "only" about 300,000 actually attended, far fewer than Woodstock's "half a million strong"), and one of the main acts on the bill was to be the Grateful Dead. Nothing wrong there, except that they were also supposed to be the headliners for our third show at the Fillmore West. We were set to play the middle spot after an American band called the Flock, who had started to

Poster for Fillmore West gig. We became the headliner when the Dead didn't show.

make some headway in the charts and featured an electric violinist who was a show all on his own. Not my cup of tea, but interesting, I suppose.

The Dead ended up not playing at Altamont because of the violence there. The problem was with the security force they had hired for the show, the Hell's Angels, who saw fit to use stabbing as a form of crowd control. The Angels killed an innocent bystander while the Stones were playing, which caused more than a little set of problems, to put it mildly. (The whole sordid tale is told in *Gimme Shelter*, the documentary about the Stones' 1969 tour.)

The beginnings of our career were strangely intertwined with the Stones. Andrew, who had just recently quit as their main man, was now our manager. Brian Jones—who had been replaced in the Stones earlier that year by Mick Taylor—died soon after he left the band, drowning in his pool. Two days earlier, he had called Steve Marriott and asked to come down and talk about jamming a bit and joining our band. Unfortunately, he never made it to our rehearsal; he chose to go for a swim instead.

So when the Altamont disaster happened, it was hardly surprising that it would somehow come back on us. This time, instead of preventing a star guitar player from showing up to play with us, it prevented an entire band from doing so. The Grateful Dead couldn't get out of Altamont to be at the Fillmore. So we ended up playing our third show at the Fillmore West as headliners, as we were the only band that could get there. The same applied to the crowd; only a very few people actually made it from Altamont, and they were so exhausted that they got in, sat down in front of the stage, and went to sleep. We must have been really impressive that night, as we managed to wake them up.

It was soon time for us to say our goodbyes to San Francisco and all that came with it. We had been told an awful lot about the drive along the old Pacific Coast Highway from San Francisco to Los Angeles and how it was one of those things in life that, if you ever get a chance to do it, you had better not miss out. So we chose to take the advice of our roadie Dave Clark, who pressed us into going for it, not that we needed a lot of pressing. He told us he could hire two brand new Mustang Mach 11 sports cars like the one Steve McQueen drove in *Bullitt*. Plus, the fact that Greg and Mandy were definitely not interested was, as sad as it is to admit it, the real driving force behind our decision to do the drive. We were all a bit Mandy'd out by this stage of the tour, so even a short break from her was a very attractive idea.

It took two days to do the drive properly, as the old road was a little, winding cliffhanger with a stunning view around every bend, so whoever was driving didn't get to see much—at least if you wanted to live. It was definitely eyes-on-the-road time. Fortunately, Dave was a hell of a driver, so he drove the lead car, with me riding shotgun and playing navigator, a role that stuck with me for the next 40 years. Steve and Jenny were in the back seat of our car, while Pete and Mary followed in the second car. As our road trip progressed, I switched back and forth between cars, depending on which couple was arguing the most.

Dave had bought a street map of LA so that we could find our digs, and, as a goof, he and I bought a map of the stars' homes so he could sound like an extremely knowledgeable road manager—which he in fact was; this just made it a bit more fun. "Over there is Cary Grant's house." "This is where Lucille Ball lives." "That's Jayne Mansfield's pink house." And so on. It was great fun; it put me into an instant mindset of Wonderland, and I loved every minute of it.

One massive mansion with an Edwardian look about it had a large plot of land in front, which I guess was the front yard (which we call the "garden" in England). There were loads of white-marble statues on pedestals all over the property, which was nothing that unusual—until an Arab with a sense of humour bought it a few years later. He decided to have pubic hair painted on the appropriate anatomical places of all his white-marble garden guests. It takes all sorts. I thought it was hysterical, but his super-conservative neighbours thought otherwise. When he refused to give the statues their dignity back, his powerful neighbours got a court order forcing him to do so. They literally had him by the short and curlies, so he left—but not before the house mysteriously burned down to the ground.

This was to be the final week of the tour and, as such, the most exciting of the entire six weeks. Here we were in Hollywood, which by itself would be thrilling enough for a 17-year-old. But added to that, with Christmas only a couple of weeks away and a whole week in which to play just four dates (which were to be recorded) at the world-famous Whisky a Go Go, we had plenty of time to see the sights.

When we got to the motel, however, we realised with a resounding wallop that things at Immediate Records were not right by a long shot. The motel was a rathole of a place, and, after checking in and going to get something to eat, we found that the hotel staff had locked us out of our rooms, put our bags in the hallway, and were very abruptly asking us to leave. Welcome to Hollyweird!

It turned out there was a problem with the credit card we had been checked in on. Paul Baines, the Immediate tour manager who was with us, was a lovely guy who did his level best to cope with the ship sinking around us. He eventually located Andrew, who had come with us to LA, and Andrew, bless his heart, fixed the problem post-haste by recruiting the help of Lou Adler. Lou, along with Elmer Valentine and Mario Maglieri, the other owners of the Whisky, hooked us up in the most exclusive hotel in town: the Hyatt House on Sunset Boulevard. It was so exclusive that they had put in place a "No Rock Bands" policy, but for us they made an exception as a favour to Lou, Elmer, and Mario. Consequently, we were the first band ever to stay in the now-infamous Riot House.

We were not due to start the shows for another three days, so we were able to put in a bit of serious socialising, and Andrew came into his element. He had so many cool friends in LA, it was hard to know where to start. The two I remember most clearly are John Phillips of the Mamas & the Papas and Elmer Valentine. We were invited to both of their houses, John's being in Bel Air, the posh part of town, and Elmer's in super-cool Laurel Canyon, up in the hills behind the Whisky.

Both houses were astonishing. John's was an old-school Tudor mansion that came with the whole shooting match: the long in-and-out semicircular drive, the big wrought-iron entrance gate that of course opened automatically, and, to complete the pretentious nonsense of it all, a butler. John was extremely nice to us and, other than being a bit distant, was a charming host. We were served a lovely meal in the formal dining room, with wine flowing and joints being smoked. John had recently hooked up with a famous model whose name I can't recall, but whose legs I'll never forget. They were sooo long: they just kept going and going and didn't stop.

At John's house, I had my first experience with seeing and hearing a home studio. By that I mean he had a full-on, top-drawer studio with all the latest equipment—in his house. It was actually quite small, way up in his cathedral-ceilinged attic, which was more like the size of a priest hole. Taking into consideration how tall John was, it's amazing he ever got any work done there. But he did record quite a bit of material there, judging by how much he played us that night. As impressed as I was with the house and the meal and the studio, however, I must admit that his music didn't move me much at all. After we managed to escape his grip in the studio, we thanked him for a pleasant evening and got the fuck out of Dodge.

The next outing a la Andrew was a trip to Elmer's house in Laurel Canyon the following afternoon for a very casual pool party. Elmer, an ex-cop from Chicago, was much more my personal cup of tea. He was a lovely man who knew how to look after musicians better than anybody I had met so far. He didn't try to impress us at all, and, in not doing so, he impressed us a great deal.

At the party, Elmer introduced us to his minders, who were much like the girls who had looked after our every need in San Francisco. Charlotte was an extravagant mass of red hair who exuded life and the love of it; I'm proud to say she is still my friend today. Although I haven't seen her for a number of years, she's the kind of person who would greet you as if you had been in her company on a daily basis. Then there was Linda: tall, blonde, and elegant. She would intimidate most fellas, but tended to get on with drummers on principal—you know, natural rhythm and all that.

This gathering was a pivotal moment in the history of Humble Pie, as it was the first time that Andrew actually put his cards on the table and informed us of what was going on. He told us in simple terms that Immediate was going belly up and that we should, at our earliest convenience, get in touch with A&M Records as they were looking to sign new acts and were interested in us thanks to his recommendation. Although this was not the best news we'd ever had, at least Andrew had the decency to forewarn us and tell us what to do. I was forever grateful for this, as it gave us hope for the immediate future—albeit a future without Immediate. Andrew told us to ask for a $250,000 advance and at least 14% in points (percentage of record sales), which is what gave us hope. As it turned out, we got nearly twice that.

(Our publishing was going to be in a muddle because our contract with Immediate allowed them to assign it [sell it on] to the highest bidder, which is precisely what the official receiver eventually did, although we fought it tooth and nail all the way.) In the meantime, though, we still had the shows to do and the live recording to make.

The Whisky a Go Go, which Elmer owned and ran with his partners Mario Maglieri and Lou Adler, was and still is the most famous club in America. It was situated right in the heart of Sunset Strip. To the west were the fancy houses I have already described, the Beverly Hills Hotel, and Bel Air and its mansions. To the east lay all the record company buildings and the upscale shops and restaurants. To the north were the Hollywood Hills and Laurel Canyon. To the south was Santa Monica Boulevard, where many other music clubs and cool restaurants were located, including the Troubadour and Barney's Beanery, where, believe it or not, they served real English-style beans on toast.

Back then, Elmer was very much hands-on. In later years, he took a back seat and let his trusted lieutenants do the day-to-day stuff. The club itself was no great shakes. It had dreadful acoustics, with a high ceiling and a balcony that literally hung over the stage. The audience sat at tables almost all the way up to the stage, with a small area right in front of the stage for the idiot dancers.

The waitresses constantly patrolled the tables in front of the stage, so there were lots of drink orders shouted across the floor, and loads of glasses clinking—or smashing if an order was dropped. On the other hand, all the merits of the club also belonged to the waitresses: they were all drop-dead gorgeous.

We were supposed to play three shows per night for a total of four nights, which for us was a bit of a stretch, as we only had enough material for two shows tops. So after we did some begging and pleading, Elmer allowed us to play just two shows per night. We were recording the shows as well, so it made for a pretty nerve-wracking four days, but we got through it without too much fussing and crying. The Whisky's audiences were a blasé lot who had seen it all and were much more interested in getting the attention of the waitresses than paying attention to us. Steve came up with a unique solution for this bad habit; he told 'em off, literally screaming at them at the top of his voice to "SHUT UP!!!"—and the remarkable thing is that they did.

We all wanted to see Disneyland while we were in LA, how you do, so it was left up to Charlotte and Linda to organise our day out, which they did with military efficiency. I had been enjoying the company of Shelly, one of the Whisky waitresses. She was lovely and truly great company. Thank God we never married; can you imagine, the poor woman's name would have been Shelly Shirley.

Charlotte took care of Steve, Jenny, Shelly, and me, while Linda looked after Peter and Mary. If you ever want to absorb the Christmas spirit in a way that beats all others, I highly recommend going to Disneyland at Christmastime with someone you love, and enjoying as much of it as is humanly possible. This was one of the greatest things I have ever experienced. Mind you, I am an incurable romantic (or was back then), so the entire day was a wonderfully natural high. Even though we had just found out that our record company was going broke and our beloved manager Andrew was losing the plot, it somehow didn't matter. I was enjoying the company of a beautiful woman who seemed to have only one mission in life, which was to cater to my every whim. I suppose this was the closest I had got to feeling what it was like to love a woman without getting carried away, as I was fully aware that this was purely a temporary arrangement. I was certainly guilty of making lots of hay while I was in California, where the sun shines all the time, and all that haymaking was exhausting me, plus I was smoking an awful lot of post-haymaking cigarettes.

Of all the Disneyland rides that touched my sentimental side, it was the "It's a Small World" ride that most did so. This is a ride you go through in floating logs dug out to resemble canoes, and at each turn you are confronted with little people from all over the world: Dutch children dressed in traditional clothes, and so on. At the grand old age of 17, all I could think of was Mum and Dad and how soon it would be before I would get to see them and spend a great Christmas with them and my brother, who I also missed terribly.

Chapter 9

Town and Country

December 1969 to June 1970

In which Mum's the word in the Shirley family; the Pie is sold to the lowest bidder, and we're damned happy about it; and I have a run-in with Old Bill and a walkout with Young Syd.

As we were on our way home, I decided to wear my glad rags, which consisted of the various things I had bought on this first tour. I looked like a complete Wally, but, of course, back then I thought I was the bee's knees. My outfit included a floor-length white corduroy overcoat and a maroon fedora that was a cross between a cowboy hat and a Forties hoodlum hat. Add to that platform shoes and velvet bellbottoms, and you can see why I now think I looked like a complete prat. I had also bought a lovely little Gibson acoustic. So, as I walked out of customs at Heathrow, I was fully expecting Dad and Angus to take the piss, what with my clothes and the guitar under my arm. But they didn't; in fact, they were uncharacteristically subdued.

After they gave me the usual welcome-home greetings, I asked if they had brought the Daimler and how it looked now it was white. They both said it looked great, but not with the same enthusiasm they would normally have, and I would soon find out why. After I had inspected the car and given it my thumbs-up, we got in, and off we went to pick up Mum.

Once we were out of the airport, I asked Dad how Mum was, and he pulled the car over and parked in the first spot he could find, which happened to be in the car park of a pub. He turned to me and, not being a man to mince words, said, "Your mother has cancer. They have operated on her and got most of it, but the doctors have told me that she has nine months to a year to live. Now, you can react any way you wish. You can get mad as hell, you can scream and shout, you can punch the car, or you can punch me if you wish, although I don't recommend that particular option. Or you can join your brother and me in making the last bit of time that your mother has with us as enjoyable and comfortable as is humanly possible."

I simply couldn't believe what I had just heard. I didn't know what to say. Of course I would do everything I could to help. I didn't even have enough time to have a good cry about it, as we were picking Mum up in about 20 minutes. Dad's reason for not beating around the bush was to emphasize just how important it was to put ourselves to one side and focus on making Mum as happy as we possibly could. The first thing I remember saying—which left me with a guilty conscience for the rest of my life, until very recently anyway—was, "Is it hereditary?" At which point my poor father said, "No, it's not," and went on to explain that Mum didn't know that she had cancer, and it was our job to make sure it stayed that way. Back then, for some reason, they didn't tell the patient if it was cancer.

We picked Mum up at the Royal Masonic Hospital and headed for home. She looked fine, and it was lovely to see her—and of course she was thrilled to welcome her travelling musician son home, as she hadn't seen me in nearly two months. In a way, it was a blessing for me to have so many things to tell her—and the whole family, come to that—simply because it acted as a diversion from dwelling on her ill health and her stay in hospital. Mum had been told that she had a twisted colon that had to be surgically fixed, and as far as she and the whole family were concerned, that was the end of that. It was a very strange façade for the three of us to have to keep up, but when you've gotta do what you've gotta do, you've gotta do it and be done with it.

With Mum home safe and sound, we set about having the best Christmas ever. It wasn't easy, but I am proud to say we did a damn good job. Looking back, I think we managed to keep up the charade as part of our denial, as the surgeon had said that in rare cases miracles do happen, or words to that effect. Dad, Angus, and I latched on to that, and I, for one, started to pray every night for my dearly beloved mother to be spared—as God had answered my nightly prayers once before, why not ask for his intervention again? Sure enough, Mum seemed to get better and behave just as she had before the operation; she even went back to work. The three of us were ecstatic, and soon thereafter, life was back to normal.

The only problems that I still had to face were all to do with keeping the band I loved so much together, as our life support system, Immediate Records, had gone bust. We no longer had a weekly wage to rely on, which meant we had to go out and earn a living the only way we knew, which was to book a bunch of gigs. Fortunately, our agent at the time was very good, and we weren't exactly a hard act to book. So, before too long, we were able to keep the wolves from the door, and we started to get better and better. The acoustic piece was removed from the show, and we began to get better still.

I clearly remember the first gig at which Steve finally came back out of his shell. It was at the old Country Club on Haverstock Hill in London. We had to do two sets; the first marked the very last time we did the unplugged bit and was followed by some electric material, with Steve still taking the back seat. During the break, Peter, Greg, and I all pleaded with Steve to let go and give this seemingly nonchalant crowd a wakeup call they were unlikely to forget—show them the old Steve we all knew and loved. So, with a little reshuffling of songs, we went on for the second show and just let rip. The response we got was outstanding. Steve got that crowd in the palm of his hand and did not let 'em go.

We started to put together a stronger set, which kept evolving and improving all the time. The more clubs we played, the more we shone. We started to see attendance increase and our audiences show much, much more appreciation. We were doing it the old-fashioned way by playing out a lot and building a reputation, which is most gratifying because it's yours and nobody else's; no one can take credit for it but you.

As we were now without a record label and in dire need of some cash, we started to shop around for a deal. Our first port of call was A&M Records, as Andrew had suggested. We got in touch with the London head of A&M, a lovely man called Larry Yaskiel. He was indeed interested in signing us. Quite frankly, if he hadn't been as enthused as he was, we would probably have folded, but because at least one major label was showing interest and talking in telephone numbers as far as the money side of things went, it gave us the impetus to continue.

So the first thing to do was for Steve to meet Larry to see the extent of the latter's interest. While he was there, we all prayed he would come back with some good news. As soon as he returned, he called each of us to say that A&M's initial offer was not $250,000, it was actually $300,000—and since there were no middlemen involved, the dosh would be all ours. We could not believe our good fortune.

We were also looking for a manager at the same time because we knew full well we would ultimately need one. Peter had got to know Chas Chandler quite well and told us of Chas's interest in managing us. Chas had been the bassist with the Animals, and had gone on to manage Jimi Hendrix when the Animals disbanded. We decided to give it a go without signing anything with Chas. At that juncture, he did something that would benefit us enormously. He was an old friend of Ahmet Ertegun, the boss of Atlantic records, who himself was an amazing musician, writer, and arranger. Ahmet and his label were the ones that would be on the top of our wish list, if for no other reason than that he was responsible for bringing Ray Charles to the attention of the public at large, producing and sometimes writing some of Ray's early hits. Atlantic Records were *the coolest* of all record companies.

As Ahmet was in London for a few days, Chas engineered a meeting for us with him, or rather an audition that was not like a normal audition. All Ahmet had to do was to meet us at our rehearsal place, the 100 Club on Oxford Street. With this all nicely in place, Chas let Larry Yaskiel know we were rehearsing at the club, and invited him to meet us there and hear how we were doing. Unfortunately, though, he neglected to inform Larry that Ahmet would also be there. This was a great example of a Dutch auction in reverse, playing one side off the other for the highest price.

It started with Ahmet offering $325,000 and 14%, the same percentage that A&M had offered. A&M responded by upping it a further $25,000, and so it went on until it reached an offer of $400,000 from A&M. But that was not the last of it; in fact, Ahmet made a further offer of $425,000. The difference was that with the A&M deal, we got the money in three yearly instalments which amounted to $133,333 upon signing and a subsequent annual payment of the same amount in each of the next two years, so that we had a nice automatic income from the advances of record royalties. That income amounted to a basic yearly wage of just over £14,000 for each of us, which was, back then, as Dave Gilmour pointed out, slightly more than the Prime Minister was getting. As Dave had just signed a deal that was worth about the same as mine, we had something in common, financially speaking. But that's where any similarity between our bank accounts ended, I'm sad to say.

After much back and forth, we decided to go for the A&M deal. Even though it was actually worth less money, in the long run it was worth much more, especially since we would have had to give Chas a piece of the Atlantic deal be-

cause he was instrumental in bringing it to the table. Plus, we would be one of the only rock bands on A&M, but not at Atlantic, who were awash with rock bands good, bad, and indifferent.

We were forever grateful to Ahmet for putting the wind up A&M and making

Promo video shoot in Germany.

them believe in signing us for such a large amount. He was no fool, though; he knew full well the potential of Humble Pie. As we finished the first song we were rehearsing that day, our version of Dr. John's "I Walk on Gilded Splinters," Ahmet was visibly astonished—and this was a man who had seen it all before. His quote was perfect and will give you some idea of how good we were becoming. He said, verbatim, "Wow, it's like having two Jimmy Pages in one band and a baby-making rhythm section that just don't quit! Outstanding!"

What happened that early spring afternoon in 1970, thanks to Ahmet and Larry, set us up for the unrelenting drive to succeed. The elements were falling into place, one by one. Looking back, I can't quite believe that we took care of our business as well as we did. That we did was due to one huge difference in our entire camp and the way it ran back then: Steve Marriott had his shit together, and, with a lot of help from his mates, especially Peter Frampton, he was on a mission. It took a lot of coercing from all of us to help him get the bit back between his teeth, but, little by little, he soon had the fire in his belly again, and I have to say it was a joyous thing to behold.

In his own way, and for a different set of reasons, Peter was also struggling to find his natural place in the band as a performer. Once he started to do this, it was wonderful to witness his ability to bounce off Steve and draw the very best out of him as a guitar player, so that pretty soon we did indeed have our "two Jimmy Pages in one band," and, in Steve, we also had the original lead singer who Robert Plant had fashioned himself after. Led Zeppelin's big hit "Whole Lotta Love" was taken from "You Need Love," an old song written by Willie Dixon for Muddy Waters. The Small Faces had done it (as "You Need Loving") on their first album and had credited the songwriting to Lane/Marriott, which was an error that was later fixed. Robert took Steve's approach to the song—I don't think Robert would mind me saying that, as he was a self-confessed huge fan of Steve's—and turned it into one of the biggest airplay hits of the Seventies and a classic-rock radio staple. I recently saw Robert, and as we discussed how he used Steve's interpretation, he said, "Yeah, while that is true, it was us [Zeppelin] who Willie Dixon's lawyer came looking for when it was time to pay the piper."

We had a minor crisis with Chas as our manager. Steve spotted something about his motives that he didn't like: Chas had pushed for us to take the Atlantic deal because he had nothing to do with getting the A&M deal, and he therefore wouldn't be entitled to any percentage from it. If we had gone along with his advice and taken the Atlantic deal, it may well not have been in our best interests, but it would have been in his. So Steve felt we needed to see what Chas would do if he were faced with having to decide which company we should sign with. When we next met with him, Steve called his bluff and told him we definitely wanted to go with A&M, and Chas did exactly what Steve predicted he would do. First, he tried to make us change our minds. When that didn't work, he suggested that he was entitled to a percentage of the A&M deal, at which point our relationship with Chas Chandler was officially at an end.

We now had to find a manager, but not just any manager. We needed a high-powered American who knew how to break an act in the States because that was both our goal and A&M's. After all, the company had just spent close to half a million dollars signing us, and I don't think Herb Alpert and Jerry Moss saw themselves recouping their investment if we continued to play Cleethorpes and Redcar, with stop-offs at Dunstable and Aberystwyth.

Greg had recommended that we hire his old chum Danny Farnham—who had been Spooky Tooth's tour manager when they went to the States—as our tour manager. Once Danny was on board, he suggested that we contact Dee Anthony, the American manager who Chris Blackwell used—for what was commonly called "service management"—when one of Chris's acts went over to America.

In the meantime, however, we had some very important business to attend to: we had our first A&M album to make, and we had some serious spending to do. I don't know exactly how much our first paycheck would amount to in today's money, but it would be worth at least 10 times what it was then. (The farmhouse I bought back then for £14,000 was recently on the market for just over a million, but that incredible rise can be accounted for by not only general inflation, but also inflation in real estate prices.) So, even by a conservative guesstimate, our first big payday in today's money would be somewhere around £250,000, which, no matter how you chop it up was a huge amount for an 18-year-old to have and be able to spend anyway he chose. *Ker-fuckin'-ching!*

Larry Yaskiel was thrilled that we chose A&M over Atlantic and immediately went to work, securing Glyn Johns as our engineer/co-producer and booking a whole month of studio time at Olympic. We had been writing as a group down at dear old Magdalen Laver Village Hall, plus we had all been writing individually, so there was no shortage of good material. We had even tried out a lot of the songs live to see what an audience would make of them, which led to some songs being chosen for definite inclusion and some given a definite

elbow. The beauty of this record deal was that, because
studio time was still relatively
cheap, A&M paid for the studio on top of our advance, so
that all of the money came
to us, plus, as we had gotten
the deal ourselves without a
manager, we didn't have to
part with any percentages,
which on $400,000 at as
much as 20% was an enor-
mous savings of $80,000.

Outside the Guildford gig on the day we signed the big A&M deal.

This period in the band's history was probably the happiest for many reasons, but mostly because of Steve's frame of mind. Simply put, he was deeply in love with his beautiful wife, Jenny; he had almost singlehandedly negotiated one of the biggest record deals ever done; and he had done it without the help of a very expensive manager—although it has to be said that his partner Peter Frampton did help him a lot with that. This truly was Steve's golden moment, and, to make it all the more special, he was the nicest man you'd ever care to meet. He had become very compassionate, understanding, and just plain content for the first time in his life.

His old bandmates had replaced him with Rod Stewart and Ronnie Wood, and they were themselves starting to make an impression, but, sadly, they had chosen for some reason to take potshots at Steve in the press. I thought that was uncalled for, as Steve had never said a bad word about them. What made matters even worse was that the person who was taking the most cheap shots at Steve was the very one he had suggested as his replacement, Ronnie Wood. Ronnie had no reason to badmouth Steve, for the Faces were doing well and were on the verge of signing a great deal with Warner Brothers. In reality, Steve had done them a huge favour, as they went on to become one of the biggest bands of that era. Oh well, rock 'n' roll does strange things to otherwise perfectly rational people.

This period was also the best in my relationship with Steve. He and I were incredibly close; he and Jenny more like my older brother and sister than mere bandmate and his wife. I was living in two places: a flat in Chelsea that I shared with Willie Wilson, the drummer with Sutherland Brothers and Quiver, and his girlfriend Monica, and at home, spending time with

117

Mum and Dad and catching up on things with Angus. We were greatly encouraged by the way Mum was recovering; the doctors were even telling Dad that her cancer was, for the time being, in remission, and, you never know, miracles do happen. The head oncologist, who was overseeing Mum's case, actually said he would never be happier to be proved wrong in his prognosis than now.

There was a lot of music press coverage about our record-breaking deal, so much so that I had people coming up to me in public and congratulating me on it. The one I remember most was Mick Ralphs, who was still with Mott the Hoople at the time. He was so sweet about it; he said it was about time the bands—not the managers only—started to directly benefit and that Steve and Peter deserved everything they got, as they were so underrated it wasn't fair. What a gentleman.

There were two things at the top of my shopping list that were mainly driven by advice I got from Mum and Dad. The first was a house (Mum's suggestion); the second was a car (Dad's suggestion), preferably a Rolls-Royce (my suggestion).

Dad was a dab hand at spotting good bargains in the house market, as he had bought, fixed up, and sold houses on so many occasions that it was second nature to him. The first house that came to our attention was in Lower Nazeing, which is situated between Broxbourne and Harlow in Essex. It was a mock Tudor with five acres of land and a host of outbuildings. The house was set a long way back off the road and had a classic in-and-out semicircular driveway, with a huge privet hedge all along the front of the property so that it could not be seen from the road.

I had loved this house ever since I was a little boy. It represented wealth to me, and here I was, barely 18 years old, and I had the means to buy this incredible place. However, there was a problem. Through his connections with the local councillors, the old man had found out that within five years of me buying the place, it would have a compulsory purchase slapped on it, so that four of the five acres would be built on with brand new houses that would be breathing down my neck. I was heartbroken, but not for long. Dad found an old Tudor farmhouse on three acres, with lots of outbuildings, plus a cottage and a huge Essex barn with a pond—all for only £14,000.

We went to see it and immediately fell in love. There was a magical feel about the place, and it was everything I wanted. It was, however, completely derelict and uninhabitable as it stood. It needed an entire rebuild. Getting a crew of guys together to do the rebuild was not a problem. The problem was that, back then, the rules that governed whether or not you got a mortgage were heavily stacked against us, as I was under 21. The fact that it was derelict meant that if they did give me a mortgage, they would not actually give me the money until *all* the necessary work had been done. I also would have to put up a deposit of at least 40%, and even then there was no guarantee that they would give me a mortgage.

My first attempt at getting the mortgage failed miserably—so did the second and the third, and the fourth was just as hopeless. By the time I got to the fifth attempt, I was told the cold hard truth: that this property was unmortgageable. I had already put a healthy cash deposit of £4,000 on it, but could not for the life of me get a mortgage, which meant I was perilously close to losing not only the farmhouse but the £4,000 as well. As always, it was Major Robert to the rescue. He simply said, "Call the farmer, and ask him for a private mortgage," because, if I was having that much trouble getting finance, so would other people.

The old man was spot on when he realised that the farmer would jump at the chance to get this house sold and off his back. So, I called the farmer and did the deal over the phone. He gave me a £10,000 loan over 10 years at 10%, which everybody at the time said was a bit fierce, but it soon turned out to be one of the best deals I have ever done.

The magnificent Green Farm in 1970 and 1995. It was recently on the market for just over £1 million.

The family mood was generally good, but, for obvious reasons, we were living on a knife edge, as Mum would only have to sneeze and her husband and sons would be thrown into a state of sheer panic on the inside, but have to hide it for Mum's sake.

By now, I was spending most of my time living in a flat on Redcliffe Gardens in Chelsea, only a 15-minute drive from Olympic in Barnes, where we were recording our first A&M album. Dave Gilmour lived literally around the corner on Old Brompton Road. Unfortunately for us, both flats had become Party Central; at almost any time, day or night, one of or both would be full of visitors, mostly freeloaders, with a sprinkling of people we actually knew. After a while, this got old, and we started to come up with clandestine plans to get around it.

Most everything we tried failed, as this was 1970, and therefore smack dab in the middle of the hippie era. Getting tough with the freeloaders wasn't an option, and telling them to piss off was also bad form, so with all this love and peace flowing though the air, other methods had to be found. The best example of this that I can recall happened one midweek afternoon when Willie and I had well and truly had enough. We sneaked into the bedroom and called Dave to see how things were at his place. He told us that it was all clear, so we went into the living room and told the gathering masses that we'd just got a call from the studio and our presence was urgently required, so we would have to leave. As soon as we had got rid of them, we shot round to Dave's flat, thrilled that we had outwitted the madding crowd. When Dave opened the door, the wry smile on his face said it all. There were our freeloaders in all their glory, having beaten us to it, settled in nicely with the kettle on, as if nothing had happened.

It was around this time that Dave, like me, decided to look for a house out in the Essex countryside, at which point an amazing twist of fate put him in touch with an estate agent who happened to have a house on his books that I had passed on. Dave decided to buy it, despite the fact that I had turned it down on the grounds of a compulsory purchase order that was going to be attached to some of the land. Screw the chance of this possibly happening later on; he just wanted out of London *now*. So it was that, by the end of the year, we had a small community of close friends, all musicians, living within a stone's throw of each other. That would mark the start of one of the best periods of my life, but for now it was still nine harrowing months away.

In the meantime, we had our first A&M album to record. The band started that with an extremely positive attitude; after all, what's not to like? We had just got rich overnight; we were being recorded by Glyn Johns, the best engineer/producer in the world; and we had plenty of great material that was mostly band-written, much of which we had played live at some of our gigs, which, by the way, kept getting better and better.

Fortunately, A&M had not signed us as a singles band by any means. They had a policy back then of signing a band and working with them to build their career over the span of the first five albums. The first two or three were the building blocks for the next two, which would be the big sellers that you could then, everyone hoped, continue to produce for as long as you were able. Sadly, this approach is long gone in the music industry; if you don't have a huge hit the first time out, they don't stay with you, although nowadays they are much better equipped to make sure your first effort succeeds. But it has to be said that, back then, there seemed to be a lot more of the human touch involved in building a band's career.

Touring was, and still is, a huge part of making your records successful. So from the record company's standpoint, it was imperative that the act had strong management who knew how to make the band's roadwork pay off. In our case, Danny's suggestion of approaching Dee Anthony to do the job was perfect. Dee was the best in the business, and he brought with him a truly great agent in Frank Barsalona. When they flew from the States to meet us, we happened to be playing the Marquee, so they could see us perform as well. As soon as they

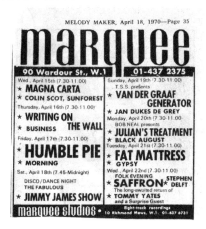

Ad for the Marquee show at which Dee Anthony scouted the band.

saw us live, they knew we had what it took to break America—but they also knew we had some work to do. That was fine by us, as we were getting more and more determined to crack the States wide open. We were ready, willing, and able to take direction on what to do and how to improve. The more we got to know about Dee and Frank, the more we were prepared to trust their judgement and have them show us how to better ourselves onstage. They were so good at what they did that it was easy to follow their direction, plus they made it all so much fun. They were two of the funniest guys we'd ever met and were so sure of themselves. With Dee and Frank, it wasn't *if* you were going to make it, it was *when*.

Recording was moving along beautifully. Glyn was doing an enormous job, and we were playing out of our skins. Everything was so perfect, I should have known something was up.

Steve and I were on our way to his house one morning after an all-night session at Olympic. I was driving Steve's Alvis, which was a lovely old car but a major attention grabber, as it was gold in colour and had chromed wire wheels. The weather was beautiful, and Steve had just lit a large joint of some of the strongest hash we had seen for a while. As we pulled up to a set of lights, I noticed a car in the rear-view mirror, with two very suspicious-looking chaps getting out of it and heading in our direction. They were two plainclothes policemen. "Old Bill," is all I said to Steve, at which point he put the joint out and stashed it under the floor mat. It was a daft thing to do, I know, but he didn't have many options, bless his heart. He also had a large lump of hash in his pocket, which he immediately shoved into his mouth and started to eat.

As soon as the plainclothes got to either side of the car, the lad on Steve's side opened his door and went straight to the joint under the floor mat. He'd obviously seen what Steve had done, plus, when he opened the door, it must have stunk of hash. Holding up the joint in front of us, he literally said, "'Ello, 'ello, what's all this, then?"

From that point on, it was a comedy of errors to beat all others. There we were, facing the distinct possibility of never going to the USA again and losing everything we had worked so hard for—and all we could do was try to fight back a serious case of the giggles. The main cop asked Steve, "Is this your car, sir?" to which I replied, "Yes, it's his car." Again to Steve: "How come you're not driving?" I replied, "He doesn't have a licence." Then the cop said to me, "What's the matter, can't he speak?" to which I responded, "That's right, lost his voice. He's been singing all night."

At this juncture, I didn't dare look at Steve for fear of setting him off, but he did nod his head in agreement, grateful, I'm sure, that I'd given him some kinda cover while he was busy trying to chew and swallow a piece of hash the size of a Milky Way bar.

The main cop got in the car with me while the other one put Steve in the police car, which I was told to follow to the local cop shop. As we started to drive off, the one with me said, "So it's his car, yeah?" "Yes, sir." "But he doesn't have a licence?" "Nah." "So you drive him?" "Yeah." "You have a licence, don't ya?" "Of course I have a licence. I wouldn't be driving if I didn't have a licence, now would I?"

At the cop shop, they kept us in separate rooms while they interviewed us. When they were done with us, I saw Steve, who looked so high I'm surprised they got any sense out of him at all. After charging us with possession of a roach and making us fill out a lot of paperwork, they let us go, giving me the keys to the car and telling me to drive carefully and make sure I didn't let Steve drive. At no time did they so much as ask to see my licence or check the records to see if I had a full licence or even a provisional one.

The only time I got to talk to Steve while we were in the police station was when they let us both go to the loo at the same time. I told him that when they ask him about his earnings, he should play it down; otherwise they will fine us more than they ought to. But when it came time to go to court, the headline read "ROCK STARS CHARGED WITH CANNABIS POSSESSION."

The story went on to say: "Drummer Jerry Shirley, 18, said that he lives at home with his parents, earns £60 a week, and pays his mum £20, whereas Steve Marriott, 23, said he earns £300 a week and gives his mum nothing." With that vital piece of information in hand, the judge fined us £300 instead of £30. But, to be fair, I couldn't exactly expect Steve Marriott, husband of top model Jenny, to say he was living at home with his mum and giving her £20 pounds a week, now could I? Plus, the court reporter's sense of humour was priceless: "earns £300 a week and gives his mum nothing" indeed. I don't think Steve felt he had to pay his mum anything, considering he had just bought the house she and his dad were to live in for the rest of their lives, bless 'em. His mum, Kay, still lives there to this day.

We had no idea how lucky we were at the time to have picked Dee and Frank as our representatives, for the simple reason that we never heard another word about the bust as far as it affecting our ability to acquire work visas for America. It was as if it just went away. God bless 'em for that; otherwise, some of the greatest performances in America by one of rock 'n' roll's true giants (Steve, all 5' 4" of him) would never have happened—all because of a roach.

Professionally speaking, things couldn't have been going any better. I kept getting asked to play on some of the most incredible sessions that any musician would be proud and honoured to do. In one nine-month period from the summer of 1970 to the late spring of 1971, I performed on Syd Barrett's two solo albums, *The Madcap Laughs* and *Barrett*; John Entwistle's first solo album, *Smash Your Head Against the Wall*; B.B. King's *Live in London*; the first two Humble Pie albums for A&M; plus three tours of the USA, including the one on which we recorded *Performance: Rockin' the Fillmore*. As if that lot wasn't enough to be getting on with, I did a number of BBC live radio sessions for Syd with Dave Gilmour on bass, plus the only live performance ever put on tape by Syd, again with Dave on bass, live from Olympia in Earls Court. Syd barely survived the first three songs of that show, and then proceeded to walk off, without any warning, during the fourth song, with a big grin on his face. David and I were stranded there with nothing but our instruments, so we walked off after him. The madcap laughs indeed.

I had become quite a good friend to Syd, bless his heart, when I was living in Redcliffe Gardens in 1970. He would often come around to the

At the B.B. King sessions, with no bass-drum spurs. We were in such a hurry to get to the session that we forgot to pack the case that had the spurs in it, so we used big theatre weights that we crammed on either side of the drum.

flat and ask me and Willie if we wanted to go to the Speakeasy. The only thing was, this being Syd, it would be eight in the morning when he arrived, all dressed up and ready to go clubbing. So Willie and I would let him in and explain that, as it was 8:00 A.M., he was welcome to hang out until 11:00 that night, when it would be a more appropriate time to go to the club.

We would spend all day hanging out, listening to records, smoking hash, drinking tea, and generally having a very normal time until it was time to go to the Speakeasy. On the way to the club, Syd would act perfectly normal and would be quite talkative. When we got there, however, and I paid the entrance fee (Syd never had any money on him), we would walk in and that would be it—he would clam up and just stare into the middle distance and become completely uncommunicative. It was extremely sad for me because, as a very young chap, I didn't understand the whys and wherefores of psychological problems; I just felt bad for Syd that going to a club would affect him like that. I even felt guilty for being the one who took him there, even though he had asked to go—albeit at eight in the morning.

The sessions for Syd were remarkable. They were extremely harrowing at the time, but I am forever grateful that I did them. After all, it was a once-in-a-lifetime thing to do that was, as we now know, never to be repeated. It is often written that I played drums on both *The Madcap Laughs* and *Barrett*, but that is not true. My good old chum Willie Wilson played the drums on *Madcap* for the most part, and Robert Wyatt also played on that record, while I only played a little bass on one track and some percussion, I think. My contribution on drums was solely for the *Barrett* album.

I would often act as Syd's ride when it was time to go to work on *Barrett* at Abbey Road. The sessions were surprisingly ordered affairs, thanks to Dave Gilmour, who was very much in charge. They consisted of two types. For some songs, everybody played live together: Syd on guitar, Dave on bass, Rick Wright on keyboards, and yours truly on drums. My favourite track in this format that got on the record was "Gigolo Aunt." It was a shuffle, so I was in my element, and it didn't take long to get on tape. I still enjoy listening to it to this day.

The other type, and this is where it got harrowing, was when we had to overdub the drums. ("Baby Lemonade" is a perfect example of that type of track.) After recording Syd playing guitar and singing, Dave would sit and figure out all the weird foibles of time structure that Syd's naturally off-the-wall way of playing would produce. Once he had done that, he would memorize all these little goofy bits and then stand in front of me, conducting me through the weirdness while I played along. In doing so, Dave made it go a whole lot faster than if I were to try and anticipate all these strange timing changes, which would have been near to impossible. Dave's patience with Syd was commendable, as was all of ours, really. All we wanted to do was help our friend make the best record he possibly could, given the circumstances, and, looking back, I think we achieved that.

I got a call from Peter one evening while I was at Greg's flat, telling me he needed a percussionist to play on George Harrison's triple debut solo album, *All Things Must Pass*. I said, "I'm sorry, Pete, I don't know one," to which Pete replied, "I mean you, yer fool!"

It was not my nature to pursue these opportunities. One of my biggest downfalls has always been my inability to pursue leads or to self-promote in any way; I'm terrible at it. I always looked upon it as an incredible honour when these things came my way, and always assumed it was because some other bugger had got sick or was otherwise unable to attend, and I got a lucky break as a result. It never occurred to me that my own talent had anything to do with it. Still doesn't, to tell the truth.

The George Harrison session was a sight to behold: more famous faces than you could shake a stick at. Phil Spector was producing, although I seem to remember him being told what to do by George more than the other way round. In particular, I remember George telling Spector to get on with it 'cos Ritchie (Ringo) had to be home for his tea. I thought that was precious, especially when you consider that this was in front of a room containing a who's who of Sixties superstars, including Eric Clapton, Billy Preston, all of Badfinger, Klaus Voormann, Ringo Starr, Peter Frampton, Carl Radle, Jim Gordon, Gary Wright, George Harrison, and… me. Go figure. We did two songs: "Ballad of Sir Frankie Crisp (Let It Roll)" and Dylan's "If Not for You." My contribution was a tambourine part in the middle eight of each song. You can clearly hear it, I'm proud to say, but you wouldn't know I played it, as I'm afraid I didn't make the list of credits.

Humble Pie's first A&M album had some very strong band performances on it. The opening track, "Live With Me," is nearly eight minutes of Goosebumps City, a tremendous performance by four excellent musicians highly tuned in to each other's playing, recorded by the best engineer/producer in the business. It was a truly stunning piece.

It felt pretty damn good to all of us. But with Glyn, we knew we'd done a good one when without us asking him, "How was that?" he would simply say, in a very calm voice, "Come in and listen." With that, we would come in, and Glyn would make sure we were each seated in our favourite position. For Greg and me, this meant the man-sized playback seats: the long couch in front of the control desk, directly below the four huge Tannoy monitor speakers. I am now deaf as a post from years of sitting in those seats, but Greg and I loved every minute of it.

Glyn would then dim the lights and, with a conspiratorial smile, hit the play button with the volume *up*. Those were the best moments for the band in general, but they were particularly special for the rhythm section because we knew that if we got it in that first take, especially if Glyn gave it his immediate thumbs-up, we had just done something pretty damn special. Plus, if, like me, you came from the generation of drummers who were seriously focused on putting your all into that first take and you pulled it off more times than not, you were doing the whole recording process a huge favour by saving enormous amounts of time and, therefore, money.

The highest compliment I have ever been paid in the 50 years that I have been playing drums was when Glyn Johns would look at me during one of these "Come in and listen" playbacks and give me one of his Cheshire cat "Well done, young man" grins. As I retell the story, I can see him doing it now, and it's giving me the same sense of achievement. So, if anybody might wonder what I got out of it all, considering that we weren't smart enough to get rich off it, Glyn's approval is one of the absolute highlights.

Chapter 10

"Woik, Woik, Woik!"

May to December 1970

In which our new label has Great Expectations;
we tour with Grand Funk; someone gets a bollocking from
Keith Moon; and we attend a Scandinavian-Lebanese
summit meeting high in the friendly skies.

A&M put some pretty big expectations upon us on the release of our first album for the label, called simply *Humble Pie*. When you, as a company, have just stumped up $400,000 ($4 million or more in today's money) on the signing of a band, you have every right to expect a lot. As I mentioned earlier, it speaks volumes about the men who were running the record companies at the time that they were prepared to stick with you through the first two or three albums before they got big returns. That was a real blessing for us because our first effort did not set the world on fire by any means. It got some decent reviews, but very little airplay and alarmingly small sales.

We were, however, starting to produce some stunning results onstage. From the moment Dee Anthony and Frank Barsalona came to England, saw us at the Marquee, and signed us, we were a changed band. Dee and Frank's ability to instil self-confidence in a band and steer you in the right direction onstage was second to none. They were old-school guys who went all the way back to almost vaudevillian stage sensibilities. Between them, they'd had a hand in the development of everybody from Tony Bennett to the Who. If they coached you on how to improve your stage show, you listened—and you saw almost immediate results. Their philosophy about success was simplicity itself: "Here's what we're gonna do, guys—we're gonna [in a

Manager Dee Anthony.

New York accent] woik, woik, woik! Then, when we're done woiking, we're gonna woik some more!"

They would fine-tune your show song by song—"Move this song here, that song there"—and tell you when to bring the show down with a slow blues and when to pick it up again with a steamin' shuffle. They were particularly good helping the frontmen. After all, when your experience goes all the way back to working with legends like Bennett and Sinatra, you know what you're talking about. So when they would try to fire you up by telling stories, in a matter-of-fact way, about the likes of Sinatra or even Sophie Tucker—who they had either worked with directly or been very close to someone who had—you would sit up and pay attention.

They were incredible together, and truly great men as individuals. Dee was a pure genius at getting the best out of some very talented people. He was also one of the funniest men I've ever met, and told some priceless stories. Dee was very clever at relating a certain story about, say, Bobby Darin to Steve or Peter that he knew would hit a nerve and therefore bring the best out of them.

He also promoted the idea that he was the "head coach" of the whole shooting match. As most musicians tend to respond well to the sports analogy, being treated like a team that has to go out and win every night brought us tremendous results. Dee even bought a referee's whistle that he would blow from the side of the stage to add the necessary impetus to the evening's proceedings.

We started our onslaught of roadwork in support of the first A&M album with a bunch of dates in and around England and Europe, which got us warmed up and ready for our first tour of the States for Dee and Frank. We kicked off that leg of the tour in Detroit in mid-September, then played multi-night engagements in Boston, Philadelphia, and Boston again before moving on to Chicago for a show that Grand Funk Railroad was headlining on October 16.

At this time, the biggest band in the States was not Led Zeppelin, although they were becoming huge: it was Grand Funk. They were the most unsung success story of the early Seventies. Their popularity was extraordinary in that it defied all logic. They got *no* airplay, and any reviews they might have got would be bad on principal, as the rock 'n' roll writers of the time seemed to be of the combined opinion that they were useless, which couldn't have been further from the truth. They did suffer some at the hands of Terry Knight, the megalomaniac manager who insisted on doing everything for them, including mixing the sound at their concerts, which was definitely not his forte. His real strength was doing everything else a great manager of that time needed to do to make his band successful, and he certainly accomplished that.

It was astonishing to witness, first hand, what Grand Funk achieved at the beginning of the Seventies. More than any other band, they were responsible for putting rock firmly into the stadiums. What the Beatles started in 1965 at Shea Stadium, Grand Funk continued by taking on Shea, the Grand Dame of stadiums, and other behemoths like it, and selling them out in minutes. They famously sold out Shea in the summer of 1971 without *any* publicity. The only ad they put out was published in, I believe, the *New York Times*—*after* the tickets were gone, a full-page ad for the show proclaimed "SOLD OUT"! (We opened for them at that historic show; more on that later.)

One of the many benefits of Dee's management was his enormous number of connections, one of whom was Terry Knight. I can't remember exactly why Terry was more than happy to do Dee lots of favours to help Humble Pie, but he was. I'm sure Frank had an awful lot to do with it, as he was known—at that time and for a long time after—as "the most powerful man in rock 'n' roll."

As our American tour commenced that fall, Dee was very excited by the news that Knight had agreed to let us open for Grand Funk at several shows, including one in Chicago, at the heart of their Midwest stronghold. They were huge everywhere, but they were *enormous* in the Midwest. The only thing that caused us some concern was that not a single band that had ever opened for Grand Funk had survived without being booed off the stage.

So it was with some trepidation that we took this challenge on. The first show with Grand Funk was at the Chicago Coliseum, which I remember holding about 12,000 people. The show was, to say the least, harrowing. It was sold out; in fact, it was oversold, packed to the rafters. Strangely, we were not that affected by the distinct possibility that we might be booed off. I can't remember why, but we just knew somehow, because of Dee's intense coaching, that we would be all right. After all, what was the worst that could happen: an early bath?

In those days, when Steve had got all his frontman confidence back, and Peter was right up there with him, this sort of situation was like a red flag to the bull. Those two took the baton and ran with it. Mind you, they did happen to have, by now, one of the most confident and uplifting rhythm sections in the business backing them up. Greg and I were like a locomotive on full speed ahead; there was no stopping us two, and Steve and Peter knew it.

We had started to open our shows with a blues shuffle that we called "Four Day Creep" (which was mistakenly credited to Ida Cox, as she'd done a tune with that title—I guess we made a few bucks for Ida's family, so no harm done there). It was the perfect opener for us. It had some really tight, punchy bits in the intro that grabbed you right away, and it rocked your socks off. The best thing about it was that it let you settle into a nice groove immediately. A good blues shuffle will do that every time, so long as it's well executed, and this was. On this occasion, we were almost thrown off course by the crowd's reaction at the end of the song. There was a split-second pause… then the audience went *nuts*. They were with us from that moment on, right to the end of our show. Plus, we got not one, but two encores. We didn't think it was kosher for us to assume our right to go on for the second one, when Terry Knight did something that oozed class: he stood on the side of the stage, insisting to Dee that we go back on for number two.

This was uncharted territory; before us, not only had no band ever got an encore when opening for Grand Funk, none had even managed to finish their show. Once we had done this, a wonderful piece of old-fashioned good luck fell into our lap. A foreign correspondent for *Melody Maker*, who happened to be there to review Grand Funk, witnessed our little bunch of Brits going down a storm and gave us the review of a lifetime. The headline read "Humble Pie blow Grand Funk off stage." Thank God the review came out in the UK, not locally in Chicago, because I'm not sure how much further Terry Knight's benevolence would have stretched had this headline been shoved under his nose the next morning!

Word of what had happened spread like wildfire, and before too long we were getting a response equal to, or better than, the response the headliners got, wherever we played. In time, this started to backfire on us as our reputation began to precede us. Bands were getting gun-shy of Humble Pie and didn't want us to open for them. Fortunately, this is where Frank's strength came into play. He was vehemently opposed to that sort of headliner insecurity or paranoia; he just wouldn't allow it. And, as he had most of the headline acts on his books or at least wishing to remain on his good side, they couldn't do a lot about it, other than to suck it up and behave like mature headliners should. After all, Frank argued, *they* were all in our position when they were on the way up, so what would have happened to them if he had folded back when others were trying to not have *them* on the bill?

On September 23 and 24, we played the Fillmore East in NYC. Since our last show there, we had moved up the bill by one spot: we now played after the opening act and before the headliners, Derek and the Dominos, Eric Clapton's new band.

We went on the first night to a standing ovation almost from the start. It was as if NYC had got advance warning of our newfound confidence and were ready, willing, and able to come along for the ride. It was such an incredible feeling conquering the NYC audiences; they stayed with us all the way to the end of our time together, and were as loyal and devoted as any audience could ever be. And there were many more like them. Up and down the Eastern Seaboard, all through the Midwest, and across to the West Coast, we were starting to get outstanding responses from every crowd we played to. It was a very special, precious, and magic time for all of us.

We still had a long, long way to go before the real glory days we all wished for were to arrive, but deep down we were starting to believe in our collective ability to crack it: to make the big time that was on show all around us. Everywhere we looked, there was another example of what was in store for us at the end of the rainbow, once we got to headline and take home the big bacon. Whether it was stories of Zeppelin's huge grosses and private jets, or the numbers of records Grand Funk were selling, it was there every day, like a hook being baited to pull us in. We were four very willing participants in this game, coveting the ultimate prizes that were there for us to go after. Still, the downsides were very clear to see and the hardships obvious, especially to the married guys: months away from home, tour after tour, constantly being reminded that getting the prizes required making huge sacrifices. It doesn't take too much of that before even the most dedicated hedonist wishes he were at home with his feet up, watching the football.

Around this time, John Entwistle (the Ox) asked me to play on his first solo album, *Smash Your Head Against the Wall*, and Dad encouraged me to do the sessions as a way of taking my mind off Mum's deteriorating health. The opportunity arose out of the Ox not wanting Keith Moon to do the sessions because of the mayhem that would have ensued were Keith involved. Not that the sessions were as peaceful as a prayer meeting; they were utter madness. But there was madness, and then there was Keith Moon lunacy—he wasn't called Moon the Loon for nothing. He was a sweetheart and at that time, I'm proud to say, a dear friend to me. I was still very young and

Smash your head against the wall.

John Entwistle.

in awe of Keith, but to his credit he treated me very well indeed. Keith made everybody who knew him feel like they were his best friend, and I was no exception.

We had come home for a longer break than we'd anticipated, and had left our equipment in the States, as it was cheaper to keep it there than to bring it home just to store it for a month. So I had to hire a kit from Drum City in the West End, which had a big attitude problem with all but the biggest-name drummers. As I was still on my way up, they weren't likely to pay a lot of attention to my needs, and when they delivered the kit on the first morning of the sessions, they didn't adhere to my one request: that I absolutely *had* to have a Ludwig Speed King bass drum pedal.

Keith happened to show up at the studio that morning, just to wish everybody, including little me, well. He immediately spotted the fact that I was distraught about Drum City's lack of attention to detail and, without being asked, went to the phone and called them to give them a serious bollocking. Keith was probably their best customer, considering how many drum kits he demolished and had to replace in a hurry when Drum City were the only supplier of Ludwig drums back in the Who's early days, when Keith was still using Ludwig. Within minutes, the Speed King pedal was delivered, and I was a very happy camper. Keith knew full well that Drum City employed a prejudiced policy towards the young up-and-coming drummers, and he hated it. It wasn't that long ago that he too was being treated poorly by them, so he couldn't be happier than to oblige with a bollocking they wouldn't soon forget.

The sessions, at Trident Studios just off Wardour Street, would start at 11:00 A.M. and go as late as 3:00 or 4:00 the next morning, with two or three pub breaks. Typically, we'd go at six in the evening to the Ship on Wardour Street, or a little later to the Chase, or to the Speakeasy at midnight to 1:00 A.M.—and still go back to the studio and record one more back track before going home. We also drank in the studio: the top of the grand piano served as our help-yourself bar, and was fully stocked at the start of each session with every kind of booze you can imagine.

John and his guys from the Who camp were what I would describe as professional drinkers. They knew how to pace themselves. On the other hand, even though I could keep up fairly well with most drinkers, I was a relative novice in this bunch. Plus, with very little sleep and a very sick mother to keep an eye on, it wasn't long before the cracks started to show in me. I ended up getting so drunk that I fell asleep one evening late in the session—*still playing.*

The guitar player on the album was Dave "Cyrano" Langston, a friend of ours who recommended me for the sessions, and who later worked for Humble Pie for a while. We were recording "Heaven and Hell," and were almost at the end. The next thing I remember, I woke up with a start, drumming away, but having missed Cy's signal for the ending. Because I blew the ending, the track was faded out instead.

Although we were keeping such a bizarre schedule, we were getting a huge amount of work done on what became one of John's best-selling solo albums. There were just the three of us—John, Cy, and me—doing the back tracks. The engineer was Roy Thomas Baker, who was just starting then, but later became a huge star producer for Queen, Foreigner, the Cars, and many others. We started on a Monday, worked all week, had the weekend off, came back the following Monday to work for one more day, and that was it: we had recorded an album's worth of back tracks and a couple of spares, including a credible version of Neil Young's "Cinnamon Girl," which didn't make the record but was released years later as a bonus track on the expanded CD.

During the sessions, three things happened that each had a profound effect on me.

I was driving myself most of the time, even though I still had only a provisional licence / learner's permit, but on these sessions I desperately needed a driver, as the schedule was intense. So I switched between two drivers: John Hammel, our new roadie, and Brian Scott, a friend of mine from Cambridge.

At the end of the third night of sessions, I went down to the Speakeasy with the rest of the crew, and was soon getting on famously with two girls who shared a flat in Clapham Common. Before you could say "crumpet," I somehow conned the keys to the Rolls-Royce from Scotty, who was driving me that night, and was on my way to Clapham with these two beauties.

Unfortunately, as I worked my way down Oxford Street, I kept nudging the cars in front of me whenever I came to a stoplight. After more than once being spotted doing this—and then, in front of a cop, doing a broadside skid around Marble Arch corner heading down Park Lane—I was surrounded by cop cars as I pulled *in* to the *outlet* of the petrol station halfway down Park Lane. The head cop came up to the car and knocked on the window. When I opened it, he said, "Would you kindly step out of the car, sir?" and opened the door for me—at which I proceeded to fall out of the car and ended up lying on my back at his feet. All I could think to say was, "It's a fair cop, sir!" which of course it was. It also cost me my licence.

The second event was a kindness that Steve and Jenny did for me. Mum had been moved into Harlow General Hospital. She had got very bad very quickly in the last couple of weeks, was heavily medicated, and often didn't recognise even her closest family, which was heartbreaking.

The doctors suggested that we try to get some people who she knew well but hadn't seen lately to pay her a visit; sometimes this gets the patient to rally a bit. I mentioned this to Steve and was amazed when he and Jenny agreed to go and visit her. Not many people have got the courage to visit someone in hospital who is that ill and may not even recognise them. But Steve and Jenny went, and a truly miraculous thing happened.

As soon as they walked into her room, she came around as if there were nothing wrong with her whatsoever. They stayed and chatted with her for almost an hour, joking and laughing, and Mum talked about how she couldn't wait to get out so she could visit them. Once they left the room, though, Mum went back to being the way she was right before they got there: completely out of it, not knowing who was who. None of us, including the doctors, could believe what we had just seen. I have never forgotten what Steve and Jenny did that day. It was so very, very kind of them to do that for me and my family.

The third thing happened on the Saturday of that week. I went over to Harlow General to visit Mum, and as I got there, I saw her sister, Aunt Ethel, running down the corridor from the direction of Mum's room, screaming and crying. Mum was dead. She had just drawn her last breath as I was coming into the hospital.

I don't remember a thing about the events of the rest of that day or the next, but writing it down now has made me remember exactly how I felt at that moment. The way my psyche was able to recall that emotion from all those years ago put a cold shiver up me.

I still miss Mum terribly. With a cut that deep, time does not heal—it just helps you learn how to cope without those you have lost, although I for one have never been able to learn quite how to do that. I was to remain a lost soul, just going through the motions, for a very long time to come.

In the short time I worked for John Entwistle, I can't honestly say I got close to him; he struck me as someone who was not easy for anybody to get close to. But when I went back to the sessions on the Monday to, if only for a short while, take my mind off the loss of the most important person in my life, he did something very sweet. He didn't mention my loss directly; he simply gave me my paycheck and said, "I thought this might come in handy, given the circumstances." When I looked at the cheque, I saw that he had paid me the same amount he was paying himself and Cy, which was twice the amount I was originally going to get. What a class act.

><

The next leg of the American tour was due to start at the end of the week. If I were to honour my professional commitments, I would miss my mother's funeral. My father insisted I should go on the tour and not in any way change my plans; he said Mum would want it that way. Angus agreed. As a young lad of only 18, I didn't know what was best, so I decided to go along with what Dad and Angus wanted me to do. I would regret this decision for the next 40 years, feeling so guilty it was often too painful to even think about.

So back we went on our never-ending journey across America. At least this leg included a stint in sunny Southern California, playing five nights at the Whisky a Go Go. This had several benefits attached to it. We were in familiar surroundings; we were being looked after by lots of familiar faces, including Elmer, Mario, Charlotte, and Linda; and, as a bonus, we were being overseen by Dee's brother, Bill Anthony, who was one of the best people in the business to be looking after you. Bill is one of life's very special people; he's funny, he's good at his job, and he has some of the best road stories in the world.

For no particular reason, I hadn't told anybody in management that I had just lost my mother. The road crew had told Bill, and he, out of respect, said nothing. But Peter Frampton, bless his heart, had said something as we got on the plane on the way over that shows how people, when talking to someone in a deep state of grief, sometimes don't realize what they are saying. Pete, who was a vegetarian and had recently taken to eating all things macrobiotic, said, "Brown rice cures everything." Now Peter obviously meant nothing by that, but, given that Mum had just been taken by the ravages of cancer, I wanted to smack him. Fortunately I didn't, because, apart from the fact that I didn't need to add getting the sack to my woes, Pete is a dear friend of mine.

So there we were in the pressure-cooker environment of our first gig in LA for Bandana (Dee's company) and A&M. The album had got some good reviews, even in *Rolling Stone*, and we were obviously a much-improved band that had benefited from the months of roadwork that we had got under our belt. We had become, as they say in the music trade, as tight as a duck's bum. We had also benefited from being on the road without Mandy: this time, the perennial fifth member of the band stayed at home, where she should have been all along, looking after Greg's kids. This gave us a chance to do some good old-fashioned male bonding,

We had also got extremely close as mates. Peter was the frail, skinny one, and Steve the tough little Artful Dodger with more front than Sainsbury's but not much to back it up, which is where Greg and I came to the fore, both on- and offstage. We also had two of the best roadies in the business in Dave Clark and John Hammel, who were also the best at looking after us all—or should I say at helping me and Greg look after Steve and Pete. Steve because he was one of those lads who would be the first with mouth but the last with self-defence. Pete because he was such a pacifist that you couldn't help but feel protective towards him. If anybody so much as thought about messing with either of them, they would have to deal with one of us—me, Greg, Dave, or John—or all four of us.

Many years before, as a young Small Faces fan, I would get very upset when Steve would blow his top at the rest of the band onstage. Even though I, as a working musician myself, was in awe of all that he and they did, I thought it was extremely bad form to be yelling at your bandmates in front of the entire audience. Fortunately, Steve had never done that with us, at least so far.

What happened next was so against the grain that it took everybody by complete surprise. We were into the last set of our second night at the Whisky a Go Go, and all hell broke loose. For no apparent reason, Steve threw one of his old-fashioned onstage wobblers à la Small Faces, and it did not go down at all well with the troops. Screaming at the top of his voice, his exact words were, "Get it together! Yer playin' like a bunch of fuckin' haddocks!"

I was mortified, as was Greg, who knew full well what it took for me to come on this tour and what a sacrifice it was for me to miss my mum's funeral. His attitude toward me seemed to radically change. In his eyes now, I was a real trouper for coming on tour in what was obviously my darkest hour, and he could not believe that a man so young could handle the situation with such grace, class, selflessness, and team spirit. I must admit that I saw it much the same, although it was really more a case of operating on automatic pilot out of respect for my father, brother, and, of course, Mum, as I, rightly or wrongly, believed that this was what she would want me to do. Keep the old British stiff upper lip and all that comes with it—"grace under pressure," as she would so beautifully put it.

So how dare Steve belittle me, Greg, and Peter in front of a crowd! Especially after I made such a sacrifice without any fuss, not even telling the management or asking for any special treatment whatsoever.

A stiff upper lip was all very well, but Greg knew I was about to blow my top in response to this awful, infuriating betrayal of trust and friendship. To add insult to injury, we weren't playing badly at all that night; Steve just fell back into old and very bad habits at the worst possible moment.

Once we got to the dressing room, my temper got the better of me, and I completely lost it. Bill Anthony had the common sense to get Steve out of harm's way, stashing him in the dressing room next to the one I was in. I was going berserk, smashing everything in sight and screaming at the top of my lungs that they had better keep him away from me. Steve, of course, heard every word, and I am assured that he was scared shitless for the first time in his life—scared by his little mate who had worshipped the ground he walked on for so many years—and also at least realised how insensitive he had been.

In any other circumstance, I would be well and truly fired, sacked, tin-tacked, given the elbow; I would have collected the pink slip. Simply put, the drummer doesn't threaten the lead singer's life or suggest that he must have developed a taste for hospital food. But that's exactly what I did.

To ensure Steve's safety, the powers that be made sure there were at least a couple of zip codes between me and him. Greg stayed with me to make sure I didn't do anything stupid, and Steve went back to the hotel with Peter and Bill, where the three of them told Dee about Mum dying.

This incident had several important lessons attached to it for Steve and the band. In the first place, it set a precedent by making Steve realise that shouting onstage at his bandmates for no apparent reason was just not on. Second, it made him see that even his closest and dearest young friend had his limits and that he could only go so far before he would face some come-back—that even he could be castigated if he went too far. Prior to this, I think Steve had pretty much got away with just about anything, with rare exception. Third, it established an unwritten law within the band that was there from the start but had never been tested, which was that we really were a democracy in the best sense: no one was fireable, and, even though we had two such powerful frontmen (who in subsequent bands had no trouble firing band members), this particular band was formed on the premise that each of us got an equal share in everything, warts and all. In fact, we actually did get... Oh no, sorry, that was crabs!

The next morning, after the dust settled, Dee called to ask me to come see him in his room. When I got there, he was kindness itself; he could not have been more understanding. He told me how much he respected my quiet, no-fuss approach and my show-must-go-on attitude, and he said that my mother would be proud of me. He understood why I lost it and got so angry, and agreed that Steve's antics were completely inexcusable. He went on to tell me a story about how his mother, on her deathbed, made him promise to look after his younger brother Bill, and how he had since seen to it that Bill never wanted for anything, financial or otherwise. I still don't quite understand the relevance of that, other than that it was his way of commiserating with me by showing that he too had lost his mother as a younger man and that looking after his younger brother was just part of his story.

While Steve never did apologise directly to me, I suppose having the manager do it on his behalf sufficed. Steve never was big on apologies anyway, but I'm sure that, while he had his own reasons for losing it onstage, he would have thought about it and at the very least realised that his timing wasn't exactly the height of tact.

In this particular story lies an insight into what it was like to deal with Steve. Here's a man who thoughtfully took the trouble to go and visit his friend's mum right before she passed away, then, within a week or two, treated the same friend with complete thoughtlessness. When anybody asked me what kind of person Steve was back then, I had a stock answer: "The one thing that is predictable about Steve Marriott is the fact that he is completely unpredictable." That remained true as long as I knew him, although, to his credit, he never again shouted at the troops onstage—small mercies, I suppose.

So we trucked on, and all was forgotten. To be honest, the rest of the tour was a bit of a blur; I was just trying to figure out which end was up.

I do know my playing was getting better all the time, primarily because one advantage of being a drummer is that it's a wonderful way to deal with anger. I always play best when I'm angry, and there's nothing like your mum dying to really piss you off.

I was still mad at God, and was refusing to talk to him because he had taken my mum away from me at a time when I needed her so badly. Don't let the word "God" put you off. It's just that, when I was a young lad of 11, doing all that praying and getting what I prayed for, my faith in the power of prayer had been considerably strengthened—wouldn't yours be? And now, what with losing Mum so young after praying so much for her not to die, my belief system had been given a serious kick in the arse. So I wasn't talking to him; I was *yelling* at him, figuring he owed me for screwing up so badly by letting Mum die.

Aside from my drumming improving because of my anger, we were all playing our arses off, getting better and better, so that even the away-from-home blues were starting to get easier for all of us to deal with. When you're tearing the place up, night after night, it cures many ills.

With a lot of nurturing and encouragement from Dee, Frank, and now Bill, Steve had become the proud, mature pro that he'd always been deep down. Don't forget, he had been trained at an early age to be a professional stage performer. Theatrical actors are the epitome of everything that Dee and Frank drummed into all their acts. The show must go on, stage presence, voice projection—all those things had been taught to Steve from the tender age of 11 onwards. In addition to his daily training at the Italia Conti Academy's drama school, he had worked with the very best—Peter Sellers, Laurence Olivier, and John Gielgud, among others.

Steve exuded masses of natural, God-given talent, and it was a joy to see how, in the hands of such brilliant coaches, he was coming to the fore again, only so much better than before. It was a privilege to be part of it. His rebirth was knocking the socks off everybody, except for one: his good friend and partner in the frontline, Peter. Pete was torn between two directions. On one hand, Humble Pie had started because Peter wanted to form his own band, even though that then developed into forming a band with me and so on. On the other hand, Steve's resurgence of stage presence was so undeniably powerful that Pete didn't want to dampen it. People sometimes forget that Peter was Steve's biggest fan… next to me!

We had a gig near the end of this leg of the tour to look forward to: opening for Grand Funk in New York. At Madison Square Garden, no less. In the meantime, though, we were stuck at some dodgy club in Chicago for a three-night stand that nobody, including the audience, wanted to be at. On the first night, there was hardly anyone there—in fact, the audience were outnumbered by the band, crew, and bar staff—which was unusual for us by this stage in a Midwest club, especially in Chicago.

Everything was working against us. The weather was atrocious, there were at least two other big-name bands playing within minutes of where we were playing, and the club was a horrendous toilet. So we were quite happy to have Steve navigate the choppy waters of pulling us out of the second and third nights we were booked to play.

Even the promoter was made to see the sense in cancelling the final two nights: he was losing money on the shows, and it became quite obvious that the crowds were spending their hard-earned cash on some other big band just up the road. Steve was in his element, and he successfully argued for us to get the fuck out of this nasty little suburb of Chicago. Ah yes: Madison Square Garden, here we come… and then home to move into the farm for Christmas.

We got to NYC full of anticipation about playing the Garden; never mind that it was only as the opening act. We had started to build our own following in the city, and they were always a tremendous crowd to play to, so we couldn't wait.

As a result of something that happened at the soundcheck for that show, we found our signature tune. Peter and I were playing onstage, just getting the sound right. Peter started playing a certain now-well-known riff, and I began to play along, followed by Greg, who had now come up onstage. When Steve heard it, he shouted to us to keep playing as he ran onstage and joined in, singing the Ray Charles hit "I Don't Need No Doctor" over Peter's chord sequence. It fit perfectly!

We opened with it that night and never looked back. in fact, of all the songs we ever played from that night on, the only one that has *always* been included in our shows is "Doctor." Even after Humble Pie, Steve would always do it, and after he and I agreed that I could use the name without him, I always played it. "Doctor" is recognised as one of the toughest, meanest-sounding blues songs of its time, and, frankly, Peter was largely responsible for it. Even more, it was the epitome of what made the chemistry between Steve and Peter so good, the shining example of what their partnership did best.

Grand Funk Railroad.

We played great that night, going down a storm, and I had one of several moments during that period when I could clearly, and in a very powerful way, see what was going to happen to us. I can't explain it, other than to say I just knew we were going to make it big in the USA. You could argue that it wasn't the meaning of life that I had got the inside track on; after all, we were getting some pretty strong indications through our hard roadwork, increased record sales, word-of-mouth crowd reactions, and the higher gig fees that Dee and Frank were slowly starting to achieve as our booking team. Even so, believe me, we were still far from being in the big league, and no one was betting their house on us getting there just yet. But I knew…

In fact, that very night, I saw the earth—or at least the dirty, great big lump of concrete that is the Garden—move. Literally.

As Grand Funk went on, Greg and I stood behind the stage, looking at how it was constructed with scaffolding. We both noticed that the crowd of 20,000 people were jumping up and down so much that the *floor* was actually moving up and down, too—by at least two or three feet! We found out later that the Garden was actually designed to move like that, so that it didn't collapse from all that stomping and excessively loud music. Ah, rock 'n' roll—don't you just love it?

We headed home on a brand-new invention that was the biggest thing I'd seen since Terry Knight's ego: one of the British Overseas Airways Corporation's first 747 jumbo jets. (I mention Terry's opinion of himself simply because, as we were doing the soundcheck at the Garden, Greg needed a light and asked him if he had a match, to which Terry replied, "Not since Superman died!" Those of you too young to get the reference might insist that Superman never died; I refer you to the sad fate of George Reeves, the actor identified with the Man of Steel at the time.)

That first flight on a 747 was remarkable. Back then, the upstairs lounges, which were in first class, were set up very extravagantly, with pianos, cocktail bars, and so on. As we were still travelling economy, we had to use whatever charm we could muster to get a quick look around at these amenities. The stewardesses who we charmed and befriended were lovely ladies. As we chatted with them, the subject somehow turned to drugs, which it often did with us. One of them, a Scandinavian, said she had some hashish with her—a fine chunk of Red Lebanese, she claimed, and she was not lying. Back then, of course, you could smoke tobacco on planes, but that didn't fix the problem of the smell of the hash. The Nordic beauty, however, came up with a solution. She took us down into the galley in the belly of the plane, and we got stoned at 35,000 feet. Ah, what a life!

Chapter 11

"RESPECT THE BOARDS!"

December 1970 to July 1971

In which we Rock On *at Olympic; Beanie-Cake meets Hector the Humping Dog; we learn a lesson from Sophie Tucker; and we rock the Fillmore... but have to rescue the mix; and we get buzzed and buzz around with the Who.*

Being home again was very strange: it was the first Christmas without Mum, and I moved into the farm over the same holiday period. I was determined to put together a crew to do the work on the farm that was made up entirely of guys I grew up with, most of them from the old Waltham Cross Mods, who were at their height a ferocious team, to say the least. I wanted to use people I could trust, and I achieved that with no problem. To a man, these lads were the best at what they did, and, just like before, when Angus and I had our various bands, they were extremely protective and conscientious about taking care of their little mate. By now, I'd become a bit of a Waltham Cross legend in a "local lad does good" sort of way.

The farm screamed out for a horticultural makeover, and, as gardening had become Dad's main hobby, it was the perfect job for him. I gave him the reins to do entirely as he wished. He was also the ideal man to oversee the house rebuild, and he did a superb job on that, too. His other job was fending off all the local widows, as he had become quite the catch from their point of view—not that he was rich or anything, but he often borrowed the Rolls-Royce, and the effect that car had on women young and old was amazing. Rolls should have taken advantage of this phenomenon in their ads—"Having trouble with your love life? Young or old, buy a Rolls and get laid!"—but they never did. I can't think why, although I suppose they would figure that if you've got the cash to buy a Roller, you should be able to get laid anyway.

On Boxing Day, Rick Wills and Lynny Parfitt came to visit for a while, and a wonderful thing happened: it snowed. The farm was beautiful; it had that pretty chocolate-box look about it. We decided to take the Rolls for a ride up to Cambridge to visit Lynny's parents and catch up with some friends—and, of course, show off with the car a bit, how you do. Our first task was to drive into the nearest village to fill the car up with petrol. We stopped at the village store / petrol station, and Mr. Newell, the dear old man who owned it, came out and asked how much gas I needed. Naturally, I told him to fill it up. As he collected the five pounds, he started to fawn all over me about the car, telling me how incredible it looked. I said something like, "Ah yes, I know, but you see, this is a *very special* Rolls," implying in a really flash-little-git sort of way that I had made sure to buy the best they had to offer. Then I went to turn the key… and the car wouldn't start. Talk about instant karma! This incident taught me very quickly that bragging about one's wealth can prove to be a treacherous enterprise.

The next step for the band, and therefore me, was to record our second A&M album. We were to use Glyn Johns and Olympic again, which was a joy to look forward to. We would record the whole album at Olympic, with the exception of "Strange Days," which we'd recorded nine months earlier (as the B-side of the "Big Black Dog" single) at Chris Blackwell's brand-new Island Studios. Humble Pie almost got in the history books by being the first band to record a full-on session at there; unfortunately, Free took that honour by recording "All Right Now" there the night before.

The material we had ready for this record was a combination of things we had been doing on the road for a while; newly written songs by Steve, Peter, and Greg; and some group-written material. There was a lovely tune by Steve and Peter called "Sour Grain." We had already nailed "Strange Days" (music by the group and lyrics by Steve) at the Island session, bringing on one of those "Come and listen" moments from Glyn. We were very happy with the results and didn't want it to die a death as the B-side to a flop single, so we decided to put it on the album. Steve had a little gem called "Red Neck Jump" that eventually was edited together with "Strange Days" as a perfect yin-yang close to the album, with "Red Neck Jump" having all the humour and "Strange Days" all the severity. Peter had written a couple of gems of his own—"Shine On" and "The Light." I remember thinking that if we were a singles-type band, "Shine On" would fit the bill. Fortunately, I had not written anything on my own, so I could not be humiliated a second time by being told to sing my own song in that awful falsetto voice of mine.

Finally, we had some group-written material we had been doing on the road for a while. One song in particular, "Stone Cold Fever," was a strong favourite live. It was built around a middle passage custom-made for one of Peter's long guitar solos, and also featured him and Steve doing a lot of call-and-response soloing. "Stone Cold Fever" ended up being the reason Glyn declined to make a third album with us and, curiously, at least part of the reason why Peter, barely six months later, decided to leave the band. I say "curiously" simply because it was in large part Peter who wrote it. Only a few months hence, that song, "Rollin' Stone," and "I Don't Need No Doctor" were used as examples of where the band's musical direction was going, causing Glyn to opt out and Pete to decide to leave.

For some reason that I can't for the life of me remember, we chose not to record studio versions of "Four Day Creep" and "Doctor." If memory serves, we did try them in the studio, but they just didn't cut it and remained in the live show only.

We had again left our equipment in the States for economic reasons, which meant that, just as with the Entwistle sessions, I had to hire a kit. This time I got lucky: I was able to hire a kick-ass little Ludwig Red Sparkle kit. It sounded great, and we got our best drum sounds yet out of it.

Steve was on fire on the piano during these sessions, but, for some reason, Peter and I played piano together on Steve's "79th and Sunset." I played the left-hand part, while Pete played the right. I don't have any idea why, considering how well Steve was playing, but it was indicative of the way we were all getting on during this period.

I've heard many so-called rock 'n' roll historians and even some of Steve's old musician mates, not least of all Ronnie Wood, go on about how Steve lost it once he left the Small Faces, or that as a guitar player he was "just a strummer," but I beg to differ. Whilst he did lose a certain degree of his natural abilities later in life, he had by no means done so at that early stage of Humble Pie. His lyrics were spot on then, and I defy anybody to find me a lyric by Mr. Wood that is any better than those that our Steve was producing at the time—not to mention his melodies, chord sequences, lead and rhythm guitar work, fabulous piano playing, remarkable harmonica skills, and sense of rhythm and harmony. Add to these his abilities as a studio sound engineer and his onstage showmanship, and I would say the only things that Ronnie had in abundance over Steve were a few inches in height—hell, everybody had that over him—and hair, which Steve was already starting to lose.

Now that I've got that rant out of the way…

Glyn brought in Bobby Keys on saxophone and Claudia Lennear on back-up vocals… and eye candy. Claudia was an absolutely gorgeous black lady whose recent claim to fame was as a back-up singer, along with Rita Coolidge and others, on Joe Cocker's "Mad Dogs & Englishmen" tour. She was enlisted, along with Doris Troy and P.P. Arnold, to do the back-up vocals on Steve's "A Song for Jenny." Bobby, of course, had been working with the Stones, and had been part of the brass section on the Cocker tour, along with Jim Price. He played a sax solo on a song by Greg called "Big George."

When we recorded "Shine On," I was proud to be able to help Peter arrange the song—not to any huge extent, just enough to feel better about myself and get a much-needed confidence boost. You see, working and keeping up with Steve, Peter, and Greg was an all-day, every-day job. All three exuded talent, and you could very easily get to feel like you weren't carrying your weight if you didn't contribute. Having said that, I am forever grateful to them for nurturing and encouraging me. If I did make a beginner's mistake or was not quite as versed at some aspect or other of this level of recording, they never took the piss or in any way tried to make me feel like anything but their equal.

I suppose you could say, "Well, you were there on merit," and I've finally admitted that to myself after 40 years. But, as I said early on in this book, I'm trying to write about how I felt at the time, and, back then, I most definitely was very insecure about my own abilities alongside those of the other three, which were breathtaking.

In any case, we were now working well together on every level. As soon as we started to get such great drum sounds at the beginning of these sessions, I knew we were onto something a notch above all that we'd done before. The record turned out to be one of our best, and the sessions were some of the most enjoyable we ever did. This was in part because of the material we had to work with, and the main reason we were producing such high-quality material was all the roadwork we'd been doing. We were fighting fit, extremely tight, and sharp as a tack. We had been writing together on the road and rearranging things at soundchecks. We had become a well-oiled machine and, as the after-show shenanigans hadn't yet turned us into the *other* kind of well-oiled machine, we were on a roll. Each session was better than the previous one, and some of the performances Glyn got on tape were sensational.

It wasn't long, though, before some big changes would hit us. Looking

back, the early warning signs were there to see, but we weren't inclined to see them—we were having too much fun just doing, without too much analysing.

Coming up with a title for the album was a no-brainer. On the last tour, in the States, we had started to use the phrase "Rock on." I don't remember why; we just did. So *Rock On* it was.

Steve came up with the idea for the cover, which was to hire a motorbike crew to ride in a pyramid shape, stand on each other's shoulders, and hold a banner that read "Rock On—Humble Pie"—not exactly thinking man's rock 'n' roll, but that's something you would never accuse us of. We were never "let's think about it" rock; we were always "let's just fucking do it" rock. John Kelly, the photographer who took the shot, found out that the only people who did the stunt were the Royal Air Force Police Display Team, and they were only allowed to charge the not-exactly-princely sum of £70. We also had him throw the bikers an all-you-can-drink party so that he could film the results, which turned out a bit tame. We couldn't believe they went to all that trouble to do the stunt and only received such a small amount, but at least they got a party out of it.

As much work on the farm as my budget would allow was completed, but the rest had to be put on hold until the next influx of A&M cash, which was not until May 19—four months away. In the meantime, there was no central heating, carpet, or furniture, save a mattress in the living room, which was warmed by the big Inglenook fireplace. It was all about roughing it through one of the coldest—but prettiest—winters we'd had for a while, with snow and the whole nine yards.

This was a very special time in my life, as you can imagine. Here I was at the tender age of 18, with a Rolls-Royce in the drive of an Elizabethan farmhouse that was nearly 400 years old, situated on three-and-a-half acres with tons of outbuildings, including an Essex barn that was bigger than the house, a three-bedroom cottage, and weeping willows hanging over the pond, which was separated from the front door of the house by a red-brick bridge. It was like heaven on earth.

Just as I was settling into Green Farm, my dear friend Gala Pinion—Syd Barrett's ex-girlfriend and one-time fiancée—was getting her life together post-Syd, and I asked her to stay at the farm once or twice to housesit, and soon after to dog-sit. Dad had found an orphaned Pyrenean Mountain Dog that needed a home—a big home. Hector was fucking *huge*, at least 160 pounds. He was young and had not been fixed, so he was ready to rock 'n' roll. He was also gay…

Hector had taken a shine to one of our part-time roadies, an asthmatic called Beanie-Cake because he always had beans and cake around his mouth. The band were rehearsing one afternoon at Magdalen Laver Village Hall. While we had a tea break in the kitchen, we heard what sounded like Beanie having what can only be described as asthmatic copulation. We rushed out to see Hector with this absurd grin on his face and his two front legs locked firmly around Beanie's midriff—from behind, naturally—going at it like a steam train.

Beanie, who only weighed 120 pounds, had been conveniently kneeling down, fixing Peter's foot pedals, and didn't notice Hector slowly amble up behind him and hop on. By the time we pulled Hector off, Beanie was in full asthmatic arrest. After he had calmed down a bit, he explained between desperate gasps for as much air as his shell-shocked lungs could muster. "He caught me by surprise, boss…" gasp, gasp, gasp… "And he's so big…" gasp, gasp, gasp… "I didn't know whether to try to beat him off…" gasp, gasp… "Or lay down and enjoy it." After all, Beanie *was* a Sixties roadie.

Once *Rock On* was finished, we did a small tour of the UK—mostly colleges, clubs, and small theatres—before embarking on what was to be our longest, and by far our most satisfying, American tour yet. With NYC, as always, our base of operations, we played all the usual suspects that we'd hit before plus markets we had a particular fondness for, but had not yet been to: we'd end up playing Texas and other parts of the Deep South, Florida, and Atlanta during various legs of a tour that went on all the way through the fall.

The album was released in March. It got some really strong airplay, and the initial sales were by far our best to date. It was not blowing the doors off the charts just yet, but it was a huge improvement on anything we had achieved thus far. We also saw a big (and immediate) improvement in the response we got, with all kinds of positive reactions. In particular, limo drivers across the country told us that other bands that used their services were all saying what a great album we had just made. That sort of word of mouth is priceless in this business. Pretty soon, everybody was talking about *Rock On*, and it kept selling a little more every week.

By now the Faces, as they were now known, were doing really well. They had recruited Rod Stewart and Ron Wood to replace Steve, and were off to a fabulous start. They recorded as a group, and Rod was releasing solo albums, which were doing particularly sensational business. I've read in a number of books how Steve would brag about the fact that it took two people to replace him. I also heard many people say to him, "Ah ha! See, Steve, it took two to replace you!" Now I can't speak about the times I spent away from Steve from then until he died, but I can say that, in all the time I did spend with him (more than any other musician dead or alive did), I never once heard him boast that it took two guys to replace him. He was happy for his ex-bandmates, and thought that being replaced by Rod and Ronnie was a huge compliment. In fact, as I mentioned before, he had suggested Ronnie as his replacement, and was never anything but pleased for Ronnie and Rod.

The American tour started, unsurprisingly, in NYC at the Fillmore East. The headliner was Cactus, featuring the original rhythm section for Vanilla Fudge, Tim Bogert on bass and Carmine Appice on drums. Greg and I were huge Vanilla Fudge fans, and Tim and Carmine were a bass-and-drums partnership that we looked up to a great deal. We were really looking forward to working with them, and they didn't disappoint. They played together superbly, and both proved to be real gentlemen. Carmine was particularly kind to me and very complimentary towards our band. We also got to see and meet some other great bands at the Fillmore on our nights off, including Traffic and Mountain. When we saw Mountain, we found our future tour manager / lighting director, a chap called Mick Brigden. Mick was a Brit who somehow managed to end up living in NYC and working for Mountain. We became good friends with the band and soon worked with them on various occasions.

We were beginning what was to become one of the most remarkable years of my (and the group's) life so far. The whole tour was a steady climb upwards in every department. Onstage we were getting better and better and, most importantly, consistent. Consistency is the holy grail of performing requirements for a band on the road. If you can deliver the same level of performance night after night, you are going to achieve a much stronger bond with not only your fans but, more important, also the promoters who employ your services. Your reputation with promoters is paramount to your ability to go forth and plunder. So far, we had developed a strong connection with these guys, and it was only getting better.

All of Dee's principles of the road were paying off in bucket loads. The one that had the most powerful effect on the front row of Steve, Peter, and Greg was illustrated by a story about Tony Bennett, who, at the time the events of the story took place, was opening for Sophie Tucker at the Sands Hotel in Las Vegas.

Tony was in the earlier part of his career, and was having a hard time at home. His wife had left him, and, out of frustration, he threw this particular show away, making it very clear that the last place in the world he wanted to be was on the stage at the Sands. Sophie was outraged, and sent for Tony and Dee to find out why he had done such an amateurish thing. When they got to the grand old dame's dressing room, they received the biggest dressing down either one of them had ever got. She tore into Tony like there was no tomorrow.

"How dare you disrespect the boards?!? Haven't you learned anything yet?!? Did you see the billboard outside?!? It says, 'Tonight: Sophie Tucker featuring her special guest Tony Bennett'! Did you notice that your name is up there as big as mine?!?" Then she pressed the point home, screaming at the top of her voice, "RESPECT THE BOARDS! ALWAYS RESPECT THE BOARDS! Why do you think I had them put your name as big as mine?!?" She went on, answering her own question: "So that they can see you are as worthy an act as the headliner; and in case there are any Tony Bennett fans out there, I want them to know you're on my bill! So while you are on my stage you better leave your problems off it, and in return for all my generosity, you had better RESPECT THE BOARDS!"

This was vintage Dee Anthony. He would tell true stories about people you knew very well as huge stars, and he would point out the lessons they had learned along the way, so as to prove that they had been torn down many times before they learned how to be pros. He took the right to be considered a pro very seriously. It was definitely an honour that had to be earned by paying your dues, not by simply being lucky and having a hit. And paying your dues meant working your arse off and sticking to the basic ground rules of the road, which he would impart to us on a daily basis. It was like going to school, and because of his amazing track record, you wanted to please him. And if you did do well, you would get complete acceptance from him as a fully paid-up member of this elite club of pros that included such mega-stars as Sinatra, Bennett, Elvis, and many more— you name them and Dee probably had a story about them. Not only was this technique psychologically very effective on all of us, but it made the whole learning process a lot of fun.

It was the beginning of the greatest period in the band's history. The four of us were getting along better than ever. Steve and Peter were individually at their very best and were playing off each other onstage better than at any time before or since. Greg and I were in a class of rhythm sections that we previously could have only dreamt of—and again Dee was responsible in large part, due to his coaching skills, which brought out a fierce combatant attitude in the pair of us. Dee would literally bring us into a huddle right before we went onstage, and once we were on, he continued to motivate us from the wings with his famous whistle.

Somewhere around the start of this tour, band and management set each other various goals related to the band's success. Dee was going to find us houses in the Caribbean that we could go to between tours—and, of course, make us rich enough to buy them. He was also going to buy us a gold Rolex each, once we got our first gold record. We in turn promised to buy Dee and Frank a Rolls-Royce each, once we got to headline our own tour. All of these promises were made in a wonderful, young guns, take-no-prisoners sort of way. They were also made with a tongue-in-cheek attitude, and it was all good clean fun. But just shortly after all this good clean fun, something entered our lives that was to put a sinister edge on our well-intended, innocent goals. It was, in a word, cocaine.

I cannot stress strongly enough how much that drug affected everything we did for the next several years. I can say that our plans for houses, Ro-lexes, and Rollers were all put up *before* the arrival of the white stuff, which is surprising because cocaine is famous for making people grandiose. Buy-ing a flash car for your manager is one thing, but pretty soon we had to be stopped from buying one for the doorman at the Ritz just because he opened the door with such panache. In our defence, we were all very in-nocent about the dark side of cocaine, as was everybody who was doing it at the time—which was, by the way, *everybody*.

Nobody knew what was around the corner back then, and even if they had, it wouldn't have stopped them, such is the nature of the beast. There was another reason why, in the early days, the blow didn't severely hamper our progress; we weren't rich enough—yet. So for now, we were running on natu-ral gas, aided and abetted by some pot and the odd drink, although we really weren't drinking that much either—yet. Everything we were doing seemed to go just right, and our overall judgement, including Dee's, was pretty sound. We were just having a ball, knocking people dead night after night.

We travelled the length of the New Jersey Turnpike so many times on that tour, we were on first-name terms with the collectors at each of the tollbooths along the way. One time, we arrived in Wildwood, immediately found out that Buddy Rich was playing in town, and arranged to have the next night off so we could see him. We had heard all kinds of horror stories about what a mean son of a bitch he was and how he would quite happily give his audience shit if he wasn't in an agreeable mood.

When we got to the cabaret / dinner club where Buddy was playing, we were more than a little unnerved when the maître d' sat us at the main ta-ble, right in front of the stage. Our fears grew enormously when we realised that, other than us, there were only a dozen people there. We were horrified at the lack of support the greatest drummer in the world was getting here and decided that, regardless of the way Buddy might treat us, we were going to give him one hell of a reception. When he finally hit the stage, he was professionalism at its finest. He put on what seemed to be an absolutely top-drawer show, even though there were only a handful of people in the club. In return, we gave him a reception to match.

Buddy did this spot in his show where he gets off the kit and comes to the front of the stage to crack a few jokes and chat with the audience. As we were right in front of him, he could hardly ignore us, so we were just waiting for him to give us some shtick. But he didn't do anything of the sort; he was a gentleman through and through. He asked what band we were, and even said he had heard of us through his teenage daughter who "keeps me up with the new groups." After his sensational show, he had his roadie give me a set of cymbal holders to use on my kit. It was only a small piece of equipment, but I have used it ever since. I suppose the moral of this little tale is: do not believe everything you hear about someone until you see them for yourself.

Soon thereafter, we opened for Black Sabbath in Alexandria, Virginia, near Washington, D.C. We played one of our best shows ever, and the crowd's reaction was better than any we had got before. This was not the first time we had given Black Sabbath a good run for their money, nor would it be the last. Ozzie watched our entire show from the wings with a look of astonishment on his face, taking in everything Steve was doing. At his best, Steve always drew other lead singers to the side of the stage to get their master class on how to be a frontman and lead singer. At this time, he was blowing them all out of the water.

At breakfast the next morning, I noticed that a couple of people sitting around us had realised who we were. Back then, before MTV, the only way anyone could figure out who you were was if they (a) saw you playing live, (b) read about you in the music papers (which were small potatoes in the States), or (c) bought the album. So, sitting there with Dee, I had a Spinal Tap moment as I turned to him and said, "The vibe is out!" He looked at me as if I had lost all reason, until I explained why I said it.

Not long after this, Dee had a minor epiphany about the band's progress and what to do next: he decided we were ready to record a live album. He was seeing our effect on an audience night after night, but, while our albums were getting better, there was an undeniable gap between our success live and our success on record. Something had to be done.

Dee had recently scored heavily with Joe Cocker's "Mad Dogs & Englishmen" tour, which was filmed and recorded for a live album, propelling Joe into the big leagues. Dee figured that if it worked once, why not try it again with us. The Fillmore East was the perfect venue, and the timing was perfect, too—the hall was about to shut up shop, and our live recording would be done in the last month of shows there.

We were still not headlining, but everything seemed to be on the up. The gigs were, for the most part, much improved, from the fee we were getting all the way through to what we got in our dressing room. We were developing strong relationships with all the top promoters of the day: Bill Graham in NYC, Don Law in Boston, Larry Magid in Philadelphia, Shelly Finkel in Rhode Island and Connecticut, Ron Delsener in Long Island, and Howard Stein in New Jersey. They were all becoming good friends, and, as they had stuck with us in the beginning, it was payback time, so they all got first dibs at booking us now we were on the way up. Bob Bageris in Detroit was another of their number; he was a supreme gentleman who went out of his way to show the business that his belief in us was not misplaced. He went on to prove it within the first year that we became headliners by booking us into Cobo Hall, a 12,000-seater in Detroit, for four shows, all of which sold out, which was a record there at the time.

The Fillmore East was already *the* place to record anybody live because of those famous acoustics and its incredible track record: each and every one of the acts that recorded a live album there ended up with one of the top live rock albums ever, including the Allman Brothers, John Mayall, Frank Zappa, Hendrix's Band of Gypsys, and us lot, to name but a few. Even Peter Frampton's live album, whilst not recorded there, showed that Peter had at least learned his lessons on how to record live; he chose the nearest thing to the Fillmore by recording his album at Winterland in San Francisco.

As we were in the middle of our longest, most gruelling tour to date, we were, by definition, firing on all cylinders. Every last drop of what we were putting out onstage was so finely tuned; we had developed a telepathy that allowed us to play so tight, and were constantly surprising ourselves to the point of laughing out loud at how good it sounded. And when an audience sees a band enjoying themselves that much, they can't help but get involved. It becomes infectious.

I recall doing a show at a college just outside Manhattan at the start of this tour, when Steve brought the house down with one of his better one-liners. At the end of "Hallelujah (I Love Her So)," he started to improvise, bringing the band down to where we were playing so quietly that he could sing full-voice without the mic and be heard all through the hall, a trick he'd perfected at previous shows at the Fillmore. The lyric was an improv around the song's title. As he sang it over and over, a stunner in the front row managed to get on her friend's shoulders right in front of Steve and run her hand up his leg to his crotch, before proceeding to rub his nuts. Steve didn't miss a beat; he simply changed the lyric to "Hallelujah, someone's stroking my balls!" This got us the only favourable review we ever had in *Rolling Stone*—plus they used Steve's line as the headline!

As the tour rolled on, we kept building momentum towards the shows at the Fillmore, which were to be recorded at the end of the tour. Fate was on our side, as the engineer who would record them turned out to be none other than Eddie Kramer, our dear old friend from Olympic Studios, who had moved to NYC to run Jimi Hendrix's Electric Lady Studios.

I knew Eddie from the Immediate days when Steve used me on those Olympic sessions; Ed would step in when Glyn couldn't do one. He also worked on some of the Humble Pie stuff and was the only guy in England who could give Glyn a run for his money. Eddie had a CV that read like a list of rock 'n roll hall-of-famers: Hendrix, Zeppelin, the Stones, Small Faces, Traffic, and many more—plus he's a hell of a nice guy. So we were in safe hands.

We had never been to Florida before, so seeing it and some of the other firsts on the date sheet was a real bonus. In the weeks leading up to the live album, we had Miami to look forward to, along with Houston, Memphis, New Orleans, and yet another run through the West Coast.

We also played Boston on this tour. Every time we played there, a band of glam rockers would show up backstage to pay their respects. We knew they were budding musicians, and I believe they already had a bit of a local following. They wore lots of makeup and had scarves hanging everywhere, and the singer had a pair of lips to match Mick Jagger's. We thought it was a bit weird to wear all that stage gear when you are just hanging out, but they were very nice, well-mannered young lads and very respectful of what we were doing. A few years later, when a hard-rocking Boston bunch hit it big with their third album, *Toys in the Attic*, I recognised them as the same band: Aerosmith.

When our truck broke down in Rockford, Illinois, we got stuck without any equipment and had to borrow some from a local band who were there to see us. This extremely talented band, who were very nice to lend us their gear, became huge later in the Seventies when they evolved into Cheap Trick.

We kept running into so many great bands who were either playing on the same bill or just at the gig to check us out. Talk about a band of brothers—a lot of genuine camaraderie existed between all the bands out there on the road. And we really were in a special time and place for rock, where it still mattered if you had talent; the musicians' ability *was* the show. All the rest was secondary, just window dressing that was nice but not the main attraction.

In Island Park, New York, T. Rex—who certainly had talent but, unfortunately, were the perfect example of what did not work onstage in America—

opened for us. Marc Bolan, God rest his soul, tried everything he could think of to win over that tough crowd, and nothing worked. The harder he tried, the worse it got for him. At one point, he decided out of complete frustration to do a Pete Townshend and threw his Les Paul up in the air. Hoping to catch it on its way down, he held his arms straight up above his head… and missed. The guitar landed on top of his head and knocked him out cold. The crowd thought it was all part of the show and finally gave him some applause—if not for knocking them out, at least for doing so to himself!

Dee's management company, Bandana, were also managing some other big-name bands, and that allowed us the luxury of being booked on long stretches of dates with one or another of these acts: the two biggest at the time were Emerson, Lake & Palmer and Ten Years After, who were both managed by English companies that had hired Dee to service their acts.

We found ourselves criss-crossing America time and time again, opening or being special guest on either ELP or TYA tours, and we could feel the momentum building all the while. The way you are treated on any tour relies entirely on the headliner and how they dictate the opener should be handled, good or bad. The headliners who have a well-grounded, mature sense of professionalism usually treat you well and give you every chance to succeed. Then there are those who treat you like shit for any number of reasons—because they were treated badly and think that's the way all openers should be treated, or simply because they don't want you to show them up—and they do all they can to make sure you don't shine. As Dee was looking after the whole shooting match, at least we were guaranteed good treatment on these two bands' shows. We seemed to be leading a charmed life when it came to knocking the audiences out night after night. We were also still doing shows with Grand Funk that promised to deliver huge dividends if we were given the opening spot on their record-breaking shows to be staged that summer.

At the Fillmore, getting ready to record the live album, we waited to find out if we would be doing the Grand Funk shows. Dee came to the soundcheck and rounded us up into the dressing room to give us the news. We were to do the entire summer of dates with them, which meant Shea Stadium, Hyde Park, and a string of stadium shows across Europe, including Germany and Italy.

I made a bet with Dee—I suppose "challenge" is a more accurate description. I challenged him to make me a millionaire by the time I was 21, which meant he had two years to make it happen. He accepted the challenge and confidently assured me he could do it. As with the Rolls-Royce pledge, this was all done very innocently, and I firmly believed Dee would meet my chal-

Fillmore East marquee, showing the dates when Performance *was recorded.*

lenge; that's how well things were going. These were truly wonderful times.

The Fillmore went beautifully, and, although Lee Michaels was the headliner and we were only the special guest, we were probably responsible for 70% of the tickets sold. When you listen to the live album, you would never know that we were not the main attraction.

To be honest, at the time of recording, we had no idea the record would be as good as it turned out to be. We knew it was an excellent performance that had been very well recorded in a great-sounding room. What we didn't know was just how well those elements had jelled. In fact, the first attempt at mixing it almost ended in us throwing away the whole project because we had mixed it as if it were a studio record and forgot the audience! The resulting mix had lost its entire atmosphere.

If Dee Anthony had done nothing else for Humble Pie, what he did next was worth every penny of the commission he earned during his entire career as our manager. We had taken the multi-track tapes home to England and booked time in Olympic studios to mix them. Dee came over to hear the results, and thank God he had the strength of character to pull us up on it, telling us in no uncertain terms that it was awful. I say "strength of character" because if you tell an extremely dedicated professional musician that his judgement is off, it sometimes falls on deaf ears—or gets a very unfriendly response, to put it mildly, if the musician is of a typically volatile demeanour, which most egotistical performers tend to be. This is not criticism; it is simply a statement of fact. You had to be a brave man to tell Steve—and, to some extent, Peter—as Dee just had, that the mix they had slaved over sucked. The fact was that we had just dropped the ball in a huge way, and if Dee had not put his foot down, we would have been sunk. All of our extremely hard work over the past two-and-a-half years would have been in vain.

It would not have been a *dreadful* record if we had used that first mix; it's just that the most important elements of a *great* live recording are the audience's participation and reaction. The room sound from the microphones placed in the auditorium to record those elements is also very important; it adds the ambience that all live music needs to portray its live sound. Without that, you may as well be mixing another studio recording. In fact, the ambient sound from mics placed some distance from the source turns an ordinary drum sound into a *huge* one, and that's just one aspect of live recording that is so beneficial to getting a great sound that it is often used to embellish regular studio recordings. All this is common knowledge and practice today, but back then, these were lessons that were still being learned.

Dee taking us to task on the first mix is a perfect example of how focused and well behaved we all were at this particular juncture. This was all pre-cocaine. We had been introduced to the blow by now, but it hadn't yet become the driving force within the band that it subsequently became. At the time, our main poison was still hashish, and lots of it. We used to daydream about becoming headliners so that we could afford all the drugs we wanted, but I don't remember our drug wish list including cocaine—yet. We were still a well-dressed bunch of hippies who liked to get stoned, listen to sounds, kick ass onstage, and spend weeks on the road horribly homesick.

As the first attempt at mixing the live album had failed so spectacularly, we had to come up with a better plan. We were about to embark on another long tour, in Europe and the States, which would take in some huge dates with Grand Funk, including the previously mentioned Shea Stadium show. Since we were going to be in and out of NYC several times, we could book mix sessions in Electric Lady Studios with Eddie Kramer as the engineer. This was, next to Dee putting his foot down, the most important decision we ever made. Eddie was by far the best choice for the job; he had, after all, recorded the show in the first place. He was extremely experienced at mixing live tapes, was one of the best 24-track tape editors in the business, and already had a track record of successful live recordings at the Fillmore, not least of all with Band of Gypsys, who he'd recorded there 18 months earlier.

The final piece of the puzzle was to elect Peter to act as the band's representative at the mixes so we could fly him in on a day off to assist Eddie and be our voice, because we couldn't afford to fly the whole band in. Steve was more than happy to let Peter do the job, which was a blessing in disguise because Steve had already started to develop a "that will do" attitude in the studio, whereas Peter was much more meticulous and had become an extremely accomplished engineer in his own right. Not that Steve wasn't—he probably taught Peter most of what he knew—but the job required a much-focused, attention-to-detail type of team, and with Eddie and Peter we had exactly that. The rest of us were too impatient, frankly, and if you had all of us in there, it would be a case of too many cooks. Also, the four of us had failed before, so once bitten…

The mix sessions did start with all of us present, but with only Peter and Eddie, and to a lesser extent Steve, doing the work. The first mixes they did came together beautifully, so Greg and I were totally confident in that team; we could relax and go back to enjoying our normal hedonistic pursuits.

One story about these sessions sums up the high level of musicality the band possessed at the time. We had done four shows in two nights and recorded them all, so we had four versions of each song to choose from. "I Walk on Gilded Splinters" was a Dr. John song that we had developed into a 30-minute-plus epic with lots of extended guitar solos. We all preferred the overall performance of the song from the second show on the first night, but Pete preferred his solo from the first show on the second night, awkward bugger! In those days, we tuned our guitars primarily by ear, with a little help from one of Steve's harmonicas, and set all our tempos by yours truly counting the band in, so there was every possibility of slight differences in pitch and speed between the two performances.

We decided to try to edit the 24-track tape by taking Pete's solo from the second night and editing it into the performance from the first night—and praying that they matched. Eddie's skills with the scissors were a very welcome addition to the proceedings. When they matched perfectly, in both tempo and pitch, we were astonished. This meant we could mix the 24-track tape as one piece instead of having to mix the two elements separately and edit them together, thus saving ourselves a lot of sodding about. In today's world, we could have digitally tweaked the tempo and the pitch to match with a couple of mouse clicks, but back then it wasn't that easy.

Although the record that was eventually released was basically the show verbatim, there turned out to be more than one occasion when a good edit was needed, as many of our songs were unacceptably long. "Gilded Splinters," for instance, was edited down from 33 minutes to a mere 23:25.

Looking back at that summer tour of '71, the warning signs that Peter wasn't feeling right about his position in the band were there, but, at the time, I did not see his imminent departure coming at all. I knew there were things about Steve's character that were getting to Pete, but that came with the territory of being in a band with him; simply put, Steve was hard work. If you were of a sensitive nature, he could get to you big-time. Don't misunderstand: Steve was like a brother to me, and for whatever reason, Greg and I were better equipped to handle him. Peter, however, just didn't have what it took to tolerate Steve's nonsense. What it took wasn't patience; Peter had far more of that than Greg or I ever had. It wasn't artistic differences; Peter and Steve understood each other on a musical level far better than they did as human beings. And that is where the problem lay. They just didn't get on as mates the way Greg and I did with Steve.

Drug taking was one of the obvious things that determined their lack of common ground. Steve was a sworn stoner, Peter wasn't. Steve came from the deep-rooted "can't relate if you are straight" line of thinking. Peter was not entirely straight; he did smoke dope from time to time, and later in life had a few demons to exorcise when Cousin Cocaine weaselled her way into everybody's life for a while. But back then he didn't get on with smoking regularly, plus, as I've said before, he didn't need it. Steve was loud and gregarious, while Peter was quiet and reserved. You could go right down the line of character traits and almost all of them were opposite between the two; they truly were the original chalk and cheese. They knew it, understood it, and accepted it later in life, but back then they were less tolerant of each other's differences, as you tend to be when you are younger. Believe it or not, I had no idea, at the time, that Peter was becoming as discontent as he was, and Steve certainly didn't see it either.

Pete was giving his all and was as excited as the rest of us about the band's future. He was doing a superb job with the remix. He was also developing in leaps and bounds as a frontman in his own right. The trouble was, so was Steve. With the encouragement of management, Steve was becoming the master of frontmanship. It must have been very confusing for Pete. After all, Humble Pie started as his band, and, although he was as big a fan of Steve, when Steve was in the Small Faces, as any of us, he knew only too well how powerful Steve was when he was given the reins. And that was exactly what was happening. Steve was going from strength to strength, and, deep down, this was having a powerful effect on Peter, who must have seen control of his band slipping away. For now, though, to his undying credit, he gave his all to the band.

At the start of the American leg of the summer tour, shortly before the Shea show, the Who were spending time in NYC, recording sessions for what was to become *Who's Next*. Pete Townshend had hurt his wrist, so they were trying to record with Leslie West from Mountain playing the lead guitar parts. Leslie is one of the finest lead guitarists the Almighty had the good sense to create, but then, so is Pete Townshend.

We knew the Who were in town and arranged to go out clubbing with them. Humble Pie and the Who (minus Roger Daltrey, who didn't come along) had a fairly subdued evening at our chosen watering hole, Le Directoire. As usual back then, I was doing a terrible job of keeping up with everybody as far as drinking was concerned. I remember everybody buzzing around the club—literally—going around pretending to be a swarm of bees. Other than

that, I remember sitting between Pete Townshend and Steve Marriott, telling them both, in a bombastic fashion, how incredible they were and getting quite drunkenly emotional about it. They were very patient with me, and I vaguely remember Townshend saying to Steve, "Your little mate don't 'arf talk a lot," or something to that effect. I think they were both a bit surprised at someone outtalking them. They were still very much like big brothers to me, and I filled the role of pain-in-the-arse little brother admirably.

Keith Moon, however, treated me as he always did—like the best mate he ever had, which was how he treated everybody. As the night wound down, he invited me back to the hotel where the Who and their crew were staying—the Pierre at Fifth Avenue and 61st Street, just across from Central Park—to keep the party going. By the time we got there, it was just Keith, Chalky (our old roadie, who Pete Frampton had fired on our very first tour, and who was now working as Keith's driver), John Hammel, and I, who was, by this time, very much worse for wear. Keith was desperately trying to scrounge up a tape player from Who soundman Bobby Pridden, who had wisely retired to his room, which happened to be next door. Bob was having none of it, and kept telling Keith to piss off and that under *no* circumstances was he going to loan Keith his beloved portable cassette player. Apart from anything else, Bobby knew only too well what might happen to it should he lend it to Keith, not to mention the noise it would generate in Keith's hands. He wanted to get as much undisturbed sleep as was humanly possible, whereas Keith, while he wanted to do the same, was quite happy to wait until the end of their NYC stay to do so.

All of a sudden, I was overwhelmed with a strong desire to throw up. I asked where the loo was and was pointed in the general direction of two doors on the other side of the room. As I opened the door to what I thought was the bathroom, I let fly with a remarkable case of projectile vomiting… only to realise I had opened the wrong door and sprayed vomit all over Keith's clothes, which were hanging in what turned out to be the closet. Instead of getting angry about it, all Keith said, in his finest Noël Coward imitation, was, "Oh, don't worry about it, dear boy; I do it all the time." He then proceeded to go about the business of trying to dig his way through the wall into Bob Pridden's room—with a room service knife and fork. I didn't stick around long enough to see if Keith succeeded, but I found out later that apparently he did. Chalky was left with the unenviable task of cleaning up his old chum's puke. What a pal.

Chapter 12
Stone Cold Fever
June to December 1971

*In which we rock Hyde Park and inadvertently influence
Whitesnake and the Sex Pistols; tanks are aimed at us in
Germany, and our reception in Milan makes us cry;
we follow the Beatles at Shea, and there isn't a dry seat
in the house when Grand Funk follow us;
Pete Frampton wants to leave and go join the Who,
but Joe Walsh doesn't want to join us; and Steve
impersonates his own brother to put off Clem Clempson.*

Dee was famous for coming up with detailed master plans. As he proceeded to map out the immediate future, his enthusiasm gave it a palpable sense of certainty and was so infectious that we began to crave his "team talks." He could see the dollar signs flying around us, and he told us step by step how we were going to achieve his plans and cash in on them. We now had the keys to the car, he explained, and were about to drive it off into the land of the filthy rich. It was inspired stuff, delivered with the intensity of a Baptist preacher in a black church, spitting out fire and brimstone for all it's worth.

There were two powerful reasons why Dee would get so fired up about our future as opposed to those of the other acts he managed. In the first place, we were *his* band exclusively. He didn't have to share the commission with anybody, plus he made all the major decisions without the chance of another manager overriding him. He didn't have to play second fiddle to *anyone*.

The second reason was the one that really wound Dee up like a coiled spring: everybody had written us off. When he originally took us on, he was warned about us by just about everybody he knew, or even spoke to, in the business. It was the classic case of the red flag to the (in Dee's case) raging bull. Dee was a typical fiery Sicilian-American tough guy who you did not want to piss off, and he couldn't wait to prove all the naysayers wrong—and

Dee and the band backstage at Hyde Park after we just blew a huge hole in the stage that Grand Funk had to try to follow us on. It was our greatest moment up till that time.

even get into fistfights about it if he had to. He had developed a genuine fatherly affection for the four of us. "You're like a son to me" was one of his favourite sayings, and, in the early days at least, he meant it wholeheartedly.

As part of Dee's master plan, we were about to embark upon the biggest, most prestigious gigs we had done so far, starting in Los Angeles. We had recently completed the shows at Santa Monica Civic Auditorium, and we were playing as special guest on an ELP show at the world-famous Hollywood Bowl.

On this leg of the tour, photographer Shepard Sherbell was shadowing our every move, taking shots that were eventually used inside the live album. I didn't realise at the time just how important that man's photos would be to me for several reasons. First, having a photographic record of that whole summer helps me remember that the whole thing really *did* happen. Second, it reminds me of how closely knit our band and all the people surrounding us were. Third, it clearly shows the size of the audiences we were playing to; at Hyde Park alone there were almost 400,000 people. And finally, it shows just how good we, especially Steve, had become at handling big audiences without any visual aids whatsoever—it's just the band and our instruments kicking arse.

On a personal level, the photos of the Hyde Park show in particular portray my past, present, and future: there, all in one shot, are my father, Steve's mum and dad, Gala, and Liz Robinson, a friend of Gala's who was soon to be my girlfriend and later, as I affectionately call her, my future ex-wife.

Hyde Park was a turning point in our career. The size of the audience meant that, from then on, we never again had to support anybody in the

UK—we were always headliners. There were a number of musicians who saw us there, thought that the show was one of the best they had ever seen, and went on to become well-known in their own right, including Neil Murray of Whitesnake and Black Sabbath, and Glen Matlock of the Sex Pistols.

As the tour began to unfold, it seemed to get better (to quote the Beatles song), better all the time. After the Hyde Park gig, we decided to go back to the farm so I could finally get to know Gala on a more carnal basis and John Hammel could show Liz his etchings. But the best laid plans of mice and midgets sometimes go not quite as one would wish: John ended up with Gala having a grand old time, and I ended up with Liz, wondering which end was up. Liz was a lovely lady who was very attractive in a unique way. She had a Joan Crawford square jawline, Bette Davis eyes, a knockout pair of legs, and a great body.

It was around this time that a worrying pattern started to form. As I started to meet a more varied class of female, I began to develop an unnerving habit of proposing marriage to them, as if the gentlemanly thing to do were some weird rite of passage. Suffice to say, after Hyde Park, quick as a flash, Liz and I were an item, and I proposed to her soon thereafter. Jerry and Liz, boyfriend and girlfriend, then fiancé and fiancée—lickety-split, there we were. All my nearest and dearest were horrified, worried sick that she would come in and rearrange the entire farm—and all that sailed in her. And that's exactly what she proceeded to do!

The next leg of the tour was in Europe with Grand Funk. It included two memorable shows, again to huge crowds, one at the US Army's Conn Barracks in Schweinfurt, Germany, and one in Milan. The Schweinfurt show was staged outdoors in front of several thousand American troops stationed there in readiness for their tours of Vietnam, plus their families and friends. The audience were incredible; soldiers always are. The stage was built out of huge flatbed military trucks designed to carry armoured cars and small tanks. Four of the biggest tanks made at that time were used as follow spotlights; we had these monsters pointed at the stage, their huge arc lights shining straight at us for the entire show. It was intimidating, to say the least.

We then moved on to Italy to play a show at a football stadium in Milan. This was in the days of free concerts, and certain elements of the public had decided it was their right to get free tickets—even when the show wasn't free, as in Milan, where 40,000 people had already paid for admission.

On the fateful day of the show, all the paid ticketholders were let into the stadium without a hitch. There were riot police outside for crowd control, as there had been a build-up of free-concert-demanding hippies who were getting extremely agitated. The promoters, in conjunction with the police, decided, without much thought about the consequences, to give in to the demands of the freeloaders outside the stadium, opening the gates and letting them in. To add insult to injury, right before the police did this, they shot tear gas from outside the stadium, over the stands and onto the ground where all the law-abiding citizens who had paid were gathered peacefully, enjoying the show. The freeloaders came storming in, infuriating the people who had paid, and all hell broke loose between the two factions. It was the biggest fistfight I have ever witnessed.

Oh, by the way, we were on stage performing while all this was going on! The last straw for us came when a tear-gas shell came over the roof of the stands, rolled down the terraces, and stopped no more than 30 feet from the stage, with the wind blowing directly at us.

Dee and Bill—like us, affected by the tear gas—had seen enough. They sprang into action to get their boys offstage and into the relative safety of the dressing room. The distance was considerable, but they somehow knew instinctively what to do. Dee had us stand in a line, with the first guy putting his hand on Dee's shoulder, the next one putting his hand on the shoulder of the guy in front of him, and so on. Bill was at the end of the line, making sure we didn't lose anybody along the way.

Dee stayed calm through the whole affair, telling us to keep our eyes shut to minimise the effects of the tear gas, while he and his brother kept theirs open and got us to the dressing room. He then administered first aid to our eyes before finally taking care of his own. Dee was one of those men who always seemed to know what to do in a crisis, and he would do whatever it took to make sure we were not harmed. He and Bill were at the peak of their powers as a management team from mid-'71 to the end of the decade. They were the best of the best. They loved us, and we loved them.

The American leg of the Grand Funk tour, which included Shea Stadium, was almost upon us. It was the first time I had ever seen Steve Marriott nervous, God bless him. In fact, we were all crapping in our pants. By now we had played to some pretty big audiences, but Shea Stadium was very intimidating. For one thing, the Beatles had been the only headlining act to play there before the Grand Funk / Humble Pie show. Also, all the tickets had sold prior to us being added to the bill, so the possibility of a partisan crowd of Grand Funk fanatics booing us off seemed highly possible as far as we were concerned—and that spectre loomed large. But Dee had a sixth sense about such matters, and he knew better. He knew we were more than capable of the task at hand, and also that the only thing that could get in our way was us. He saw that we were getting ourselves in a right state over the gig and began to work on us, as a group and as individuals, making sure that each of us was suitably coached and made to focus on our separate tasks for that very special show.

In a dressing room around the time of the Shea Stadium show.

Shea Stadium was a strange place to play, simply because of the way they insisted you set up the stage. The stage itself was built over home plate, and the audience were not allowed onto the playing field. They could only occupy the regular seats, which in turn created a huge empty space between the band and the audience. It's tough enough trying to communicate with a crowd of that size at the best of times, but it's damn near impossible when there's an enormous void between you and them—the nearest audience member was the best part of a hundred yards away. To make matters worse, it was an early show, which meant we were going on in the late afternoon and playing our entire show in daylight, so we were not going to get the advantage of stage lighting. As Shea is a very large stadium in terms of height, not a lot of sunlight got in, and we were playing in a constant state of what seemed like twilight. As if that wasn't enough, the weather had been playing up all day, with rain developing one minute and sunshine the next. All those years ago, we did not have the technology we have today that protects you against the ugly possibility of electric shock in the rain. When it was raining, the only thing you could do to be safe was not play.

As it got closer to showtime, we made sure our limo was in the correct place for us to make a quick exit. That was a must because of all the bedlam that a 56,000-strong Grand Funk audience would create, plus we had been told they were going to both arrive and leave by helicopter, and we didn't want to inadvertently get in its way. As we did our soundcheck, we couldn't believe how small we felt on the stage. I couldn't help but imagine the Beatles on that same stage, using nothing more than a small PA system not much bigger than the one used to tell the crowd at a baseball game that someone's car needs to be moved.

When we were about to go on, Dee gave us the best dressing-room talk we ever had. He ended this epic speech with his favourite saying: "I wanna see a pint of blood on that stage!" Once he said that, we knew it was showtime.

We walked out onto the playing field and headed toward the stage, which seemed like a long distance away, but was probably only a few yards. As we walked up the stairs to the stage, the audience remained fairly quiet, which didn't surprise us but did make us a little apprehensive as to what would happen when we started playing. The adrenaline that rushed through me was intense as I looked out and saw this huge crowd in a city that was known to be tough on bands. We were opening for a band whose followers were notoriously partisan, and I completely forgot all the hard work we had put in at venues all over NYC.

Whenever we played a special gig in the NYC area, Dee had Scott Muni, the well-known and respected DJ, announce us. Muni knew what he was doing, and really helped break the ice at Shea, so once we started we could at least tell we had the crowd's attention. We played well and were wholeheartedly in the groove. At the end of our first song we got a polite response, which was far better than getting booed off—but we were not knocking them out. Then a piece of rock 'n' magic happened, courtesy of Steve Marriott.

Steve took a potential disaster and turned it around in our favour. It started to rain, bucketing down. This was not good. Back then, the usual response by any band was to beat a hasty retreat, and walking off in such circumstances wouldn't necessarily be held against you. Steve, however, wasn't going to let anything get in the way of him grabbing this audience by the scruff of the neck and making them ours. How he did it was priceless, a real Marriott special. As the rain worsened, Steve ad-libbed to the audience: "We don't care if it rains all night long! Nothin's gonna stop us from rockin' our ass off for you tonight!"

That might not seem a lot when you read it on a page, but when he yelled it at that huge crowd, the place went absolutely nuts. They were so bowled over by this cocky little man's bravado that he had them in the palm of his hand for the rest of our show. If I remember correctly, we played one encore but could have done several.

This was typical of the kind of brilliance that Steve would repeat many times over the next few years. His masterful ability to read a crowd and grab their attention was second to none.

The band were dying to get to Atlanta for a number of reasons. It conjured up all kinds of mental pictures of the Old South: the blues, *Gone With the Wind*, pawn shops selling guitars, Southern belles, Southern hospitality, and on and on. I, however, had only one reason to want to play there—the Playboy Club. Ever since puberty, I had dreamt of certain conquests that only a rock star or a rich bastard could accomplish. One was a nurse (in uniform, of course), then a stewardess (also uniformed), and last, but not least, a Playboy Bunny.

By the early Seventies, the previously successful chain of Playboy Clubs had started to hit a rough patch, the result of which was the closure of most of their number. But Atlanta had so far survived. So it was with extreme excitement that I went along to the Atlanta Playboy Club with our roadie, John Hammel. John, as the other bachelor in our midst, and I would always be partners in such capers.

The waitresses were all wearing the classic Bunny outfit, and in the dimmed lighting they looked sensational. They were polite, friendly, and off limits to the clientele—or so we were told. Not to be put off by a silly regulation like that, we both pursued a bunny each. As the night wore on, the possibility of hitting pay dirt was looking decidedly iffy; it seemed far more likely that we would go home alone. As the club was about to close, John gave up and said he was leaving, just as I had started to make headway. I said a hurried goodbye to John and immediately turned my attention back to the strawberry-blond beauty I felt I had a chance with. Sure enough, she told me to meet her in a coffee shop around the corner in 15 minutes, and, as the Bunnies weren't allowed to fraternise with the punters in the club, it was the only way the evening could progress.

As I waited at the coffee shop for her to show, it occurred to me that this could have been an easy way of getting rid of me. Just as I was about to give up, I noticed a nondescript girl coming through the door with a small rucksack slung over her shoulder. She started to walk towards me and the penny dropped: it was her! Amazed at her transformation, I managed to maintain my composure and tried desperately to hide my disappointment. She obviously had crossed this hurdle before, as the first thing she said was whispered in my ear: "Don't worry, I've got the uniform in my bag." Somewhat embarrassed by my lack of subterfuge, I was nonetheless thrilled by her upfront approach to copulation.

I have always been an admirer of American women and their approach to matters of the flesh. I can't comment on how things are today but, back then, there was a distinct difference between American women and their British counterparts. The British woman would put you through weeks of coy shyness and a "not on the first date" attitude that would sometimes last for weeks or even months. All this did was turn you into a liar par excellence— "Of course I love you, darling; I've almost remembered your name"—and cause your nuts to damn nearly explode. As a travelling musician, you didn't have time to sod about with all the niceties that a normal budding relationship would demand. You were always moving on the next day so, as a young man bursting with testosterone, you much appreciated the more direct "Hi, wanna fuck?" approach of American women like my Atlanta Bunny.

We took a cab out into the suburbs and were dropped off in a fairly decent-looking neighbourhood, although I must admit that, even in my horny gotta-get-laid mindset, I couldn't help but notice the fact that we had to travel through the ghetto to get to her house.

Once inside, we went straight to the bedroom and started to get busy. She told me to get my kit off and that she would be right back. (Note to my non-British readers: in this context, "kit" means clothes; I didn't have my drums with me at the time!) Off she went to the bathroom, and in no time at all reappeared in her Bunny outfit, minus the ears, which were, after all, surplus to requirements.

This friendship was hardly one that was based on lengthy conversations about each other's backgrounds; all I knew was that we were two young, single people who both wanted to get laid. I had no reason to believe otherwise until she mentioned, in a matter-of-fact way, that she had a boyfriend, but he was away and was not coming back for several hours. Although I had a twinge of apprehension, her assurance that there was nothing to worry about was all I needed to relax and enjoy what was happening. She was back to looking fabulous, and I was back to letting my little head do the thinking for his big brother.

Just as we were getting serious, there was a noise outside the front door that sounded like someone letting himself in. "Shoosh, he's home!" said the Bunny. "It's my boyfriend; he's home! "Quick, you'll have to go!" As pleased as I was that she had grasped the essence of the situation so accurately and was able to state the stunningly obvious with such precision, I still couldn't believe what was unfolding around me. I'm butt naked; she's dressed as a Playboy Bunny. In a display of quick thinking second to none, she scooped up what bits of my clothing were on her side of the bed, threw them at me, pointed to the window, blew me a kiss goodbye, slid into the front room, shutting the bedroom door behind her, and said to her boyfriend, "Surprise! I thought I'd give you a welcome-home present!" I have never got my kit on that fast. As I climbed out the window, thankful that the bedroom was on the ground floor, I caught a glimpse of a pair of work boots the size of small house. Not making their owner's acquaintance was fine by me.

As soon as I was far enough away from the house, I stopped to catch my breath and get my bearings. It dawned on me that I was right in the middle of the ghetto with no idea of my whereabouts or those of the hotel. I was on foot, and the natives were noticeably restless. As I started to walk—running would have brought attention to this little white boy—I realised that I didn't even know if I had any money with me. So, if I could find a cab, I would have to blag my way to a safe journey home, and American cabbies aren't known for their generosity of spirit—not in the low-rent part of town anyway. Just as I was about to give up hope, I looked skyward and said, "Now listen up. I know I have not been talking to you lately, but if you could see it in your heart to help me out of this spot, I would be forever grateful." As soon as I said that, from out of nowhere came an old, beat-up yellow cab.

The driver was a hippie with long, straight, brown hair parted in the middle, a full beard, and a thin face. Sound familiar? Having got over the irony of the cabbie looking like a certain saviour of worldwide renown, I was still overwhelmed by this cabbie being my saviour in a more down-to-earth fashion. I jumped in the cab, and, before I told him where I was going, he told me I was lucky that he came along when he did because the chance of a young white boy surviving for very long in that area on his own were not good. This cheered me up no end, as you can imagine. I proceeded to tell him why I was in the spot I was in and that I didn't even know where the hotel was, only that it was near the Playboy Club. He started to warm towards my plight, but I still had not told him that I had no cash. He asked me what I was doing in Atlanta, as I was obviously not a local, and I told him I was in a band called Humble Pie. He freaked right out, as they used to say: "You're kidding me! I don't believe it! You guys are my favourite band! I love you guys! Far out, man!" He was a real gem of a guy, and if he hadn't been there when he was, I could have easily been mugged—and killed for no apparent reason other than that the muggers were angry because I didn't have any money on me.

Between us, we figured out which Marriott the band were staying in, and, when it came time for me to pay him, he wouldn't hear of it. As much as I tried, he wouldn't take any money for the ride; he said it was an honour to have had a member of Humble Pie in his cab. If he only knew that I didn't have any money on me! I could have got the money for him by waking up half the hotel looking for the tour manager's room, but instead I took his name and put him and his wife on the guest list for that night's show. This was the first of many situations where dropping the name of the band got me out of trouble. The difference was that, this being the first time, it struck me how much our sheer hard work was starting to pay off.

When I told this story to Dee, I got a fatherly bollocking for sodding off without leaving any way for them to find me, and he told me what an extremely dangerous thing I had done.

If we thought we had been busy before, we had no idea what the word meant until now. Just when we were about to step up to the plate as headliners, Steve thought we would be able to kick back a bit. But management were on the "make hay while the sun shines" side of things, mainly because they had seen it all before and knew how fickle audiences could be. As for me, I was all for the "woik, woik, woik" approach. I wasn't married, and I could see the benefits of working hard now so we could earn and stash as much money as was humanly possible.

Pretty soon we were known as the hardest-working British band on the road. We went back and forth to the States, criss-crossing the good old US of A in six-week stints that entire summer. Including the shows in Europe opening for Grand Funk, we had been seen by approximately 2,300,000 people, and had left every last one of them literally screaming for more.

As is often the case, the band were the last to realise the potential success that the upcoming live album had to offer. We knew it was a great-sounding piece of work that we were very proud of, but it was, after all, a live album, and we had almost gotten used to albums that sold only in moderate amounts. With the exception of Steve, none of us had known any different, and it wasn't as if he had reaped any significant benefit from the Small Faces' huge record sales.

We finally came home to stay for a while at the end of the summer. The live album was soon to be released in the States, and we had earned enough on the last tour to bring home the first of many lump sums of cash. We each got $5,000, which doesn't sound like much now but was a nice little chunk (about $50,000 in today's money) back then. Plus, we had received the second instalment of the A&M money in the spring, so things were definitely on the up.

Dee was a great believer in using catch phrases, most of which he said with tongue firmly in cheek, and all of which he intoned in his big, deep voice in mock-Hollywood-gangster "I gave him an offer he couldn't refuse" mode. "I wanna see a pint of blood on that stage!" was his favourite. My own favourite was "Nobody leaves this group alive!" Little did he, or we, know how relevant that one would soon prove to be.

The Who were playing in London, and Peter wanted to see them. The problem was that we had booked a day's rehearsal out at Magdalen Laver, and Steve was insistent that we should rehearse. Back then, the Steve Marriott that we all had the privilege to work with was still extremely conscientious about rehearsing and his commitment to the band in general. He would not listen to Pete about going to the Who show; as far as Steve was concerned, not rehearsing was a slap in the band's face, and he would not have it. "Show up for rehearsals, or else" was his attitude, as Peter was soon to find out.

I recently discussed this crucial tipping point in the band's history with Peter to get his side of the story. He was kind enough to write up a few words and to let me share them with you here.

Over to you, Peter…

My mind was pretty well already made up that I was going to leave the band, but the "storm in a tea cup" over the rehearsal was the last straw for me. My actual conversation with Steve came about while I was meeting with our manager, Dee. He had flown into London to show us all the artwork for the live album, and I went to see him in his hotel. I sat and looked at the artwork and said, "It's wonderful; I really like it. But there's something I need to tell you, and you had better sit down… I'm leaving the band!"

Dee obviously couldn't believe what he had just heard. Once he had calmed down and listened to my reasons, he realized that this had been coming for some time. He could also see that my mind was fully made up. We then both decided that it was a good idea to call the band as soon as possible, so I called Steve right away. I could tell that he was extremely upset and hurt, and very soon he lost his temper. I could understand, but it was hard to listen to. Steve had always been there to encourage me, starting from the end of my Herd days. First my dream had been to join the Small Faces—I wanted to play guitar with him while he sang. Now I was leaving the band we had cofounded.

I learnt more about music from Steve than any other musician in my whole career. He truly was a huge inspiration and the best singer I have ever had the pleasure of picking my licks behind. I miss him terribly.

On reflection, this bust-up was an accident waiting to happen because, along with Steve's newfound onstage confidence, he had a somewhat heavy-handed way of dealing with people. There was some merit to his wish for us to be diligent in our work ethic, but, in this particular circumstance, a little give-and-take would have sorted everybody's needs. It wasn't as if we needed the rehearsal: we were tight as a drum. And we weren't pressed for time: for the first time in the band's existence, we had an extended break from the road, so we could rehearse at our leisure.

But there was no give-and-take. It was a classic Mexican standoff that neither side was about to back down from. At the end of that heated phone call with Pete, Steve basically said, in a loud voice, "*We are going to rehearsals—we'll see you there!*" Then he hung up. Peter never showed. When we got back to Beehive Cottage, there was a message from Dee that Peter had left the group. Just like that, we were a three-piece.

I was devastated, and so was Greg. Steve, on the other hand, was giving one of his all-time great performances as the wounded but not defeated warrior who was going to carry on with the fight, no matter what.

Peter's reasons for leaving were hardly surprising. Steve's overwhelming side had finally got the better of Pete, and he just couldn't handle it any longer. There were some musical differences as well, but not nearly as much as was made out by the press at the time. It had been said that the band was getting too heavy for Peter's taste, but I for one never did buy that, for one simple reason: the heavier material that we had started to develop was initially brought to the table by Peter. The idea that he was into softer rock 'n' roll was nonsense—unless you consider "Stone Cold Fever" or "I Don't Need No Doctor" soft rock.

It is true that Peter went on to have some big solo hits with acoustically based songs, but he also had that sort of song in Humble Pie, so it didn't make any sense that he would leave the group over the choice of material. It might have been a small contributing factor if he looked ahead and thought Steve might start vetoing his songs based on their softer approach—but why would he fear that, as Steve had never done that before?

So there we were with an album that was about to be released that heavily featured two guitar players playing off each other, and now we only had one. It was time to start figuring out what sort of guitarists were out there, and whether or not they would fit in.

Our first choice was Joe Walsh, who had just left the James Gang, or was about to. Dee called Mike Belkin, the promoter from Cleveland, Ohio, who we had worked for many times, and who was also Joe's manager. He presented the offer to Joe, but Joe gracefully declined, as he was putting his Barnstorm and solo projects together and wanted to see them through to fruition. On reflection, I think Joe made the right choice—he had great success as a solo artist and, later, mega-success when he joined the Eagles. Musically speaking, it would have made for an astonishing line-up with Joe in Humble Pie, although I suspect that hotel chains across the US would have run for cover.

The next candidate was Mick Abrahams, who we knew a bit from Jethro Tull. He had left Tull and formed his own band called Blodwyn Pig. Mick was a lovely guy who we thought would fit in perfectly, and we were really looking forward to playing with him, so we set up some rehearsals at Magdalen Laver. It hadn't taken us long to write some new material, and even though we were only firing on three cylinders, it was sounding pretty damn good to me. We started to play a couple of the new songs—"The Fixer" and "Sweet Peace and Time"—that we had worked up into near-as-damn-it arrangements so that Mick could get an idea of what we sounded like and what he would have to fit into. He listened while we ran through the two songs, and once we had finished, a remarkable thing happened. Mick said, "That sounds amazing! It's such a big sound! There's nothing I could add to that—it's too good! I couldn't improve on it!" His guitar never left its case.

We were starting to get a little nervous, as the live album was about to be released both in England and the USA, and we still didn't have the right replacement for Peter. Then, out of nowhere, Steve got a phone call from a guy he'd never heard of who played guitar in Colosseum, a band Steve had never heard. Steve had no idea what this guy's playing was like; all he knew was that Colosseum were a jazz-rock fusion band, which wasn't exactly our cup of tea. Steve told the guy that he—Steve—was out, and that he was Steve's brother. He said he'd give Steve the message, and that Steve would get back to the guitarist. This ploy gave Steve time to find out more about the guy. So he went to the local record shop and found a Colosseum live album. When he listened to it at home, the record did nothing for him—except that he was knocked out by a guitar solo in a long, slow blues.

As far as Steve was concerned, there was no need to look any further; this guy was the bee's knees. His name was Dave "Clem" Clempson, and he was a brilliant blues guitarist, which was precisely what we wanted.

Clem could not have joined the band at a better time. Everything was on the ascent. We couldn't believe our luck: all we touched now seemed to turn golden. The live album had just been released and was doing well on both sides of the Atlantic. The sales figures coming in from the States were sounding like those of a much more successful band. We had got used to Dee telling us about other bands' successes as examples of what we would eventually get if we worked at it—and that we had most definitely done. The album was shooting up the *Billboard* chart in the US, and was doing such good numbers that it went gold long before we arrived in the States to promote it. Also, we had booked a small tour of England and Europe first to get the new line-up worked in, and to our amazement we were doing great business there too. Finally we had it all going on.

I was amazed at what was happening to us in England, as we had not really worked there that much. But Dee reminded me that we had played in front of almost 400,000 people in Hyde Park only three months before and had knocked them out—more strong proof of his methods working to perfection.

The first gig of the new tour was at the Roundhouse, London. It was packed to the rafters, and the crowd were going nuts. There were a few other bands on, but all the audience wanted to see that night was our little lot, and they virtually booed the other bands off.

The place officially holds approximately 3,300 people standing, but on this night there were definitely more than that; you could not move. All of our old friends showed up to cheer us on. Dave Gilmour came to see what the band was like now. We had a real mutual respect for each other's music; I never missed one of his shows, and he never missed one of mine.

The excitement kept building. Every time our head roadie, Dave Clark, came into the dressing room, he told us how much the crowd had grown or how they were yelling for us during another act's show. Then, finally, when our equipment was being put on the stage, there was a huge roar as the crowd saw my bass drum with the Humble Pie logo on it.

The audience were pushed up like sardines against the safety barrier in front of the stage. Prior to this night, we had played many, many shows where the crowds were much, much bigger, but this was something special, outstanding in every way. It was the first bona fide headlining gig we had done in England since Dee took over as manager. The sound was great. The audience didn't quit from start to finish. Steve was at his fiery best, and we didn't put a foot wrong. That gig is up there on my list of the best we ever played. From there on down, we never played another show in support of someone else, except at some big festivals where we were in the "special guest" spot. In less than two years, we had gone from being perceived as a bunch of one-hit teenyboppers to one of the most dynamic hard rock 'n' roll bands out there.

Early press photo with Clem (first left).

Chapter 13
C'mon Everybody
December 1971 to May 1972

In which various slices of the Pie are treated to Rollers
and Rolexes; big slice Steve Marriott does his crust in
with Steve Stills; the Whisky burns and we go up in Smokin';
Procol Harum has enough class not to turn a greener shade
of envious; and things go worse with coke.

The live album was gaining momentum; in just a few weeks, it had gone gold in the States, and it wasn't long before it did the same in England. We had succeeded in making the transition from a pop group that the girls came to scream at to a highly respected, rocking blues band. After the Roundhouse and a few other shows around the UK, we went over to Europe to test the waters there. It was more of the same in Germany, Belgium, Holland, Italy, and France—we played to sold-out crowds that went nuts. All of this work gave us a chance to get the new show with Clem up to scratch so we would be well and truly ready for our first tour of America as a headliner.

Dee and Frank had decided, based upon how well the live album was doing, to book a short headlining tour, just 10 shows, in our strong markets. In case we were not ready, the last thing they wanted was to send us out there on a massive tour playing to half-empty houses. They reasoned that if it didn't quite live up to expectations, it wouldn't be a devastating blow; we could regroup and go to Plan B. The only problem was that we didn't have a Plan B. So it was up to us to deliver the goods so that we could start 1972 as a bona fide headliner.

As we got ready to go on the tour, we were getting fantastic reports of the box office activity: some of the bigger shows were already sold out. Dee had promised a large cash lump to each of us if the tour sold out, and we could afford to buy those two Rolls-Royces for him and Frank. It was a wildly exciting time for us, as each day we got a call from Dee, telling us that yet another show had sold out and that we were getting ever nearer to the whole tour being sold out.

Meanwhile, Liz was busy turning Green Farm into a cattery, which I didn't mind too terribly, but I had heard rumblings that she was neglecting the dogs in favour of the cats, plus committing a few other indiscretions that I will not go into.

We had already written a couple of new tunes, "The Fixer" and "Sweet Peace and Time," plus we had a cover of an old Eddie Cochran tune, "C'mon Everybody," and an old Ray Charles blues called "I Wonder." Between those and the songs we planned to keep onboard from the show we did with Peter, we had the basis of our new show.

Clem was fitting in perfectly, although he was of a nervous disposition. If he'd had the time to absorb what was happening around him, he probably would have blown a fuse, but it was all happening at such a pace that he wasn't able to let it get to him. All he could do was keep his head down and hope the pace of things would change after a little time had passed, which it did. It got faster.

There were a few things we had long since promised ourselves we'd do once we became headliners. As I had lost my driver's licence over my drink-drive bust during the Entwistle album sessions, I had planned to hire my old mate Chalky to be my driver as soon as I could afford it, and now was the time.

The tour consisted of 10 dates in 15 days, primarily in cities up and down the Eastern Seaboard: New York (two nights), Boston, Philadelphia, Pittsburgh, Washington D.C. (two nights), Long Island, and Asbury Park, New Jersey, where we had a band supporting us called Dr. Zoom & the Sonic Boom. The good doctor was a young local lad better known to his mum and dad as Bruce, and he made Mr. and Mrs. Springsteen very proud about five years later.

The tour didn't go any farther west than Detroit. Every ticket for every show was sold out, and we could have sold many more. The first dates were in NYC at the Academy of Music, the venue that took over where the Fillmore East had left off when it closed in 1971. It was very similar to the Fillmore, but held a few more people. It was there that Clem, who had never been to the States, got a pretty rude awakening to life in the big city, USA style.

We were not a band that spent hours soundchecking. We would just make sure that everything was where it was supposed to be, have a bit of a play, and leave so the roadies could get a chance to relax a bit before showtime, rather than driving them nuts by blasting away for no apparent reason.

Clem's stage fright was palpable and sometimes intense, so, as we arrived for our soundcheck in the middle of the afternoon on a sunny winter's day, the last thing he needed was some kind of sudden shock to his already nervous temperament. But as he was walking down the typical NYC alleyway that led to the Academy's back door, a guy came out of nowhere and literally fell into his arms. The guy's coat came open, and Clem saw that he was covered in blood; he had been stabbed several times. As soon as he could, Clem raised the alarm with the backstage crew and got his first glimpse of NYC's blasé attitude towards such matters; the crew were used to such occurrenc-

Poster ad, mistakenly stating that "I Don't Need No Doctor" was on Rock On. *(It also states that* Rock On *was our second album, when in fact it was our fourth, although only our second on A&M, who, of course, created the ad.)*

es happening all the time. Understandably, this incident shook Clem up something fierce, although, to his credit, it didn't interfere with his performance—he went on to play a blinder that night.

In this early period, when Clem had just joined the band and all this success was coming at us, it seemed like life without Peter would be fine, but in truth it never was quite the same. Don't get me wrong; we had a lot of good music in us yet—in particular, *Smokin'*, the first album we made with Clem, and the first year of shows after its release.

We had the best of times on this first headlining tour. Everything was going exactly to plan or better. This time we came solo (without Mandy), which was a blessing, as it allowed the band to really bond in much the same way the original line-up did when she wasn't around.

We sailed through the tour, knocking everybody out. The audiences were going nuts every night; it was encore after encore. We were causing such a ruckus that everybody was now really paying attention to what we were doing. All the naysayers were suddenly turned into "Ah, see, I told you so!" bandwagon-jumping twats.

Consistency was our strong suit. We never did a bad show, and our worst show was far better than the best efforts of most. It was a joyous experience to be part of, night after night. As you can probably tell, it was something

I am very proud of. It has taken me many years of keeping quiet and not bragging about it to finally say, yes that's right—we *were* one of the very best in the business.

One of our first dates after NYC was the Spectrum in Philadelphia; it went on to be one of the biggest venues we would regularly play, although this was our first time at the top of the bill. Philadelphia was considered a very good barometer to measure your success nationally; those bands that did well there usually went on to do well all over the country. It was one of a number of markets in the Northeast and Midwest that you could almost set your watch to; others included Detroit, Chicago, Cleveland, Pittsburgh, Baltimore, and Boston. If you did strong business in one of those places, you could rest assured that you would do so in a large majority of the rest of the big cities and most of the secondary markets, too.

Once we finished the show in Philly, we had a particularly steaming party, as we had just scored in a big way. I always found out the gross amount we earned on every date we ever played and wrote it down in a ledger book. This gig was our first that broke the $30,000 mark; we brought in $33,500, which was a strong sign of things to come.

The tour was our first to make a decent profit. At some of the venues we played, we could have done at least two more shows, but Dee and Frank did not want to get too ambitious at this stage of our career and were definitely erring on the side of caution. By the end of the tour, the live album had gone gold and was showing no signs of slowing down any time soon.

After all the expenses and commissions were paid and the money for the two Rolls-Royces was taken out, we each brought home $10,000 (the equivalent of about $100,000 in today's money). When I got home, I pulled out that hefty sum and plonked it on the kitchen table. Expecting a positive reaction from Liz, how you do when you go away for two weeks and come back with $10,000, all she said was, "That's all very well, Jerry, but when are you going to get a real job?" at which point our relationship was effectively over, although we stayed together for a little longer before we called it quits.

I had installed Chalky at the farm in readiness for my return, and I now enlisted his help in buying a car we could use as band transport. With the money from the tour, I was able to buy the perfect car for the job, an immaculate early-Sixties Mercedes Benz 600 in dark maroon, with a blue-grey leather interior, plus curtains to keep the prying eyes of our adoring fans at arm's length. Everything inside this beautiful brute was run off an intricate hydraulic system: the windows, the seats, and all that good stuff. We also fitted it with a state-of-the-art audio system that sounded magnificent.

Although the tour had been a test of our pulling power, it was also done to help promote the live album, which of course featured Peter on lead guitar. We were coming up with ideas for the all-important follow-up, and we had made sure that we played most of the material from that big success, while also playing a good portion of the upcoming album. We

Humble Pie

L To R   Jerry Shirley   Steve Marriott   Greg Ridley   Dave "Clem" Clempson

probably could have ridden on the strength of the live album alone for some time to come, but we were impatient to move on to a new studio album with Clem on lead guitar.

When Clem joined, he had brought with him a tremendous amount of talent as a lead guitar player, and also, to his undying credit, a tremendous amount of praise regarding Steve's lead guitar abilities. Peter had also done that, but it had been three years since the original line-up got going, and as Peter and Steve had marked their territories a long time ago, it was a fresh shot in the arm for Steve to hear an obviously talented guitarist point out his strengths on the instrument. The biggest compliment Steve ever got about his playing came via Clem, who had hung out with Jimi Hendrix on a couple of occasions and had talked shop with him. Jimi had told Clem that the guitar solo on the Small Faces record "Whatcha Gonna Do About It" was his all-time favourite, which, coming from Jimi, was as good as it gets.

So, with a newly invigorated style of twin guitar playing, the band went about the task of putting together the material for the next record. As I mentioned, we had already played some of the new songs on the road—which, if possible, is always the best way to do things—so there was no need to do any rehearsals to speak of. We just kept getting better and better, and nothing seemed to be getting in our way… yet.

The destruction that cocaine can wreak upon perfectly good people and their relationships had not yet been done to us and our families. If anything, the stuff was *enhancing* everybody's relationships—with their spouses, within the group, and even with our businesspeople, primarily because they were all indulging in it as well. It was without a doubt a classic case of "Everybody's doing it, doing it, doing it," to quote the old song.

For the time being, Chalky was serving dual roles: living at the farm and driving me around, and also driving the band to and from the studio to record what would become our most successful record.

We were still very much on the ascension and, as such, were bulletproof. So it was that when we started work on our next album, we were at the very top of our game. Everything was going just the way we wanted, all of Dee's predictions were coming to fruition, and our record deal with A&M was in the black so that everything we released from now on, if we left the deal the way it was, would mean instant profit. All things considered, 1972 was fast stacking up to be our best year yet.

We decided to record at Olympic as we always did and to use "Irish" Alan O'Duffy to run the board. Glyn Johns had committed to another project and was not entirely enamoured with the direction we were taking, to say the least. Peter's departure had influenced his thinking somewhat, and as much as he appreciated Steve's talent, Glyn, like many others, found Steve too much to handle, and he did not relish the idea of working with him again.

The songs we had road-tested were all recorded in the first take or soon thereafter, and the new songs we wrote as a band, which began as jams in the studio, were also, in the main, one-take wonders.

One of our best-known songs came out of nowhere. "Hot 'n' Nasty" started with Steve jamming away on the Hammond organ and me behind the kit. As soon as Clem and Greg heard what we were playing, they joined in, and, before we knew it, we had the back track on tape.

The same was true of "(I'm a) Road Runner / Road Runner's 'G' Jam." The track consisted of two songs put together into one long jam, on top of which Steve sang the words of the Junior Walker hit. We gave it two titles so that we could pick up publishing royalties from the long "Road Runner's 'G' Jam" section.

We were working so well and so quickly that we had the majority of the back tracks recorded in less than a week, with two exceptions, "Old Time Feelin'" and "Hot 'n' Nasty." The overdubbing stage also went by in a week or so.

Shortly after we started to record "Old Time Feelin'," we were interrupted by a street fight outside the studio. Chalky and I had popped to the pub to pick up some supplies, Ted the roadie was washing Greg's Bentley, and everything seemed normal. As Chalky and I walked back towards the studio, he shouted some friendly banter across the road to Ted. Before Ted could think of what to say back, out of nowhere appeared six Asian men who obviously thought that Chalky was shouting abuse at them. They came across the road clearly looking for trouble, and I saw no point in giving them the chance to utilise their obvious numeric superiority. So I told Chalky to get inside the studio and lock the front door on them, hoping they would calm down, lose interest, and move on.

Instead of just doing that, Chalky had to get brave. Once we were in the studio, safe and sound, and I had called out for help, he decided to try to get these lads to move on. He took the fire extinguisher off of the wall and opened the glass front door just a little to squirt the extinguisher at our Asian friends, who immediately saw the advantage and pulled the door open. They then proceeded to grab Chalky and drag him through the door, breaking the glass and pushing him down onto the long slivers that were still stuck in the door frame and pointing dangerously skyward, straight at his anus.

At that point, I knocked out one of the attackers and went at it with another. As I held him in a headlock and punched his head, a piece of his hair came off in my hand; this tough guy was wearing a wig. He then gave up all attempts at fighting, so I let go and he dropped to the floor.

By this time, reinforcements had arrived in the shape of Greg, Cyrano, Dave and John (the other two roadies), and, of all people, Alexis Korner. Alexis had to be the staunchest pacifist you could possibly imagine, but there he was, God bless him, wielding a mic stand as a weapon. Greg did the same with his Precision bass. Cyrano distinguished himself by jumping into the middle of the affray and shouting some ridiculous bit of supposed karate-speak that one of his mates had told him to use at the start of a fight. But all it did was to attract the attention of one of the Asian gentlemen, who turned on Cyrano and administered one of the best roundhouse kicks to the head I have ever seen, making Cyrano and his alleged knowledge of karate look very silly indeed.

I was very lucky to come out of this mini-battle more or less unscathed, with only a couple of bruised and slightly swollen knuckles. It could have been much worse, as I learned much later in life when I took up karate myself—not the smartest thing a drummer can do as a pastime—and caused many injuries to my hands.

It was all over, but Chalky was nowhere to be seen. When he finally reappeared, he told us what had happened. Apparently, in the midst of the action, he had slid out of sight into the graveyard adjacent to the building that housed Olympic. While the brawl that he instigated raged onwards and upwards, he was hiding behind a gravestone and planning his escape to the hospital that happened to be just a block away from the melee. So when he showed back up, he was already suited and booted with the appropriate bandages and medication to take care of what can only be described as a second asshole.

When this storm in a handbag was over and done with, we went back to putting together "Old Time Feelin'," an old New Orleans-style rollin' piano blues that Steve and Alexis had dug up from the formidable library of traditional blues they kept in their heads. Steve never failed to amaze me with his knowledge of the blues and old country music; he didn't know just the titles of the songs, he also knew all the lyrics, chord sequences, and so on. His personal mental jukebox was enormous and a tremendous resource when you were stuck for an idea.

There were a number of reasons why recording this album was such fun. We had a new guitar player who was putting a slightly different bluesy slant on the sound of the band; we were coming off an extremely successful tour of the States; and we were, all of a sudden, flavour of the month in good old Blighty, which was a status that we hadn't previously held. We were now attracting all kinds of stars who would drop by from Studio No. 2 just to see what was happening and/or to see how much coke we had.

It was extremely gratifying that other big names wanted to be our Steve's best mate all of a sudden, and it was especially great to see the way that Steve handled it. He was, by then, a past master at sorting out the men from the boys. If their motive was musical, he would spend an inordinate amount of time and trouble getting to know them. If, however, someone was only interested in being his buddy for self-serving reasons—"Hey, look at me; I'm Steve Marriott's best mate!"—he would spot it a mile away. His response was usually hilarious and sometimes a bit cruel, but always fair.

One of the wonderfully over-the-top examples of the Steve's-best-mate syndrome involved a big American rock star, and happened when we were doing the session for "Hot 'n' Nasty." From start to finish, our work on this song, one of those jams that immediately took shape, was special. After we wrote and recorded it in less than 30 minutes, all that remained to be done was Steve's lead vocal. At that point, Chuck Kaye, A&M's head of  publishing, stopped by to show his respects and get high; we were happy to oblige. After the mind-altering substances had been smoked and snorted, we played "Hot 'n' Nasty" for Chuck, and it knocked him out—and that was without the lead vocal. When we asked what he thought about it, he replied "Smokin'"… and so we now had the name for our new album.

In the meantime, we needed Steve to sing the lead, if for no other reason than so Chuck could hear the finished track. Steve had told me earlier that he hadn't got a grasp on what the lyrics should be just yet, so I sent him off to the toilet. So there was Chuck Kaye, watching the hottest band on his label send their lead singer off to the loo—to do what, he couldn't imagine. Finally his curiosity got the better of him, and he asked, "Why have you sent him to the john?" "Because that is where Steve writes his best lyrics," I replied. When Steve returned, words and melody at the ready, Chuck must have wondered what Steve had eaten recently when he started to sing, "Hot 'n' nasty."

A little later, Steve Stills, who was recording in Studio No. 2 next door, popped his head in to see what was happening. We were all huge fans of Stills and his recent solo work. He had just finished his day's work, so he and his percussionist, Joe Lala, wanted somewhere to work off their adrenaline.

What followed was definitely one of rock 'n' roll's finer moments of instant musical brotherhood, when that was working for the best of everybody concerned. We were at the tail end of the day's session, and all we needed to do was mix the track. Wrong. Stills was armed with a large pill bottle containing at least an ounce of the best coke in town. We knew what he had without asking, because we were also getting our gear from the best source, we had the exact same stuff, and we had just about the same amount—although ours had taken a severe beating, as it was supplying a larger number of nostrils than were present at the Stills session, which consisted of only him and Joe recording some overdubs.

I struck up an immediate rapport with Joe, him being a percussionist and all and, to my utter amazement, found out that he was a huge fan of Humble Pie. It was one of the first "I'm not worthy" moments in my long career as a drummer. As we settled into our mutual-respect drummer chat, we almost didn't notice what the two Steves were up to. We did see that they were getting along famously and that they were getting stuck into their respective stashes of coke. They seemed to be matching each other snort for snort, and pretty soon it was apparent that they were in for the long haul. The first voice of concern came from Joe, who said, "Oh no, here we go. He's found a new playmate." "Yeah, but all they seem to be doing is working on some backing vocals," pointed out uninitiated me, to which Joe replied, "Just wait and see; this could go on for *days*." After a long contemplative pause, he added, "I don't know what your guy is holding, but my guy has got at least two days' worth. So if your guy's got about the same, we're in for a long ride."

He was spot on. After hanging in there for a considerable length of time, I finally got to the end of my tether and decided to throw in the towel. I noticed that Joe was also getting ready to call it a day, so I asked him if that meant that his Steve was getting to the end of his fuse. His reply stunned me: "Are you kidding? He's just warming up!" Our Steve was not going to be outdone in the "who can keep going the longest" stakes, and, as he had been doing most of the providing, he was determined to keep going, if for no other reason than to help Steve Stills burn as big a hole in his own stash as he had in our Steve's. I had a vested interest in that side of this coming together of two mighty midgets; you see, Steve's stash was not exactly his. It was, in fact, mine. So I wanted to see what would happen, whether my mate would outdo Stills.

Once we had run out of coke and our supplier couldn't be found, I had to go. Chalky, who had to drive that big old Mercedes and me home safely, went over to Stills and asked if he could have a snort for the road, which seemed fair enough, as Chalky and I had been putting out the lines for him all night. At this point, Stills showed us what he was really made of—he looked at his ginormous stash of at least a half ounce and said, "Sorry, man, I'm getting a little low. I can't help ya." Ah, superstars. You gotta love 'em.

Chalky and I finally left after the two Steves had been at it for 12 hours straight, which was in addition to their own sessions that had also run for about 12 hours. They then kept going for a further *48 hours*, God bless their cotton socks. The end result for the backing vocals was simplicity itself: a catchline that had more hooks than Jane Russell's bra. They layered that one line over and over, singing, "Do you get the message?" and it arguably made the difference between the song being a hit or a miss. So, in spite of his miserly ways with his drugs, Steve Stills turned out to be more than generous with his musical talents.

I knew we were onto something. It just felt right. Nineteen seventy-two was standing up to be a right-on-the-money time for good old Stumble By. We were off and running. Feets, don't fail me now.

Steve had a song he had been working on for some time. I was particularly familiar with it, as he often came to my room to ask what I thought of a certain rhyme or middle eight, or used me as a general bouncing board for some "What do yer think of that?" type of help or encouragement. This is often the role that a songwriting partner fills on one particular song, while he will be a full-on collaborator, maybe writing the words and some of the music, on the next.

As things had gone so horribly wrong with Steve's previous songwriting partnership, with Ronnie Lane, I was overly careful not to step into waters that were untested from my point of view. I had to make it painfully clear that I was not interested in getting *any* credit unless I had written 50% or more of the song in question. Still, although it was a privilege to be the one who Steve solicited an opinion from on this particular occasion, it was just my luck that this would be the one song that I would have been very grateful to get a share of…

Dee had recently told Steve and me a cute story about a street fight he had with another motorist in Manhattan. The guy had threatened Dee with a crowbar and Dee, in legitimate self-defence, had punched him once, knocking him out. The police were called, and Dee and the other guy were hauled in front of the judge a week later so that the judge could decide who the guilty party was. The other guy arrived at court bandaged up to the eyeballs to try to make a case for damages, and the judge bought it, to the extent that he offered Dee a deal: either pay the fine for assault or get "*30 days in the hole.*" At this point in the story, Steve cracked up laughing and made a mental note, as all great songwriters do when they hear a word or a phrase that has potential.

He had been messing with this thing—an homage to the Stones way of elegant debauchery—for a good while, and it had been just sitting there minding its own business until now. Steve had been recruiting my help for the druggy references; I couldn't imagine why, but at the time I took it as a compliment.

The beginnings of the song go all the way back to when we were on the road with ELP leading up to the tour on which we played the Hollywood Bowl. We were set to play a gruelling four-day stint at the Whisky a Go Go, but we only got as far as the first night, when we were handed a three-day rest, not because we couldn't play, but because we no longer had a club to play in.

After our show on the first night, we were in the dressing room when some LA woman staggered in and passed out on the couch. Nobody knew who she was, which was a shame because she was a real cutie, not quite a knockout, but close. The trouble was, she was so stoned on downers that she wasn't winning any popularity contests. When it was time for us to clear the dressing room, we left, and security helped her to her feet and out of the club.

The next thing I know, it's about four in the morning, and my phone rings and wakes me up. It's our head roadie, Dave Clark, and he tells me that the Whisky has gone up in flames, the whole building destroyed. Miraculously, though, all of our equipment had been saved by a very efficient fire brigade, who apparently were Humble Pie fans. They managed to cover our gear with their fireproof blankets while they attended to the fire, which was so intense that mirrors and all forms of glass were reduced to melted warps of their former selves.

We were told that an electrical fault had caused the blaze, although we suspected that it might have been a touch of "Italian lightning." Years later, however, we found out that it was actually caused by Madam Barbiturate. Apparently, when she had collapsed, the lit cigarette in her hand fell down the back of the couch. Nobody noticed. It sat there for a little while, started to smoulder, and eventually let rip. Those big old couches back then were filled with horsehair and other highly combustible substances, and you could probably get high on the smoke when they burned.

We were very pleased with this unexpected time off. We shouldn't have been, as the owners, Elmer and Mario, were very good friends of ours who had done nothing but help us and be kind and supportive. But man, was their club hard work, plus we had been on the road *forever*.

During this break, Steve came to me with many of the one-liners he was putting together to make up the basis for "30 Days in the Hole": "Black Nepalese make you weak in the knees"; "Newcastle Brown will sure smack you down"; "Live on the road, where there's a new highway code"; and my personal favourite, "Urban noise 'n' Durban Poison." He had been working on the lyrics over a period of months, adding a line here, a line there, until he had a whole slew of them, and he finally made some sense out it all when he heard Dee's story. I had the great privilege of being Steve's board to bounce his ideas off on a number of occasions, but none was more fulfilling than with this song, both because of what it became and because of what I *didn't* ask for or expect to get from him for being there when he asked me the simple question, "Here, Jel, what do you think of this?"

As we grew closer to completing the recording of *Smokin'*, we were also setting up a small tour of England to get our feet wet with a new show that would include all the material from the album. The problem was, we were exhausted, Steve especially. We didn't have to do much other than reschedule some of the shows, but it did mark the start of a pattern—brought about by the heady mix of success, money, and cocaine—of pushing ourselves to the limits and beyond.

Steve was developing a "fuck the gig" attitude, and I was determined to gently nudge and cajole him into getting rid of it. It just had to go, mainly because the hangover from the Small Faces' no-show reputation had adversely affected Steve's own rep.

Your reputation in show business will make you or break you. No matter how big or successful you may become, if you continue missing shows, you will not last very long at all. Dee was so good at the coaching side of management that he had all but eradicated that sort of behaviour in Steve. It was amazing to witness the change that Dee instilled in Steve and his professional behaviour during that period. Steve was truly devoted to Dee and Frank from the beginning, so that once we got to this stage where there was so very much at stake, the intensity of their commitment to each other and to the band was profound, to say the least.

Nineteen seventy-two had got off to a stunning start. Everything that we had worked so very hard for was coming to fruition, and then some. *Smokin'* had come out of the box living up to its title; it was on fire. There have been bigger beginnings for rock albums, some much bigger, but most of the massive out-of-the-box sales were still in the future, with rare exception. This, for us, was by far the best start we had ever seen, and it was right on the heels of the live album, which was still on the charts.

Once we got some rest and recuperation, we went ahead and did the British dates, which went down a storm. We were on such a roll; it truly was one of the peaks in our career, and I have always cherished it.

My relationship with Liz just wasn't built to last, and by now it had well and truly ended. The final straw for me was when I had to negotiate a place in the bed that did not disturb the cats, all 12 of them, just so that I could get some sleep.

As we readied ourselves for the next big tour of the States, I made sure that all the plans for the farm, while I was away, were completely in place. The shows were sold out or as close as can be, night after night. We were starting to take steps to ensure our long-term financial well-being, and nothing seemed to be going wrong. We still, however, had Cyrano with us, which was a potential nightmare, as it was by now fairly common knowledge that he and Mandy were more than just good friends. Plus, Dee couldn't stand the guy, so plans were made to replace him at the end of the tour with Mick Brigden, our buddy from Mountain, who was doing this tour as our lighting director while Mountain were off the road.

I had made that challenge/bet with Dee back in the Fillmore days that he couldn't make me a dollar millionaire by the time I was 21. He had taken it up with both hands and always got into these "I'll make you a million yet; how much longer do I have?" wind-ups that were all good clean fun between a manager and one of his lads. But as this tour continued, he was getting more and more serious about the possibility of making it happen on or before my 21st birthday. If he was gonna pull it off, he now had just under a year to do it.

Dee's renegotiation of our A&M contract was a work in progress; the third and final advance to us was due in May, and it was his intention to have a new, much bigger and better record deal in place by then. He had been filling us in on his progress every now and then, but as the album kept selling and going further up the charts, he was getting more and more excited about completing the deal.

Somewhere around the middle of the tour, we were playing a show in Baltimore, and Dee flew in with some "incredible news." We were all summoned to his suite and sat down to hear his announcement. He told us that the new deal was not only gonna make a dollar millionaire out of me, it was gonna do so for all four of us!

He went on to explain the ins and outs of the deal, which was so sophisticated and complex that none of us rock 'n' rollers understood a word of it. In fact, once he got into using words like "cross-collateralization," even the most polite of us were finding it hard to keep a straight face, as we didn't want to offend him. He had just gone to bat for us and apparently brought home the bacon; the only trouble was that it was written in Chinese as far as we were concerned. All we wanted to know was, "Where's the blow?"; we were ready to celebrate. Even if we were not quite sure exactly what it was we were celebrating, it sure sounded important, and we were freshly awash with the vital information that, apparently, we were all filthy rich.

I remember waking up the next day, looking in the mirror, and saying to myself out loud, after my huge smile had dissipated, "You know, Jerry, nothing has changed really. You still don't have all this money in the bank or in a form in which you could spend it, so get over yourself and keep it on the island." I then called home and ordered a brand-new Range Rover.

In the meantime, the tour kept rolling on. With *Smokin'* now a great success—it was in the *Billboard* Top 10, at Number Eight with a bullet—dates were added to the tour, and so it kept getting longer. I had bought a secret weapon to help me keep going: a gram of crystal methedrine that you only required a tiny snort of to keep you moving all day. To give you an idea of how strong this speed was, I bought it at the beginning of the tour and did the last of it when we eventually reached Hawaii some eight weeks later, and I was giving more than the occasional snort to anybody amongst us who asked.

Sometime around the middle of the tour, we had our triumphant return to Cobo Hall to look forward to. As we flew into Detroit for the show, Cyrano decided to behave on the plane in a fashion that guaranteed us unwanted attention at the airport when we landed—and could have cost us the tour. It was a close call as to which part of his behaviour sealed our fate, but it was probably a combination of abusing the flight attendants, being generally loud and obnoxious, and threatening the flight engineer when he came back from the cockpit to try to calm things down.

As soon as the plane pulled up to the gate, our reception committee came on board so that the flight staff could identify all of us. Steve quietly said to Bill, "The cocaine is in my wash bag." His wash bag was in the overnight bag that Bill was carrying for him, thank God.

Once we were taken into separate rooms to be interviewed, Bill Anthony earned his right to be part of our management for the rest of our existence with his pure, unadulterated brilliance in the art of quick thinking. When the security guys started to search everybody's luggage, Bill, knowing that there was the best part of an ounce of the purest cocaine that money could buy in Steve's bag, immediately grabbed the bag as if it was his own, then proceeded to throw a complete wobbler. He complained loudly that this was a severe breach of his rights as an American citizen, that he had done no wrong, and that it was his job to get us to Cobo on time—otherwise there would be a riot, as there was a sold-out crowd of 14,000 waiting for us to perform for them that evening. He managed to do this with such class that they didn't know what hit them.

The attention that Bill drew to himself, and therefore away from us, saved the day. He was not the one they were interested in, and, because he was an American citizen, immigration was not an issue. And, as he had done nothing wrong, he had the right to free passage; even if they were going to detain us, he, at least, should be allowed to proceed so that he could go and inform the promoters that we may not get there in time, and therefore help to organise control of the riot that was almost certainly going to occur.

It was Oscar-winning stuff. Bill looked squeaky clean and all-American, and he knew that, so long as he and his luggage went through, the biggest problem we faced would be solved. The immigration officials, Feds, and local law enforcement who had all been summoned to deal with this dangerous band of nefarious malefactors were, thanks to Bill's tirade, extremely unsure of what to do. As all our work visas were kosher and their extensive search had come up empty, they ended up giving us a strong warning against that sort of behaviour on aeroplanes, as it was a federal offence and could have put us in deep trouble. If they only knew.

We were extremely grateful to Bill. All that Cy had done was further seal his fate, as he had in four short weeks managed to almost destroy our entire career in America *twice*, between this and an incident involving Chalky, which isn't worth going into now. He was remarkably lucky to keep his job until the end of the tour.

The album was now at Number Six with a bullet and had been officially certified gold, which meant that in less than six months we had achieved two gold albums, each of which was fast heading towards a million albums sold. Plus, A&M had recently bought the rights to rerelease our first two Immediate albums as a double-album package called *Lost and Found*. All of the paperwork for the new A&M deal had been drawn up, and it was just a matter of us signing on the dotted line to instate the new contract in place of the old one. As we were on our way to California to play sold-out shows at Long Beach Arena, the Sports Arena in San Diego, and the Swing Auditorium in San Bernardino, it was the perfect opportunity for a contract signing get-together with all the bigwigs from A&M, Dee and Bill, and, of course, us little lot.

We had arranged to stay at the Beverly Hills Hotel to mark the importance of the occasion. Each of us had a bungalow to himself, which was a long, long way from sharing rooms together at the Holiday Inn on 57th Street in NYC when we first came to the States almost four years before. Dee had arranged for his suite to be decked out with plenty of food and drink, and we made sure a certain South American stimulus was present in abundance so that everybody could converse readily and freely in celebration

Outtake from Smokin' *cover shoot.*

of this momentous occasion. When we arrived at his suite, we all sat cross-legged in a circle on the floor, and watched as the accountants and lawyers got all the paperwork together and passed it around for us to sign one by one in an orderly fashion—while the only thing we were interested in was the large porcelain plate that had a small mountain of coke on it for us to indulge in. We didn't care nor understand what was written in the paperwork, other than the fact that it was suffering from this nasty-sounding condition called cross-collateralization. We all hoped it would get better soon, but in the meantime, "Do ya wanna line?"

When a band signs a record contract, it is their responsibility to have it vetted by their own independent counsel; nowadays it is the law, I believe. These contracts were very complex and should have been examined by someone on our side. The only problem was that we used the same lawyer as Dee, and none of us ever read this legal complexity that was put in front of us—we just went ahead and signed it, smiled for the camera, went back to the Peruvian love dust, and continued with our ongoing career as good-time Charlies. Don't misunderstand: there's a lot of hindsight in the summarising that I'm doing here. Believe me, we were having the time of our lives back then. We didn't think we needed to go over those papers, because we implicitly trusted everybody concerned. Their job was to take care of all of that stuff while we went about the business of kicking ass onstage, which we did better than just about everybody.

We were young and still extremely naïve, but it wouldn't be long before we understood the importance of reading and understanding everything you ever sign. Even more important, you should only sign something when you are stone cold sober, otherwise you only have yourself to blame if it doesn't work out quite the way you thought it would.

One of the most interesting things about Dee and Bill as managers was their history. The stories they would tell about their time with Tony Bennett were priceless. You could also learn a lot from their stories—there was always a lesson regarding decorum and the dos and don'ts of true professionalism.

As we were getting ready to leave for Hawaii, Bill told us that Tony Bennett was also staying in the Beverly Hills Hotel and had agreed to meet us. We pulled the limos around to the bungalow that Tony was staying in and all filed out to go have a meet-and-greet with the man. He was outstanding, the most gracious gentleman I had ever met. He asked us how things were and showed genuine interest in our end of the street, which of course was a million miles away from his, although he made us realise that they really weren't that far apart, that we were, after all was said and done, in the same game. As he asked us if Dee and Bill were looking after us properly, he looked at Bill like a father asking his son if he has done his homework, and Bill replied in the way a son would. There was obviously a lot of respect between these two men, and I don't know anybody on God's earth who has a bad thing to say about Bill Anthony or Tony Bennett.

We were in Hawaii to play two shows with Procol Harum. Our first show got such a powerful reception that when Procol went on after us, it was heavy going for them, bless their hearts. They were a great band, but they had a very stoic appearance onstage; they just stood there and showed no emotion whatsoever. There's nothing wrong with that, but by the time we had finished with the audience, they were wound up like a coiled spring and wanted to keep on rocking, not just stand there and get deep, man. Once the house was cleared after the first show and the venue was ready to let the next show's audience in, Procol came to us and said, "Listen, why don't we open this show, and you go ahead and close it," to which we replied, "No problem." We therefore went in Hawaii from opening act to headliner all in one evening.

After the tour ended, I travelled to New York and went to Dee's office to pick up some gifts and goodies to take home and distribute to the troops: some gold records, some cash, and a couple of gold Rolex watches for Clem and Greg. The cash was our tour bonus of $20,000 each; as Steve had already taken his bonus with him, I had to bring the remaining $60,000 for myself, Clem, and Greg. I felt like a street flyboy from the East End of London, with gold watches up my sleeve and a briefcase with a zipped-up side pocket full of cash. I wasn't sure what would happen if the Customs and Excise guys stopped me and searched my luggage; the good news is that they didn't, and anyway, once the cash was securely deposited, the appropriate taxes were duly paid. So off I went with Chalky, who had come to pick me up in the Mercedes.

I was so glad to be back in England, on my way home. Chalky had made sure the car was nice and clean and looked like a million bucks. After he filled me in on what was happening at the farm, how much work had been done, and how all the animals were, I got a little nervous because he seemed a bit suspect and edgy, as if there were things he didn't want to tell me. He mentioned that he had uncovered a beautiful red-brick fireplace in the kitchen and worked hard to try to bring it up to scratch before I got home, but he hadn't found the time to finish it. I should bear with him, he said, as it was a work in progress, and he left it at that. He also told me how he had found an excellent source for cocaine, and that the price was only £240 an ounce. With that, he reached into his pocket, handed me a small bottle and a spoon, and said, "Try this." It was of the highest quality, but I started to think, "Hmm, what is he doing talking about ounces, and why is he so on edge about everything?" It wouldn't be long before I would find out.

When we got home, I discovered that Chalky had managed to completely destroy what was left of the fireplace once he had got all the plaster that was covering it off. He had chosen the night before I was due home to attempt this harebrained idea, so there was still a thick layer of brick dust lying all over the kitchen.

To say I was annoyed would be an understatement. I was livid. A good friend of mine, Jack McCulloch (the older brother of Wings guitarist Jimmie McCulloch), had stayed at the farm with Chalky to try to give a helping hand; he didn't know what to say other than to tell Chalky that he shouldn't have messed with it. Once the shambles was cleared up and Chalky was suitably castigated, all was forgiven, especially when the real culprit was revealed: a large quantity of cocaine. Chalky had, without my knowledge, purchased an ounce of it for my homecoming. The trouble was, he had gone and got his nose in it, so that there was only less than half of it left. Suddenly, all was clear; he had got himself well and truly engulfed by the stuff, and all his irrational behaviour was explained in an instant.

I went through my mail and saw a letter from a local farmer, who complained that my Mercedes was being driven around the small farm roads "so fast that it was throwing gravel up in the face of any poor, unsuspecting pedestrian," and that "if the driver was working for me, I'd give him a severe bollocking." I should have fired Chalky right there and then, but he was an old friend, so I chose to give him a strong warning, tell him that if it happened again, etc., etc., and leave it at that, hoping he would shape up. Sadly, he didn't, and eventually I had to let him go. I loved him like a brother. I just found out that he recently passed away, having lived a happy and productive life far away from the rock 'n' roll business, which just doesn't suit everybody; it's as simple as that.

Steve and Jenny arguing was nothing new, but what they were arguing about had changed, and the way they went about it had become much more aggressive. Steve had taken to getting physical with Jenny in fits of rage, which was in complete contrast to the way he was before he started to get recognition for his efforts onstage in America. Unbeknownst to us, he had stopped being able to turn his stage persona off once he got home.

It started to become apparent that Steve wasn't handling the rigors of the road nearly as well as we thought he was. When he was on tour, his phone bills were always big, but recently they had become enormous. I found out that things weren't good, because both Steve and Jenny were using me as a shoulder to cry on. Steve would tell me how things were getting tough for him because he was on the road all the time. Jenny would confide in me that she sometimes wished Steve was on the road *more*, as he had become a nightmare to live with. I couldn't argue with her, because he had changed, especially now that the studio we were having built above his garage was nearly finished. When he was home, all he wanted to do was spend time in the studio, making music and getting high; the thing was, where cocaine goes, trouble follows, as we all were soon to find out.

BEST SEAT IN THE HOUSE

By now, Steve was clearly in trouble, or at least his marriage was. As far as I was concerned, building the studio right there in his house was a huge mistake, and it led to a myriad of problems that unfolded as we went along on our journey. The people who were starting to show up at the studio were pretty grim; they were often dealers who would hang around 'cos they thought it was cool, whereas Steve was happy to have them hang out so that he could get free cocaine. The most dangerous thing to come out of this situation was Steve's penchant for staying up as long as five days or more in a row, without so much as a catnap.

Fortunately, these horrors were not yet a daily occurrence, and, for all their arguments, Steve and Jenny were still dedicated to each other. We had a lot of touring to do during that summer, and the offers that were coming in were much huger than anything we had previously experienced. We started doing stadium shows as "special guest," which at the time was the best place to be. You didn't have the responsibility of the headliner, as far as the box office receipts were concerned, but you still got paid a king's ransom to get up there and kick some ass. In our case, we always did exactly that, often to the chagrin of the headliner.

Chapter 14
Hot 'n' Nasty
May to November 1972

In which we ramp up the showmanship, and Alice Cooper's crowd love it to death; Steve loses his wife—and his rag; Rod Stewart and Ronnie Lane get in each other's faces; I meet Cindy, incidentally; we leave Ozzie speechless and make Jeff Beck jump up and shout; and the Blackberries sing sweetly, but sour grapes nearly ensue.

The summer tours in 1972 were marked by two changes in the way we took care of business. First, we were playing a lot of stadium shows; second, our mode of transport altered radically, thanks to our new tour manager / lighting director, Mick Brigden. During Mick's time with Mountain, he had hired a private Learjet for the band, and he was now telling our management that it could be cost effective compared to the price of first-class airline tickets for everybody. It also made for a much less stressful way to travel and, in some cases, made it possible for us to play dates that we otherwise might not be able to do when regular commercial flights couldn't get us there on time.

Our maiden Learjet voyage was to Pittsburgh to do a stadium show with Alice Cooper. For Steve, it was love at first flight; he was absolutely wild about it and said to Dee and the other powers that be at Bandana, "If I could travel like that all the time, I would be able to tour as long as you like." This was heavy stuff coming from a guy who had previously been scared to death of flying.

The show at the Three Rivers Stadium in Pittsburgh stands out in my mind as one of the greatest we ever did. It also epitomized Steve Marriott at his very best—and when he was at his very best, there was not a living soul who could do what he did better than he.

A ramp that protruded about 25 feet from the centre of the stage had been built for Alice. No one told us that we could or could not use it, so, as we were going down a storm, Steve chose to go out onto it at the end of our show and get the whole crowd wound up like a spinning top.

It got a little hairy when a bunch of people from the audience climbed up and started to jump and shout and shake it all about; as soon as they did, everybody backstage panicked, and so did little me, because this ramp was only designed to carry the weight of one person, and we were now looking at a potential nightmare. We managed to get to the end of the show without incident, and the crowd were ready and waiting for Alice to start his show. As we started to wind down in the dressing room, Alice came in, leaned against the wall, and said, "How the fuck do you expect me to follow that?"—and with that, he went and did his show. It was such a gracious way to behave, given the circumstances. By the way, he also went down a storm. What a pro.

The management had made some concessions in the way we were booked, so as to accommodate Steve's deepening paranoia about his home life. On the one hand, he would be on the phone encouraging Jenny to go out more as an answer to her fears about being at Beehive Cottage all on her own. This was not because Jenny disliked the place—on the contrary, she loved it. She had several dogs to act as guard dogs; the trouble was, they were not trained in any way to protect her, so their barking only worried her and made her think there was someone out there. It simply is not healthy for a young lady to spend all her time isolated out in the middle of nowhere; no matter how many dogs she has for company, after a while it will get scary.

On the other hand, if Jenny did go in to London to visit friends, Steve would start accusing her of all sorts of things, and would end up screaming at her about her imaginary transgressions.

To sum it up, Steve was becoming impossible to live with; whether at home or away, he was hard work. He was even starting to be that way on the road with his best mates: the band, as well as Dee and Bill. Dee especially had become a father figure to Steve, spending hours and hours with him, locked in a bathroom or a spare bedroom of the Party Suite, in the company of the gods of cocaine. They weren't doing anything bad whilst in this self-imposed lockdown, and others could sometimes be granted admission. The conversation at these meetings of the minds consisted of the usual cocaine-driven rearrangement of the world as we know it, coupled with Steve's paranoid ravings about what his wife was or was not up to in his absence. This was also where his wish to do solo work started to take shape.

Since Steve's Learjet epiphany, we knew we had really arrived. Being able to afford a big suite wherever we went and a Learjet to get us there

Aerial view of Beehive Cottage.

was, to quote Eddie Cochran, "something else." We would hire a suite in our hotel so that we could come to the party and leave when we wanted to, as opposed to the party coming to any one of our rooms. Steve saw the opportunity to get a Party Suite for himself by taking it over as his own, and, as he was always the one who was up the longest, it made sense for him to have it. Besides the suite, the other requirement for one of these parties was a snorting contest, whereby a line of coke about a foot and a half long would be chopped out along the top of a table to see if you could snort it—and I don't remember any band member or Dee ever failing to succeed in this endeavour. So it is hardly surprising that we would reinvent the wheel every night after we played.

It's all very well to play stadiums and festivals as the drummer in a tremendously successful rock 'n' roll band, but the most important job I had that summer was to act as my father's best man.

About a year after Mum died, Dad had started to see a woman called Jo. He had wanted to get out of the family house as quickly as possible, and was also trying to avoid all the local widows who were trying to snag him, but he had known Jo and her husband for years, and she had lost her husband at roughly the same as Dad lost Mum. Jo owned the local garden centre, which was in need of some help. So she and Dad decided to combine their

Dad's wedding to my stepmother, Jo. Can you spot the drummer?

resources, live together in her house (which was attached to the garden centre), and use Dad's money from the sale of his house to start making the garden centre a better place in which to do business. Shortly after Dad moved in with Jo, they announced their engagement. We were thrilled for him, as Jo was known to us and because he would have something to work on—redoing the garden centre was right up his street.

On the day of the wedding, I knew that Steve and Jenny were in trouble —both of them had come up with excuses as to why they wouldn't be coming. Jenny had gone up to London to get away from Steve for a day. Steve just said he wouldn't be able to make it and that witnessing a wedding might be a bit too much for him at the moment, but he wished Dad and Jo all the best. Angus was in India on the hippie trail and wouldn't be able to get back in time; his wife, Peggy, came in his place. After the ceremony, we went to the local pub for the reception.

Less than an hour into the reception, I got a message to call Steve—who knew where I was because the invitation we had sent him included the pub's address—as soon as I could. When I phoned him, he was beside himself, mumbling on about Jenny leaving him, which, at the time, was nonsense. She had gone to town to meet up with Chrissie Shrimpton, her friend and fellow model, and do some shopping. Chrissie was Steve's old girlfriend, so I guess that got his paranoia working overtime. He was desperately trying to find his wife because not knowing where she was, even though he had told her to get out more, was driving him nuts. He kept asking me to come over to Beehive Cottage to help him figure out what to do, and could I bring some booze and some blow to ease the pain? I tried to make him realise that I was at my father's wedding reception and that I couldn't just get up and leave, but it wasn't registering with him; he wanted me to get over to Beehive, pronto. I told Dad what was happening, and, bless him, he said, "Get over there, son. If Steve is hurting that bad, you should go."

When I got to Beehive, the first thing Steve wanted to do was get high, then he proceeded to pour his heart out to me. I didn't know what to do, so I just listened for what seemed like hours. Then he said something that really shook me up—he asked if I would call Chrissie's house, pretend to be a heavy, and tell her that if she saw Jenny again, she would be in some serious trouble. He kept on and on about it until I finally agreed to do it, and off we went to the nearest working phone booth. I went in, dialled, put on my best tough guy voice, and, while Steve looked on from the car, I had a serious talk with… the speaking clock. I made it look like I was strong-arming Chrissie, and all the clock would say in return was, "At the third stroke, it will be two thirty-five and ten seconds… Beep, beep, beep."

After this episode, Jenny went home from her shopping day in London and was none the wiser. Steve finally calmed down, and things seemed to be on a much more even keel—for now anyway.

While we were in England, we had a couple of festivals to play; one was in the Midlands at a town called Lincoln. Slade were on the bill, and Ian Wallace, a fellow drummer and a good friend, was there—I can't recall which band he was playing with.

Steve was on particularly good form at the festival. This was the first time that we had played in front of such a huge audience since we scored so heavily at Hyde Park on the Grand Funk bill. The reception we got when we walked onstage was fit for the return of a conquering hero. England was obviously thrilled to see their old favourite Steve Marriott back in front of a great band, playing music that they loved. The performance he gave that night was breathtaking; he was at his pinnacle, and he not only played for the audience, but also with them, making them do whatever he wanted them to do.

That might not seem like a big deal, because it is commonplace in today's live music scene, but, back then, what with the hippies and their beloved progressive rock—or, as we would call it, thinking man's rock—it wasn't that often that an audience would go nuts and let their hair down, so a band like us, with such strength up front, was a breath of fresh air. Steve wasn't about to let an audience sit on their hands; he would use every trick in the book to make them remember us and forget whoever else was on the bill. It was also at this festival that I started to notice a phenomenon whereby all the other musicians on the bill would pack the stage wings and watch us, not moving an inch while we were out there kicking ass. Professionally, Steve was back on top.

Ian Wallace came back to the farm to celebrate Steve's return to form with me and Chalky. I had bought an ounce of top-grade Peruvian love dust for £250 just before we had gone up to the festival, so there was a large amount left. The three of us had a deep and meaningful drive home to the farm; amongst other topics, we discussed my position in Humble Pie.

Cocaine will make you say and do almost anything that you would not say or do sober. As we drove back, Ian, God bless him, said something that was a perfect example of this. He told me he could do my job better than I. I was amazed. Then he spent the next 48 hours helping Chalky and I put a big hole in the cocaine. After the second day, he had to get back to London, so we drove him to the station and bid him farewell. Several years later, I went to see Steve, with Ian as his drummer, play a gig in the States near the place where I was living. After the show, Ian took me to one side, apologised for what he'd said, told me that playing drums behind Steve was not the cakewalk he had thought it would be, and congratulated me for having done it so well.

I continued on with the party and was still indulging in the rocket fuel when I had Chalky drive me over to Greg's house. Sitting there at Greg's, I decided—to this day, I still don't know why—that all this snorting had to go, for me anyway. I looked at the quarter ounce that was still in the bottle, put it down on the coffee table in front of me, and said, "Here, Greg, have fun. I'm done." I remember the look on Greg's face that seemed to say, "I'm glad you said it; you saved me having to do so." I let Chalky stay at Greg's; Jenny Roff, a dear friend of mine, drove me home and looked after me for a couple of days.

I didn't stop using until a long time after this, but I did stop going on long binges. I couldn't stand the way that staying up with no sleep made me feel: completely hollow, as if my entire soul had been ripped from within. Empty.

There are so many cool venues to play during festival season in the States. Just about every major market, as well as some secondary ones, had some sort of permanent facility that was originally built for orchestras playing either classical music or big band stuff. We were in the first wave of rock bands that opened the door to playing these places, which today are commonplace venues for rock shows and are known as "the sheds." They usually seat about 20,000 people, with the first 5,000 seated under a covered area, and the rest on a grass hill that rises up on an incline away from the stage. These facilities all have a festival atmosphere to

Newspaper concert ad from '72.

them, and the sound in them is perfect. We played a number of them in that summer of 1972.

It was curious that the other band who had a similar reputation then for giving the audience a good time were Steve's old compadres the Faces, who had become big in their own right—and Rod Stewart, bless his heart, had become really huge as a solo artist. We were booked on one festival in the Pocono Mountains, along with the Faces, ELP, J. Geils Band, Badfinger, and Three Dog Night, amongst others. The attendance was huge; they stopped counting at close to 600,000 people, which made it the biggest rock festival so far. But the evening's entertainment soon went south when, thanks to the weather, the whole thing became a nightmare.

Helicopters were shuttling the bands back and forth from the Holiday Inn, where we were all staying, to the festival site, an enormous oval stock-car raceway. All the top bands were due to go on when it got dark. By then, unfortunately, it started to rain periodically; worse than that, it was getting so foggy that it was becoming impossible to get the bands to and from the site, and equally hard for the audience to see the bands at all.

Before we were taken to the gig, there were already problems brewing about who was playing when. Nobody wanted us to go on immediately before them or after them. We were told that the Faces wanted to avoid either scenario, and that their manager suggested that Badfinger be used as a buffer between us and them. This did not go down well at all with Dee; although he was nothing to do with Badfinger's management, he was not about to be party to such miserable behaviour. I remember seeing Rod Stewart and Ronnie Lane in a heated argument on the balcony of the Holiday Inn. They could have been arguing about football for all I know, but, as we were told that the Faces camp was split between the desire not to follow us and for us not to follow them, when my young mind saw these two yelling at each other, it was easy to surmise that this split really did exist.

With all this backstage bullshit going on, Dee had a slight advantage that had the potential to affect the whole show: he managed or represented several of the bands that were still to play. Humble Pie, ELP, and J. Geils Band were all his, whereas the Faces, Three Dog Night, and Badfinger were managed by others. The highlight of the management squabbles was watching the Faces' manager, a little gay guy called Billy Gaff, running for his life away from Dee, tripping over his own feet, and landing face first in several inches of mud. If he had foolishly decided to stand his ground and duke it out with Dee, we would have had to bail Dee out of jail for attempted manslaughter. Dee was a man you wouldn't want to piss off; he was famous for his hair-trigger temper, which, in today's world, would get him sued and/or jailed several times over. I have to say, though, that he would only lose his rag over something that was clearly detrimental to one of his acts, as opposed to getting physical just to throw his weight around. Dee couldn't abide a bully, and, if he found himself confronted by one, he would do his level best to put him in his place.

Once we were at the site, we just wanted to get on with it. With all this politicking going on around us, the various managements who were involved were suddenly made to focus on just doing the show because the longer they took sodding about, trying to satisfy all egos involved, the more likely they were to end up trapping their acts in the confines of Pocono Raceway indefinitely—the fog that was forecast was now becoming a reality. I cannot remember the exact final order of play, but I do recall ELP going on directly after us and the Faces some time after that. In the meantime, the fog was getting thicker by the hour, and all we heard about the end of the show was that when Three Dog Night, the actual headliner, and the Faces before them, to a certain extent, played to the greatly reduced crowd of 200,000 people, the fog was preventing anybody past the fifth row from seeing what was happening onstage. The newspapers reported the next day that when Three Dog Night finally went on, it was seven o'clock in the morning and, unless you were lucky enough to be in the first row, you didn't see a thing.

We definitely had the best spot on the bill because the audience could at least still see us and it hadn't got super-cold just yet—although I have seen footage of us playing "I Don't Need No Doctor" at this show, and there Steve is, wearing an overcoat in the middle of summer.

I was somewhat saddened to see the reaction of Steve's former bandmates when they saw him. He went with open arms to greet them, but, with the exception of Kenney, who was his usual kind-hearted self, they chose to give him a bit of a cold shoulder. It was heartbreaking to witness, considering the fact that they had actually prospered from Steve leaving them when he did. It had been rough for them in the beginning, but once they knuckled down to the job at hand, they went on to become one of the biggest bands in the world and were selling more tickets and records than we were—and, if you take into consideration Rod Stewart's solo career, they were miles ahead of us. So I would have thought that by then the hatchet would have been well and truly six feet under. Oh well, boys will be girls.

The next outdoor show we were scheduled to play was in Saratoga Springs, settled in the foothills of the Adirondack Mountains in eastern upstate New York and famous for its place in the racehorse fraternity. The show was oversold, so that the capacity crowd of about 25,000 people was bursting at the seams and raring to go.

The album was still in the Top 10, and we had two singles taken off it as what would today be called airplay singles; they weren't necessarily put out to generate their own sales, but more to perpetuate sales of the album. The first, soon after the album was released, was "Hot 'n' Nasty"; the second, about three months later, was "30 Days in the Hole." The latter was somewhat butchered by a record company guy who edited out an offensive line. (I can't recall for sure, but I think he may have excised the bit about the "greasy whore.") It made us laugh out loud when we heard what he had done, then we rejected it out of hand and thought no more on the subject. It turned out that they released the single anyway, and I was glad they did, simply because it gave the album even more legs than it already had. So way to go, A&M.

This gig personified everything that was good and great about our successful run. It was a beautiful night for a rock 'n' roll show, and you could tell that the area had become one of our strongholds. Many New Yorkers head upstate in the summer, especially to the Saratoga area for its natural springs, horse racing, and gambling. It felt like we had uprooted our NYC fans and plonked them all down en masse in Saratoga Springs. After the opening act were done and their equipment was cleared from stage, as soon as the crowd saw my drum kit—which was my pride and joy, as I had just had it delivered from Ludwig—they went berserk. It wasn't just a roar at the beginning of the show; it was a continual roar that went from strength to strength.

By now we were closing the show with "30 Days" and using "Doctor" as the encore. But on this occasion, by the time we got to the end of "Doctor," the audience would not let us go. The only song we hadn't played yet was "Hot 'n' Nasty," so we finally acquiesced to their demand for more and played it for the

A gig in Gaelic Park, the Bronx, where Joe Satriani pretended to be a roadie so he could see us. He has said that show influenced him to become a musician.

first time in front of a huge audience. We could literally feel the earth move under our feet, and before you could say "midget," there were waves of audience members jumping up onto the stage to join us, until, before too long, it was downright dangerous. There were people jumping up onto the drum riser and making it move around in a way that it was not designed to do. At one point, a guy and his girl grabbed onto the tom-tom that was mounted in a holder on top of the bass drum and used it to stop being knocked off the riser and trampled underfoot. In doing so, they pulled the tom-tom right out of its holder and all but ruined my brand new kit.

We had developed such a strong reputation in the first six months of being a headliner that we were stuck in an unusual position. On the one hand, big headliners didn't want to have us as a special guest in the middle spot of their show, because, while we were guaranteed to boost their box office, they were not inclined to be blown off their own stage. On the other hand, we weren't quite big enough just yet to headline the stadiums—but we were selling out the theatres and coliseum-sized places, which suited us fine, thank you very much. Through all this, we didn't care—just give us a stage, and we'll do the rest. Everybody in and around our camp deserved to be proud of what we had achieved, and while Steve was not a man to brag or get all full of himself, he was immensely proud of the band at that time in our career.

Angus had come home from India with a nasty morphine habit and checked into Harlow Hospital to withdraw from it. Some good came out of this; until now, since Mum died, Dad and Angus were not seeing eye to eye at all. Dad had got into the routine of visiting Angus—and doing it sober, thankfully—when one evening he walked into the small four-bed ward that Angus was in. The nursing staff were running around like crazy trying to look after the three frail old men, all in their eighties and nineties, who occupied the other beds. The nurses were giving them oxygen and generally helping them with breathing disorders, while Angus was lying there with this cat-that-got-the-cream grin on his face. When Dad asked him what was going on, Angus told him that the old guys hadn't believed him when he told them he could light his farts, so he gave them a practical demonstration of flatulence ignition. However, because he was coming off all that morphine, he had a lot of gas, and, as a result, he was blowing blue flames a yard long out of his ass. The subsequent belly laughs nearly killed his ward-mates. What a way to go!

It was around about now that Steve's unpredictability reached new heights. To be fair to him, he had, as I mentioned earlier, been promised an extended break to help shore up his marriage and get his home life back on track. But these assurances were given prior to a huge offer that came in out of the blue.

I am telling this story not out of any kind of sour grapes; I let those feelings go a long, long time ago. I am telling it only to illustrate just how out of kilter we had become. We were having almost a whole month off during this period when we were at our most successful, and therefore strongest in terms of our bargaining power, which is usually *not* the time to put your foot on the brake, but rather to woik, woik, woik. That said, for the long-term good of the whole team, it was adjudged to be more important to help Steve in any way we could, within reason, to put some footings under the walls of his home life. What was a week here or there between friends to help him mend some fences at home, right? Wrong. Out of nowhere, a promoter made us an offer we couldn't refuse, if we were dealing with a full deck, that is. We were asked to play four festival-size shows over a long weekend at $75,000 dollars per show, with all expenses paid plus first-class air tickets.

It didn't take a genius to work out the maths to see that our little quorum of dramatis personae would earn, after commissions and expenses, at least $54,000 each, which, in today's money would amount to at least $540,000. Steve said *no*, there would be other offers, and his extra time out was *that* important to him. I was too dumbfounded to cry or otherwise react; I think we all were. We're still waiting for those other offers to materialise…

We were only talking about rescheduling a few days off. When I discussed it with Jenny years later, she said that Steve never told her about the offer and that had she known, she would have told him to go and would have gone with him if need be. This was the kind of irrational behaviour we were starting to have to deal with: the man could moan about getting horribly ripped off one minute, then go and throw away offers like this the next.

Me and Sadie.

The even bigger heartbreaker is that the extra time Steve had off was not put to good use at all. He spent most of it either sodding about in his half-built studio or running roughshod over Jenny and not making any real effort to put things right. The Steve we all knew and loved so deeply had gone, and gone somewhere none of us seemed to be able to reach. It was fast becoming a tragedy of Shakespearean proportions.

After this, we all went about the business of at least enjoying an extended time at home. I was about to get my provisional licence back, so I decided to mark the occasion the same way that every self-obsessed young hedonist does: I went and bought a BMW 3.0S. When I got the licence, I started to really enjoy the fun of driving a different car each day. Talk about flash, dear oh lord, what a cocky little sod I was—and I have to say I loved every minute of it. I had overlooked one minor point, though, but I didn't let it get in the way of all this fun: I still hadn't passed my driving test so that I could get my full licence.

The next tour of the States would turn out to be the best of the bunch and the most profound in its effect on my personal life. We were scheduled to go back to Texas, which was always a highlight of any tour in more ways than one. We had shows scheduled in Houston, Dallas, and San Antonio, and then a trip into Louisiana to play New Orleans. Dupuy Bateman, a close friend of the band, met us at the airport in Dallas to inform us that all the Texas dates were sold out and that we were about to break box office records in Houston at the Sam Houston Coliseum and in the Dallas / Fort Worth area at the Civic Center in Irving. And the dates in San Antonio and New Orleans date were already all but sold out.

When we went onstage in Houston, the huge crowd went berserk, giving us just about the loudest response I could recall us ever getting so far. They kept getting more and more involved, and Steve was at his masterful best. He was the master of crescendo and dynamics in general; the way he could control a crowd and get them to do whatever he wanted was a joy to watch and be part of. For every move he would make, it was my job to follow him:

louder now, then quieter, and with lots of ad libs. From day one, he and I always had a sixth sense as to what he wanted to do in an ad lib. It was one of those uncanny things that, from the very beginning, the whole band had with each other. Peter and Steve had it, Pete and Greg, Greg and Steve, and Greg and I *always*. We two had that glue between us, and once Clem joined, he picked up the telepathic thing that was a trademark of our band and today remains a benchmark for all bands to strive for.

The noise from the audience was almost overwhelming. I remember actually thinking, "Thank God we've done this for a while." If we hadn't, it would have thrown us right off; they were making that much noise. I also thought, "Thank God we've got Steve driving this train" 'cos no one did it better; we definitely had the best in front of our band. Once all these split-second epiphanies were past, I got this tremendous surge of inner power that only came behind the kit when I was mad or really Steve-proud, and I was definitely proud of him that night. Lots of people who, for one reason or another, had witnessed Steve at his most obnoxious would say, "How the fuck do you put up with him?" I could only reply, "Because when he's good, he's the best"—plus I loved him like a brother.

Once we were into the third song, "The Fixer," which I could take at least a little breather in, I looked over to my left and saw something that would change my life forever: the most beautiful pair of eyes I had ever seen. I could not stop looking at them. Fortunately, the show was going so well it was able to keep my attention; otherwise I would have lost it completely. I kept looking over, and the face that surrounded the eyes was even more beautiful to look at than the eyes alone. The show kept getting stronger, and it was as if my attraction to this beautiful face grew in direct relation to how much better the show was going. I didn't know her name or who she was, but I knew somehow that I had to get to know her and fast, because I was determined that this one was not going to get away.

As I came offstage, I said to John Hammel, "Find out who she is, and see if I can meet her." We got through the usual dressing room after-show madness and then headed back to the hotel. As we went up to our rooms, I thought, "Oh well, it wasn't to be," and went off to the Party Suite extremely deflated. After a short while, John came in, pulled me to one side, and said, "Come with me; I've got something to show you." I followed him to a room close to mine, and, as he opened the door, there she was—the most beautiful woman I had seen so far in my young life, other than those on a movie screen.

Her name was Cindy. She had long, fair hair, and she had high cheekbones from the American Indian half of her family. She was like Cher when Cher was at her best; i.e., after she had the nose job. Cindy's nose was au naturel just like the rest of her; she was a natural beauty. She carried herself with grace, beauty, and charm, and oozed sensuality from her large mouth, surrounded as it was by lips to die for. She was a knockout. We talked a lot and got to know each other. She spent the night, but more because it was very late than for any other reason.

When you live on the road you have to get to know someone quick, although as soon as I saw Cindy, even though I didn't yet know her, she went right to the top of my shortlist of future ex-wives. This was, quite literally, love at first sight. I remember something about that night that is a great example of road life. Everything about Cindy was perfect; the only question mark was to do with her legs, which I didn't see at first, because she was wearing jeans. So I said to myself, "If her legs are cool, then she's the one." As the night wore on, it came to the point when I asked her if she would like to stay, and she said yes. As we got our kit off, I tried not to be too obvious about checking her legs out and was so relieved to find out that they were spot on.

In the morning, she looked just as good as she did the night before; if anything, she looked better. She had to leave early to sort things out so that she could come with me to Dallas, San Antonio, and New Orleans. As she was getting ready to leave, she said there was something she needed to tell me. "Oh dear," I thought, "here we go. She's married, she's a high-class hooker, she's a stripper; what is it?" She said she had a child. He was 18 months old, and she had divorced his dad soon after the boy's birth. It was a bit of a blow, but not the end of the world. She waited for my reply to see if it had put me off. I thought for a brief moment, then said, "Can you be back by twelve, ready to go to Dallas?" She smiled, genuinely relieved, and took off to get her life organised to come on the road for a few days.

Looking back now, I knew then that she was the one, but, for some strange reason, I was a lot more thoughtful and measured at that time about making decisions on whether I got involved with her or not; I suppose it was because of the child. This was not my normal style—I would usually act first, think later—but I knew deep down that there was more than enough fire down below to make this one worth the trouble.

Cindy spent those next few days with me, and we had a really good time in each other's company. As a young man, I was very picky about ladies I spent more than an odd night with; in fact, if I didn't care too much for one, I knew right away because if they tried to be touchy-feely or cuddly, I would very quickly run for cover. Use 'em and lose 'em, I'm ashamed to admit, was my M.O. But this one was different.

During the rest of that fantastic summer, the band kept putting in tremendous shows, selling out most everywhere we played. We continued to do big stadium gigs as the special guest on Black Sabbath shows and others as the headliner with J. Geils Band as special guest for us.

We had some shows to do in Florida, the last of which was at the arena in Tampa. Because Florida is the Sunshine State and generally associated with sun, fun, gorgeous women, Disney World, and a fairly liberal take on life, people forget that it is in the Deep South of the good old US of A and, as such, can be an extremely redneck place. Steve wasn't the first rock 'n' roller to fall foul of this misconception back in the late Sixties and early Seventies; Jim Morrison had been arrested in Miami in 1969 on several charges, including lewd and lascivious behaviour onstage. That wasn't Steve's style, but he had developed a nasty habit of using foul language onstage—not exactly the kind of thing that would corrupt the youth of yesterday, or today, but typical of Steve in that it was guaranteed to anger the bible-belting rednecks of that time. "Goddamn motherfucker" was Steve's idea of savoir-faire; you should have heard him when he was being rude and lewd. From the rednecks' point of view, this was not only foul-mouthed behaviour, it was blasphemous foul-mouthed behaviour of the worst kind, even though it probably represented at least 20% of their own limited vocabularies.

At this show in Tampa, we were sailing very close to the wind, as they had warned us on a previous occasion to behave or be nicked. Telling Steve Marriott that he was on a short leash was just asking for trouble—you may as well have told him to head straight for the chief of police and to call him a limp-wristed faggot; Steve would have done that, too. So as we went onstage, in addition to the various cautions Steve had received from his own people prior to showtime, he was told in no uncertain terms by the head of the police in the building, the head of the venue's in-house security, *and* the promoter's in-house security that any blatant profanity onstage would lead to his *immediate* arrest. As soon as I saw the little curl in the corner of Steve's half-smile, accompanied by an almost sinister chuckle and a stare at his shoes through those trouble-making Chinese eyes, I knew we were in for a long night and the possibility of an extended stay in Tampa.

As the lights dimmed and the audience let rip with a huge roar, on we went. Steve shouts into the mike, "'Ello, Tampa! How the 'uck are yer?" then blasts out the huge chords of our first tune, "Up Our Sleeve." Between the roar of the crowd and the sheer volume of that opening explosion of *loud* rock 'n' roll, plus the way the little bugger almost said "fuck," but actually only let out the "'uck," we just about got away with it, for now. We still had another 90 minutes to get through before we emerged on the other side as free men.

As the evening went on, Steve was in his element of mischievous bliss. This was the stuff that made him tick: any and all forms of authority in all its glory, just waiting for him to fuck with in any way he chose. He loved to get away with it if he could, not that he cared that much about any of the repercussions that might have come our way as a result of his messing with the cops. That was always Steve's way: fuck with someone first, think about it second, or, more accurately, don't think about it at all. Consequences, what consequences? Fuck consequences. While this is all immensely entertaining and sometimes hysterically funny, after the hundredth time when you are one of the guys who has to cover his arse, it can become extremely irritating.

But sometimes things go so ridiculously that it makes it all worthwhile, like on this hot summer's night in Tampa. He kept on *almost* saying "fuck" and "shit" and "motherfucker," at which point he had lulled the crowd and the band into a false sense of security. But as we started to get close to the end, he let out one of the biggies: "Goddamn motherfuckin' rock 'n' roll!" The head of police could hardly believe his ears—or his luck. "That's it, we've got him!" was his reaction, and he started to get his officers in place to arrest Steve as we came offstage.

The new management representative, who Dee and Bill had brought onboard for precisely this sort of situation, was a perfect crisis-management guy called John Doumanian, who had worked with Woody Allen, amongst others. John got wind of the intended arrest and started to make his contingency plans. He told one of the limo drivers to park at the top of the entrance ramp that led down to the backstage area and told our truck driver to pull his rig across the bottom of the ramp so that he could delay the cops getting their cars out of the backstage area. Next, he told the driver of another limo to head off in the opposite direction from the private airfield where our plane was ready and waiting. He then had a third car wait at a different entrance to the backstage area, ready for him and Steve.

When Steve came offstage, John had the roadies grab him, throw a coat over him, and run him in the opposite direction from the rest of us, shouting, "Emergency! Emergency!" while we were all walking towards the dressing room. The cops followed, thinking Steve was with us. Once they got into the dressing room and realised that Steve wasn't there, they were so pissed off that they ran off frantically looking for their dastardly criminal midget. At the same time, we nipped off straight to the airport where our plane was all fired up, with Steve and John safely inside, waiting for us and laughing their asses off.

We got in the plane with Bill Anthony, who was with us, running interference. As the plane pulled up to the top of the runway, we could see at least 10 police cars, with their lights flashing, screaming into the entrance of the little airport. It was a tongue-in-cheek police car chase right out of the Mel Gibson / Goldie Hawn film, "Bird on a Wire"—but almost 20 years before that movie was released. As we took off, I looked down in hysterics at the cop cars and said to John, "Well, this is something I can tell the grandchildren when I'm 60 and writing my autobiography."

Alex King, who usually worked in the office back in Manhattan, was on the road with us then for reasons I forget. He was the only casualty, poor guy. Back at the arena, as he was walking along with the police to the truck, taking his sweet time to respond to their requests to get it moved, one of them swiped him across the side of his head with a billy club, which must have hurt like hell. When asked about it, all Alex said, with typical British dry understatement, was, "That's the trouble with these southern chaps: no sense of humour."

This was one of the most contentious times in American history. The Vietnam War and the public outcry it created were peaking in these early years of the Seventies. Kent State had only just happened barely two years before, and rumblings about the Watergate affair were starting to break. There were those amongst us who were getting ever more nervous about the possibility of us English travelling musicians being called up for military service in the US, based on how long we were spending in the States, our immigration status, and so on. It turned out that all of this was hysteria brought on by certain Brits who had got their green cards only to find out that there was a remote chance the immigration laws could include them as eligible for the draft.

Vietnam veterans represented a large percentage of Humble Pie's audience both then, when it was happening, and for years after the war, when they would remain loyal fans of the band. We had many of the disabled guys in their wheelchairs at our shows and would make a point of inviting them back to party and at least trying to make them feel better about themselves.

They came to our rescue more than once, the most memorable such occasion being when they saved Steve from a bunch of Cajun pool hustlers who had played him like a fiddle and hustled him to the tune of several thousand dollars. Steve was not a stupid man by any means—in fact, he was extremely bright—however, sometimes his actions made you wonder.

We had played two sold-out shows at the famous Warehouse in New Orleans. Although, strictly speaking, the Warehouse was a club, it was a *huge* club. It was built in one of the old warehouses down in the rail yard, which gave it a very realistic blues feel. The club's promoter, Don Fox, was a good friend who would always join us for the after-show revelries. He was a true gentleman who always made sure we wanted for nothing. Don warned us on more than one occasion how dangerous the dark side of the French Quarter can be.

After the gig, once we were back at the Royal Orleans Hotel and the party was in full swing, two vets who had been to the show were getting ready to leave to go play some pool and maybe win a few bucks. We all wished them well and good luck. No one was quite sure how the ensuing events came about, but apparently the image of a couple of guys heading up and down the French Quarter looking for a pool game appealed to our Steve. He headed into the night with someone from the party to play out this fantasy of being a pool-hall hustler. Steve did this a lot, usually when he was high on cocaine; he'd take on a character and play it for a while.

In this particular instance, he had chosen a very dangerous part to play out on the back streets of the Big Easy. At the party, Don Fox, the vets, and others had told him in graphic terms how the Cajun pool hustlers would find a sucker, gain his trust, and let him win a bunch, then turn the play in their favour and take him to the cleaners. If for some reason the mark couldn't pay his debt, he would be taken out into the bayou and disappear. The alligators made sure of that.

Sure enough, Steve found a suitable bar and was soon befriended by a bunch of Cajun rednecks who followed the script perfectly and started to let him win, and win big. Steve took the bait hook, line, and sinker, and before you knew it, he was several thousand dollars in debt. When it came time to pay the piper, he didn't have a dime left, but he had been playing the part so well, these hustlers thought he at least had the money to back up his arrogance. As far as they were concerned, they were gonna collect their cash or take Steve out for a trip into the bayou.

All of Steve's "Don't you know who I am?" protestations were not getting him anywhere. Just as things were getting out of hand and he was about to become gator meat, our vet friends from the party happened to walk into the bar. They brokered a peace whereby everyone went back to the hotel, where Steve found Bill Anthony, got the cash, and paid the guys off. Thanks to Steve, the band's coffers were several thousand dollars lighter. Thanks to our veteran buddies, we still had our Steve. As mad at him as we were, we were very, very grateful that he was still there to be mad at, silly bugger.

One of the stadium shows we were booked for that summer was at the Akron Rubber Bowl, with Black Sabbath as the headliner and us as special guest. We had started using a Hansa Jet, as it was a little bigger than a Lear-jet, you could stand up in it (if you were short-arse lads like most of us), and it had a decent loo that was a big improvement on the Lear's accommodations. We were in full swing and having a superb time.

Then the Pie curse hit. Every time we were booked on an open-air show from then on, it would rain. Actually, it wouldn't just rain; it would utterly piss down. As the technology was not in place to play in the rain safely the way it is today, a serious downpour meant a reschedule or a complete cancellation. On the day of the Rubber Bowl show, it started to bucket down fairly early, so that it was soon apparent that we would have to reschedule. Fortunately, we were able to do this almost immediately, and the second attempt went without intervention from the gods of aquamarinus interruptus maximus.

By now it was commonplace for the wings of the stage to be packed with all the other musicians on the bill while we were performing. It was not something that we ever got cocky or complacent about—well, not complacent anyway—it was purely something that we were grateful for. However, there were still naughty schoolboys within us who were almost always instigated by Steve and his habits from his acting days. Stage plays are notorious for their backstage pranks. Steve had taken that tradition with him into his days on the package tours the Small Faces did in the Sixties, and we continued it when we were touring the UK in the first year of the band's existence. Our road crew were also steeped in playing silly buggers when it was doable. All of this is commonplace now, but we were in on the early days.

On this particular night, Ozzie Osbourne was standing on the side of the stage with his mouth open in awe of Steve and his performance as the band put in its now-standard crowd-destroying show. Sabbath were well aware of our abilities by this time, as they had kindly let us do several shows with them while we were on our way up, and they were certainly men enough not to be afraid of us. They did, however, put together an insurance policy on this show to try and ensure that the audience would be suitably impressed with their entrance after we had been on—they had a fireworks display that went off as they were coming onstage.

The private airport that we flew into was right next to the Rubber Bowl. In previous weeks, we had been introduced to the wonderful world of aerobatics: flying upside down, doing barrel rolls, flying into deliberate weightlessness, and so on. The road crew told us about the fireworks and suggested we get the pilot to do a low flyover, with a victory roll thrown in for good measure, as Sabbath took to the stage, so as to rain on their parade—of fireworks, that is. The pilot, who was a game chap, drew the line at a complete victory roll over the stage, but said he would be able to roar across the sky directly above the Rubber Bowl and maybe execute a half roll as he did a steep bank away from the stadium.

With all this nonsense in place, we went straight from the stage to the plane and took off just as Sabbath went on. The sensation of taking off low and fast across the stadium felt great, but of course we couldn't appreciate what it felt like down in the stadium itself. When we spoke to the roadies the next day, they said it was outrageous. As Sabbath took their places, with Oz centre stage, at the precise moment the fireworks went off, we shot across the top of the stadium and completely drowned out the fireworks, and everybody rubbernecked to see what was causing all that noise. The road crew said that the look on Ozzie's face was priceless. He was gazing skyward, with his mouth wide open with incredulity, and his arms raised above his head as he normally does to wind up the crowd—only this time, his raised arms took on a Biblical twist, like Moses receiving the Ten Commandments. Way to go, Oz. You gotta love the man. In truth, our little stunt probably enhanced Sabbath's entrance.

With the new record deal in place, it was time to turn our attention to the making of the next album. The studio in Steve's home was nearly finished, and all indications were that the sound quality was extraordinary. We had spent a fortune on getting it right. Anything Steve wanted for the studio, Steve got; after all, it was actually *our* studio, and, as such, it behoved us as a business venture to spend the money to make sure that it was spot on because once it was in place, we would no longer need to pay for studio time. The band's natural togetherness, sound-wise, was easily being captured on tape thanks to the brilliance of the mixing desk designed by Dick Swettenham and built by his company, Helios. (Dick had also designed and built the desk at Olympic Studios in Barnes, where we had recorded our previous best sellers.) The tape machines were state-of-the-art 16-track Studers, the best that money could buy. The whole process was being looked after by Irish, the best engineer there was, after Glyn. He had done a superb job on *Smokin'*, and he got on well with everybody.

His strong people skills were to prove extremely important, as we were about to introduce three ladies to the line-up in the form of the Blackberries: ex-Raelette Clydie King, ex-Ikette Venetta Fields, and Billie Barnum, the sister of H.B. Barnum, an arranger and sometimes conductor of Aretha Franklin's orchestra. These girls were the very best of the very best.

Humble Pie & The Blackberries
L To R Vanetta Fields, Billie Barnum, Clydie King, Steve Marriott
Jerry Shirley, Dave "Clem" Clempson, Greg Ridley

The inclusion of the Blackberries was something the band had on the back burner for a long time. Once we knew that we were going to start recording this big make-or-break record, we gave Dee our wish list of singers for the three-piece back-up. Steve's original dream roster consisted of Venetta, whose work he loved on an Ike and Tina Turner live record; Marjorie Hendricks, who sang on *Ray Charles in Person*; and Lorraine Ellison, whose single "Stay With Me Baby" was one of our favourite records. It was quite a wish list, but what Dee came up with was actually better. Steve's choices were not all available, so Dee found Clydie, Venetta, and Billie, who turned out to be doing sessions together under the name of the Blackberries.

So, by the beginning of September 1972, the studio was finished, the Blackberries were hired, and we had already started to put down some of the back tracks for the new record. At the end of the last tour, I had gone to Houston to see if Cindy was still as keen on me as I was on her. On that weekend, I took her on a shopping spree and thoroughly spoiled her. We had an altogether wonderful long romantic weekend together. At one point in the proceedings, after Cindy had surveyed all the clothes I had bought for her, she said, "Oh honey, you shouldn't have! At this rate, I'll end up spending *all* your money!" to which I replied, "Cindy, my dear, you couldn't if you tried!" What an obnoxious, condescending thing to say. Oh well, the things we do when we're trying to impress. But, as they say, "Payback's a bitch," and Cindy had plenty of time yet to prove me wrong.

John Doumanian had already proved to be a priceless addition to our extended family after his brilliant save in Tampa. He was now recruited to take care of the Blackberries and bring them to England so that everything would go smoothly. When the girls got to NYC, he met with them and Dee in the Bandana office, where they went over all their wants and needs, then called to tell me what flight they were coming in on and to ask if I could meet them. I said I would be glad to and that I would break out the Mercedes to mark the occasion. Dee said jokingly that he would expect me to give them a big brass-band reception, to which I said "Fine, no problem." Dee bet me $100 that I couldn't pull it off, and I took the bet. I immediately called Bob Kerr's Whoopee Band and booked them for $50 to meet the flight at Heathrow.

When we got to the airport, the authorities almost put the kibosh on our plans because they wouldn't allow live music in the main terminal. So we had Bob set his band up in the parking lot, and when the girls came off the lift, they were greeted by a rousing chorus of "There's No Business Like Show Business." They loved it, and it was a great way to break the ice. It was also the fastest 50 bucks I'd ever made.

As the sessions got underway, it was obvious that there was something truly special between us and the girls. We gelled in every way. The music we were producing together was nothing short of sensational, we liked the same drugs, and we shared the same sense of the utterly ridiculous. They were a treasure trove of musical knowledge, and the two main girls had been with our all-time favourite bands and singers. Having the best Raelette to ever sing with our hero Ray Charles *and* the all-time best Ikette was worth the price of admission alone. Add to that Billie, their choice for third-part harmonising, and you've got an experience that made every moment we spent together special.

The fact that we had these fine examples of rock and soul royalty living and breathing in our house felt pretty damn good, especially as they were there on merit. We weren't by any means the only people interested in employing them; the list of those who wished to have the Blackberries come on board was long and impressive. Even more impressive was how much longer that list became as a result of their work with us. In fact, the Pink Floyd had them sing on *Wish You Were Here*, their follow-up to *Dark Side of the Moon*, because Dave Gilmour had seen them and got to know them at our gigs, and it was a no-brainer to use them—they were that good. Not bad for our little bunch of white punks on drugs, I thought.

You would think the girls impressed us with all their stories about the musical integrity of their pasts, and that is in part true, but I remember being most impressed by their little humorous and human-condition stories, such as Clydie King telling us that, "In order for you to become a Raelette, first you gotta let Ray!" Or Venetta's story about Ike Turner: as they were about to go onstage, he would line the Ikettes up, grab on to their wigs, and pull on them with all his might to make sure they would not come off. Then, if the wigs did so much as move, he would fine the girls, fucking prick that he was.

These were indeed golden years for us four little boys from the UK, and nothing in the world could get in our way, or so it seemed at the time. Beware the ill wind… For some reason—maybe it was the brash arrogance we were starting to show—I began to hear my inner voice telling me that something's gonna give, something's *gotta* give. We were starting to believe way too much of the ego-boosting side of life on cocaine. As a wise old compadre of Steve's once wrote, "I wish that I knew what I know now when I was younger." It would have saved us all a hell of a lot of heartache and an even bigger amount of money, but man, were we having fun.

One of the big things we tried to keep Steve's mind off of the impending doom surrounding his collapsed relationship was to tell him that we would support his musical wishes 100% on this album. He would be in total charge; he could make whatever record he wished to make, and we would be behind him. He could whistle Dixie if he wanted, and we would back him. We did this in good faith, but it turned out to be one of the worst things we could ever have done.

Angus had spent a while straight, which was a blessing, especially as we realised that we would need someone to drive the girls back and forth from the studio—someone who was one of us and didn't mind the weird hours we were keeping.

The astonishing thing about the way the Blackberries worked was how quickly and precisely they sorted out their arrangements. They would stand around the microphone, spend just a few minutes figuring out what they were going to sing, and, in no more than one or two takes, they would nail it. They not only nailed it, they turned every bit of their backgrounds into something spectacular every time. They also managed to do this in the same condition we were in, with the exception of Billie Barnum, who is and always has been as straight as an arrow.

The material we were recording was strong, the sound Irish was getting in the new studio was wonderful, and the band, as always, were playing out of their skins. We had decided to make this record a double album for no particular reason other than the fact that we could. We had an electric side, a covers side, an acoustic side, and a live side.

Within the first week of work, the girls had completed almost all of their backing vocals and recorded some tracks for an upcoming Blackberries album that A&M were planning to release. One of the songs we recorded with them for their own record was a knockout version of "Twist and Shout." The drum sound on it was one of the best we had ever got, thanks to our Steve and Irish—they had been working together for a long time and had the same upbringing as far as drum sounds were concerned.

Months later, we were partying with Jeff Beck's band in Japan. Carmine Appice was playing with Jeff, and, as he was an old friend of mine, it was good to see him. He was very proud of some of the material that he and Jeff had recently recorded, and he offered to play it to us. Jeff did not seem too thrilled with this idea, but soldiered on anyway, grudgingly allowing Carmine to have the floor. After listening to one or two tracks of what Steve and I thought was not necessarily the greatest Jeff Beck music ever written or performed, our Steve decided to put the girls' version of "Twist and Shout" on the tape player. As soon as it started with a huge *crack* on the snare drum, Jeff literally jumped out of his seat, said, "Now that's what I call a drum sound!" and sat down again. Whilst I might sound boastful by telling you this story, it's not every day that a man as talented as Jeff jumps up and effectively says that your drum sound is better than that of one of the greatest drummers in the world. Jeff probably doesn't remember this, as it happened nearly 40 years ago, but I remember it as if it were yesterday. Wouldn't you?

The girls had been given a reasonable offer by Dee prior to coming over to England, and they had accepted it: £3,600 a week for the whole group, plus all expenses and a private jet to travel in. That kind of pay wasn't exactly chump change in 1972, and it seemed to me that the jet was certainly a notch or two up from travelling on a drafty old bus doing the chitlin circuit.

But when Clydie told Steve that Dee's pay scale was a bit on the cheap side compared to what she was used to getting as an LA session singer and that, frankly, she wasn't sure if she would want to continue much past making the album, she hit Steve right where it hurt—here was another woman telling him that she might bail if he didn't shape up. Of course there was no real comparison between Steve's wife and his newly found musical compadre, but it's not as daft as it seems; he desperately wanted both women to stay with him, but didn't seem to know how to convince them to do so. With Clydie, his solution was simple—pay the piper—but the trouble was, he offered to pay her with everybody's money, as opposed to just his own, without discussing it with any of us.

To give you a clearer picture, this is the offer that Steve gave the girls on that fateful first night… Our newly promoted business tycoon Stephen Peter Marriott promised them £3,600 *each* per week, making management the bad guys who had obviously made a mistake and misunderstood what he wanted to pay his singers. On top of that, for no understandable reason whatsoever, he offered to buy them each a mink or sable coat—I can't remember the type of animals that lost their lives to supply the fur for these extravagances. This was certainly not my dear old friend Steve, a devout animal lover, engaging in this absurd flurry of spending. It was the *other* Steve, who right around now we were starting to see, more often than not, taking over. All because he had gone and got so high that he was offering anything and everything to get his own way.

Steve, as only Steve could, had told the girls that their pay scale would be so huge that if we were to abide by it, the entire band and crew would be working for the Blackberries. When he promised them riches beyond their wildest dreams, they must have each thought they had gone to sleep and woken up as Mrs. Howard Hughes. If I had been there, I would have pulled them to one side as soon as I saw the opportunity, and explained that Steve had got carried away. After this unpleasant situation, in fact, they came to me whenever they wanted to know the real skinny, but at the beginning, they had no reason to not believe Steve.

Thank God we had someone else at the helm to make business decisions, or we would have been sunk. This little example of Steve's character at its worst portrays how frustrating working with him could sometimes be. After all, we had built this band from the very start on the premise, right or wrong, that it was a completely equal democracy both musically and businesswise. For a man who revelled in not being a bread-head (as he would put it), he sure liked to be the one who dictated how and when the group's money was spent. This was where the mistake of giving Steve complete control of this record started to show its slip. It was like giving a loaded gun to a man who wasn't a very accurate shot, then standing right in front of him just to make absolutely sure he doesn't miss.

After the initial misunderstanding over their finances, Venetta stepped in and took over the position of spokesperson for the Blackberries. As she was supposed to be in that position in the first place before Clydie gave Steve her sob story about money, this would prevent any further misunderstandings. It was clear early on that Clydie was not the person to be making business decisions for the group. It might have been true that she came to England unaware of the exact numbers—again, coke was making everybody's decisions for them at the time. I know I keep harping on about the cocaine, but I have to stress how strongly it affected everybody's decision making and, therefore, their lives.

Chapter 15
All or Nothing
December 1972 to May 1973

In which the sound of Eat It *bass-ically bites;*
I P.O. the Jamaican PM; we meet our new lead singer, Melvin;
Steve is saved from becoming another McCartney, but
Clem suffers the same fate as Clapton; Japan rubs Sir Harold
the right way; and we look in the mirror and see Elvis.

By now we were starting to adjust to the new Steve that had entered our world. There was still a lot of the old Steve in this new version, but for those of us who loved the old one like a brother, it took some getting used to. Jenny was still there in the physical sense, but emotionally she was gone. I felt so bad for Steve, but I also fully understood how Jenny felt, and I equally hurt for her. Every time there was an attempt to try to patch things up, New Steve would act on Old Steve's behalf and royally blow it. He was so angry with the whole situation—and deep down so angry with himself—that he was doing crazy things to try to rekindle Jenny's love for him, which had gone cold through months and months of ill treatment.

Everybody involved with the recording sessions for what became *Eat It* was thrilled with the way they were developing. It was going to be a double album with something for everyone: a cool live side, new original electric and acoustic songs, and some cool covers. Not bad for a bunch of white boys, or so we thought. There were some great songs. "Get Down To It" was a raucous, bluesy, Hammond organ gem of Steve's, while "Black Coffee" was a lovely Ike and Tina cover. There were some beautiful acoustic songs from Steve: "Oh, Bella" was a typically sweet and gentle ballad he wrote about his grandma. Plus, the live side included our new show opener, "Up Our Sleeve," which has got to rank as the toughest opening song I have ever had to play. This tune ain't for sissies, believe me. I was so fit back then; I had to be. I didn't work out or anything—playing drums for an hour and 45 minutes every night behind Steve Marriott was plenty workout for me, thank you very much.

The addition of the girls, who, after all, we had used before, was no great departure for us. The band's collective and individual performances were as good as, or better than, any we'd done. We were absolutely delighted with the way the studio had turned out, even if it had cost an arm and a leg to build. From where we were sitting, it was money well spent—and it was right there to occupy Steve while he rode out the storm of his perpetually on-again, off-again marriage.

Once we had completed most of the recording, with the exception of some of the finishing touches, we had a short British tour to do. Then we went to the States to play some dates before Christmas, then back home for Christmas, then back to the States to do a special two-show gig in Asbury Park, New Jersey, at the Sunshine Inn, with a certain Dr. Zoom opening for us. Next it was up to Toronto to play a New Year's Eve gig at the Maple Leaf Gardens, with Badfinger opening the show.

After the show in Toronto, we flew down to Miami on a Learjet to clear American Immigration, then went on to the Bahamas. Dee and our accountant, Bert Padell, had bought with the group's funds a magnificent property they had found in Nassau, which we had christened Rock's Rest. It was a complex of six houses on five acres, with its own beach that ran the length of the property, located at the end of the road that led to the exclusive Lyford Cay yacht club. The houses were built three on each side of a private driveway that ran from the entrance gates down to the beach. Each had two bedrooms with en suite bathrooms, a large living room, a kitchen, and a sundeck/patio that was built on the front of the house, looking out towards the sea. The houses took up half of the property; the other half featured beautifully manicured tropical gardens that included well-kept grass, loads of palm trees, and a variety of tropical fruit trees. Halfway down the private drive, there was a large fountain in a circular wishing well. It was complete and absolute paradise.

Steve took the first house on the right of the drive nearest the beach, and I took the one on the left. Clem's was behind Steve's, and Greg's behind mine. The two houses nearest the road were for guests, but actually belonged to Dee and Bert. The groundskeeper and his wife lived in the one that belonged to Dee.

The idea of the property was that we would use it to get some rest and relaxation between tours and rent it out to other resting rock stars while we were not there; hence "Rock's Rest." Dee thought of the name and meant it to be tongue in cheek, so we went along with it; it was so cheesy, it was great. The entire property was bought for $180,000. I have no idea what it would be worth today, but I did hear that a few years later, the person who Dee sold it to went on to sell it for five million dollars.

So there we were in Nassau at the beginning of 1973, which was shaping up to be our biggest year yet, and everything that was being planned for it was extremely exciting. As we arrived on the island, Dee told us that he had just heard that Richard Nixon had announced the beginning of the winding down of the Vietnam War, which was huge news. He also heard that comet Kahoutek was going to be visible above the Bahamas at 6:00 in the morning of the third day we were going to be there. Dee's daughter Michele was down in the Bahamas on holiday with her dad. She and I volunteered to go out on Dee's boat with him to spot the comet.

The morning came, and we three intrepid comet spotters headed out onto the ocean on Dee's boat "Smokin'" to see what we could see. We took all kinds of binoculars with us, as the comet was supposed to be visible to the naked eye. From the ocean, the sky in that part of the world is an incredible sight just around sunrise, with or without Kahoutek, and while we spent a great deal of time looking at high-flying jets through our binoculars, we never did spot good old Kahoutek. He remained ever elusive, but we convinced ourselves that we had seen a number of highly suspicious flying something-or-others. I am sure I had taken something or other to heighten my sense of vision, but the fact that we never did see the bloody comet did not stop us from telling more than a few people that we had.

The rest of the guys chose to go straight home or only stay in Nassau briefly before returning home. As I was the footloose and fancy-free member of the band, I stayed a little longer. I had volunteered to fly home to pick up the *Eat It* artwork, and then to LA to deliver it to A&M. While staying at Green Farm, Sheena McCall, an artist friend of Steve's from the early Small Faces days, had illustrated a beautiful booklet—which Dee, with a characteristically Italian touch, called the "libretto"—to go in the album sleeve. Her artwork was wonderful, and everybody was thrilled with it. Each page included a high-class caricature of a band member, along with an appropriate quote at the bottom of the page. I was depicted sitting on the end of my four-poster bed as if I were sitting behind a drum kit playing drums—except that my right hand wasn't holding a drumstick, but rather a bullwhip in full swing! The implication was fairly obvious, on which subject I claim the

Eat It interior artwork by Sheena McCall.

fifth, although it was rumoured that the corner posts of the bed were used to tie up more than just the bed curtains. The quote accompanying this illustration was, "I don't use it as a rule." Oh well.

Just when things were looking better than ever before, that blasted ill wind started to blow cold and strong. The first indication that things weren't exactly tickety-boo came when it was time to cut the master discs. While I was in England to pick up the artwork, I also took the master tapes to Apple's cutting room, the best in the country at the time, and gave them to the most respected master cutter in the country, George "Porky" Peckham. I stayed there when he did his work. The tapes were so bass-heavy that he could barely keep the cutting needle on the acetate discs that are used at the factory to press millions of copies, you hope, of your most recent masterpiece from. It was bleak and horrifying, to put it mildly.

When you build a studio, the most important thing to do is to scope the control room with sound meters that tell you if the room is true. Some rooms have too much treble, others have too much bass, and yet others have not enough of one or the other. The idea is to get the control room, where you are going to listen to what's been recorded, to be as neutral as possible so that you get a totally true-sounding end result. If you are recording or mixing down too much treble, middle, or bass onto tape, you will know it when you listen in the control room because the room doesn't lie. If, however, you have a great-sounding room from the get-go and don't think you need to go to all the trouble and expense of having the room scoped and fitted with the appropriate acoustic tiles or wall coverings to equalise the room properly, you are playing with fire and asking for some serious trouble. To do that would be tantamount to treason and nothing short of professional suicide. And that is exactly what we—or, should I say, Steve—did, and no one questioned him.

To understand how something like that could possibly happen, you have to grasp the atmosphere in which the studio was put together. Steve had always had his two-track equipment and fabulous playback system in place in the rooms above the garage that eventually became the studio. He and I had made several demos there that sometimes sounded as good as masters, and Steve would often go in there on his own and do the same. He understood the technical side of running a home studio from the early days of the Small Faces, when he was making demos that sometimes ended up being used as part of the masters they were working on. His generation of writers did this all the time. However, recording technology had come a long way in a very short time, and, unfortunately, Steve had not bothered to check out the sonic values of the control room. It's not that he made some grievous error; all he knew was that everything sounded great in that room. The trouble was, *Eat It* marked the first time that anything coming out of that room was going to be put to the ultimate test—being listened to by the masses over the air, or in their cars, or on their stereos at home.

What I don't understand is how *nobody* said *anything* at all until it was too late. That would never happen today to anybody who was about to put out such an important record, the first release on a multimillion-dollar record deal from a band that had put so much hard work into building a long-term career. It's not as if we were on the one-hit-wonder, pop-single side of the business. Absolutely everything we had done was specifically designed for the long haul. Everybody from the record company to the management to the agents were all on the long-term side of the business, and yet they all allowed this absurd mistake to get by them. It's not as if they hadn't said, "Wow, stop; there's something wrong here. Let's fix it before we go any further" before—they had said that about our big breakthrough live album barely a year prior. So why not now?

Still, back then, if the sonic values of a master weren't pristine, it didn't automatically mean that the work was no good. George Peckham told us a story about Lennon's "Instant Karma." When George received the master tape, he called John to tell him there was a lot of distortion on it as a result of the echo and double-tracking that had been used on Alan White's drum part. John told him in no uncertain terms that he knew about this, and that's the way he liked it, so leave it like that or else! The single was released and went straight to the Top Five on both sides of the Atlantic.

After finishing my business in England, off I flew, with the master discs and artwork in hand, to LA. Once there, I went to A&M, dropped off the discs, took the artwork to the art department, did the rounds of the company to say hello to everybody, hung out with the Blackberries a bit, and tried to figure out whether I could swing by Texas on the way home to see Cindy. It didn't work out, so John Doumanian, who was with me, helped me pick out a nice present to send to Cindy to make up for not being able to see her. We then started to make our plans for the return trip. I was pretty down about not seeing Cindy, and John, bless him, commiserated with me about it.

Dee called to ask if I wanted to go home via Jamaica to see the Joe Frazier-George Foreman fight. "Of course, I'd love to!" Our lawyer, Elliot Hoffman, had been appointed as the intermediary who acts as a referee between the two fighters' lawyers, and he held an awful lot of clout. He had already invited Dee, Frank, and someone else who had dropped out.

The plan was to spend a couple of days relaxing in Nassau, then head to Jamaica and spend a couple of days there—as guests of the prime minister of Jamaica, no less—before heading home to England via Bermuda. All of this in January 1973, and I still hadn't turned 21. When we arrived in Jamaica, it soon became apparent what a huge deal this fight was. Everybody and their mother was there: Louis Bellson, Pearl Bailey, F. Lee Bailey, James Caan, Jack Nicholson, Johnny Carson, Don Rickles, Faye Dunaway, Barbra Streisand, Aretha Franklin, and… me!

The prime minister hosted a cocktail party for his guests—those I just mentioned and many others—at his private residence. There were more celebrities than you could shake a rattle or roll at, and everybody was dressed up to the nines in their Sunday best. It's not the easiest task to get all spruced up when the temperature is 103 degrees, because the more you wear, the easier it is for your preparations to go astray: wilting hairdos, running make-up, and so on. Thankfully, this was not something I had to concern myself with, but it was amazing to see how others coped.

The Jamaican staff at the pool party were intriguing to watch as they, poor sods, were all dressed in the most ornate uniforms I've ever seen up close. Their jackets were white, with lots of gold embroidery and resplendent rows of medals. Their trousers were dark blue or black, with red and gold stripes down the sides. The security staff were wearing the equivalent of a British bobby's helmet either in black or white, which I guessed had something to do with rank. The waiters wore either black caps or nothing on their heads at all.

I was a big gin-and-tonic drinker at the time, and all this standing around in the heat, celebrity watching, was hard and thirsty work. I had managed to befriend one or two of the waiters and had been suitably stocked with my favourite libation. But as the number of guests grew considerably, it started to turn into a dipsomaniac's nightmare—the waiters had become impossible to find. Just as I was about to give up, I finally spotted what had to be the head waiter. He had the most elaborate uniform of the lot, and his military-style cap had more gold braid on it than the rest of the staff put together. He must have been taking a breather, as he wasn't dashing about serving people; in fact, he was standing there with a solitary drink in his hand—waiting for the person who had ordered it to return from the bathroom perhaps?

I took the opportunity to jump in and ask for a refill. He smiled at me and nodded his head, but declined to take my glass to get it refilled. Odd, I thought. I asked again and saw that he was getting mildly irritated. Just as I was about to get a little miffed myself, one of the security guards came up to this head waiter, who was now trying to ignore me completely, and said, "Excuse me, Prime Minister. Pearl Bailey and her husband, Louis Bellson, would like to meet you." Ain't life great?

Sometime during this period, I had decided to ask Cindy to spend the rest of her life married to me. I was so thrilled at the idea of bringing her and her son, Aaron, to England that I couldn't wait to get on tour, call her, and tell her to pack her bags to come home with me. The only minor problem in all of this was that I forgot, as a result of my ludicrous and ever-growing selfishness, to warn her of my impending proposal. It was now mid-March, and I had not spoken to her since early January, when I had called to tell her that I couldn't come to visit her in Houston, because, it turned out, I had an important date with Joe Frazier and George Foreman in Jamaica. Oops.

So I guess it was hardly surprising that when I called her, less than a week before I was due to play in Houston, I couldn't find her. I tried every number I had for everybody I knew in Houston and… nothing. She was MIA, and I was frantic. When I called Dupuy Bateman, he said to leave it with him; he would find her. I was overreacting to such an extent that I didn't hear the calm assurance in his voice that should have told me to relax. Poor me, poor me, pour me a drink—I proceeded to get stinking rotten drunk.

Dupuy called the next day. He had spoken to Cindy, told her that I was trying to reach her, and alluded to the reasons why. I was ecstatic and called her immediately. Whether or not she disappeared on purpose to make me show my hand I didn't know, but she made it very clear that she was not prepared to sit around and put her and Aaron's lives completely on hold on the off chance that I might decide to call her. All I could do was tell her how much I loved her and wanted her to come home with me and set up shop in England, and that I was prepared to do my best to try to be whatever Aaron wanted me to be for him: his friend, his stepfather, whatever.

We had moved up in the world of private jets; we were now using a Falcon Jet, which was much bigger. It held between eight and 10 people, and had a proper loo and a stewardess. The pilot, Jim, was a Vietnam vet who used to fly B-52 bombers; he was absolutely brilliant. He did all the classic aerobatic manoeuvres: barrel rolls, victory rolls, flying upside down, and the coup de grace—aerobatic weightlessness.

Experiencing zero gravity ranks as one of the truly great experiences of my life. The pilot puts the plane into a steep climb. At the top of the climb, he puts the plane into a sharp decline, and as the plane goes into this accelerated freefall, it dives down at a speed that makes it immune to the pull of gravity; you become weightless and start to float around in the cabin, which can prove to be a touch hazardous. If you choose instead to keep yourself strapped in, you can sit and watch all manner of things float about. A favourite of mine and Steve's: hold on to your glass of whiskey while you watch the whiskey leave the glass and float around the cabin, and make bets on who it is likely to splash down onto once the pilot pulls the plane out of the dive and goes back to normal flight. The boom box you forgot to hang onto calmly floats around aimlessly, going nowhere in particular—until it drops from mid-air into someone's lap. There are certain precautions you have to take in the toilet; whiskey is not the only amber liquid that can float around the cabin to its heart's content if the toilet seat and lid are left up.

The stewardess's name was Nancy. She was a nice lady and reasonably attractive. To my utter amazement, she survived the entire time with us without one of the troops having their evil way with her. The Blackberries' presence did bring about a certain amount of good behaviour from the rotters' club. They kept their collective eye on us, and if you started to develop a roving eye or two, they would come down on you like a ton of bricks in that tough-ass way that only black women can. Their liberal use of the word "nigger" towards us, as they would use it with their black bandmates, felt like a compliment, inasmuch as they were accepting us into their way of doing things. It followed in the time-honoured American tradition of black and white musicians working together as equals during the segregated Sixties. There we were, performing as a unit similar to the great partnerships of Stax and Tamla Motown, where blacks and whites performed side by side, supplying the soundtrack to those turbulent times in the Deep South of Memphis and at the heart of the Detroit race riots, as if there was nothing in the world wrong with it—which, of course, there wasn't. They set such a good example for all to see. I'm not suggesting that we did anything musically that compared to those giants of the business—we were definitely not worthy—but you can't condemn young lads for living out their dreams, can you? And the world still needed good examples back then, as racism was still going strong when we collaborated with the Blackberries, as you soon will see.

It was around this time that the steady disappearance of the Steve who didn't consume anything stronger than a joint was becoming painfully apparent. Simply put, he wasn't the same man. When the girls arrived on the scene at the tail end of 1972, we were, on the face of things, having a ball. Their arrival, however, coincided with a division between the management and the band that was sad and regrettable in all kinds of different ways, which will unfold in front of you as my story follows us through the most successful—and the most destructive—year in Humble Pie's history. That story was supposed to climax in unimaginable wealth for all concerned, but instead it culminated in the band's demise.

Looking back, there were, for me, three musically superb highlights of our time together on the road in the early Seventies: the summers of '71, '72, and '73. The band was a tight, perfectly tuned, steaming machine ready to roll all over the concert circuit of the USA, England, and Europe.

In the summer of '73, we were starting to look at spreading our wings. At the end of this first leg of the tour, with the Blackberries firmly entrenched into our line-up, we headlined a sold-out show at the Baltimore Civic Center, with Edgar Winter and Gentle Giant supporting. *Eat It* was selling really well and steadily climbing the charts. No one had yet mentioned any reservations about the sound, as it was still in the honeymoon period where it had its precious bullet in the Billboard chart and had just broken into the Top 20. Cindy and Aaron were on their way to meet me and head back to England after the show.

There must be something about Baltimore. It was where I famously said, "The vibe is out" in '71. It was also where Dee came in '72 with the news about the record deal making us dollar millionaires. And now it was again Baltimore that he came to with an incredible game plan that was being set up to seal our place amongst the rock 'n' roll elite.

What Dee proposed was basically a repeat of what he did with Joe Cocker on the "Mad Dogs & Englishmen" tour in 1970, which was to take a film crew on the road with the tour and film and record the whole affair. The only difference was the location. With Joe, they only filmed in the USA, whereas they were going to follow us in two countries. First, a swing across the States that would include Madison Square Garden in NYC and the Forum in LA, plus a few other choice dates in Detroit, Pittsburgh, and Philadelphia. Then they would come to Japan with us on a 707 jet that could hold 130 people. We would have loads of reporters and our families with us, film the whole shooting match, and release the film and soundtrack. This would be the thing that did for us what Joe's movie did for him; it seemed only logical. Dee had such a proven track record of making his acts successful that it didn't for a moment occur to us that there was any reason whatsoever to question this plan of action. He hadn't steered us wrong yet, and when he came to Baltimore and explained his entire game plan, he was so excited and animated about the whole thing that he got us totally wound up about it also.

I finally met Aaron on the day Cindy came home to England with me at the end of this leg of the tour. Talk about leaving it to the last minute. What if we didn't get along with each other? But it was always going to be simply accepted as a fait accompli.

When Cindy arrived, I was waiting for her in the hotel suite I had hired so that we could have more space, so Aaron could be put to bed without us having to go to bed at the same time. When she knocked on the door, I opened it to find a shy little boy hiding behind his mother's skirts. I let them in, and Aaron immediately made a beeline for the bathroom and hid from this big bad world he had just stepped into.

I'm not sure what made me do it, but I somehow instinctively knew how to break down any barriers that might have existed when this young lad and I first met: I got down on my hands and knees, crawled into the bathroom, stuck my head around the door, and pulled a silly face. This made him laugh, and from that moment on, we got on famously. By the time we were on the plane going home, Aaron and I were inseparable. We made each other laugh; it was that simple. Once we got home, he charmed everybody he met right off their feet. My father and Jo adored him, as did Sheena and Jack McCulloch, who had been house-sitting the farm.

Aaron was a very special young lad who was very easy to love. He was the sweetest child I'd ever met by a long shot, and he was a testament to how well Cindy had raised him. She had obviously done a superb job bringing him up with a lot of help from her immediate family, who were as sweet as sweet can be. Virginia, Cindy's mum, and Virginia's mum, Grandma Carey, were two of the kindest-hearted women I had ever met, and they had clearly been a great help in Aaron's upbringing. Virginia later endeared herself to both the well-spoken middle-class side of my family and the more rough-and-ready Northeast London lot at our wedding, when, having only just met them, she told them a story about a burglar who had tried to climb in the window once when she was babysitting at Cindy's Houston apartment. "Oh, you poor thing. What did you do?" asked my Aunty Marjorie, to which Virginia replied (in a slow Texan drawl), "I shot him." What a gal.

Soon after we arrived home from the tour, we had a little welcome-home party at the farm for Cindy and Aaron. At one point in the evening, we were all sitting around the kitchen table. Cindy was sitting on my lap, and Steve was on the bench along the side of the table. Dee had recently given me an early Polaroid camera as a gift. Steve picked it up and took a picture of Cindy and me sitting at the end of the table. Once the photo developed, Steve wrote one word along the bottom: "Bliss". Now Steve wasn't one to openly remark on my personal happiness, probably because, for the most part during those heady days, he assumed I was a happy chappy, and I certainly gave him no reason to think otherwise. I thought it was very sad that he wrote that on the picture for me, as it spoke volumes about the way he felt—almost envious, in a perfectly decent way—and it told me an awful lot about how my dear old friend was hurting inside. It struck such a deep nerve inside me that I almost felt guilty for being so happy and content. He did not do it to make me feel that way, bless his heart; I think it was his way of expressing both his happiness for me and his sadness about his home life, which was collapsing around him.

Mind you, when Steve was good, he was really good; in fact, he was outstanding. There was no one quite like him, and he was still performing, playing, and singing at the peak of his game. Any deterioration in his professional skills as a direct result of cocaine abuse or the subsequent breakdown of his relationship had yet to rear its ugly head. Bobby Tench once said about Steve that he constantly amazed Bobby with his ability to burn the candle at both ends—and at the middle—and still be able to perform at the top of his game. Ask just about any lead singer, and they will tell you that the worst thing you can do to yourself is to stay up yelling and hollering and not getting your rest. You will notice that while Keith was having a good old time staying up for days on end, Mick was in his bed, getting rest every night and jogging in the morning. That's why he is one of the greatest performers of the Sixties era to ever grace a stage.

I certainly do not wish to give the impression that Steve was the only one amongst us who had developed an extreme liking for Cousin Cocaine. We were all to blame for letting that godawful stuff control our every move. However, like alcohol, it affects each person's demeanour in vastly different ways.

You never knew which way was up with coke; it could bring the best and the worst out of people. Sadly, in Steve's case, it was definitely bringing out the worst. He became someone else. A recent book made a big song and dance about Steve's supposed schizophrenia. Everybody is entitled to their own opinion, but I—having spent more time with Steve than any other human being on God's earth, other than his Mum and his sister Kay—can tell you that he was not a schizophrenic. No, he was someone who became an asshole when he was drunk or high.

Later, in Dallas during the '74 tour, Steve decided to trash a hotel room one night, only he didn't just trash a room—with Greg's assistance, he *completely* trashed an entire *suite*. There was very little left that you could identify as a hotel suite; it was totally messed up. This was not our usual MO, and it would cost a fortune. If Steve were responsible, he would have to personally pay the bill. Ouch. He had to do some quick thinking. He noticed an American Wrestling Federation "Welcome, Wrestlers" sign in the lobby. So when he was asked by an exasperated Bill Anthony the following morning what had happened, he said, in his typically convincing way, that the party had been gate-crashed by a bald wrestler called Melvin, who had run riot through the suite and trashed the whole place. So convincing was he that the hotel bought it.

Thus Steve's drunken, coked-up, pain-in-the-arse alter ego was born and christened Melvin. So much for his schizophrenia—silly buggers they were for writing it in the first place. Mind you, Steve would have got a real chuckle over someone taking his beloved Melvin so seriously. His penchant for giving everybody a nickname was paying off in spades; from his wonderfully sick point of view, he had now become Melvin, the bald, professional wrestling sociopath.

From our first meeting, Aaron and I got on like father and son. Without any coaching or prompting whatsoever, he was calling me Daddy in no time at all. It was as if he was just waiting to find someone to call his dad. Even though his real father was still available for him in Texas on a part-time basis, Cindy wanted an all-day, every-day father for him. I was more than ready, willing, and, I hoped, able to be that for him.

We never prompted Aaron to call me Daddy; it just happened over time. I started as Daddy Jerry and soon become plain old Daddy. He had this adorable little Texan accent that often became entwined with an English one. The longer he was in England, the more English he sounded. He had brought a teddy bear with him, and when he said, "Where's my bear?" his Texan accent made it come out as "Wire's ma buyer?" which of course made everybody roar with laughter. Once he realised that all these new people thought he was really funny, there was no stopping him. All our married friends adored him so much that it wasn't long before many of them started to have kids. Aaron is probably responsible for many, many grown children of rock stars today. The curious part of it was that I was by far the youngest in my circle, and yet here I was with an instant family.

With the upcoming super-tour almost upon us, Cindy and I got busy finishing up all our arrangements so that we could leave house and home for a few weeks. The babysitters were in place, and she and I were ready to rock 'n' roll on our first full road trip together as a couple.

We arrived in LA, with everybody and his mother along for the ride, to start this extraordinary leg of what was being billed as our big push into the major leagues. We even brought Ernie, Dee's chauffeur from the limo service that he used from time to time whilst in London. My own brother was now in on the act as the guy who makes sure all the luggage is accounted for, which was a poor excuse for us desperately trying to find a title for him. What had actually happened was that Clydie had pulled him in London when he was hired to be the Blackberries' driver. So as the tour grew closer, she had started to make noises about how she couldn't go a day without her newfound man. Angus had moved to LA to live with her, and whereas I had inherited an instant family of one child, he walked into a family of four. Clydie's boys ranged from five to 15, and Angus seemed to fit right in from the beginning.

The band, the Blackberries, the crew, and the management all congregated to get ready for the first show at the Los Angeles Forum. Bill Graham and Concerts West, who were normally in competition with each other, joined forces on this show and promoted it together for reasons I have long since forgotten, but it was a compliment to us that they both wanted to be involved. The show was sold out well in advance, and we brought in our biggest gross for one night so far: $48,000. (Again, if you put another zero on the end of that, it will tell you what today's rough equivalent would be.)

The Forum was followed by two sold-out shows at Winterland in San Francisco, which were recorded for the King Biscuit Flower Hour, a radio show that broadcast acts live from various venues. This recording is arguably the band's and the Blackberries' finest hour. It is so big and tight sounding that it takes your breath away trying to keep up. It is exhausting to listen to, in the best possible sense of the word. We didn't think twice about it at that time; in fact, I'm not sure we even heard the recording until much later. It wasn't the first time we were featured on that show, so I suppose we took it for granted. Listening to it many years later, however, when the company that owned the tapes re-released it, it truly sounded breathtaking—there's just no other word to describe it. The version of "Hot 'n' Nasty" on it left me gobsmacked.

The next day, on our way to the airport to fly to Japan, "Get Down to It" came on the radio, and we got our first frightening taste of how bad the album sounded over the air. There was so much bass on it—or, should I say, across it—that everything was affected. It sounded like someone trying to talk with a sock in his mouth. It was truly horrific. Greg and I were in one limo, and the other guys were in another, along with the girls. When we all got out at the airport, the mood was grim. We were amazed at how bad it was. We asked the limo driver if his sound system had blown a speaker, or if it had ever sounded that bad before. His answer was "No," at which point we knew we were in deep, deep trouble. I guess we were having such a good time, what with going to Japan and having our families along for the ride, that we had just put the issue of the record's awful sound behind us, either not thinking about it or trying to ignore it.

When we got on the 707, we started to notice there was something wrong with Dee's movie concept—there were no cameras! Plus, there were only three reporters. And there were only 35 people on a plane that was built to hold 130. The weird thing was that nobody said anything about it; the only thing we said was, "Where's the blow?" For some reason or other, we could not take off right away. It was something to do with the weight of the plane—too much fuel, I think, and not enough people. While we were waiting, we ran out of drugs. Don't forget, we were on our way to Japan, which has one of the strictest drug policies anywhere in the world; in 1980, they almost put Paul McCartney in jail for many years for a little bit of pot.

It makes me shudder to think what they might have done to us if we were caught with a big bag of cocaine, but that didn't seem to stop us from making a call, while we were waiting for the plane to get sorted out, to a friendly local dealer who drove another bunch of coke out to the plane for us. Greg, bless his heart, had decided to pop a couple of Valium and sleep his way to Japan; the problem was, it took so long to resolve the plane's weight problem that he eventually woke up and thought we had arrived, only to find out that we still hadn't taken off. He was not a happy camper, although the blow was softened by the blow, of which there was now a new abundance, thanks to that friendly dealer.

The size of our party was remarkable when you consider that we were only a four-piece band going to Japan for the first time and not exactly being paid a king's ransom to do so. Each band guy had his wife with him, and Dee had his wife, all three of his children, his father, and his chauffeur. We never did figure out why Ernie came along for the ride. His only claim to fame was being found stark naked, wandering the halls of the Regency Hotel in

NYC. Then there was my brother, who was looking after both the luggage and Clydie. We also had our regular crew, which consisted of 12 people. And then there was the press corps, all three of them: one guy from *Rolling Stone*, our old friend Pete Erskine, who wrote for *Sounds*; and a guy from *Record Mirror*. When you consider that those 35 people drank the plane dry before it took off, when it was fully stocked to serve 130, you can imagine how that set the tone for the journey ahead.

In actual fact, though, we were reasonably well behaved, and, after all, it was our plane—well, for the duration of the flight to Japan anyway. After that, we would go back to using regular transport, and when we were finished in Japan we would fly back via Hawaii on a regular jumbo jet, some of us in first class, some of us not. The expense of all of this was astronomical, and we were all spending money like it was going out of style—in Japan, we would all end up buying Nikon cameras, fancy silk kimonos, watches, more Nikon cameras, more fancy silk kimonos, and on and on it went.

We were to be in Japan for a total of 10 days with five dates to play, which meant there would be a considerable amount of sightseeing time and general having-fun time. It looked like it was gonna be a hell of a good trip—the problem was, it almost didn't happen. By the time we landed in Tokyo, most of us had got well and truly thank-you-very-much on the plane, courtesy of all the booze we drank for the hundred people who weren't there with us. After all, it was only fair; as they were unable to show up, the least we could do was drink their alcohol for them. By the time we landed, most of us were just tired and wanted to get through customs and immigration and to the hotel to sleep, with one exception: our dearly beloved, do-it-all-and-still-keep-going Steve.

The Japanese Customs and Immigration officials are notorious for being the strictest anywhere in the world, or they certainly were back then. Steve had decided to dive headlong into an extremely heated argument with Jenny right before we were due to get off the plane. He continued this dispute right the way into the Customs area, while brandishing a bottle of brandy that he was taking generous gulps from. We almost didn't make it into the country because of this, and I really don't remember how things turned in our favour, but the combined bargaining skills of Dee and Bill Anthony and John Doumanian saved our bacon, and we entered Japan safely.

The first thing that greeted us as we appeared from the Customs hall was a big sign some fans were holding; it read, "Welcome Hamble Pie," which I suppose wasn't too dreadful when you consider all the possible calamities that can happen when the Japanese get their teeth into the English language. (Eric Clapton apparently loves playing Japan, where he is referred to

Entering Japan (center). We would not have been allowed in were it not for the efforts of Dee and Bill Anthony. Our road crew (surrounding, clockwise from top left): Mick Brigden, Randy Burton, Dave Clark, John Hammel, and Ted Sellen.

as Eric Crapton.) We fared reasonably well on the dodgy-English front, with one exception. Not long after arriving, we visited a radio station, where the effervescent disc jockey chose to announce us individually. It went along in a reasonably safe manner. He introduced Steve Marriott without problems, then moved on to Jerry Shirrey, which didn't turn too many heads, and then Greg Ridrey. We hadn't thought too much about it until he got to Clem, who was announced like this: "Radies and gentremen, prease wercome *Crem Crempson!*" Clem, bless his heart, took it manfully, but from that day on, much to Steve's delight, he remained Crem Crempson.

We were to do two shows in Tokyo and one each in Kyoto, Nagoya, and Osaka. We were being paid $10,000 per gig, so our gross for the 10 days was $50,000. Considering this was our first time up to bat in Japan, it didn't seem such a bad deal if the expenditure side of things had not got so out of hand. The shows were all sold out except Osaka, which did reasonable business. The promoters said there was no particular reason that show didn't sell out. It was held in the broad daylight of afternoon in what looked like a school hall. Very strange.

The Japanese promoter of this tour was a legend in the business called Mr. Udo. He prided himself in being the most caring promoter out there, and he was. He certainly was on a par with all the top guys we worked with across the USA, and it helped to have the sort of thoughtful relationship that Mr. Udo thrived on working for you when you were half a world away from home. He had several little trademark hospitality manoeuvres he would do for the bands that came through Japan, so his reputation preceded him.

He took us to fabulous restaurants, where we were introduced to the wonderful world of Kobe beef. This was the tenderest beef I have ever tasted; there is no meat like it. Apparently, they massage the animals from the time they are babies, and they feed them on totally natural food that contains no chemicals whatsoever. Of course the icing on the cake is watching those hibachi chefs show their knife-wielding expertise, which is worth the price of admission all on its own.

One of the perks of going to Japan and working for Mr. Udo was summed up in two words: bath house! It's all you hear about prior to going there. Never mind the great audiences, the supremely efficient stage crews, or the big money that can eventually be earned there; it's the bath houses that everybody wants to experience. Those places are, without a doubt, legends in their own lunch break. They are absolutely extraordinary.

Mr. Udo arranged for all the band members to go to a bath house on the second night we were in Tokyo. Our ladies were fine about it, with one exception; Mandy would not hear of it. Greg going to have the massage of a lifetime? Not a chance. She arranged a regular massage for both of them in their hotel room; I'm sure it was nice, but not quite the same.

As Steve, Clem, and I arrived at the bath house, the first thing we had to do was take off our shoes. "Okay, that's a start," I thought. We went up the stairs and at the top entered a small lounge where there were cushions to sit on cross-legged and wait, while a Japanese beauty in a lovely silk kimono took our drinks order. Once we were served, a steady stream of Japanese babes soon started to file into the room one by one, and we were asked to take our partners in no particular order, until the last girl came in and there was only me left. This was one example of how nice guys don't always finish last—she was gorgeous.

I had let the others go before me for no real reason, but I do remember one or two of them walking into the back of the house where all the action happened with big, self-satisfied smirks on their faces, thinking they were the cats who got the cream. Right away I had something to smile about, as we had seen a couple of guys who were finished being escorted back into the lounge by the girls who took care of them, so I knew Steve and Clem would see my beauty when we were done.

My knockout escorted me back along a corridor lined with those Japanese screens that are often lit up and have black silhouette scenes painted on them. When we got to her room, she pulled open the sliding door and beckoned me to walk in, then followed me.

The room was remarkable. There was a small stream running through the middle, with a little humpback bridge over it. I couldn't help chuckling over this, given that it was not the only thing in the room that had something to do with humping. The massage table was on one side of the stream, while the Turkish bath and a small stool were on the other. Once I got my kit off, she had me sit on the stool while she lathered me up all over. She then rinsed me off and had me sit in the Turkish bath, one of those that close in around you while your head sticks out of the top with a large towel around your neck. When I was suitably cooked, she had me sit on the stool while she rinsed me off again, then dried me with a towel before pointing to the massage table. I was cleaner than I have ever been; she had washed me in places that I was previously unaware even existed.

Once I was on the table, she started giving me the greatest massage I have ever had. The reputation of these beauties was that they could make a man cum by using a form of massage that only they know how to administer. All I will say on the matter is that their reputation is extremely well deserved. Having completed her task, she had me sit on the stool while I got my last rinse and dry, then proceeded to escort me back to the lounge, where I could gloat ever so slightly over her beauty.

After my bath house visit, I felt it was only proper to organise a trip there for our road crew for all the hard work and loyalty they had shown us over the last few years. I told them I was personally going to spoil them by taking them on my tab. They say that lightning never strikes twice; however, once I was in the bath house on this second visit, I had to wonder. The same thing happened, except this time I watched as the crew were taken back one by one. Seeing that they had got some excellent-looking ladies, I was not worried about my outcome; I just assumed I was in for a letdown, given my good fortune on the previous visit.

And then, what do you know, it happened again. Only this time, she was even more beautiful than Number One. Number Two was a serious stunner. I almost felt bad about what the crew would think, but then… nah! Once back in the lounge, I sat there and openly gloated over her gorgeous face and her figure to die for. The crew loved me for taking the time to consider them in this endeavour, but they were a good bunch of lads who had more than earned it.

By now, it was more than clear that the film was not going to happen. I would like to tell you that the reason was something to do with the normal stuff, like contracts couldn't be agreed to on time or the film crew's equipment was lost in flight—only that wouldn't work, as we had hired the plane for them to fly on. The strange part of this entire episode was that nobody questioned it, and no one gave an explanation. It simply didn't happen. So there we were with all the trappings of a big-shot movie crew, without one major ingredient: the movie crew.

This minor oversight on somebody's part did not stop us from having a good time. All the gigs went extremely well, although we couldn't figure out the Japanese audiences at first. They would just sit there, very quiet and well behaved, until the end of each song, when they would go nuts in a very orderly fashion, and then go back to being very quiet and polite, all for no apparent reason.

We eventually found out the reason. The promoters had experienced some extremely wild crowds in the past, so they had decided to up the police presence and show the audiences in no uncertain terms what would happen should they start any trouble. We were told how these policemen had conducted themselves at previous gigs with other bands, and it wasn't pretty. So our audiences dealt with the prospect of police violence by sitting there as quietly as they could, and then using the breaks between the songs to let rip. It was such a strange experience, but once we had come to terms with it, it was fine, and pretty soon we were enjoying ourselves immensely.

Clem's wife Kathy got some terrible news from England: her father had passed away. This left us in a bit if a jam, as Clem wasn't in a position to leave the tour, but Kathy obviously had to go home right away. The solution was simple—Dee's daughter Michele volunteered to fly back with Kathy to make sure everything was okay. Even though Michele was only 16 at the time, she did a fabulous job and showed the maturity of someone twice her age.

After Japan, we headed back to mainland USA, but not before we stopped in Honolulu, Hawaii, to do a show in the H.I.C., the same building we had played the year before, except this time we played the H.I.C. Arena, the big room that the Osmonds had played in '72. Elvis had also recently played there as part of his comeback tour. The place holds about 8,500 people, and the crowd there is fantastic.

We nearly didn't do the H.I.C. Arena show at all, thanks to yours truly. I have said before that Steve did not have exclusivity on bad behaviour, and what happened next was one of my own contributions to our Hall of Infamy. On the flight from Tokyo to Hawaii, after drinking all the sake in first class, I decided to go back into economy and sit with all my drinking partners, the road crew, with whom I proceeded to drink economy dry of sake. We then moved on to any libation that took our fancy.

I had gone back and sat with the crew because Cindy had asked, if I was going to get ripped, could I please do it in the back with the lads, as she wanted to get some sleep.

As I stood up to go back into economy, Jenny, who was sat across the aisle from me, said in a scornful manner, "That's the trouble with you, Jerry. You're a real pain in the arse when you're drunk."

Although I was pie-eyed at the time, her words really struck a chord with me, primarily because it was Jenny, but also because I figured that if she felt that way about me, so must others. I was mortified. Her comment did not, however, stop me from drinking right away, but it did plant a little seed in my subconscious that I kept watering for many years to come.

When we landed in Honolulu, I hadn't slept much, and I was obviously plastered. I must have stunk of booze because even if I had brushed my teeth before we disembarked, which I did not, I would still have smelled like a distillery. As we stood in line waiting to show our passports to Immigration, I swayed back and forth. I could barely stand up. When it was my turn, I staggered into the Immigration officer's booth and handed over my passport.

"Have you got your immigration form?" asked the lady officer in the booth.

"What immigration form?" I replied in a drunken, bossy voice.

"One like this; they give it to all passengers during the flight," she said. "Here; take this over there, fill it out, then come back and we can start again, okay?"

I grudgingly went over to the side of the booth, filled out the form, took it back to her, and threw it down on her desk in a very intoxicated, pissed-off manner.

"Go and do it again," she said. "It's illegible," which it was.

So I went and did it again in a slightly improved hand, took it back to her, threw it down, and said something like, "You could have read it the first time if you weren't so fucking blind and ugly, you soppy old cow."

Before I knew what was happening, she beckoned two armed police-men to come and take me away to be interviewed and searched. When we got into the interview room, they told me to take my clothes off. As I started to strip, they asked what I was doing in Hawaii. I told them I was playing the following night in the H.I.C., at which point one of them said, "Wait a minute—you're not in Humble Pie, are you?" I replied that I was. They immediately told me to stop taking my kit off, and could they get an autograph instead? It turned out they were both huge fans of the band and had bought their tickets to our show months before. I gave them my autograph and told them I would put some backstage passes at the Will Call window for them. I was a very lucky boy; if they had wanted to, they could have stopped me from entering the country, and that would have been disastrous.

Once sober, I started to think that maybe I should have a look at my drinking. For Jenny to say something about it really did bother me a great deal, and pondering what nearly happened at Immigration gave me some serious food for thought. It took me another 20 years to actually do something about it, but I am forever grateful for these two incidents for at least getting me started on the road to recovery, even if it took a long time for me to surrender to it. So, by then, being a member of Humble Pie had not only given me a blessed life, it had also made me rich and had saved my bacon on more than one occasion.

Mick Brigden had managed to get us approval to use these huge mirrors onstage that Elvis had used as a backdrop behind his orchestra when he played at the H.I.C. Arena, and Mick did a fine job utilizing them for our show. I remember thinking how big we had become and how efficient our crew was, getting all our staging and amplifiers and lighting to fit in one truck. They really were the best at what they did, and we were very lucky to have them.

The rest of the stay was short and sweet, unlike the last time we were in Ho-

In Hawaii with Steve, who's wearing a daft swimming hat left behind at the pool by an old lady.

nolulu, and it was tremendously satisfying to see that we'd upgraded from playing a place the previous year where we only drew a couple of thousand at best to the venue's big room that held 8,500 people.

The album had got near the Top 10 with a bullet in *Billboard* as we took off for a string of dates that would lead up to Madison Square Garden in NYC. The first stop was Des Moines, Iowa, and then it was on to Pittsburgh, Philadelphia, Detroit, and the Garden. Cindy flew home to see and look af-

Reaching back and going for it at Cobo Hall, Detroit.

ter Aaron, while Sheena and Jack flew to NYC to see the show. All the dates leading up to the Garden were sold out, with one exception: Des Moines. This of course gave Steve's "only play in big cities" argument plenty of steam. He firmly believed that we were a big-city band and had no business messing around in the secondary markets. Zeppelin, though, had recently done a three-week tour of the States in which they played almost entirely in secondary and tertiary markets. So Steve's attitude was another good example of how he would often frustrate our attempts to progress into wider markets and to adopt conventional business practices that other bands had been following for a long time. It didn't help matters that whenever we got a gig that was even slightly off the beaten track, it made Steve misbehave something wicked.

The pre-Garden gigs all had a level of performance that was above anything we had achieved so far. It had a lot to do with the Blackberries being with us, as they had a really positive effect on Steve, and in doing so had an amazing effect on the rest of the band. For some reason, having them on board made us get even sharper and tighter musically. The band had always had great backing vocals, but now, with the girls along for the ride, there was a fullness to the vocals like never before. As time went on, we found more and more places to feature the girls' individual talents in the show. They were also a lot of fun to look at. It was a joy to witness all this going on around me.

With that string of sellouts under our belt and the album doing big business, everything in the garden seemed to be rosy, but the cold, hard facts were not good by any means. We were about to fly into New York to play our first date as headliners at the Garden. During the couple of days before the Garden show, a number of small things added up to make me fully aware of how bad things actually were.

When we arrived at the airport to fly from Detroit to NYC, we had two stretch Learjets instead of our beloved Falcon. Steve loved the girls to travel with us, so we had figured out that we could in fact travel together if we used one of the planes for luggage and one for humans—but they were originally rented so the band could fit in one and the girls in the other. While that seemed fine and dandy at first, it now hit me that we were hiring a private jet to transport *luggage*. Not a good sign. Until now, we had been reasonably sensible with our expenditures; the problem was that we had recently doubled our wage bill and all the things that go along with it, but hadn't increased our income. Yes, we were doing considerably better than the year before, but not *that* much better; certainly our income hadn't doubled. We had also, long before, budgeted for the three-day stay in NYC to accommodate our families to come over and see their boys play in the world-famous Madison Square Garden. While I may not be the brightest spark in the fire, it didn't take a rocket scientist to figure out that things may have got a little out of hand.

I was keeping a tab on what we were making, so that if we ever had to, we could use my records and compare them to the actual figures. The band were more than happy for me to do the job, as it meant that one of us was keeping an eye on the store—and that they didn't have to do it. I'd been doing this from the beginning of the band. At first, I suppose it was just a little hobby. However, the more money we made, the more important it was that I kept track of it. I made some really good friends among the promoters across the USA by asking what the night's take was. Actually, most of the time I wouldn't have to ask—they would tell me. It taught me a lot about the business and how things worked on their side of the fence, plus I made some long-lasting friendships that, sadly, I don't keep up, simply because I now live in the UK and they all live in the US. I got to learn all these cool words whose meanings I previously had no idea of, but which I soon found out came in handy on the rare occasion when we were on the road without anybody from the office.

I found generally that the promoters respected me for showing an interest in our financial affairs. Steve took great pride in his negative attitude regarding the business and took the piss relentlessly out of anybody who even tried to keep an eye on it. The cruel irony was that all of Steve's heroes who got to the top, and stayed there for a very long time, care a great deal about their business; otherwise they too would be condemned to a lifetime of playing in pubs and clubs and bars. But I'm getting ahead of myself here. For now, the whole band was enjoying the top flight as much as anybody. While you are there, you can't imagine being anywhere else.

Dee was very good at giving out wise counsel that, if you listened, would be good for you. If you chose not to pay attention, you would end up at the dry end of the oil stick. The most profound example of this happened in the restaurant at the top of the Holiday Inn in Des Moines, where we played right after Japan.

After we ate, Dee and I decided to have a look at the band that was playing in the bar; everybody else chose to go to their rooms instead. The band was one I had never heard of: the Four Lads. In between sets, Dee went over to them, shook their hands, chatted for a minute, and came back to the table. When he returned, he just sat there pensively, without saying a word.

After what seemed to be forever, I finally said, "So, you know those guys?"

"Yeah, kinda," he replied.

"Really? How come?"

"They used to be huge. We worked with them on a couple of occasions when I was with Tony Bennett."

"Really? Wow, what a comedown to end up playing in this pisshole," said I.

"Yeah," Dee agreed. "And if some of us don't wake up and smell the roses, this is where they will end up also."

I was fairly confident that he didn't mean me, and, after thinking about it, it hit me that he didn't mean anybody in particular; he simply meant it as a generalization—pay attention, or this is where you'll end up—and as history shows, he was right.

So here we were in NYC, getting ready to do the biggest gig of our career. We had played to bigger audiences, but never as the headliner. Back then, the Garden was a notoriously tough place to sell out, and some said we weren't ready to headline it. But Dee was so proud of his band—"Ma boys," as he used to call us—and he loved it every time he got to prove them wrong.

At the hotel, I found Dad and Jo and took them out for lunch. Dad asked me to choose an affordable place 'cos the prices at the Regency were so outrageous. So I took them to a favourite place just around the corner that Greg and I went to all the time when we were in NYC. I also told Dad not to worry; he and Jo could put anything they ate at the hotel on the bill, and I would pay it when we checked out.

Dad wouldn't hear of it; he insisted it was bad form to take advantage of his son's good fortune. I was proud of my old man's show of good manners—even though I could afford it, you were not going to ever catch Major Robert freeloading from anybody, least of all his own son. He told me how much was being spent in the bar by Steve's family—it was astronomical. And it wasn't even Steve's mum and dad; it was his second-string Auntie Something and Uncle Whatever who were helping themselves to room service. Anyway, I told Dad not to be silly; the meals were on me. I think I managed to buy him and Jo dinner one night, but that was it.

Before the show, we had a day or two off so that we could be well and truly ready for our big night at the Garden. Each of us had his own way of dealing with the nerves that come with doing a gig that prestigious. Clem walked into a large cathedral on Park Avenue and prayed for a good show. As far as I recall, he was not religiously minded. I didn't do much of anything, other than buy some cool new stage clothes for the Garden show from North Beach Leather, which had just opened up a store in NYC. Then I headed over to the accountant's office to see how things were.

Even though there had been a few signs of that ill wind blowing again, I was in for a huge shock. Considering that we had just played some of the biggest arenas in the US, toured Japan, and on the way back played another run of the big arenas, nothing could have prepared me for what I was about to find out.

Our accountant, Bert Padell, was the same one Dee used, which was Bad Move No. 1. He let us do things that we never should have done from an accounting point of view—Bad Move No. 2. And he was too timid to at least try to make us see how things were—Bad Move No. 3.

Bert seemed to be a nice, soft-spoken New Yorker, and we had come to see him as another father figure, so when I went to his office that day, I was shocked to see the state he was in. He was nervous, sweating, really jumpy, and finding it hard to string two words together.

"We're sunk, Jer," he said. "I mean *really* sunk, Jer. We gotta do something." He was pacing back and forth, so I told him to sit down and tell me what was up.

"You guys are over $100,000 in debt; that's what's up," he said.

That couldn't be right. There must be a mistake. After all that work?

"Yeah, but what with the big jet to Japan, plus the big wages for the girls—although they sing beautifully—it's costing you guys a fortune. And then there's the studio. Wow! How does Steve manage to spend over a hundred thousand bucks on a little studio in his barn?"

I nearly fainted. Steve had led us to believe that the studio only cost $10,000.

Bert asked me if Dee knew I was coming to see him. I said no; why should it matter? He said that he should be the one to tell Dee about our meeting. I said I thought we should do it together. He said no, he should do it, and in any case, it should wait until after the Garden show. On that we were in agreement.

This was quite a lot to take in all at once, particularly when you consider that I was barely 21 years old, and as proud as I was that the band were happy for me to watch the money for everyone, it was nonetheless a lot of responsibility.

Now that the band's relatives were in town, we were in a celebratory mood. Everyone was having a good old time, and why not? I chose not to say anything to anyone until after the show. I figured, what's the point? It would only serve to ruin everybody's night at the Garden, and who knows, this may turn out to be the only time we get to headline the place.

Our sold-out headlining show at Madison Square Garden in NYC.

We just managed to sell out, with moments to spare. There was so much anticipation leading up to the show that the actual event was almost a letdown. It wasn't bad or anything, but when you get that wound up about one gig, you can easily let yourself down come showtime. But the presence of the relatives stopped the show from being a disappointment and, in fact, made it rather great, believe it or not. In a room of 20,000 people, our families could be heard above the madding crowd on occasion, plus they had found some Union Jack flags somewhere that they were waving above their heads, which didn't please the people sat directly behind them. Mind you, if those poor sods behind our lot would even think about complaining, they would get the double whammy from Steve's mum and my dad, her screaming and him punching. Ah, what a life I led.

Despite the band's nerves, we played wonderfully. Steve looked at the top of his game and never sounded better. I think the fact that his mum Kath, dad Bill, and sister Kay were there helped him to behave himself offstage, and it certainly helped onstage, as the one thing he'd always wanted to do was appear on the top of the bill at MSG in front of his mum and dad. I was equally chuffed that my dad and brother got to see me do the same, and especially thrilled to be the drummer behind Steve when he was performing in front of his family. All of this only goes to show that life with Steve Marriott always was "All or Nothing."

After the show I was faced with a serious dilemma. Who was I going to tell what to? Years later, I heard my dear friend Tommy Cusick say something that would have fit perfectly in these circumstances: "When in doubt, do nothing." That is pretty much what I did to begin with, but after a little while I obviously had to say something. We had a lot to do, and something like this could cause irreparable damage to everything we had worked so hard to achieve, so I decided to have the two men sort it out. I told Dee what Dr. Doom had told me. He was furious—how dare Bert lay something like that on one of us right before a show like the Garden! He gave Bert an appropriate bollocking and worked out the apparent shortfall so that we could continue onwards and upwards.

This was a great relief to all concerned, although I must be honest: I could have done without it being laid on my young little shoulders. Also, it put me in the position of middle man for everybody, so that, after this incident, if one of us had a problem with something that another one of us had done, he would come to me with his grief.

All I wanted was for us to go forward without hindrance. After all, we were making some pretty decent dosh at the time, so if we were in hock to the extent of a hundred grand, it wouldn't take that long to work our way out of it. However, that wasn't the only problem that we were facing. The album was starting to collapse around us. It took a considerable tumble down the charts—on the *Cashbox* chart, I recall it going from Number 10 with a bullet to 10 without a bullet to 23—in the three weeks that surrounded the Garden show. By the time we were back home for a couple of weeks, it was off the charts entirely.

The doom and gloom I got from Bert also served to put the magnifying glass on all things financial. Up until now we had no reason to question anything, as everything seemed fine, and any financial requests that we had were dealt with in a timely manner. Looking back, I can see that this was where the rot started to set in.

Steve commanding attention at Madison Square Garden.

There was a little incident on the flight home from the Garden show that summed up the changes in our Steve extremely well.

The band had got tickets for first class, and the families were to sit in economy. This wasn't done with any sort of malice; it just made common sense all round—there were so many people being flown to and from NYC, especially Steve's family and friends, as he had invited many more people over and above his mum, dad, and sister Kay, bless 'em. Though band and family were originally booked on separate flights back to London, Steve, for reasons that I forget, chose to fly home on the same flight as his parents and Kay. As they were about to get on the plane, Steve realized that his ticket was in first, while his folks and sister were in economy, so he threw one of his famous wobblers and insisted that his family should be flying home in first with him. His family were trying to say it didn't matter, and can we please just get on the plane and go home without any fuss. They had, after all, flown over in economy along with the other families, Dad and Jo included.

The upshot of it all was that the band paid several thousand dollars more than originally planned on the flights for Steve's family and friends. So, after all this nonsense, off they went back home, probably a little embarrassed that Steve's behaviour had blown a huge hole in the band's finances.

When I arrived later at the airport with Dad and Jo (Cindy was already home ahead of me), we didn't know about Steve's song and dance, as we were on a different flight. As we boarded the plane, the stewardess realized we were together, although the tickets were first for me and economy for Dad and Jo, and asked Dad if he would like to sit in first class with his son.

"No, that's okay, thank you," he replied. "I wouldn't want to put any more strain on my son's money. He's already done enough."

"Don't worry, Mr. Shirley," said the stewardess. "Let's see if there's any room left. If there is, we can bump you up to first class without you having to pay anything extra." And that is how my father was able to boast in the pub for the rest of his days that he flew home from NYC first class.

Chapter 16
Strange Days
June 1973 to January 1974

*In which we learn that, no matter what anyone says,
the Average White Band are indisputably better than
Pink Floyd—but David Gilmour's mum is the Killer queen;
Paul Stanley talks about going to church; we outdraw
Led Zep, but their record remains the same; there's a riot goin'
on at Summerfest; I don't quite see eye to eye with Peter Wolf;
and Steve invests in chips instead of Jenny's antiques.*

Once back in England, we went about making the farm into a family home. It really didn't take much doing, as the place already had a really nice homey feel. After Cindy and Aaron settled in and we found a good kindergarten for him, there wasn't a lot to be done. Cindy fell right into the English country way of doing things, which is not that dissimilar to the Texan way: both are very laid back.

Clem and I had become good mates, as we had a lot of common interests, the biggest being football. We decided to form a band soccer team and started by playing amongst ourselves in one of the fields on my land behind the house. Clem was an extremely good inside forward, or midfielder as they are more commonly known. We were joined by our roadie Ted Sellen, who looked after my kit and was living upstairs in one of the attic rooms at the farm; he played a hair-raising version of a fullback. We also recruited a number of my old Waltham Cross mates, who were all pretty good at football and even better at protecting us from any excess aggression on the field from jealous plumbers. The local plumber/builder/carpenter-type lads often put a team together for no other reason than to take a potshot at the long-haired rich guys in "that rock band." They also didn't appreciate all the Rolls-Royces and BMWs that were parked outside the farm.

Steve, being Steve, was not a big football player, as he was the first to admit, but he still wanted to be part of it, and, as only he could, he created the position of trainer/doctor who would dash on to the field at the drop of a hat, administer some of his super-medicated goo, and make us all laugh. The only problem was that his ability to put together an extremely effective potion soon became a thing of legend, and you would find guys diving and screaming for the trainer to come to their aid just so they could get a swig of grog and a bump.

Steve did his bit on our inaugural match on the field, as we first had to make it playable, before we got semi-serious about it. To celebrate this auspicious occasion, he had Sheena and Cindy make him up and dress him like an old East End charlady, a regular Widow Twankey. It was hysterical, and, of course, he stole the show, which was the one habit Steve never did find a cure for, thank God.

This made for some pretty hysterical weekends at Green Farm. Everyone would show up on Friday night or Saturday morning, depending on how much drinking and dart playing they wished to partake in as a lead-up to the Sunday afternoon football match with whoever chose to put themselves in the line of fire. When we were not playing the aforementioned tradesmen, we would ply our trade on other bands. Some were dreadful, as in the Sutherland Brothers & Quiver; some were not bad, as in Pink Floyd; and some were excellent, as in the Average White Band. On some occasions when it wasn't football season, we got together for marathon dart matches. The two most memorable started at local gigs that the Sutherlands were playing on the Saturday night and progressed to my local pub, where the publican, Joe, would gladly shut the doors at closing time so that we could continue without being disturbed by the local constabulary. We would even-

The Humble Pie football team ready for action. I'm at bottom left, with Clem next to me. We're looking up at Greg, who is making a wisecrack. He's in black, as he was playing in goal that day. Angus, with beard, is in the front row, second right. Far left, out of uniform, is Jack McCullough, Jimmy's older brother, who was the "trainer" for that day. The bag across his shoulder contained the all-important "medicated goo." The recommended dosage was a swig of brandy and a line of coke to revive one's spirits.

tually end up at the farm for marathons of Killer, a dart game based upon a knockout system whereby the last man standing is the winner.

A normal game of Killer usually runs for up to 40 minutes, with four people playing, but there were at least 20 playing on these two occasions, which started at the farm at about midnight and went on and on—and after they had gone on and on, they went on and on again. Dave Gilmour and his mum, Sylvia, happened to be there for both of these marathons. There were all these supposed hotshot dart players who were taking it really seriously; then there were people like me and Dave, who were not exactly taking it seriously. And then there was Sylvia, who was just having a ball, without taking it as anything but fun. At the first marathon, almost eight hours after we began, we crowned the new Killer champ—Mrs. Sylvia Gilmour, bless her heart. And a few months later, she did it again!

The band spent the rest of the summer going back and forth across the good old US of A, with one significant change to our line-up. Clydie had had enough, and decided to call it quits and go back to LA and the sessions she was doing before we took her on the road. We had learned a lot from her, and it had been a privilege to work with such an esteemed member of Ray Charles' extended family. At least she was in love with my dear brother, God bless her and him. Years later, Angus told me some lovely little stories about answering the phone at Clydie's house and the voice on the other end saying, "Hey, little brother. Tell her it's Brother Ray on the phone."

To fill the void left by Clydie, Venetta brought in an old friend of hers from Buffalo called Carlena Williams. Carlena was an outstanding singer, a big lady with a big voice who was so good that the Blackberries didn't miss a beat. As a group, they were just as powerful, possibly more so. Clydie's solo voice was so unique that it would always be missed, but it's a testament to how good Carlena's voice was that it enabled us to keep moving forward and minimized the loss of Clydie to where you didn't miss her nearly as much as you would have if she hadn't been replaced by the force of nature that was Carlena. Her roots were in the black church—which in my book is the best place any singer could possibly be from—and Steve loved her to bits.

There was, however, a negative side to the Blackberries coming on board. It was not anything they did; they were now more reasonable to deal with from a business perspective. Clydie's only shortcoming had been her tendency to be somewhat demanding, whereas with Carlena in the fold, Venetta was able to keep a better hold on things; she didn't have Clydie constantly moaning about one thing or another.

The problem was a particularly despicable form of racism that went across the board from certain people in our audience to certain areas of the industry. It's strange to look back on it now because I can't help being filled with pride and shame at the same time. I'm proud because we were the first major white British rock 'n' roll band that so blatantly stood for an equal stance on stage and record between black and white musicians. There had been Americans who'd done it before us—among others, the Stax family of singers and musicians, who, after all, were the model we were trying to emulate in terms of total equality. My shame is due to the way our audience, particularly in the southern States, chose to turn off to us as a result of the nature of our new show.

Paul Stanley of Kiss said that watching Steve in Humble Pie "was like being at a church revival," and that about sums it up. It was very much what Steve had always wanted to do one day, and we did our level best to support him all the way. We did not notice any difference in the way we were received when we played live; it was more subtle than that. Instead, it was the aftermath—the fact that the record did not catch on in the South, where we had been super-strong before; people there were just turning their backs on our new direction. Those in the more cosmopolitan areas of the States were far more accepting. This kind of prejudice was horrifying. But, as I said, I'm proud of the way we worked with those great ladies and took no notice whatsoever of all that bullshit; we just played and sang our asses off and loved every minute of it.

At the Spectrum in Philly, from the collection of roadie Ted Sellen.

The racism that was so deeply entrenched in some parts of the American South was graphically illustrated to me on one of our tours around this time, when, as Cindy had recently moved to England and was going to marry me, I met the rest of her family.

Cindy's Grandma Carey, who I had met previously, had grown very fond of me, and I absolutely adored her. She had recently moved from Port Arthur to the infamous Vidor, Texas, not far from Beaumont. And now I met Cindy's two redneck uncles, Milt and Junior, better known as June. These guys were so redneck that they would consider being referred to as such a compliment. We all sat down to dinner, and Grandma Carey gave me a detailed history of Vidor, whose population back then consisted of about 5,000 people, all of whom were white. I assumed that all of them were also members of the Ku Klux Klan, as Grandma Carey's husband, Arthur, pointed out that Vidor was a stronghold of that godawful band of reprobates.

I withheld the little nugget of information that Humble Pie was going to be touring the Deep South with three black ladies, as discretion seemed by far the better half of valour… especially in Vidor.

Milt and June did not say a word at dinner; all they did was glare at me. Each had an identical greased black hairstyle a la Elvis and wore a white t-shirt with his Lucky Strikes tucked up under the sleeve on the shoulder, James Dean style, showing off what looked like a prison tattoo on his large biceps. The difference was that, unlike Elvis or James Dean, these two were ugly bastards with beer bellies. The only time their demeanour changed was during Arthur's explanation of Vidor's place in the history of the KKK, when they shared a knowing look, full of pride.

After dinner, we all went and sat in the living room and tried to get comfortable in the sweltering heat and humidity of the Texan summer evening. There was no air conditioning, just a fan that made lots of noise but did bugger-all else. Milt and June chose to sit either side of me. Still they said nothing as they drank their shots of Old Grand-Dad whiskey chased with Pabst Blue Ribbon beer.

Finally, after what seemed an eternity, Uncles Milt and June leant in towards me, and, with a conspiratorial hooking of his index finger, Milt motioned for me to listen to some dark secret he wanted to whisper in my ear. "We ain't got no niggers around here!" he said, then leant back with a proud smile on his face that June shared, as if to agree. I was stunned, but not surprised. I figured that an anti-prejudice rant would probably not be a good idea, so, in my best BBC accent, I said, "Absolutely, old chap! Fine show! Well done, dear boy!"

I was disgusted with myself, although deep down I at least got a little satisfaction out of the knowledge that they had no idea I was mocking them. I did get a little nervous when I saw the look Vern gave me when I used the words "dear boy," but, as he didn't suggest lynching me, I guessed that I had got away with it. After all, even though I was a Goddamned Long-Haired Hippy, I was a filthy rich one who was marrying his niece.

As we were leaving an hour or so later, Vern finally said something, almost as an afterthought, following on along the intellectual lines of his brother:

"There was a nigger who came through Vidor once, a long time ago."

"What happened?" I asked in a half-hearted attempt to feign interest.

"He stopped to get directions," Vern replied.

"And then what?"

"He got lost and came back through to ask again."

"And then what?"

"They lynched him," was the succinct reply.

I couldn't help but notice how Steve and Dee were both being horribly distorted in very similar ways by that stinking white powder that was now around us at all times. Gone were the days of Dee being a strong father figure who could tell us where we were going wrong before we went *too* wrong, a good case in point being his insistence that we remix the live album because we hadn't done a good enough job on the first mix.

When he and Steve were working well together and behaving almost like father and son, it was a joy to witness and be part of, and it produced spectacular results. But then, once money was no object and the cocaine was around *all* the time in large quantities, they both went into free fall. Not to be outdone by their shenanigans—after all, this was an equal opportunity screw-up—the rest of us didn't help matters. We did plenty of moaning and groaning, our own fair share of cocaine, and very little else. The trouble was, we ended up being not-so-innocent bystanders.

So here we were with Steve and his seditious and utterly subversive approach to everything that was being attempted for him by us and others who were trying to help and had no axe to grind whatsoever. Bill Curbishley is probably the best example of someone who offered a helping hand only to have it almost bitten off by Steve for no other reason than it was easier and more rebellious than to graciously accept it: "Why cooperate when I can be an awkward bastard?" Bill was the Who's manager and had been asked by Dee to help out with the day-to-day management of Humble Pie while we were working in Europe, in much the same way that Dee used to service-manage English bands in America for Chris Blackwell and others. Mark Fenwick was another good example. He had got involved in helping to manage us in the UK, as Dee had done the same for him and his partners when their acts, which included ELP and Roxy Music, came to the States. These were two of the brightest young things of their time, and Steve did his level best to work against them, rather than with them.

Then there was Dee. Instead of confronting us about the sound quality of *Eat It* as he had with the live album, he just allowed it to be released and made all these grandiose plans that failed to go the distance.

We still had lots of touring to do right through the summer. Many of the dates were more of the big outdoor shows that we had become masters at playing. There is a certain "take no prisoners" attitude that comes with performing to a huge crowd, and our approach was perfectly suited to it. It also has to be said how remarkable it is that Steve was at his very best in front of 100,000-plus people, especially back then, without the assistance of huge video screens to help him. I have seen that man hold more than 400,000 in the palm of his hand and cause complete mayhem in the audience.

Soon after the start of the next leg, we were due to play at a festival called Summerfest, right on the lake in downtown Milwaukee. I was looking forward to seeing some friends of Mick Brigden—Sprout to his mates—who I had got to know.

Benedetta "Benny" Balistrieri, daughter of Frank Balistrieri, the infamous Seventies mob boss from Milwaukee, met the Falcon Jet in her Mercedes, which she was able to pull right up to the plane on the tarmac, and took a couple of us while the limo took the rest. Benny had been to England the year before and stayed at the farm as my houseguest. I looked after her really well, and she was grateful, so picking me up in her Merc was the least she could do. She also put on a big party for us the following day, but that's another story.

It was a lovely day; for once, the weather was on our side. As we drove into the city, the radio station reported on the size of the crowd that were showing up. The DJ told the listeners that Steve Stills had broken the attendance record when he drew 72,000 people the previous year, then started a running commentary on how many ticket-holders were coming through the turnstiles this year.

As we pulled out of the airport, he started with, "The crowd is already looking like it might get close to last year's record," then went on to say, "Hey, guys, you're the greatest! You just broke the record—the latest box office figure is 80,000," then, "You're not gonna believe it; we're now at 90,000," and so on. By the time we got checked into the hotel, the final figure had got to 125,000 people. We couldn't believe what we were hearing. This was at about four in the afternoon, and we weren't due on until the early evening. Zeppelin had recently broken the record for a single band, drawing somewhere around 75,000 in Tampa, Florida. They had taken full advantage of this, buying full-page ads in all the major publications so that the whole world knew that Led Zeppelin were the biggest draw in the business. Little us had just pulled 125,000, but because we had Joe Blow and His Blue-Veined Flutes as our warm-up act, we missed out on a technicality: it wasn't a single-band show. JB and His Flutes' enormous pulling power made all the difference—they must have had at least eight people come to see them, as each guy in the four-piece band brought along his mum and dad.

The only way to get to and fro from the site was by boat, as the stage was on one side of the water and the civilised world on the other. It was a hot day, and a local brewer was supplying vast quantities of beer to a very thirsty crowd, which magnified their excitement and caused the natives to get restless to see us—JB and the boys were just not doing it for them. So the promoters came up with the ingenious plan of asking us to go on earlier than scheduled. We didn't care—with a crowd that big, the sooner you let us at them, the better. It was a great gig, but the crowd got a bit too boisterous, to say the least. They ended up onstage with us—not all 125,000 of them, but enough to make the promoter lose his sphincter over it. There ended up being a fair bit of mini-rioting going on, so much so that rock music was banned at Summerfest for the next few years.

The return trip back across the water was packed with self-congratulatory fervour. Someone reminded us of the Zeppelin ad, and in our puffed-up state we thought that this was a felicitous comparison and proceeded to call Frank, at home in NY on a weekend, to tell him how well we had done. As pleased as he was, he was also the voice of reason and advised us *not* to put any full-page ads in the papers, because we might be seen as a bunch of upstarts who were trying to outdo the big guys—which was precisely what we were trying to do. All of this could have got ugly, so we had to thank Frank, as trying to upstage Zep was a losing battle from the get-go; those guys were so big at that stage that we would have made ourselves look pretty silly. This was a good example of the role Frank played in our career. Not only was he Super Agent, he could get through to Steve when nobody else could. Steve respected Frank even above Dee, which was saying something.

Still, the cold, hard facts were that, in the summer of 1973, we were top of the bill at Summerfest in Milwaukee, performing in front of 125,000 people, which was no mean feat however you cut the cake. Normal, right-minded thinking would have shown us the error of our ways when it came to comparisons with Zep; however, sybaritic amounts of Peruvian love dust made us get a bit carried away with ourselves… again.

We had also recently played a one-day festival in Waterford Park in Chester, West Virginia, where we had flown into the local private airport and then taken a helicopter into the site. It was a red-hot summer's day, and the humidity was brutal. The bill included Peter Frampton, J. Geils Band, and some other acts I forget. I remember that when Mick Gallagher, Peter's keyboard player, spotted me checking out the stage, he beckoned me over to look at his Hammond organ. He pointed at the keyboard and said, "Play that." When I went to do so, it was so scorching that my hand reflexively pulled away from it as if I'd just touched a hot plate in a restaurant. Mick had to put an umbrella over it to allow it to cool down and become playable.

As he and I were walking away from the stage towards the mobile-home dressing rooms, I noticed something strange happening to the audience, all 50,000-plus of them—it looked like the parting of the Red Sea. They were all, to a person, making way in a very orderly fashion for somebody to walk through their midst. We stood transfixed, as did everyone backstage, while this beautiful, extremely tall, long-blond-haired woman casually walked, with her head held high and her more than adequate bosom (which gravity had yet to get the better of) standing upright, through the crowd and towards the backstage area… stark bollock naked. As she drew closer to the rope barrier that she, strictly speaking, needed a backstage pass to get through, we held our collective breath, praying that the security guard would show some leniency—or plain old common sense—and let her in.

What happened next was pure poetry in motion. Just as she got to the guard, he raised the rope without skipping a beat, and she walked straight in without stopping or being asked for her pass, which, it was plain for all to see, she did not have—although you could argue that she had the best possible form of backstage pass very clearly on display. Once backstage, she kept heading in a straight line towards the dressing room area and disappeared between two of the mobile homes, never to be seen again. The security guard got a standing ovation for his part in this early-afternoon entertainment. Watching him take an extremely theatrical thespian bow for his efforts was priceless.

Where else in this wonderful world of ours can you see a beautiful, stark naked lady walk casually through your workplace as you are getting your coffee ready to start your hard day's work? A brothel or a strip club, perhaps... or a Humble Pie show.

I had my own little gaff during that leg of the tour with Peter Wolf, the lead singer of the J. Geils Band. Peter and I are very good friends, and he is a true gentleman. We were just getting to know each other back then, and he had recently met his future ex-wife while on the road with us. She had been a dinner guest at Dee's flat in London, and no one recognised her. She wasn't dressed up—all she was wearing was an old pair of blue jeans and a sweater—and her hair was a mess, or, should I say, not coiffured. Frankly, no one paid much attention to her sitting in the corner of the room. Her name was Faye Dunaway.

Peter always wore black shades on- and offstage, and I always wondered why. So, at one point on the tour, as I sat with him, just chatting, getting to know each other, and talking music (a subject that he is a walking encyclopaedia on; he used to be a disc jockey on a black radio station), I finally plucked up enough courage to ask him if his sunglasses were worn as a medical necessity. After carefully preparing his reply, he turned to me with all the natural sincerity he could muster and, after a perfectly timed pause, said, "No." He then kept on with the conversation as if nothing whatsoever had happened. Brilliant; timing *is* everything.

Dee's dinner parties were always fun because he would invite someone—either from the entertainment world or from the business side of things—who would make the evening interesting. When the entire *Godfather* thing was going strong, he invited John Marley, the actor who played Jack Woltz, the film producer who finds the horse's head in his bed. John told us how they used phoney ones and real ones, and how the phoney ones smelled much worse.

Once home in the fall of 1973, we went about the task of making the follow-up to *Eat It*. Even though that record had not performed as well as we had hoped, we were confident that we could produce one that would not suffer from the same sound problems that had plagued the last one. We had some good material written and had chosen a few covers that were also very strong. The group's work ethic in the studio was still potent, plus we were determined to show the powers that be and our fans that we hadn't lost it and were still perfectly capable of recording a great album, although we didn't think we had produced a bad one.

While the band still had our close, all-for-one feeling going strong, the cracks were starting to show. Growing more and more frustrated by Steve's erratic behaviour, Dee was developing this routine of calling anybody but Steve and going on and on about how much Steve was going to screw up everything if he didn't shape up and sort himself and his marriage out, one way or another. The person he chose to call the most was me. We, in turn, did our own bitching and moaning about the way Steve was behaving, particularly when it came to the money. The trouble was, he was spending it faster than we could earn it. So long as we were all getting our fair share out of all the hard work we were doing, it was fine. But when Steve started to get into the habit of spending all of his share and then going on to effectively spend ours as well, it wasn't long before that began to grate on our nerves, for the simple reason that it was not fair—we all worked just as hard as each other, and we were supposed to split things four ways, so there was no excuse.

The way that Steve tackled this was weird and wonderful, pure Steve. He used the studio as a red herring to draw us away from the real issue of his overspending. I have to say again that this was all a product of his reasoning while he was on coke, which by now, sadly, was pretty much all the time. He insisted that the money being spent on the studio was a fraction of what we were told it was, and this was a sign of our money being systematically ripped off.

He also came up with an interesting way of rationalising the expenditure, which was not dissimilar to the way he was toward Ronnie Lane five years earlier about who wrote the lion's share of the songs. He said that, as he would be owed more money from the publishing royalties when they came in, he felt that the studio should be all his and not the property of the group, even though it was the group's money that had paid for it so far. And as his and our publishing money was tied up in a dispute between our old publisher, Immediate (who had sold our rights to United Artists) and Almo Music (A&M's publishing branch), Steve, for all intents and purposes, didn't have any publishing royalties to bargain with—not yet, anyway. (When he finally did, he was paid a small fortune by Freddie Bienstock and Carlin Music, and we didn't receive a penny.) So, effectively, the band paid for the studio and Steve kept it as his own.

There was over a hundred thousand dollars spent on the place, or should I say that amount was sent to Steve and was supposed to be for the studio—whether he spent all of it on the studio, I don't know. He always claimed it didn't cost nearly that much and that this was just a smokescreen to cover up all the money that was being ripped off from us, as I mentioned earlier. This all led to an atmosphere of back biting and Chinese whispers that was to, slowly but surely, erode the wonderfully strong bond between us.

When mistrust develops in an atmosphere such as this, where the main players in the story are all under the influence of a paranoia-inducing substance such as cocaine, it is truly astonishing just how warped things can get in no time at all. At this stage, we were all new to the effects of cocaine and the various innuendos—pure confabulation of the actual facts—that it can make you put upon your surroundings, so as to suit your version of the events as you wish them to be.

None of us were immune from this dark, seedy way of behaving. Clem turned from being an easygoing, normal, well-balanced young lad from the Midlands into a scheming, back-biting menace to society, or to his own lunch break anyway. Greg just wanted to pick a fight with the world, and with Greg being Greg, if you were a betting man, you would clearly see that the world was in big trouble. So that left me, in my newly loved-up state of mind, planning my nuptials on the one hand, and on the other desperately trying to play piggy in the middle and referee all of this nonsense that had so quickly plunged our previously euphoric state of mind into a downward spiral in a vehicle with no brakes.

Again, I was just as bad as everybody else, in that all I seemed to be able to do was piss and moan behind Steve's back rather than confronting him face to face with what I thought he should or could be doing. It has to be said that Steve was not the best person to confront; he didn't do confront, he just exploded. It wasn't necessarily his exploding that bothered me so much as what might happen if he did explode. I wasn't physically scared of Steve, bless his heart—he was a tiny little thing—but I was frightened of what might happen if *I* exploded, as I had almost lost it with him before. My temper back then was terrible. I used to lay in bed imagining what I could say to him to bring him back to reality, and there would always be a lot of anger in what I thought I might say. So there was a big part of me that was subduing the strong urge to tell him off because deep down I knew that losing my temper with him would not do any good whatsoever; even if it was well and truly deserved, I would run the risk of losing him altogether. The rational part of me was determined to never lay a finger on him. The trouble was, I wasn't that rational in those days.

For the time being, we were still very much into making the next album, and we hadn't lost any of our spark when it came to playing together. We had recruited Alan O'Duffy again to engineer the record, as he had a vested interest in proving that the sound could be fixed at the studio; after all, his pride must have had a little knock as a result of the rough sound that came out on the finished record the last time round. He had a point to prove.

The sessions started wonderfully, with the basic sound of the back tracks turning out as well as we had ever done; the drum sound in particular was fabulous. We were cutting some of our best grooves so far, both on the originals and the covers. One of the covers, "I Can't Stand the Rain," originally recorded by Ann Peebles, was a standout for me. It has since gone on to be a hit for a number of people. Sadly, it was not a hit for us, although we at least had the satisfaction of knowing that Ann Peebles herself loved our version; she was quoted as saying that she loved the groove, which is my department, and I was flattered that a black lady soul singer would praise us like that.

When we had just begun work on the record, I called Dave Gilmour and we compared notes, as he had just started the new Pink Floyd record. We did this a lot back then, as we lived so close to each other. When one of us had done something, he would play it to the other to see how we were doing. It was a friendly rivalry, although after *Dark Side of the Moon*, they had gone on to such heights that we were hardly rivals any more, but Dave hadn't changed a bit and still had a genuine interest in his little mate's band.

After about a month had gone by, I called Dave again and told him how proud I was of all the back tracks and the overdubs, and that all we had left to do were some vocals and the mix. I then asked him how the Floyd's album was coming along, to which he replied with a deep sigh that they were still getting drum sounds. Mind you, our record, *Thunderbox*, ended up selling fewer than 200,000 copies, whereas Pink Floyd were recording *Wish You Were Here*, which has sold 8,000,000 and counting. There's a moral in there somewhere.

Dave had visited us at the studio as we were starting to record the original back track for "I Can't Stand the Rain," and he had tried to record a little piano intro on it. I had played some straight 4/4 time on the hi-hats at the start, so that this simple intro could be played over it. My timing had varied just slightly, so that I was the only one who could figure it out; everybody tried, but couldn't get it. So Dave said, "Okay, you're so smart—*you* play the piano over it!" I did, and to my amazement, it worked. Not that I'm so smart; it was more a case of "You fucked it up, you fix it."

Cindy and I had chosen May 11, 1974, as our wedding day, so we had at least six months to plan it—decide where it was going to be and all that good stuff. We found a big old stately home called Down Hall near the farm to hold the reception in and booked it way ahead of time so we'd know we had it.

The Blackberries had hired themselves out to Pink Floyd here and there to keep themselves employed on this side of the Atlantic; this helped us a bit, as we were able to use them on a couple of tracks on *Thunderbox* without it being quite so costly. All in all, we were having a great time making the record, and, as we had definitely fixed the sound problems, we were, not without reason, pretty confident that it would redress the setback that *Eat It* had put us through.

We were set to do one more tour of the States before Christmas, and then to go to Nassau to spend the holiday there. We did a few shows in England before we left for the USA that went wonderfully, as had all the gigs we'd done in England that year, including ones at the Palladium in London and the Sundown in Edmonton, which was in my back yard, what with Tottenham's ground being just up the road. Steve shone whenever he played in London; it didn't matter where. Our show had become extremely well paced and tight as it gets, as we'd had it on the road for the entire year. The Blackberries were now totally assimilated into it, and I don't recall any feelings of resistance from English audiences towards the show like those we had seen in some places across America.

By the time we got to the States, the band were every bit as good as we had ever been onstage. We were still knocking them dead on the night, every night—so much so that I think, even in the areas that were resistant earlier in the year, we were seeing them start to come around in the main, because we were simply that dynamic live. You couldn't help but enjoy yourself. If the rhythm section makes your hips move and the singers pull on your heartstrings, you really *have* to love it.

The last leg of the tour included shows in LA, San Diego, San Jose, Bakersfield, Fresno, Salt Lake City, Portland, Seattle, Denver, Kansas, Tulsa, Fort Worth, San Antonio, and Houston. We played about 30 dates in England and America on this leg, for a yearly total of about 120 shows all the way around the world and back. In the same year, we also finished off one album and recorded another. No one could accuse us of slacking, that's for sure.

Jenny joined the tour on the last date or two to be with Steve. After the tour was over, we spent a couple of days visiting in Houston, and then Cindy, Steve, Jenny, and I headed down to Nassau to spend Christmas there. Clem and Kathy also came along. We all prayed that this break would help Steve and Jenny's relationship to mend. Greg and Mandy chose to go home, which I could never figure out, considering what a sun worshipper Greg was.

I had never spent Christmas away from home, and being in a place where it definitely will not snow at Christmas was something I was looking forward to, purely from a curiosity standpoint. I was determined to make this stopover a success. Cindy and I had a good time. Aaron loved it, as did Rick and Lynny, who had come down to enjoy the holiday in the hot weather for a change of pace.

During the Christmas period, the casinos do phenomenal amounts of business. They see all the easy-money punters who think they are big shots coming through the doors, and let them win until the house is almost bust. Then they convince these poor hapless souls that they have never seen someone beat the bank like this and let them leave thinking they are superb card sharks, knowing all along they will be back. This is what happened to Steve.

Relaxing with stepson Aaron on the patio at Rock's Rest.

After they got him on the first night, allowing him to win close to $15,000, he returned home full of beans. Sure enough, he went back the following night to clean up again, only this time he didn't do quite as well. The casino got all their money back and more; they cleaned him out, only by now he was gambling with someone else's money. It was money that Dee had given to him for Jenny to start her antique shop in London, this being one way to try to convince her to stay. She didn't know about Steve gambling it away in the casinos, but she was a little sceptical when he didn't want to call the police or bring the matter up with the Customs and Excise when the cash turned up missing. He claimed that he threw it on top of his clothes when he was packing his bag, so the Customs men must have pinched it at the airport.

Funnily enough, it wasn't that particular incident that put the kibosh on their marriage, although it certainly didn't help matters much. The real reason Jenny finally walked was that she couldn't stick around to watch what Steve was doing to himself—and what he was doing to her by leaving her out at the cottage week after week, month after month, isolated from the rest of the world, cut off from almost any form of human contact, and with little or no financial support. He also seemed to forget that she was trying to run a household care for the animals, of which there were many. Neither of them drove a car, which made living in the country very difficult at the best of times, but when you are trying to do it on a shoestring in a world where you need a mini-cab just to go to the grocery shop or the vet, it becomes stressful—and it was made worse by Steve not making sure she had all the money she needed to get from one day to the next.

This Christmas break was their last-ditch attempt to pull together, but, sad to say, it didn't work. Once they got home, Jenny just packed her things without a huge amount of fuss and left. She couldn't live under the same roof as Steve anymore. Enough was enough. He was always a handful, but with his new friend Charlie staking claim on just about all of his time, it was very easy to get to the point where you just wanted to scream at him or smack some sense into him. Nobody had attempted either of those courses of action, and as fractious as things were at that time, either one would almost certainly have caused Steve to say, "See yer," so to a certain extent everybody was on thin ice. We didn't know from day to day which Steve we would be dealing with, so even the smallest band get-together was fraught with danger. Nothing seemed to work unless there was some coke around, and even then all it did was make him be the old mate who would be ready to do this and do that—but when the following day came, he would run for cover and wouldn't do any of it.

Again, it all goes back to my reply when someone asked me what it was like to play in a band with Steve: "The one thing about Steve Marriott that is very predictable is the fact that he is totally unpredictable." That was my mantra the entire time I knew him. His unpredictability never stopped me loving him as a brother, but as with real brothers, there are times when you want to slap the shit out of each other. Although the kinds of things that bring those emotions to the surface were always there in abundance, I never laid a finger on him, but years later I finally did give him a serious bollocking. And I was guilty of almost getting physical with him on two occasions, the first of which came at one of those fruitless meetings with Dee and the accountant, Bert.

Chapter 17
A Screaming Match a Day...
January to May 1974

In which I sting Steve badly at Beehive Cottage; the Piano Man is suggested to replace our frontman, who can't get no satisfaction with the Stones; Thunderbox fails to go down a storm; Cindy and I have a quiet honeymoon with the quiet Beatle; and God blesses both the 'Oo and our 'Umble little lot.

Dee and Bert had come to England to have a meeting of the minds and hear *Thunderbox*, the new album we had just finished, which some consider our best. We loved making it, and we had done what we had been asked to do—make the sound quality up to scratch—plus, without being told, we had also done some other things—there was more of the heavy rockin' and rollin' that we were known for, and less of the girls.

The two men came down to Beehive Cottage and started to put some of the issues that were bothering Steve in perspective: where the money had gone, what it had been spent on, who owned what and why. As our finances were being channelled into a corporation in NYC called Oven Development, we wanted to know the whys and wherefores of it all. On the other side of the fence, they wanted the group, aka Steve, to get a grip on spending. So, although this meeting was supposed to be a clearing of the air between group and manager, it was really about getting the two people who mattered the most, Steve and Dee, to come to the table and start playing cards again without cheating.

I was hoping upon hope that Dee and Steve could clear the air and sort themselves out because I was getting very tired of being the carrier pigeon between the two sides. Dee would tell me that this was wrong and that was wrong, and that Steve needed to do this and that to sort things out. Steve would counter that Dee and Bert were taking advantage of my inexperience or naïveté and couldn't be trusted, because of this being wrong and that being screwed up... And on and on they both went.

Steve had this bizarre game plan for the meeting that involved a trick question—if they answer this way, it means this; if they answer the other way, it means that. By this time, he had convinced himself that the powers that be had somehow got me under their spell, mainly because during this period, when his life was falling apart, they were all using me as the telephone go-between. Steve was certain that all who represented the business side of the group's life were Al Capone's right-hand men and were using me to manipulate him, which was utterly ridiculous for one simple reason: I'm not that clever. If I were, I would be a millionaire. As you may have noticed in these pages, Steve Marriott was impossible to manipulate; there was only one person who could make Steve do anything, and that was Steve. He was always his own master, right or wrong; sadly, by this stage in the proceedings, he was more wrong than right. His spending was out of control, and his financial demands were only being met by severely diminishing the band's money.

The meeting started to get a little uncomfortable as I made it obvious to Steve that I refused to get involved with the little codeword nonsense that he had got together. Once he had got that message and Dee had got the message that there was trouble at mill, all hell broke loose. It blew up into a huge row that went back and forth between Steve and me until he finally said, in an extremely sarcastic manner, "Oh sorry, man. I didn't realise I was hanging you up lately."

That did it for me. All the aggression that had been building up in me from all the times when Steve had caused huge amounts of aggravation for me and the people around us... I'm afraid I flew at him. I was so angry, I might have killed him had not Dee and Bert, who weighed 220 pounds each, stepped in and stopped me.

I screamed at him, "*You've been hanging me up for fucking years!*" while they restrained me. I remember the look of shock on Steve's face as he, possibly for the first time in his life, saw one of his old mates letting him know in no uncertain terms exactly how he felt. There is not a day that goes by that I don't thank God for Dee and Bert's intervention, because if I had got physical with Steve, I would have not been able to deal with it after he passed away years later. I was messed up enough by his death, and it would have made it much, much worse if I had hurt him physically. Sadly, this wouldn't be the last time I would get to the point where I almost hit him.

This incident was awful. The adrenalin running through my veins was so strong that it took the strength of both Dee and Bert to hold me back, and even then I almost got away from them. With all things that end up in a row as intense as this, the adrenalin leaves you in such a state of shock that you don't remember too many details, but I do recall one thing above all the rest: the stunned look on Steve's face, a look of absolute disbelief.

It wasn't so much the fact that I had lost it. After all, losing it was a daily endeavour for him; "A Screaming Match a Day Will Keep Reality Checks Away" would have been a good album title for Steve back then. What shook him up was what I said, not the volume I said it at. "You've been hanging me up for fucking *years*"—the last word was the one that got to him. That his closest friend for a good long time had said he had been bugging him for years certainly gave Steve pause for thought. Here I was, the young lad he had discovered all those years ago, who had worshipped him and looked up to him like a brother, who he had helped to shape as a musician, whose mum thought the world of him—the list was endless. But he had ignored one very important point; he hadn't noticed that the young kid had grown up and in some ways had become *his* big brother, in that I had looked after him and got him out of any number of scrapes. Here I was, all grown up and arguing the toss with him—telling *him* what was what and not believing in his word as gospel.

Although Steve had every right to quit right there and then—he had just been threatened, in his own house, by his drummer with grievous bodily harm—I don't remember him quitting. All I remember is that, a short while after this bust-up, we were looking for a new lead singer and that, unbeknownst to us, Steve had auditioned for another band.

The singer we wanted was Bobby Tench, who we knew from his work with the Jeff Beck Group, and we thought he was looking for a gig. So I went up to see Derek Green, the head of A&M in England, and told him some "exciting news": we had found the perfect man for the job. When I said it was Bob Tench, he almost fainted—he had just signed Bob to A&M as part of a group called Hummingbird. In all our arrogance, we had neglected to check if Bob was in fact looking, and apparently he was not. (Dee had suggested Billy Joel, which I must say, was a stretch of everybody's imagination. Humble Pie doing "Just the Way You Are"? I don't think so.)

Steve, on the other hand, had set his sights even higher than we had by accepting an audition as second guitarist with the biggest band in the world: the Rolling Stones.

What happened next conspired to keep us together for another year. Apparently, when Steve went for the audition, he got carried away with the excitement of actually playing with his favourite group. I don't blame him,

God bless him; Keith Richards was one of his all-time heroes, and they had become good mates. Unfortunately, the groove the band were playing at the audition was too good for Steve to just kick back on, which was the friendly advice that Keith had given him. But Steve, after all, had spent his entire professional life as a frontman and wouldn't have been able to play second fiddle to anybody for any length of time, even if the frontman was Mick Jagger and the band were the Rolling Stones. The interesting part of this story is the fact that both our original guitar players, Steve and Peter, were on the Stones' shortlist for the job.

After the dust had settled a bit, Dee called to tell me that there was a slight problem: a number of big promoters had booked shows for the upcoming tour and sent in their deposits; therefore we had an obligation to at least do those shows. Whether or not what Dee said was true, it at least got the ball rolling for Steve and me to mend fences between us. So I took a deep breath and called him. First, I apologised for screaming at him in his own house. Then I got down to the nitty-gritty and explained that there was a tour for us to do and that I felt we should do it—would he consider it?

He said he wasn't sure, as he had joined another group, referring, of course, to the Stones, although I didn't know it at the time. He went on to say that he would see if he could do the tour, implying that he needed to make sure that it wouldn't interfere with this other group's schedule. He got back to us promptly and said that he could; as we all know now, his gig with the Stones didn't pan out.

So it was with extreme apprehension that we all went into the penultimate tour of America that Humble Pie, in its original form, would do. Although Jenny was gone, she suggested that Sally Miles—a young, good-looking friend who occasionally looked after the animals and was also a brilliant artist—come on the tour to help look after Steve. Sally agreed to this; I'm sure it seemed exciting, as she had never been to the States before.

We went back to basics on this tour: it was just the four of us, and we flew on regular airlines. Our first date was at a raceway in Orlando, Florida. Spooky Tooth were on the bill, with the lovely Mike Patto singing for them. Mike, who

Concert poster from '74 .

is, sadly, no longer with us, played a big part in pulling us back together by listening to both sides of the story and suggesting that life's too short and that all this bullshit is not worth losing lifelong friendships over. How right he was.

Cindy came to the first shows in Florida and then went to Nassau to stay at the beach house—so far, so good. The next thing I know, she has been arrested by the Immigration people for possession of drugs. Someone had put a few grass joints in her box of Nat Sherman cigarettes, and she had forgotten they were there. I freaked, as I had been told that jail in Nassau was a nightmare; I immediately thought the worst and feared for her safety. Bill Anthony, who had flown to Nassau with her, came to the rescue by speaking to the right people and greasing the palm of the right hand. Had he not been there with her, God only knows what might have happened.

Soon thereafter, we played at the Nassau Coliseum in Long Island, New York. I remember thinking how long this American trip of ours had been: we had been touring the States virtually non-stop for the last five years, with about 25 tea breaks along the way. After the show, we were having the usual after-gig get-together in our NYC hotel, but it had a subdued atmosphere that got the best of me. For no apparent reason, I burst into tears. It was a "What have I done?" kind of breakdown, and I couldn't control it; it kept on keeping on. Steve was not in the room, which I thought was a blessing at the time, and I have often wondered what his reaction might have been.

The tour went on through the East Coast, the Midwest, the Mid-South, and the Deep South, taking in such places as Mobile, St. Louis, Knoxville, Chattanooga, Boston, Baltimore, Hershey, Pennsylvania (where the street lamps are made in the shape of a Hershey kiss), Buffalo, and Atlanta. In Chattanooga, we got to stay in the Chattanooga Choo Choo. The carriages were made up just the way they used to be, with all the fancy trimmings and antique furniture. Each carriage was a suite with both living area and a bedroom, and all of them were parked on what looked like an old station; it was great fun. This was all part of the fine job that Mick Brigden constantly did for us in his advance work for our tours. If there was something different to break up the monotony of the road, Mick would find it.

The failure of *Thunderbox* was a big shock and general letdown. I thought we had at least redeemed ourselves in the studio, but it was not a hit. You almost didn't notice that it had been released, and to this day I still can't tell you why it flopped so magnificently, but it did. I think A&M had lost their faith in us and were probably allowed to know too much about our problems—but that was more than 35 years ago, so it's hardly worth second-

guessing now. It was a great record, though, and we were proved to be right about our choice of material when Tina Turner (among others) had a big hit with "I Can't Stand the Rain," but we were the first to cover it.

After the last gig, in Atlanta, Cindy and I went to Houston and were followed by almost the entire road crew. We were to be married in May, and the American crew wouldn't be able to get there, so they came to Houston along with some of the English crew who stopped there on the way home from Atlanta for a pre-nuptial party.

Cindy and I stayed for a week or so and visited with all of our Texan friends. We visited Austin with a good pal of mine, Sanford Radinsky, and his lady, Linda Azios, who was Cindy's closest friend. While there, we got to see the Charlie Daniels Band. The following day, we went to Ed Wilson's house, where we were welcomed with typical Texan hospitality, as he was a friend of the Wild West Productions guys. Ed was also the owner of the biggest club in Texas, the Armadillo. We met Charlie at Ed's house; he was an extremely nice, congenial man who we got along with immediately as if we had known each other for years. What a lovely man, a true gentleman. The thing I remember the most was the size of the pile of grass he was cleaning on a tray on his lap—it was, like him, huge. The reason I bring up meeting Charlie is that it shows how diverse the music scene was back in the early Seventies. You would get the same audience showing up for both the Charlie Daniels Band and Humble Pie.

A very memorable offstage incident happened on the same break in Texas, way off the back roads of Austin. Steve had befriended Sanford and Linda, and we all went to stay at a ranch on the way to Austin that belonged to another good friend of ours, Craig Christie, and his lovely wife, Pam. Steve decided to take in the local surroundings and went with Sanford to visit yet another good old Texan friend, Junior, at his place, appropriately named Junior's Farm. (For you trainspotting rock fans, no, that's *not* the same place that Paul McCartney wrote about in the hit Wings single of the same name.) After an afternoon of fun riding some of Junior's horses, Steve and Sanford went with Junior to his local watering hole, the Hitching Post.

You have to picture this little dirt-trail shack of a bar out in the Texas backwaters, with nothing but a bunch of good old boys hanging out and a big old jukebox with just about every great country music record ever made on it. The joint also had a tiny stage at one end with just a stool on it, and in front of the stool there was a stand holding a mic that was plugged into a modest PA.

When I walked in, Steve was sat on the stool and was starting things off with one of his at-the-top-of-his-voice greetings to the bartender, which usually went something like this: "'ELLO, MATE! 'OW'S YER BUM FER PIMPLES, EH? LARGE BRANDY, PLEASE, AND ONE FOR ME MATE SANFORD, AND ONE FOR YERSELF. ANYBODY ELSE NEED A DRINK?" Then he began to sing his heart out, performing some of the old classic country songs that he had known since he was a youngster, including the aforementioned "I Worship the Ground You Walk On." Steve had long since had the whole place in the palm of his hand. He apparently had been entertaining them for hours without a care in the world. I just smiled, as I had seen him do this before. It always filled me with immense

Backstage with Cindy. The late photographer Chuck Pulin gave us this shot as an early wedding present.

pride to witness my old mate completely blowing people's minds with just an old, borrowed acoustic guitar and that incredible voice. He was the master at singing with such power and soulfulness that when people heard it up close like that, it was just that bit more impressive than it was in a stadium. The man was a vocal genius, plain and simple, a fucking genius who all those cowboys in the Hitching Post would not forget in a hurry, just as all those people in Prickwillow hadn't years before.

Once we got home, there was much to do, as the wedding was to be in the first week of May. That meant we had about six weeks to get everything that had yet to be done—meaning *everything*—sorted out. We knew where the wedding would be held, and that was about it. But with the help of the road crew, what seemed a daunting task was soon taken care of. Cindy had her dress designed by Ossie Clark, an old friend of Jenny and Steve. I had a great suit handmade by a tailor friend of Greg and Mandy whose name escapes me after all these years; he did a superb job. I had him design it based on a suit I remembered Steve wearing with the Small Faces when they

From the Sunday Express *coverage of our wedding.*

went to Number One with "All or Nothing" in 1966—it was a white, three-piece job with cool-looking stitching all along the edge of the jacket and waistcoat. I was looking forward to Steve seeing it because I wondered if he would remember it.

Sadly, Steve didn't get to the wedding; he'd been arrested in the Bahamas for being a public nuisance. Jenny didn't come, for fear of Steve being there and possibly making a scene. There was speculation that Steve had got himself arrested so that he didn't have to come. I personally don't put much credibility in that particular theory—Steve may have been off the wall, but he wasn't off the chart.

Down Hall is a huge stately home about halfway between the farm and Dad's place. It is still being used for weddings and the like to this day. The main reason we hired the place was that it had loads of bedrooms, so that those who had too much drink to drive could grab a bedroom, sleep it off, and not have to risk it. As Cindy had been married before, we were not allowed to actually get married in a church, but we could have the wedding *blessed* in a church. This meant we had to go to the registry office first to have the actual legal marriage performed by the local registrar, and then we could go to the church for the blessing. We chose a beautiful church at Nazeing Common that was built by the Normans in the ninth century.

The guests at the church didn't even notice the difference between the blessing and an actual wedding. I don't recall how many people were there, but there were a lot. It was, as they say, a Big Wedding. We had set up some equipment for any of us who wished to get up and play. Other than that, it was one huge piss-up and drug-up. Although Steve wasn't there in the literal sense, he was there in spirit...

A few months earlier, while Steve was on one of his five-day stints in the studio, the roadies John and Ted were very worried about the state he was getting into, so they called me to ask what they should do. I told them to keep an eye on him and, as soon as he finally crashed out, to pinch the cocaine and let him sleep it off. They did exactly that, and, once they were positive that he was in a deep sleep and someone was there to watch him, they came over to the farm to give me a rundown of what had happened. We all sat around the kitchen table for a match report.

Ted had got Steve's large pill bottle, which was half-full of coke. While we sat there, Ted spotted a fly that had landed on the table, and he managed to put an empty glass over it. Then he took the top of the bottle and manoeuvred the fly to the edge of the table and into the bottle of coke.

With the top firmly on the bottle, we watched as this fly sat on top of the cocaine in disbelief of its good fortune. It then started to feed on the coke in a state of extreme agitation, took a couple of fast laps around the bottle, and then—BOSH! It collapsed on its back, dead as a doornail.

So it was that, unbeknownst to me, we had a stash at the wedding courtesy of Steve, via the roadies. While this was just one of the many occasions that the road crew and/or the rest of the band had saved Steve's life by separating him from his beloved cocaine, it's ironic that it was at the humorous expense of a fly like the one in the Happiness Stan suite on *Ogdens' Nut Gone Flake*—although this fly was enjoying sustenance a little stronger than the shepherd's pie that Stan had shared with the Faces' "hungry intruder."

It has to be said that this was not a one-way street—Steve came to my rescue more than once, as did the crew. However, I am dealing with the story in a chronological fashion, and the cocaine abuse and its effects were peaking in Steve's life at this particular time. And, as he was the lead singer, frontman, and main writer in the band, it was his behaviour both on- and offstage that concerned the powers that be much, much more than that of the drummer, bass player, or lead guitarist. We were all replaceable; Steve wasn't. There was only one Steve Marriott.

Steve always said there was a five-year gap between the time he got into or did something—music, clothes, spiritual beliefs, marriage, divorce, whatever—and the time I got into or did it. This recurring pattern mirrored our age gap; we were almost exactly five years apart. I certainly fell foul of any number of the things that hit Steve at around this time, and sure enough, they—including divorce, which was the biggest cross to bear (but that, as they say, is another story)—hit me about five years after they hit him.

Andrew Oldham came to the wedding. A&M had given Steve a "You must get an outside producer for the next record" ultimatum, and when he named Andrew, I think he was as surprised as Andrew was when A&M said yes. Andrew asked for and got an astronomical sum to produce the record. At the time, the going rate for a top producer to record an album was an advance of $25,000 to $50,000, plus 2% to 5% in royalty points, meaning that if your royalty rate was between 14% and 16%, you gave up as much as one third of your royalties to the producer. Andrew apparently gave A&M an exorbitant set of numbers to see if they would go away, not expecting for a moment that they would agree to such a huge fee. When they did agree, it meant that the band were committed to each other for at least the next 12 months or so. Oh well, God loves a trier.

Andrew had recently cleaned up his act by going through the Arica Foundation program, a 40-day cleansing of the soul from the inside out— ever so New Age, enlightening stuff that seemed to agree with him a great deal. He has always been very good about such matters, in that he might sing their praises but only in a sensible and subdued fashion with a bunch of rough and ready old pals such as ourselves. There were a couple of reasons for this approach: one, so that he had an out, should it prove to be not quite the transcendental floss medication it had originally claimed to be, and two, so that he minimized the potential for piss-taking sceptical bastards like us to go to town on him. Frankly, I was very impressed with the results, as he seemed to be in better shape than he had been in for a long time; I don't think I had ever seen him so clear headed, down to earth, and easy to get along with. These character traits would prove to be invaluable in the upcoming few weeks, as Melvin was at his most exasperating, to the point where the one thing Andrew would achieve was to cross the finishing line. Even if we could have secured one of the top producers of the day, I guarantee you that not a one of 'em could have completed the project. While the finished product turned out to be nothing special, it was at least finished.

The first sign that Andrew had joined the real world for me was the fact that he had come to my wedding. He was bright, alert, happy, and frankly more down to earth than I had ever seen him, and he was seemingly content to take the back seat and allow the spotlight to shine on the person it was supposed to shine on: Cindy. While that might sound like a strange thing to say, you have to remember that the Andrew I knew had always been the centre of attention wherever he went. He himself had that star quality that he always strived to find in the people he worked with, which was why he was so good at spotting and nurturing it in others. At the wedding, his manners were immaculate; you could have described him, I suppose, as a man of wealth and taste.

Dee's behaviour at the wedding, on the other hand, was uncharacteristically ill mannered. Only Cindy and I noticed it, as he confined it to the privacy of the bridal car on the way to the reception after giving the bride away at the ceremony. In the limo, he went into a rant about Steve—how he was this and that and blah, blah, blah, blah. Frankly, I had heard it all before, and so had Cindy. He could have spared us the earful on our wedding day in our wedding car, don't ya think? All he did was show how beside himself he was about the whole situation; he wasn't going to cure the problem by raving on at me or anybody else—except for Steve. The truth was, he was barking up the wrong midget.

By the time we got to the wedding, as much fun as the day itself was, we could see by the looks on some of the faces that there were a lot of worried people in amongst the troops. Steve had, after all, been arrested in the Bahamas, and we didn't know for sure that he was all right until the day after the wedding. He turned out to be fine, thank God, and it made what he did at our next show all the more wonderful.

It was just after the wedding, and Steve had at least had a little break from Melvin World, even though it was in part thanks to a short stay in the Bahamian penal system. He was relatively stable when he arrived back in the UK. Bill Curbishley had booked us as second on the bill to the Who at Charlton Athletic Football Ground, supported by Montrose (with Sammy Hagar), Bad Company on their first big gig, Lou Reed, Lindisfarne, and the lovely Maggie Bell. Steve couldn't wait to get out there, grab the British audience by the nuts, and give 'em a good old squeeze. For the few days of rehearsal and on the day of the show, we had our old mate back, and it was a magnificent thing to see. It is no coincidence that he had no cocaine for that week. I think the experience in the Bahamas gave him at least a slight pause for thought, not that he would ever admit it, as he put on his brave face, but jail down there can be a very scary place.

I don't remember this show being billed as a return of the Mods or using any such promotional gimmick, but I shamelessly drilled it into Steve's head that this was what it was going to be like, and, lo and behold, that did the trick. I suggested that, instead of trying to compete with the Who, we would be better served to go out there, kick ass, and let the audience see how much respect we had for the Who as one of the all-time great British rock bands. To my overwhelming surprise, Steve bought into the Mod revivification angle, so much so that a couple of master strokes came about through one of the last few great group ideas that we had—and they worked so wonderfully that we very nearly stole the entire show.

The first of these was our opening song. I suggested the Small Faces' "Whatcha Gonna Do About It" and was thrilled when Steve said yeah, he got the point, especially when we rehearsed it and it sounded *so* good. He could never resist the idea of knocking people out musically, surprising them with a song or an arrangement of a song that they were least expecting. He loved doing that and was fucking great at it, I must say. He was in his element when he took an audience by the scruff of the neck and said, "'Ere, get a load of *this*!"

Next up was how we were gonna look. Steve rose even higher to the occasion by having his hair cut off in a classic Moddy crew cut and wearing blue jeans with bright silver braces and turn-ups on the bottom of the legs. Greg and Clem both wore really smart tailored jackets. Greg's was a Teddy Boy drape, which wasn't strictly Mod wear, but

he looked so sharp in it that it definitely met the Mods' expression of esprit de corps: always look cool, which Greg always did. I went and bought a white track suit like a footballer in training would wear, only on the front of the top I had, in large letters, "God Bless the 'Oo" written like the press always wrote and spelled it, which paid huge dividends when the photographers got a shot of Clem and me taking our bow at the end of the show. The resulting photo made the front page of *Sounds*, one of the big three music papers.

If I remember correctly, they put poor old Maggie Bell on in between us and the Who; now that is a serious rock 'n' roll sandwich, to be caught between us and the lads. It was made tougher for her as no one had quite been ready for exactly how well Steve got hold of that audience and squeezed, and consequently how well Humble Pie went down. We nailed it, completely tore the place up. If it were not for the Who doing one of the best shows that I've ever seen them do, we would have blown them right off their own stage. As it was, we pretty much shared the spoils—if it had been a football match, it would have been a draw. *Melody Maker*, the biggest music paper of the time, did a huge two-page spread on it. The headline read, "Who eat Humble Pie," which had enough ambiguity in it that each band could claim a victory.

The wedding had been the Saturday before Charlton, and the week leading up to the show was important both to the band and in my personal life. Cindy and I had to cancel our honeymoon so that I could play the gig, as the band needed those few days leading up to the show to rehearse and so on. We had booked our honeymoon trip to Paris months before, but when the Charlton gig came in, it was too good to not do. Cindy was great about it, partly because I was able to soften the blow a bit by accepting an invite from Apple honcho Terry Doran to spend the night as his guest at Friar Park, George and Pattie Harrison's Victorian pile near Henley-on-Thames. There's nothing like meeting one of the Beatles to ease the pain of a woman who's had her honeymoon cancelled, especially if she spent her teenage years in the Sixties and had a mad crush on George. God bless Terry; he got me out of a serious spot there. Well done, Tel.

Everyone was very nice to us that night, Pattie in particular. She even helped us sort out what I was going to wear by assisting with putting the "God Bless the 'Oo" on my track suit. A lot of champagne was consumed, and I avoided one of my projectile waste removals by the skin of my teeth for one simple reason: I managed to hang in there for all it was worth, literally praying for the overwhelming urge to throw up to desist. The Almighty was kind to me that night and prevented me from making a complete and utter cunt of myself, and for that I was most grateful. I don't do champagne very well; it always got me too drunk too quick and invariably dished out a ferocious headache and a trip to the loo to add a customised pebble dashing that the owners of said loo invariably did not appreciate.

In the spring of 1974, I was going through such extreme opposites, what with my personal happiness as a newlywed and my professional life falling apart at the seams, that it's a fucking miracle I didn't go totally gaga. Mind you, considering the five-year rule, I still had plenty of time to achieve equal bragging rights with Steve in the I've-lost-more-marbles-than-you-have contest. We should have, and in some ways did, break up at that time, but something kept us together—Andrew Oldham for one, bless his heart.

Jerry Moss was hoping that using an outside producer would help the situation, but it didn't, and agreeing to Steve's choice of producer was the worst possible thing he could have done, considering the condition Steve was in at the time. Jerry had played into Steve's—or should I say Melvin's—arms, which meant that from Steve's/Melvin's point of view, he could twist Andrew around his little finger. However, Steve had forgotten that this was Andrew he was going to be working with, and if Andrew had anything to do with it, he was not going to be easily led by this alien being he had not previously experienced. If there was one thing that would work in Andrew's favour, it was his stubbornness and sizeable ego. He also genuinely cared about the real Steve, who was then being overshadowed by his cocaine cous-in, Mel—so much so that Andrew, like us, was prepared to go to just about any length to get through to Steve.

The horrible truth was that he would find out in short order just how unreachable Steve had become.

Chapter 18
Why on Earth...?
June 1974 to February 1975

In which many sad things happen that simply can't be spun into any sort of remotely amusing, celebrity-filled, reader-baiting wordplay here, but I'll give it a half-hearted go anyway— well, let's see... Roger Daltrey says we sound too much like another London-based four-piece, Who shall go unnamed... (street) rats begin to desert the sinking ship... and... erm... ah, fuck it... just read it and weep.

As I drew closer to writing this chapter, I researched the way each person felt about what was going on at the time. Regardless of who I talked to, including people of substantial position and sizeable renown who I had never met, I kept getting asked the same question: "Why on earth did such a great band as Humble Pie break up? You had everything going for you."

Looking back from the outside in, I can see that it was the most asinine and nonsensical decision we could have possibly entertained, let alone made. What was I thinking? So many better, smarter, far more sensible options were available. Why on earth did I choose the most harmful, destructive, and plain stupid of all the choices available to me at the time?

Surely, after all that hard work together, the more sensible alternative would have been to figure out what was wrong and fix it. After all, I had just got married and had a young child to support, so, more than ever, I should have paid attention to the old saying that "the choices we make dictate the lives we lead." We had the best band, run by the best management and the best road crew money could buy. We were led onstage by the best frontman and lead singer in the business, bar none, and he was driven by one of the most powerful rhythm sections around. Quitting made no sense, and yet, within less than a year, it seemed to me to be the only choice available.

What transpired over the next nine months was so life changing—and, some might say, character building, while others would suggest soul destroying, depending on which street they choose to walk on, Optimism Avenue or Pessimism Grove—that I find it hard to believe that it all happened in such a short space of time. As time goes by, I find it even more incredible that so much was at stake and yet nobody intervened to stop us making such a ridiculous decision. We needed slapping, quite frankly, but of course, as with all things in my little story, when you consider that Melvin was by now taking sole ownership of centre stage, nothing was easily achieved.

When Andrew Oldham was brought on board to record the next album, he had no idea just how bad the animosity within the band was. He hadn't seen or been around us since Immediate went bust. He had obviously been through a pretty rough patch himself, what with having to deal with the Immediate bankruptcy and several cracks in his personal life, as he was in the throes of separating from his first wife, Sheila. He had been living in America, mostly in a beautiful house in Connecticut. His own set of demons were starting to make inroads into his personal well-being; however, he, like most people in the music business at that time, was managing to hide the ill effects of coke from the outside world considerably better than our dear Steve, who, thanks to Melvin, wasn't able to hide them that all.

Andrew hadn't had a hit, musically speaking, for a considerable time, nothing substantial anyway. So, in a way, working with us could and should have been a golden opportunity for him to redeem himself in the eyes of the business by pulling a rabbit out of the hat. Unfortunately for Andrew, and us, this would prove to be mission impossible. As he so eloquently put it in Act Two of his autobiography, "No one told me the band had broken up!" He was absolutely right: we had broken up in every way, but there had been no formal announcement. It ain't over till it's over, as they say, except we just hadn't officially admitted it.

Things were just horrible. When it came time to take a band shot for the album, the label had to send a photographer to each of our houses so they could

Andrew Loog Oldham in Italy in 1979. He has always been like an older brother to me.

take their precious "group picture" separately, then splice them together to make one good photo. This was quite ironic, as the infighting that had led to us needing to have separate shots taken had actually started as a result of several disagreements over the artwork for *Thunderbox*. I have to say, however, that the resulting black-and-white pho-

Humble Pie
(L to R) JERRY SHIRLEY, GREG RIDLEY, STEVE MARRIOTT, DAVE CLEMPSON

tos were actually quite good, and given that the album was called *Street Rats*, we did—surprise, surprise—manage to look like a right bunch of Herberts.

Sadly, once Charlton was under our belt, it was not long before Steve was back to his old ways. His all-night/all-day/all-night coke sessions started back up apace, and even though we were committed to making this album as part of our record deal with A&M, Steve treated it as an inconvenience that he would grudgingly tolerate. He had recruited a few additions to his list of usual suspects in the never-ending round robin of hangers-on, drug dealers, musicians, and drug dealers posing as musicians. Some of these would invariably have a wife or girlfriend in tow that Steve fancied, so their presence was requested on a regular basis, so much so that the poor, hapless souls would mistake this wish as either genuine friendship or respect for their musicianship, when all Melvin really wanted was a crack at the old lady. This was the Seventies, don't forget, and I'm sure that some of these guys weren't that stupid; they were, in fact, quite happy to have their missus used as bait so that they could try and muscle in and gain entry into what they saw as a great band that lacked only one thing: their prolific talents as a musician/songwriter. Again, Steve would offer them all kinds of things that he really had no place offering, like, "Yeah, man, come and join the band. We could do with a keyboard player." Apart from anything else we didn't need, we already had a keyboard player when we needed one: Steve.

Steve knew all of this, so when Melvin was promising the earth to every Tom, Dick, and drug addict that crossed the threshold of his studio door, Steve knew full well that we wouldn't have it—which of course was his perfect out: "Sorry, man, the band won't have it; nothing I can do." By that time, he had usually done whatever it was he wanted to do, musically speaking, with the future ex-band member, and I'll leave it up to your imagination what he did with the poor guy's future ex-wife.

One example of this was a keyboard player called Tim Hinckley. He tried everything in his power to join the band, even told some people that he had. He did get to appear on a couple of tracks on *Street Rats*, and came on the road in Europe for a few dates in that summer of 1974, but we wouldn't allow him onstage with us. As far as we were concerned, with Melvin screwing us around every chance he had, the one thing that was sacrosanct was the live show. This was our patch that we had worked very hard to achieve, and no Johnny-come-lately was going to muscle in just because he had Melvin's drugged-up ear in the studio at Steve's house, which by now we saw as a very negative place to be.

The studio had become so bad that there was more than one occasion when I walked into the place and bumped into a complete stranger who asked me, "Who the fuck are you?" to which I would reply, "Oh, don't mind me; I'm just the cunt who helped pay for this place." It was all such a shame, as it could have been so very different.

Unfortunately, by then, I think that Dee and A&M had all but given up on the whole shooting match. They hoped and prayed that Andrew might, just might, pull off some bit of magic in the place where it all started, Olympic Studios in Barnes. We also held a certain amount of hope for what was looking like a last-ditch effort to pull us all together and make something special like the things we did there so many times before. Five years earlier, Steve would have bitten your arm off for a 24/7 booking in Olympic Studio No. 1; now you could barely get him to show up, let alone take advantage of what was still one of the best studios in the world.

As spring turned to summer, we did what we could to get some material on tape. The only way we could achieve that was to come to a compromise and do some work at the cottage. The problem was not so much the sound issues that existed before—with *Thunderbox*, we had managed to fix most of those, and Andrew had been smart enough to ensure that we had Irish as the engineer. It was more a case of having to see this person who represented everything that was going wrong in full flight at Beehive. It was not that Steve was doing coke and everybody else was clean—far from it. We were all still doing it when and if it was around, but the quality of it wasn't very good in England anymore, at least during that summer. Also, money wasn't as readily available as it used to be, unless we did some shows in England or Europe; we weren't getting any financial support from the States, which had long since made my attempts to stand up for management's side of the story unviable.

I felt extremely betrayed because management had put me in the position of being their messenger, which was all fine and dandy, but they weren't making it possible to stick up for them anymore, as they were not doing anything to disprove or allay our fears; in fact, they were confirming most of them. Steve's fears were extreme, as was his paranoia in general; that's what excessive use of coke does

Our final release.

to you. The truth was, he had been really bad with the finances over the past year or so, and so here the rest of the band were in the middle of two camps of misbehaving men who frankly were just as bad as each other. They should have sat down and sorted it out, but, sadly, too much cocaine was being done on both sides of the fence, and the band were suffering as a direct result.

There was one potentially shining light: Bill Curbishley looked like he might be able to sort things out. Bill had recently taken over full control of the Who's management from Kit Lambert and Chris Stamp, the original partners who managed them. The Who had to be one of the most difficult bands to manage from a behavioural point of view; after all, they had Keith Moon, bless his heart, who was a nightmare to try to organise and run a top professional band around. To the band's undying credit, they stuck together and figured out how to roll with the punches (sometimes literally) and keep the original line-up together, which must have been very hard. With someone as volatile as Keith in the band, there are times when the unthinkable becomes thinkable: "Shall we get rid of him?" They didn't, thank God, but, sadly, overindulgence did it for them a few years later.

Bill was a breath of fresh air. He took on the task of helping us as much as he could, and we helped him by keeping the Who's road crew in work during that summer, hiring them to do our sound and lights. The combination of their crew and ours was fabulous, as they were both the best in the business. They were all old mates—our head roadie, Dave Clark, had worked with the Who guys on and off for years, going all the way back to when he was the Small Faces' head roadie and the Who and Small Faces worked together many times. Now that we were using them, it was just like working with a bunch of old mates; we got on great. One of the lads from their crew, Bill Harrison, was particularly helpful with me and the drum stuff, even though that wasn't his gig—he was part of the lighting crew, if I remember correctly. They were all great guys, though, just the very best.

I haven't given our road crew nearly enough credit in these pages, but I honestly believe they were the best in the business. They put up with a lot of nonsense, as most crews do, but they never moaned or groaned about any of it. They were loyal, dedicated, and remarkably efficient—the entire time that we headlined all across America, Europe, and Japan, leaving audiences screaming for more everywhere we played, we only ever used one 48-foot truck. *One* truck, think about that. The average headliner tour today hauls anywhere between 12 and 24 trucks; with us, sound, lights, backline, specials, and the whole shooting match were transported in just one truck. It still amazes me that we were able to do that. It is true that we didn't carry a lot of special effects and the like, but we never left an audience wanting, we only ever left them wanting more.

I am fully aware that you couldn't get away with that sort of thing today in the age of super productions such as the shows put on by the Stones, U2, and Genesis and Pink Floyd, if they were still out there—it's what audiences have come to expect. However, there is hope. I saw Eric Clapton and Steve Winwood in Madison Square Garden, which holds 20,000 people, doing a one-off reunion featuring the Blind Faith stuff and a selection of their individual material. Just the two of them with a drummer, bass player, and a second keyboard player, and it was superb; the musicianship is all the special effects you need when it's that good.

As we moved into the summer of 1974, Bill Curbishley very kindly took over the day-to-day managerial chores, starting with the road. He was able to find us ways of getting money from some of the European promoters so that we could function, as there was no money forthcoming from America. It wasn't brain surgery; it was simply him giving us an advance on the money that had already been advanced to him from the promoters. It was, however, an extreme leap of faith on his part. For him to have that much trust in us was something that I will never forget, because, frankly, Steve, when he was in the Small Faces, had developed a bad reputation for being a no-show, and, while we had a spotless track record in the States from all the work we had done over there, we hadn't done that much in England and Europe to alleviate his reputation. But with Bill as our representative, the promoters in Europe were not concerned about us. Plus, he was financially able to advance us money from upcoming gigs, whether the promoters sent a deposit or not. (In America, the promoters advance 50% of the money up front.) Technically, the artist is not supposed to spend any of the deposit money until the date is played, so the promoters have to have a huge amount of trust in the band and their management in order to do business with them.

Bill, having managed the Who for a while, had developed an immaculate reputation with promoters; after all, if he could guarantee the appearance of the Who, surely he could guarantee the appearance of our little lot. On one occasion, he agreed to advance us £8,000 on a week or so worth of dates, as we were completely broke and Christmas was coming—hurrah, hurrah! I remember very clearly how much money we didn't have around this time, because Dave Gilmour asked me if I would mind picking up the wine he had ordered from Harrods for Xmas. He gave me the check to pay them with, which was about £300, and that was more money than I had to spend on Xmas for *everything*. Even though we had just been advanced £2,000 each, by the time all the bills were paid there wasn't a lot left.

On a lighter note, when the money had got really tight and we were scrambling around trying to get some from one source or another, Steve came up with a novel way of alleviating his financial problems: he bought a brand-new Aston Martin DBS Vantage. Way to go, Steve! What made this particular transaction so remarkable was that Steve could not drive; whenever he did get behind the wheel, he needed a cushion to sit on so he could see over the hood. The other part of this ingenious plan of financial recovery was the monthly payment for the car, which was considerably larger than his mortgage. Brilliant! Go for it, Steve, attaboy! As if to put icing on the cake, he hadn't had the car for very long before he decided to try to drive it over to Greg's house. As he pulled out of his driveway, he had an argument with the humpbacked bridge that was no more than 500 yards from his house. Steve usually won arguments by sheer force of will, but the bridge was having none of it. He wrote the car off from the front bumper all the way up to the windscreen. The bill to fix it was almost as much as he paid for it in the first place. Not to be outdone, the bridge also required considerable surgery to rebuild the small brick wall that was there to stop people driving into the stream that it spanned. Steve did at least fool the bridge and proved that putting the little wall there was sheer folly, as he managed to plant his DBS right into the stream up to the aforementioned windscreen.

What happened to our record deal drove all of us nuts. Whereas we had each got a large lump sum every year before, now, what with all this corporation-in-New-York business that had been supposedly set up for our benefit with the taxman, we effectively received nothing. We had recorded three albums since the deal was put in place, and all we got was a certain amount of things paid for and a wages scheme that was meant to pay us all a weekly wage to live on. It did do that for a while, but after all the accusations and vitriol that were going back and forth, we stopped receiving the monthly cheques—the argument being that we/Steve had spent far too much for management to sustain our outgoings.

This was where any argument in favour of the management in New York was stopped dead on its feet, as I no longer had any grounds to argue on their behalf. I do not, however, believe that there were millions of dollars of our money skimmed off the top of our record deal and/or road receipts, for one simple reason: mathematics. It was all very well to sit there and bitch about the way things were, and I do think there was a lot wrong, but because we were sitting there in a cocaine-induced wonderland of godfathers and the like, the idea that there were any number of Mafiosi scamming millions off the top of our hard-earned money is very much like *The Godfather*: they are both works of fiction. We had not earned millions for them to skim from. I, at least, kept a record of everything we earned each night on the road, getting the figures directly from the box office at every venue we ever played in. And I knew how much we were supposed to get each time we made a record.

The more I pressed for a more businesslike approach, the more Steve would derail the whole idea. All I was asking for was a get-together so that all parties could air their differences, but no one would take the initiative and sit down face to face to sort things out. Steve didn't want to do so for reasons known only to him or, should I say, to Melvin.

As Christmas drew nearer, we had a few dates in Europe that would at least give us some money to get through the holiday. Again, all the necessary management work was done by Bill Curbishley and his staff—not that there was a lot to do, but what they did was done with extreme professionalism, and, as I said before, the guys from his crew that worked for the Who were a real pleasure to work with. Bill was our kind of man and would have made a perfect manager for us. We all liked and trusted him, including Steve, which was a godsend and obviously a necessary ingredient for it to work.

Once Christmas had come and gone, we were asked to do the back track for a song on Roger Daltrey's next solo album. Clem had already done some work on the album, which is how we got the job. We were given a tape of the song and had a go at it in Steve's studio; it turned out great. But we had tried to make it as much like the Who as we possibly could, and that was where we went wrong. When Roger and Bill came down to hear it, they liked it; however, Roger pointed out in a gentlemanly way that we had done too good a job, as it was so Who-like. Let's face it: if he had wanted it to sound like the Who, he could have got the Who to do it. Once Roger had left, we talked to Bill about managing us for real and asked if he could talk to Dee to see what could be done. At last, someone who knew what they were doing and who wouldn't be intimidated by Dee was going to talk to him man to man. I was ecstatic. I couldn't wait for him to meet with Dee.

I don't remember how long it was before Bill met with Dee, but it wasn't that long. So, when he called to say that we should meet with him so that he could tell us what had transpired with Dee, I was thrilled and eager to hear what he had to say. We decided to meet at Steve's, as it was central to everybody, and I hoped and prayed that Steve would be straight and cooperative, as he had assured me he would be. When I arrived, I had a very profound sense of "This is it; it will be either make or break."

As I walked into the studio, my heart sank. There was Steve, messing around with something he had recently recorded and trying to avoid eye contact. I'd seen it all a thousand times before: the little dance, the look of absentmindedness, the half-smile that he would do this sinister little chuckle through, as if he alone had just got the point of a joke that you hadn't got, the snorting paraphernalia, and the limited conversation we had as he told me how long he had been up to get this masterpiece finished. It was all I needed to know just how fried he was. He still had a white ring around his nostrils, for Christ's sake. It was heartbreaking because my friend who had done so many good things for me and my family was gone, for all intents and purposes, for good.

I gently suggested that he clean his nose, as it possibly might not look good to Bill, who was going out of his way to try to help us. Steve at least saw the sense in that and had a look in the mirror to help him clean his nose as opposed to fill it. I was very grateful that I had arrived first so that I could try to help him retain some of his dignity. Even if he didn't seem to care about such matters himself, I still did, and watching my hero and best friend disintegrating in front of me was horrific and devastating. Don't misunderstand me: he was not mentally losing it in the way that Syd Barrett did. He still had all his faculties; it was just the way that he used them that was so upsetting. Frankly, he had become an entirely different person to the one I knew and loved like a brother; the person that he now was had become embittered and disillusioned and impossible to reach.

When Bill arrived with Clem and Greg, he looked at Steve and then at me and winced as if in physical pain—and I am sure he was; it hurt to witness this person he had so much respect for become someone who no one could get through to, including himself. Without all the coke and subsequent bitterness on Steve's part, Bill could have done so much good for us all.

I barely remember the rest of the time that Bill was down at the studio that day, other than him saying that he was not able to get much out of Dee except that, as far as Dee was concerned, we were under contract to him and still would be five years hence. No sooner was that said than Steve said something like, "Oh well, sorry you couldn't help, Bill," in a very flippant way and went back to what he was doing before we all arrived. At that moment I knew I couldn't do this anymore. I said my goodbyes and left Steve's house/studio for what turned out to be the very last time.

Once home, I called Clem and told him what I thought about the meeting, which wasn't much, and that under the circumstances, I quit. His response was that if I was quitting, then so was he. Then I called Greg and told him; he was very sad, but completely understood. Then I called Dee to tell him about my decision, and he suggested that we should at least think about one final, farewell tour, as he had already booked some dates, expecting us to tour as we usually did at that time of year. Finally, I called Steve, told him how I felt, and said that we should maybe do a farewell tour, and he agreed. If anything, I think he was relieved.

So there I was, 23 years old and I had quit the band of my dreams, which also happened to be a very lucrative job doing what I loved to do—and the only reason I got the job in the first place was the same reason that I quit. It was all due to Steve Marriott. When I quit, it never occurred to me that I was only 23 and had seen and done more than most people do in their entire lives. Walking away from a band like that was, I suppose, both stupid and brave, but it was also a powerful indication of how much my dear old mate had changed. I just couldn't stand watching him short-change himself to that extent anymore. I had tried everything that I knew to get Steve to come back to being the person I knew and loved like a brother for all those years before his marriage fell apart. It really did turn him into a monster that only the people who came along with cocaine could put up with, for all the obvious reasons.

Chapter 19
I'll Go Alone
February to March 1975

*In which an ace Face introduces me to the Band's bass;
our farewell tour fares well, with a little help from
Robin Trower; Grandpa Munster saves our arses;
Stephen meets Stephens; and we ride off triumphantly into
the sunset, despite the vindaloo (and tequila, too).*

The tour was much the same as all the others we had done in the late winter / early spring, with a couple of exceptions. The first was more of a reliance upon a strong opening act to sell tickets than before; in this case it was mainly Robin Trower, whose huge second album, *Bridge of Sighs*, had been released in 1974 and was still on the charts. The second was the fact that it was our farewell tour, which we were doing as part of a deal with our accountants, whereby we assured them that we would send a large sum of money to placate the British taxman, who was getting more and more annoyed with our broken promises.

But we had been led to believe that the Inland Revenue had already received substantial payments from our previous tours of the USA. Just as we were in the throes of breaking up, the taxman had informed us that we had not made a payment for some considerable time and that we *must* do something about it *now*—no more empty promises. Milton Marks, our accountant, was adamant that we play the game and give over some of the receipts to the government, so we told Dee that we would do a farewell tour, so long as the taxman got £10,000 (about £100,000 in today's money) from the gate receipts as soon as it had been earned. Dee agreed to making the payment, and we went about the business of getting ready to tour for the very last time as Humble Pie. When we were on the tour, there was a serious misunderstanding about this that resulted in some considerable anger and unfortunate accusations, but it eventually got sorted out.

Before we even got on the plane, I thought how weird it would be to play "I Don't Need No Doctor" for the very last time, and wondered if I would ever play any of those songs again. (This was long before everybody started to reform at various levels of legitimacy.)

There was a beneficial side effect of this being a farewell tour. Each of us had our own reasons for being angry at what had transpired, and anger, as I've mentioned before, brings out the best in a hard-hitting rock band like Humble Pie when it comes to giving their all onstage. Bob Tench used to call it heft, but it's more commonly known as balls—either way, it's the one thing we had plenty of.

Although it was a long time ago by then, I saw how the rest of the Small Faces must have felt when Steve walked; while the circumstances were slightly different, I'm sure the feeling was similar. I felt completely empty and very frightened of what was to come. Walking away from such an amazing job without any game plan would put me and my family in an extremely precarious position. As the band were preparing for the farewell tour, Cindy and I talked about the possibility of moving to live in the USA and whether it might be a better place for me to find another gig. I certainly did not want to make such a big change at that stage in the proceedings, but I didn't blow the idea out completely, as we had started to hear some unnerving things about what the Inland Revenue planned to do to people like us, who in their opinion were filthy rich. Apparently they were going to take 90% of all our earnings, which was ridiculous, as we weren't anywhere near that tax bracket. Some were, but we were not. I wish!

Ever since the band broke up, I have been amazed at the level of respect we get from other bands—so much high regard from others, but sometimes very little from me. In today's language, it's called low self-esteem. It wasn't until we had actually broken up, or were about to, that I really got to grips with how good we were in other people's eyes.

The first and possibly most gratifying example of this was in the last throw of the dice, about six months before we did the final tour. We had played some gigs with the Faces, and the animosity they'd had for us had all but disappeared. I got a phone call from Kenney's now ex-wife, Jan Jones. She invited Cindy and me to a surprise birthday party for Ken. We had just seen each other backstage at a big gig at Wembley Stadium with Joni Mitchell, Bob Dylan, and the Band. My main reason for going was to see the Band, as they were such a huge influence on us. The old Wembley Stadium was not the greatest place to see a band, let alone *the* Band, but that didn't matter to me, as it was the only way I could see them at all on this tour. At the show, I saw a few familiar Faces, quite literally.

The party was to be the next day or the next weekend, I can't remember which. Jan asked if I could get Steve to come to the bash. I told her that it was getting harder to get Steve to go out than it ever had been. Jan knew full well how Steve could be about such matters; she had known Steve longer than any of us, as she had also gone to the Italia Conti Academy's drama school.

Ron Wood knew Rick Danko, the Band's bass player, who was considered to be the best in the business. On the day of the party, Ron arrived with his wife and with Rick as his guest. Once the party had thinned out a bit and Ron was going around introducing Rick to all and sundry, he got to Cindy and me and started to introduce Rick to us. He got as far as "And this is Jerry Shirley, the drummer from Humble Pie," when Rick, who had been fairly subdued until that moment, got noticeably wound up. He said, "Hey, man, that's really cool, man. Humble Pie are a great band; we love you guys," which completely bowled me over. He was such a nice man; he didn't have to say a word about the Band's opinion of us, but he did. Plus, I hadn't had a chance to say anything, so it was an instant reaction, not a polite response to anything I had said. It still puts a smile on my face now, more than 35 years later. What a gentleman, and what a nice guy.

A load of us piled into my BMW and headed to Ron's house. The car was built to take a maximum of five people, and we had squeezed a lot more than that into it, so the back of the car was sitting on the tyres. We did make it to Ron's house, but only just.

As the night moved on to the next day and we were the only two men left standing, Ron played me his solo album, which had just been released to, in some papers, lukewarm reviews. I couldn't understand that reaction, as it was a great record, and I had the privilege of being able to tell him so. As the time ticked away, Ron had to go to do an interview for one of the music papers. Cindy and I crashed in one of the guest bedrooms and slept the party off. Later on, once I was legal, we left.

When we got on the road from Ron's house, we were moving right along, crossing Richmond Bridge, when *bang!*—the car was instantly immobilised. I managed to get it over to the side of the road, got out, and looked under the back. The rear axle had separated itself from the rest of the car. We were so lucky; if it had happened on the motorway, we would have been in big trouble.

The following week, in the article that Ron was interviewed for, he was quoted as saying that I had said that neither Humble Pie nor the Faces had come near to doing something as good as *Ogdens' Nut Gone Flake*, to which he had replied that the Faces were currently in the process of doing so. But they never did, nor did we—*Ogdens'* was too much of a one-off piece of Sixties brilliance.

Steve decided to stay under Dee's wing and did so for at least another two years. He also instantly got money to pursue his solo career, whereas the rest of us were pretty much left to fend for ourselves. There were so many financial issues to deal with that I didn't know which end was up. First and foremost was the tour we were about to do. It was made crystal clear to us that each man had to watch what he spent if he wanted to walk away with any cash, which suited me down to the ground, as it was what I thought we should have been doing all along. If somebody used what was available at that time without having to consider the consequences, it would be human nature to take advantage of the situation.

All I knew was that I needed to make as much money as possible from the tour, as I would have to fend for myself pretty soon—in fact, only about a month down the road. The irony of all this was that the one who was pissing and moaning about his lot in life under Dee's managerial umbrella was the very same person who was walking away with the biggest financial help that Dee's company could provide.

I pro-offered my share of the Bahamas property in exchange for my freedom, writing in a one-paragraph letter that it was in lieu of any debts I may have had then or in the future to Dee or Bandana. That was it. No fuss, no "behind the door marked 'Vito Spunduli.'" Dee was very happy with it—mind you, this is where being a drummer comes in handy; from the manager's point of view, you are not a big earner like the singer or lead guitarist is.

I had always been close to the crew and the management, purely as a friend, and I was the go-between who was always there for the crew when they needed something from the management or vice versa. This was not a one-way street, believe me; I had to go to both of them for my personal needs on many occasions.

As mad as I was at Dee over the tax-money situation (which, as I have said, was eventually resolved), I can honestly say that neither he nor the crew wanted to see us break up like this. But, mainly because Steve was in such an advanced state of Melvinosity, he, and therefore we, were unapproachable on the subject. It was a done deal, and that was that. Steve was going solo, and we were going nowhere in particular but home to lick our self-inflicted wounds.

Looking back, it is amazing that everything went as well as it did. There were no particularly bad things that happened as a result of it being the last tour we were ever going to play together as Humble Pie. It was typical of us that our farewell tour would be simply another walk in the park. It was as if we were doing just another tour, another string of dates; we even had an album to go with it, although we were not particularly interested in the album. It was horrible, as far as we were concerned. It would be easy to put the blame at Andrews's feet, but that would not be fair, as he tried as best he could to make something out of nothing, but all he could do was get the best out of what we gave him, which wasn't much.

The last tour started on the East Coast with two shows at the Academy of Music in NYC on February 15, 1975. I had only just turned 23, although in some ways I felt more like I was 53. My home life and the responsibilities that went with it were more akin to those of someone much older than me. Cindy and I had so far not succumbed to the pressures of not knowing what the future was going to bring; the more I think about it now, the more amazed I am that we weren't terribly affected by the great unknown.

We were scheduled to play at the Spectrum in Philadelphia a few weeks into the tour. When we played there the previous year, Steve had nearly got us all killed in a great example of how much front that little chap had. We were halfway through our set when one of the security guards, an enormous black man, 6' 4" and 300-plus pounds, started to pick our fans out from the front of the stage by their hair and generally mistreat them in a misguided attempt to protect us. The fans were getting crushed, and Steve had screamed at the guard to stop what he was doing, but the guy didn't understand what Steve was trying to tell him; he just saw this little white guy, who he thought he was protecting, yelling at him.

The situation was already tense enough, but when Steve went up behind the guy in front of 20,000 white kids and kicked him up the arse as hard as he could, it made the crowd cheer in approval, and all bets were off. This giant of a man started toward Steve, and just as he got to where Steve was standing, all of the other security guards stepped in and pulled him offstage just in the nick of time. But this was not by any means the end of it. As we continued on with our show, the security guard, who just happened to be the *head* security guard, got a posse of his men together and stood in wait for us to come offstage.

Frank Barsalona did not always make the drive down to Philadelphia from New York City, but, as luck would have it, he did choose to come that night; it was a good excuse to take the Rolls-Royce that we had bought him for a spin. Frank did not drive himself; he had a driver called Willie, a lovely, middle-aged gentleman who resembled Grandpa from *The Munsters*, but without the makeup. It was typical of Frank to hire someone who looked very unimportant and inconsequential to do an important job that carried a lot of responsibility. (Frank was a laidback man who nonetheless wore large amounts of bling—gold jewellery and very expensive, one-of-a-kind gold Rolex watches—long before bling was invented.) Although we didn't know it until this fateful night, Willie carried a piece legally and knew how to use it, although he was proud of the fact that he had not needed to, even though he was more than capable of doing so in the defence of his boss. His weapon of choice was a .38 Special that he wore in a holster under his jacket.

As we came off and walked down the ramp from the stage to the ground level, we saw Mr. Big standing there with his large posse, who were just waiting for the word from their boss as to which limb was to be torn off which short-arse first. Steve was man enough to lead the march toward certain death—albeit flanked by Greg on one side, using his Fender bass as a baseball bat, and me on the other side, using nothing. Who was I kidding? Now, bearing in mind that we were unaware of Willie's firepower, you would be right in assuming that we were about to get the living crap beaten out of us; we certainly thought so. Just as it was about to tip off, though, Willie very casually walked up to Mr. Big and leaned into him. We watched as the big guy bent down slightly and became, all of a sudden, extremely attentive to everything that Willie had to say.

Not to be outdone in the show of paternal instinct toward us from the wonderful Willie, earlier in the evening Dee had been arguing with promoter Larry Magid over some of our backstage wish list. It got so heated that Larry turned to Dee and said, "Take your band and stick 'em up your ass!" at which point Dee turned on Larry and decked him with a straight right to the chin, which knocked him out cold. Dee was instantly arrested and was put on bail for a large amount of cash, which we put up to get him out. When Larry woke up and it was clear that he was okay, he told the powers that be to drop any charges that Dee would ordinarily have to face. There was way too much business at stake among Larry, Dee, and Frank to let a straight right get in the way.

On the farewell tour show at the Spectrum, we went onstage with an extra added hump in our engine room, which made this night one of the best we ever played, bar none. We were on fire. The gig was preserved for posterity by the King Biscuit Flower Hour.

After the show, we played back a rough mix taken from the King Biscuit feed. It was the one time on that tour that we all were in the room at the same time, listening. We came so close to saying, "What are we doing? We must be crazy!" but for some reason we didn't. We just let it happen. There had been way too much water under the bridge by then, I guess.

The crazy part of all this was that the two people who had caused the most damage and dissension amongst the troops were the very two who seemed the least affected: Steve and Dee. While our world was falling apart, the two of them were making plans and moving right along. It was totally unfathomable to witness. Here we were, watching every penny, having no idea what would happen after this tour, while Steve and Dee had the whole thing sorted out. Dee had very quickly put into place Steve's right to make a solo record under the terms of the record deal as it stood. Steve's spending, therefore, went on unabated, as he knew he was going to be walking straight into a solo record deal that gave him $25,000 when he started recording and a further $25,000 when he delivered the final mixes—and possibly yet another $25,000 when the album was released. (I'm not entirely sure about that last part, as the record was released long after we had broken up, and I was no longer privy to what was going on in Steve's life, businesswise.)

What I do know about Steve's solo deal was that it was—wait for it—"cross-collateralized," which meant that if it did not make a profit, the record company were allowed to recoup their costs from the profit on Humble Pie's successful albums, which is precisely what happened. Our last three albums were not big money-makers as such, but, with the exception of *Street Rats*, they probably just about broke even. So, by the time a couple of years had gone by, there would have been royalties to receive. Steve's first solo album, however, ended up costing a fortune, and it took more than 15 years for the costs to be recouped—and once they were, the royalties that came in every six months were greatly reduced. Still, I have to say that I am extremely grateful for those royalties when they come in twice a year.

In order to get their freedom to move on, the other guys had to sign away their future earnings from Humble Pie records, which back then were fairly inconsequential and were not going to appear, as I've just explained, for another 15 years. I used my share of the Bahamas property to pay off any debts I may have had with Dee. I didn't wait to find out whether I actually owned my share; I just took their word for it that I did, signed it over, and was on my way.

I was lucky that I didn't have to sign away my royalties. Back then, the fact was that drummers were not considered big currency like lead singers, lead guitarists, or bass players who were great singers. Drummers were allowed to just amble off into the sunset, so I never had to sign my future royalties away in order to get my freedom. This was not because of any smart maneuvring on my part; I just got lucky for once, although it took me 25 years to find out about this little bit of good fortune. It took 10 years after the royalties were forthcoming for me to discover, almost by accident, that this was the case, and once I sent off the appropriate letters, they began coming in without problems.

During the farewell tour, we played Atlanta, another stronghold for us. In fact, the entire tour was made up of our strongholds, almost without exception. It would hardly have made sense to play our farewell out in front of audiences who were not our biggest supporters. After Atlanta, we had a couple of days off, which was fortuitous, as Steve went AWOL. This was a habit he got into later in life—disappearing with the first person who had a party to go to. It can be very unnerving when it first happens and you have a band and crew all waiting to find out if their fearless leader, who has pissed off and not bothered to leave a forwarding address, is returning anytime soon. We got lucky on this occasion, as Steve ended up in the company of one of the best women he had ever had the good fortune to meet, his future second wife, Pam Stephens, bless her heart.

I don't recall the exact details, but I do remember that there was not a huge panic about his absence, so either he must have let one of us know where he was or Pam got him back to us in good time for the tour to continue unabated. I immediately felt extremely grateful to her, and at the same time very sorry for her, as she had no idea what she was getting herself into. She certainly was in for a baptism of fire in the wonderful world of Steve and his buddy Melvin. I don't mean I was sorry for her in any condescending way—she was a very smart woman who was fun and easy to get to know, a typical laidback southern lady. Once she had been on the tour for a short while, I think she was relieved to find there was another southern lady amongst our ranks in Cindy.

As the tour trucked on, we had more than the odd "Maybe breaking up is not a good idea" moment, but not nearly as many as the blistering shows we were playing should have produced. The plain and simple truth was that we were exhausted from it all. Nearly seven years of almost non-stop touring, writing, rehearsing, recording, and touring again will get to you after a while. All four of us loved the 90-plus minutes that we were onstage because no matter what was going on offstage—good, bad, or indifferent—what happened once we got onstage was nothing short of fucking brilliant every night. The absolute worst show we ever played was way better than the vast majority of our contemporaries' best shows. We were gobsmackingly good.

Every show on the farewell tour was sold out. It would be easy to claim all the credit for such good business and simply put it down to the fact that it was the last tour we were ever gonna do, but that would be unfair to the tremendous amount of help we got from the support acts we had on that tour. We always had the very best bands opening up for us, although we were never blown offstage by any of 'em. This partial list shows the calibre of act that opened for us or appeared as our special guest in the last year or two of our existence: ZZ Top, Journey, Robin Trower, Thin Lizzy, Montrose, the Eagles, Linda Ronstadt, Tower of Power, Edgar Winter's White Trash, Yes, J. Geils Band, Slade, T. Rex, Boz Scaggs, Lynyrd Skynyrd, Foghat, and Earth, Wind & Fire.

In the main, our ticket sales were helped by Robin Trower, who led a great, Hendrixesque three-piece who were definitely putting many bums in many seats. (They were also responsible for some *nice* people buying tickets!) This was typical of Premier Talent's way of doing things and Frank Barsalona's way of guaranteeing the success of our last tour. Night after night, during the last week or two, we got huge receptions from all these big crowds, who just went ape-shit and gave us a send-off to remember.

In Pam, Steve had found himself a new girlfriend who seemed to agree with him. I would like to tell you that this made him behave better, but this is Steve we are talking about, so that was never gonna happen. But he did, at least, try, and I seem to recall him treating Pam very well (by Steve's standards) in those first weeks that he knew her. If I remember correctly, her dad got sick, and Steve flew her home from wherever we were in a Learjet so she could get to her dad in a hurry. While Steve could be the most infuriating SOB on God's earth, he was not the Devil incarnate—although sometimes he could make those whose job it was to look after him wonder.

The tour ended in Houston, *not* in Philadelphia as an error-filled book about Steve by Paolo Hewitt and John Hellier stated. The book also said that we did the last tour as a five-piece with Tim Hinckley on keyboards, which is also completely untrue. It's a shame; the book was great, but it was shot through with incredible errors like those. It also stated that our live album, which was recorded at the Fillmore East in NYC, was recorded at the Fillmore West in San Francisco, nearly 3,000 miles away. The authors should have known better. They were at least gentlemen enough to admit the error of their ways in subsequent editions of their book. It takes a big man to admit when he is wrong, and I applaud them for that.

But before Houston, we played the Municipal Auditorium in San Antonio, one of the hottest, sweatiest venues in all of America, thanks to both geography and tequila. Being in the Deep South, San Antonio can be extremely hot, and the favourite local libation is tequila in all its forms; some of the hardcore locals virtually brush their teeth with the stuff. So, unless you are accustomed to the weather, it's not the kind of environment where you would be inclined to eat a hot curry, unless you were able to lay down and take a long nap immediately afterwards. Unless, of course, you were Steve Marriott.

Steve had been feeling no pain for several days before San Antonio, and had not seen a bed in over a week. As we got to the hotel, he noticed that there was an Indian restaurant that had just opened adjacent to the hotel lobby. Having not had a good vindaloo for a while, he—being extremely hungry and forgetting that he was in 105-degree heat and 100% humidity—walked straight into the air-conditioned Indian restaurant and ordered up, hot and large.

Later that afternoon, I rescued him from the restaurant, where he had passed out at the table after eating his fill and consuming several strong local tequila specials—rum-punch-type drinks, only made with 100-proof tequila. I got him up to his room and laid him on his side on the bed. We were not due at the gig until 9:00 that evening.

As I was getting ready to go to the show, I got a frantic call from John Doumanian, saying that they can't find Steve and no one knows where he is. "Have you checked his room?" I asked. "Yes, I've been calling it for ages; there's no reply," John answered. "Doesn't mean he's not in there," said I, "Get a pass key; I'll meet you at his room."

When John, Bill Anthony, and I got to Steve's room, we opened the door, and, sure enough, there he was, fast asleep and snoring like a trooper. I woke him up and helped him—he was still in his clothes—into the shower. I volunteered to do this because we figured if it was one of the others, Steve might get ornery and start objecting in an "against the suits" kind of way, whereas if it was a band member, he would wake up and maybe realise that being helped into the shower with his clothes on was necessary.

By now we were running incredibly late, which was unheard of for us. The audience had been kept waiting for over an hour, and things were starting to get ugly. Everybody was worried that Steve was not going to get through the gig, except me; I knew he would pull it off. He didn't disappoint me or the sold-out crowd: he proceeded to put on one of the best shows I had ever seen him do. It filled me with incredible pride in my little mate, the way he showed everybody that he was the very best at what he did, even when he had been comatose 20 minutes earlier and had just been manhandled into a cold shower and then almost directly from getting his dry clothes on to putting his guitar on to going onstage. The place went *nuts*. He was hot as a pistol that night. While the crew was on tenterhooks at the start of the show—even I was watching him like a hawk for any signs of a problem—he soon put everybody at ease.

At the end of the second song, Steve turned to me as we hit the last bash and gave me a little grin and a wink, which put a huge smile on my face. It was the closest thing to a thanks he was ever gonna give me. How he pulled off going from a deep sleep to putting on such a fantastic performance in such a short time, I didn't know then and I never will. But I did know that I'd had the privilege of playing drums behind the greatest white-soul frontman that rock 'n' roll had ever seen, then or now, and I couldn't help but wonder if I was ever going to play for him again after the end of that tour.

I hoped deep down, and somehow believed, that I would.

Epilogue

All in all, Steve Marriott and I worked together, on and off, from New Year's Day 1969 to December 12, 1986, the first and longest period being from the start of 1969 until the spring of 1975—the period that this book is primarily concerned with. We got back together in the autumn of 1979 to reform Humble Pie, and subsequently worked together for another two years, producing two strong albums for Atco and co-writing a single called "Fool for a Pretty Face," which actually got into the American Top 40. The only other person to co-write an American Top 40 hit with Steve was Ronnie Lane, God bless him; that song was a little ditty called "Itchycoo Park." Ronnie got to be Steve's partner through an immense amount of talent as a songwriter. I got to do so through an immense amount of good fortune and the occasional ear for a tune.

Once that version of Humble Pie—which featured Bobby Tench on lead guitar and vocals, and Anthony Jones on bass—broke up in 1981, Steve and I moved back to England, having lived in the States for several years. We got together again in 1985 when Steve called and asked me to play drums with his great three-piece blues band, Packet of Three.

This, sadly, is where my long friendship with Steve hit one of its many bumpy patches, which ended up with him having someone else tell me that he no longer wanted me in his band. I was devastated. It wasn't one of Steve's finer moments, as he used me, his old friend, as a scapegoat to get himself off the hook in a set of circumstances that I won't go into here, because it doesn't matter anymore. He knew that what he had done was wrong, and, as always, whenever he behaved appallingly towards one of his close friends, he would eventually get back in touch, with yet another invite to play some steamin' rock 'n' roll, and all would be forgiven.

The problem was, this time there wasn't going to be a next time, and we were denied the opportunity for his behaviour to be forgiven and forgotten when Steve died in a horrendous house fire on April 20, 1991, right when he was on the brink of a big comeback. He had even started to work with his old partner Peter Frampton again. The pain of losing Steve, especially in that fashion, was too much to bear for a long, long time. It still hurts like hell to this day. What hurts the most is that we were never able to say to each other, "Sorry, mate."

Me and my baby Isobel with Steve and his Molly.

This book is, in some ways, my way of saying "Sorry, mate" for my part in the wrongdoing between us, and, trust me, being the brothers that we were, there were plenty of times that we fought, cussed each other out, and almost came to blows, just as real brothers do.

I could have written a "dig up the dirt" kind of book; believe me there was lots of dirt to dig up. But, I am afraid to say to all you dirt lovers, that is just not my style. I will let others do that. I am far more concerned with writing about a very young upstart kid who was given a hell of a big break by one bighearted superstar and then went on to be treated like an equal by a long line of generous, kind-hearted, and enormously talented gentlemen.

This is the real story, and I wanted to tell it: how a young kid can have his dreams come true and how show business doesn't always have to be a cold, callous, mean-spirited place to be. It *can* be a whole lot of fun and a joy to be part of, and that's what was important to me: to tell you how it felt for a young lad to go through the experience of a lifetime, and years later still be able to look back and be filled with gratitude and struck by the wonder of it all.

Dee Anthony is also no longer with us, and while I didn't get to see him in the later part of his life, I had long since forgiven any perceived or real hurt that Dee may have caused me, because in his own way he helped me in my subsequent career with other bands with a generosity of spirit that was second to none. He got a lot of blame for many things that he simply did not do, by people who really didn't know. So I wanted, in the main, to focus on what an incredible job he did as our manager, friend, and father figure. When he passed away, he had over 15 years of sobriety under his belt. That is a joy to know and typical of the man's strength of character that he could do that at the age he was when he found sobriety, given that he died at 83.

I would be remiss if I didn't mention the sad loss of my dear partner in crime in the rhythm section, Greg Ridley, who died in 2003 from complications that came back after he had initially beaten throat cancer like a real trooper. He was the finest bass player I have ever played with, a wonderful singer, and the best big brother I could have had the extreme pleasure of sharing my teenage years and early twenties with.

Greg and I even got back together towards the end of his life and recorded a Humble Pie album called *Back on Track*, which didn't sell squat, but sounded great. The band we put together to write it and play on it was another dream come true—it included Zoot Money, one of my boyhood heroes, and Bobby Tench, who is one of the best blues singers I have every played with. The line-up also included a good friend of mine (who my mother taught when he was a young boy) called Dave "Bucket" Caldwell, who played with Bad Company for a while on second guitar behind Mick Ralphs.

As a result of this fabulous start in the music business that was so generously given to me, I have been able to carve out a livelihood as a professional musician for the vast majority of my adult life.

I formed two bands in the second half of the Seventies that both succeeded in generating huge record deals of several hundreds of thousands of dollars. The first was Natural Gas, with Joey Molland of Badfinger, Mark Clarke of Colosseum, and Pete Wood of the Sutherland Brothers & Quiver. We toured extensively, supporting Peter Frampton on his "Comes Alive" stadium tour. It was a great band, but eventually failed.

Next was a band called Magnet, with me, Pete Wood, Les Nicol from Leo Sayers' band, NYC bass player Mike Neville, and Bob James, who sang lead for Montrose after Sammy Hagar left. Speaking of Sammy, he kindly asked me to play drums on four tracks on his first solo album shortly after the Pie first split up. He and I had been buddies ever since the days Montrose opened for the Pie.

I had a great time putting a band together in the Eighties called Fastway, with "Fast" Eddie Clarke from Motorhead. I was also able to turn my hand to broadcasting for a while on a classic rock station in Cleveland, Ohio, as a direct result of being a working musician with the odd story to tell. In fact, it was during my time there that I first thought seriously about writing this book. I was forever telling stories on the air, and I eventually asked myself, "Why don't I wrote all this down?" So I made my first attempt at starting the book with a legal pad and a pen all those years ago in Cleveland. I think my ex-wife Cheryl still has those first

The punch that won the fight—learning to defend myself in NYC in '77.

few handwritten pages locked up somewhere in Cleveland. I must ask her to see them one day.

I've had a long and varied life in rock 'n' roll, and there is an awful lot of it that I haven't even been able to mention in these pages—maybe some other time, if you enjoyed this one well enough. We shall see what we shall see.

All of this could never have been achieved if it were not for those two very Small Faces who first watched me at the side of the stage when I was barely 14 years old. It wasn't until I was writing this book that I asked Kenney Jones about the circumstances surrounding him and Steve doing that. It turns out, as I had suspected all along, that Dad, who was always on my side, had politely asked them if they wouldn't mind checking out his young son, as it would make my day. And he was right: it most certainly did. It made my day then, and it made many days for me, for many years thereafter.

With Dad, his beloved doves, and the house he built for them, 1978.

Humble Pie and Jerry Shirley Discography

Humble Pie: Original Albums, 1969 to 1975

As Safe as Yesterday Is recorded at Olympic Studios, Barnes, London, England; Morgan Studios, Willesden, London, England; and mobile, Magdalen Laver Village Hall, Essex, England—Immediate Records, 1969

Town and Country recorded at Morgan Studios, Willesden, London, England—Immediate Records, 1969

Humble Pie recorded at Olympic Studios, Barnes, London, England—A&M Records, 1970

Rock On recorded at Olympic Studios, Barnes, London, England—A&M Records, 1971

Performance—Rockin' the Fillmore recorded at the Fillmore East, New York City, May 28–29, 1971, and mixed at Electric Lady Studios, New York City—A&M Records, 1971

Smokin' recorded at Olympic Studios, Barnes, London, England—A&M Records, 1972

Eat It recorded at Beehive Cottage, Essex, England—A&M Records, 1973

Thunderbox recorded at Beehive Cottage, Essex, England—A&M Records, 1974

Street Rats recorded at Olympic Studios, Barnes, London, England, and Beehive Cottage, Essex, England—A&M Records, 1975

(Humble Pie has been well served by a plethora of compilations, albeit perhaps nothing definitive and comprehensive. For information on such releases, the interested reader is directed to such online resources as AllMusic, Amazon, iTunes, Wikipedia, etc.)

Jerry Shirley: Selected Session Work, 1968 to 1975

Would You Believe by Billy Nicholls, recorded at IBC Studios, Portland Place, London, England—Drums on "Girl From New York"—Immediate Records, 1968

The Madcap Laughs by Syd Barrett, recorded at Abbey Road Studios, St. John's Wood, London, England—Some percussion and some bass guitar—Harvest Records, 1970

Barrett by Syd Barrett, recorded at Abbey Road Studios, St. John's Wood, London, England—Most drums, some percussion—Harvest Records, 1970

The Peel Session by Syd Barrett, recorded live February 24, 1970, at the BBC, London, England—percussion—Strange Fruit, 1987

All Things Must Pass by George Harrison, recorded at Abbey Road Studios, St. John's Wood, London, England—Some percussion on "Ballad of Sir Frankie Crisp (Let it Roll)" and "If Not For You"—Apple/EMI, 1970

B.B. King in London by B.B. King, recorded at Olympic Studios, Barnes, London, England—Drums on "Alexis Boogie"—ABC Records, 1971

Smash Your Head Against the Wall by John Entwistle, recorded at Trident Studios, Soho, London, England—All drums—Track Records (UK) and Decca Records (US), 1971

Nine on a Ten Scale by Sammy Hagar, recorded at the Record Plant, Sausalito, California—Drums on four songs—Capitol Records, 1976

Humble Pie Tour Dates

Humble Pie toured Europe, North America, and Japan nearly non-stop from 1969 to 1975. This Tour Archive attempts to catalog all of Humble Pie's gigs, from the beginnings in 1969 until the breakup in 1975. However, we are aware that this does not account for every show; Jerry estimates that this list includes about 60% to 70% of the shows the band played in the timeframe covered. If you can add to the Humble Pie Tour Archive, please contact tourarchive@aol.com. Thanks to Greg Vick for allowing us to use his extensively researched gig list, and to all the other fans and concertgoers who have helped us out with missing dates. © Copyright 2004 Tour Archive. All Rights Reserved. Reproduction in whole or in part in any form or medium without express written permission of Tour Archive is prohibited.

August 1969 – October 1971
Humble Pie #1 (Marriott, Frampton, Ridley, Shirley)

1969

8/8/1969 London, ENG, Ronnie Scott's Club (debut gig)

8/22/1969 Bilzen, BEL, Jazz & Pop Festival *Deep Purple, Soft Machine, Shocking Blue, Bonzo Dog Band, Taste, Moody Blues, Marsha Hunt & White Trash, Brian Auger's Trinity*

8/23/1969 Amsterdam, NLD, Paradiso *Deep Purple, Brian Auger's Trinity*

8/24/1969 Amsterdam, NLD, Paradiso *Deep Purple, Brian Auger's Trinity*

10/8/1969 Coventry, ENG, Coventry Theatre *David Bowie*

10/9/1969 Leeds, ENG, Town Hall *David Bowie*

10/10/1969 Birmingham, ENG, Town Hall *David Bowie*

10/11/1969 Brighton, ENG, The Dome *David Bowie*

10/13/1969 Colston, ENG, Colston Hall *David Bowie*

10/16/1969 London, ENG, All Saints Church Hall, Powis Gardens *David Bowie*

10/17/1969 Exeter, ENG, Tiffany's *David Bowie*

10/19/1969 Birmingham, ENG, Rebecca's Club *David Bowie*

10/21/1969 London, ENG, Queen Elizabeth Hall *David Bowie*

10/23/1969 Edinburgh, SCT, Usher Hall *David Bowie*

10/24/1969 Sunderland, ENG, Empire *David Bowie*

10/25/1969 Manchester, ENG, Odeon Theatre *David Bowie*

10/26/1969 Liverpool, ENG, Empire Theatre *David Bowie*

10/30/1969 Gravesend, ENG, General Gordon *David Bowie*

10/31/1969 Gillingham, ENG, Aurora Hotel *David Bowie*

11/7/1969 New York, NY, Fillmore East *Santana, Butterfield Blues Band*

11/8/1969 New York, NY, Fillmore East *Santana, Butterfield Blues Band*

11/12/1969 College Park, MD, University of Maryland, Ritchie Coliseum *Neil Diamond (HL)*

11/14/1969 Cincinnati, OH, Ludlow Garage *Kinks, Glass Harp*

11/15/1969 Cincinnati, OH, Ludlow Garage *Kinks, Glass Harp*

11/27/1969 Grand Rapids, MI, Fountain Street Church *Moody Blues (HL)*

11/28/1969 Detroit, MI, Grande Ballroom *Moody Blues (HL), Savage Grace*

11/29/1969 Toronto, CAN, Massey Hall *Moody Blues (HL)*

11/30/1969 Chicago, IL, Auditorium *Moody Blues (HL)*

12/4/1969 San Francisco, CA, Fillmore West *Grateful Dead, Flock*

12/5/1969 San Francisco, CA, Fillmore West *Grateful Dead, Flock*

12/6/1969 San Francisco, CA, Fillmore West *Grateful Dead, Flock*

12/7/1969 San Francisco, CA, Fillmore West *Grateful Dead, Flock*

12/8/1969 West Hollywood, CA, Thema

12/9/1969 West Hollywood, CA, Thema

12/15/1969 West Hollywood, CA, Whisky A Go Go *Grand Funk Railroad*

12/16/1969 West Hollywood, CA, Whisky A Go Go *Grand Funk Railroad*

12/19/1969 Woodland Hills, CA, Valley Music Theater *Smith, Bigfoot*

1970

3/7/1970 Birmingham, ENG, Mothers

4/12/1970 Croyden, ENG, Greyhound

4/17/1970 London, ENG, Marquee *Morning*

4/22/1970 Guildford, ENG, Civic Hall *Mott The Hoople, If*

4/24/1970 Sunderland, ENG, Locarno *Roy Harper*

4/25/1970 Dudley, ENG, Dudley Tech College

5/1/1970 London, ENG, Hampstead Country Club

5/2/1970 Dagenham, ENG, Village Roundhouse

5/9/1970 Leeds, ENG, Leeds University *Procol Harum*

5/11/1970 Dunstable, ENG, Civic Hall

5/23/1970 Birmingham, ENG, Mothers

5/24/1970 Redcar, ENG, Coatham Hotel, Jazz Club

5/26/1970 Colchester, ENG, Essex University *Heaven, Trader Horne*

5/30/1970 Little Bardfield, ENG, Barn Club

6/2/1970 London, ENG, Marquee *Da Da*

6/6/1970 Sheffield, ENG, Sheffield University

6/8/1970 Edmonton, ENG, Cooks Ferry Inn

6/22/1970 Essen, DEU, Hamburg Big Gig Festival Colosseum, *Family, Rare Bird, Black Sabbath, Uriah Heep, Gentle Giant*

7/26/1970 London, ENG, The Roundhouse *MC5, Matthew's Southern Comfort, May Blitz*

7/27/1970 London, ENG, Aeolian Hall, Studio 2 BBC

8/4/1970 London, ENG, Marquee *Cochise*

8/14/1970 Newcastle, ENG, Mayfair

8/14/1970 Newcastle, ENG, City Hall

9/10/1970 London ENG, Paris Cinema BBC

9/18/1970 Detroit, MI, Eastown Theatre *Mountain, Cradle, Mutzie*

9/19/1970 Detroit, MI, Eastown Theatre *Mountain, Cradle, Mutzie*

9/24/1970 Boston, MA, Tea Party *James Gang, Hard Meat*

9/25/1970 Boston, MA, Tea Party *James Gang, Hard Meat*

9/26/1970 Boston, MA, Tea Party *James Gang, Hard Meat*

10/2/1970 Philadelphia, PA, Electric Factory *Mungo Jerry*

10/3/1970 Philadelphia, PA, Electric Factory *Mungo Jerry*

10/8/1970 Boston, MA, Tea Party *Mungo Jerry, Spider John Koerner*

10/9/1970 Boston, MA, Tea Party *Mungo Jerry, Spider John Koerner*

10/10/1970 Boston, MA, Tea Party *Mungo Jerry, Spider John Koerner*

10/16/1970 Chicago, IL, Syndrome. Coliseum *Grand Funk Railroad (HL), Brethren, Chase*

10/23/1970 New York, NY, Fillmore East *Derek & The Dominos, Ballin' Jack*

10/24/1970 New York, NY, Fillmore East *Derek & The Dominos, Ballin' Jack*

11/28/1970 San Antonio, TX, Municipal Auditorium *Grand Funk (HL)*

12/3/1970 San Francisco, CA, Fillmore West *Savoy Brown, Seatrain, Ry Cooder*

12/4/1970 San Francisco, CA, Fillmore West *Savoy Brown, Seatrain, Ry Cooder*

12/5/1970 San Francisco, CA, Fillmore West *Savoy Brown, Seatrain, Ry Cooder*

12/6/1970 San Francisco, CA, Fillmore West *Savoy Brown, Seatrain, Ry Cooder*

12/9/1970 Los Angeles, CA, Whisky A Go Go *Edward Bear*

12/10/1970 Los Angeles, CA, Whisky A Go Go *Edward Bear*

12/11/1970 Los Angeles, CA, Whisky A Go Go *Edward Bear*

12/12/1970 Los Angeles, CA, Whisky A Go Go *Edward Bear*

12/13/1970 Los Angeles, CA, Whisky A Go Go *Edward Bear*

12/14/1970 Memphis, TN, Mid-South Coliseum *Grand Funk (HL)*

12/18/1970 New York, NY, Madison Square Garden *Grand Funk (HL), Brethren, Chase*

12/19/1970 Birmingham, MI, The Palladium *May Blitz, Julia*

1971

2/9/1971 London, ENG, Marquee

2/26/1971 London, ENG, Lyceum *Forevermore, Comus, Trader Horne*

3/1/1971 London, ENG, Shepherds Bush, Kensington House, Studio T1 BBC

3/10/1971 Leeds, ENG, Town Hall *Comus*

3/11/1971 London, ENG, Marquee *Paul Brett Sage*

3/15/1971 Birmingham, ENG, Town Hall *Comus*

3/19/1971 New York, NY, Fillmore East *Cactus, Dada*

3/20/1971 New York, NY, Fillmore East *Cactus, Dada*

3/27/1971 Detroit, MI, Eastown Theater *Johnny Winter, Dada*

3/28/1971 Detroit, MI, Eastown Theater *Johnny Winter, Dada*

4/2/1971 Philadelphia, PA, Spectrum *Mountain (HL), Black Sabbath*

4/4/1971 Alexandria, VA, Alexandria Roller Rink *Black Sabbath (HL)*

4/5/1971 New York, NY, Fillmore East (replaced Jethro Tull) *Edgar Winter, Cactus, Tin House*

4/6/1971 New York, NY, Fillmore East (replaced Jethro Tull) *Edgar Winter, Cactus, Tin House*

4/8/1971 Rockford, IL, Sherwood Lodge

4/10/1971 Winnipeg, MN, Winnipeg Arena *Ten Years After (HL)*

4/16/1971 Boston, MA, Boston Garden *Ten Years After, Cactus*

4/17/1971 Syracuse, NY, State Fair Coliseum *Ten Years After*

4/21/1971 New Orleans, LA, Warehouse *Cat Stevens*

4/23/1971 Dania, FL, Pirates World *Ten Years After (HL)*

4/24/1971 Dania, FL, Pirates World *Ten Years After (HL)*

4/30/1971 Island Park, NY, The Rockpile *Tyrannosaurus Rex*

5/1/1971 Island Park, NY, The Rockpile *Tyrannosaurus Rex*

5/2/1971 Long Beach, CA, Arena *Ten Years After, Cactus*

5/4/1971 Los Angeles, CA, Whisky A Go Go *Jo Jo Gunne*

5/13/1971 San Francisco, CA, Fillmore West *Swamp Dog, Shanti*

5/14/1971 San Francisco, CA, Fillmore West *Swamp Dog, Shanti*

5/15/1971 San Francisco, CA, Fillmore West *Swamp Dog, Shanti*

5/16/1971 San Francisco, CA, Fillmore West *Swamp Dog, Shanti*

5/21/1971 Crawfordsville, IN, Wabash College Gym *Johnny Winter, Emerson, Lake & Palmer*

5/28/1971 New York, NY, Fillmore East *Lee Michaels (HL), Fanny*

5/29/1971 New York, NY, Fillmore East *Lee Michaels (HL), Fanny*

5/30/1971 Cleveland, OH, Public Hall *Frank Zappa & Mothers of Invention, Free, Head Over Heels*

6/10/1971 Birmingham, ENG

6/12/1971 Durham, ENG, Durham University

6/16/1971 Brighton, ENG, Brighton College of Education

6/18/1971 Leicester, ENG, Leicester University *Hookfoot*

6/19/1971 Felixstowe, ENG, Pier Pavilion

6/20/1971 Frankfurt, DEU *Grand Funk (HL)*

6/22/1971 Schweinfurt, DEU, Conn Barracks Airstrip *Grand Funk (HL)*

6/23/1971 Twickenham, ENG, Winning Post

6/25/1971 Rotterdam, NLD, De Doelen *Grand Funk (HL)*

6/25/1971 Swansea, ENG, Top Rank *Manfred Mann's Earth Band*

6/26/1971 Amsterdam, NLD *Grand Funk (HL)*

6/28/1971 Paris, FRA, Olympia *Grand Funk (HL)*

6/30/1971 Rome, ITA *Grand Funk (HL)*

7/1/1971 Milan, ITA *Grand Funk (HL)*

7/3/1971 London, ENG, Hyde Park *Grand Funk (HL), Heads, Hands & Feet*

7/9/1971 New York, NY, Shea Stadium *Grand Funk (HL)*

7/11/1971 Asbury Park, NJ, Sunshine Inn *Bruce Springsteen Band*

7/14/1971 Port Chester, NY, Capitol Theatre *Black Sabbath, Yes*

7/15/1971 Port Chester, NY, Capitol Theatre *Black Sabbath, Yes*

7/16/1971 Detroit, MI, Eastown Theater *Soft Machine, Savage Grace, Yes*

7/17/1971 Detroit, MI, Eastown Theater *Soft Machine, Savage Grace, Yes*

7/18/1971 Toronto, ON, York Stadium, "Beggars' Banquet" *Three Dog Night, Black Sabbath, Grease Band, Steel River*

7/19/1971 Hollywood, CA, Hollywood Bowl *Emerson, Lake & Palmer (HL), Edgar Winter*

November 1971 – March 1975
Humble Pie #2 (Marriott, Clempson, Ridley, Shirley)

11/18/1971 Frankfurt, DEU, Jahrhunderthalle *Velvet Underground*

11/28/1971 London, ENG, Roundhouse *Michael Chapman, Yamash'ta, Phillip Goodhand-Tait, Jerusalem*

12/3/1971 New York, NY, Academy of Music *Edgar Winter White Trash, Bell & Arc*

12/4/1971 New York, NY, Academy of Music *Edgar Winter White Trash, Bell & Arc*

12/5/1971 Plattsburgh, NY, SUNY Plattsburgh, Memorial Gymnasium *Yes*

12/6/1971 New York, NY, Ritz Theatre *King Crimson*

12/8/1971 Chicago, IL, Auditorium Theater

12/9/1971 Detroit, MI, East Town Theater *J. Geils Band, The Frut*

12/10/1971 Detroit, MI, East Town Theater *J. Geils Band, The Frut*

12/11/1971 Philadelphia, PA, Spectrum *J. Geils Band, King Crimson*

12/12/1971 University Heights, OH, John Carroll University *Glass Harp*

12/14/1971 Boston, MA, Orpheum Theatre *Yes, Glass Harp*

12/16/1971 Passaic, NJ, Capitol Theatre (2 shows) *J. Geils Band*

12/17/1971 Gaithersburg, MD, Shady Grove Music Fair (2 shows) *Yes*

12/18/1971 New Orleans, LA, The Warehouse *Yes*

1972

2/9/1972 Cardiff, ENG, Cardiff University

2/10/1972 Bristol, ENG, Bristol Polytechnic

2/11/1972 Bath, ENG, Bath University

2/12/1972 Manchester, ENG, Manchester University

2/14/1972 Portsmouth, ENG, Portsmouth Technical College

2/17/1972 Oxford, ENG, Oxford Polytechnic

2/18/1972 Kensington, ENG, City & Guilds College *Hookfoot, Al Stewart, Wild Angels, Linda Lewis, Dando Shaft*

2/19/1972 Leicester, ENG, Leicester Polytechnic

2/21/1972 Wolverhampton, ENG, Civic Hall

2/22/1972 Bangor, WLS, University of Wales

2/23/1972 Aberystwyth, WLS, University of Wales

2/24/1972 Chelterham, ENG, Chelterham Hall

2/25/1972 Reading, ENG, Reading University, Top Rank Suite *Lindisfarne, Hookfoot*

2/26/1972 Hull, ENG, Hull University

3/2/1972 Warwick, ENG, Warwick University

3/3/1972 Durham, ENG, Durham University

3/4/1972 Loughborough, ENG, Loughborough University

3/8/1972 Essex, ENG, Harlow Technical College

3/10/1972 London, ENG, Rainbow Theatre *Hookfoot, Trapeze*

3/16/1972 Boston, MA, Aquarius Theater *Black Oak Arkansas*

3/17/1972 New York, NY, Academy of Music *Sweathog, Black Oak Arkansas*

3/18/1972 New York, NY, Academy of Music *Sweathog, Black Oak Arkansas*

3/20/1972 New Haven, CT, New Haven Arena *J. Geils Band, Alexis Koerner*

3/23/1972 Brookville, NY, C.W. Post College

3/24/1972 Buffalo, NY, Memorial Auditorium *King Crimson, Sweathog*

3/25/1972 Bangor, ME, Municipal Auditorium

3/26/1972 Alexandria, VA, Alexandria Roller Rink (2 shows 3:00 pm & 8:30 pm) *King Crimson*

3/30/1972 Louisville, KY

3/31/1972 Cincinnati, OH, Music Hall

4/1/1972 Cleveland, OH, Public Hall *J. Geils Band, Five Man Electrical Band*

4/2/1972 Dayton, OH, Hara Arena *J. Geils Band, Five Man Electrical Band*

4/3/1972 Hershey, PA

4/4/1972 Orlando, FL, Kemp Coliseum

4/5/1972 Tampa, FL, Bayfront Arena

4/6/1972 Atlanta, GA, Municipal Auditorium

4/7/1972 Miami, FL, Auditorium

4/8/1972 New Orleans, LA, Warehouse *Alexis Koerner*

4/9/1972 Detroit, MI, Cobo Arena *Edgar Winter's White Trash Band, Dr. John*

4/11/1972 Chicago, IL, Arie Crown Theater *Snape (Alexis Koerner, Peter Thorup, Ian Wallace, Mel Collins & Boz Burrell)*

4/12/1972 St. Louis, MO, Keil Auditorium

4/13/1972 St. Paul, MN, Auditorium

4/14/1972 San Diego, CA, Sports Arena *Sweathog*

4/15/1972 Santa Monica, CA, Civic Auditorium *Sweathog*

4/16/1972 Long Beach, CA, Auditorium *Sweathog*

4/17/1972 Phoenix, AZ, Travelodge Theater *Loggins & Messina*

4/20/1972 Salt Lake City, UT, Salt Palace

4/21/1972 San Francisco, SF, Winterland *Edgar Winter, Osibisa*

4/22/1972 San Francisco, SF, Winterland *Edgar Winter, Osibisa*

4/23/1972 Honolulu, HI, Civic Auditorium *Procol Harum, Deep Purple*

5/29/1972 Lincoln, ENG, Great Western Express Festival *Joe Cocker, Genesis, Vinegar Joe, Jackson Heights*

6/22/1972 Baltimore, MD, Civic Center *Edgar Winter*

6/23/1972 Pittsburgh, PA, Three Rivers Stadium cancelled due to flooding *Alice Cooper, Uriah Heep, Groundhogs*

6/26/1972 Toronto, ON, Maple Leaf Gardens *Groundhogs, Edgar Winter*

6/29/1972 Saratoga Springs, NY, Saratoga Springs Arts Center

7/1/1972 Tampa, FL, Tampa Stadium *Three Dog Night (HL), Bang*

7/2/1972 Memphis, TN, Memphis-Ellis Auditorium

7/4/1972 New Orleans, LA, Warehouse *Ramatam*

7/6/1972 New York, NY, Gaelic Park (cancelled & rescheduled) *Groundhogs, Edgar Winter*

7/8/1972 Long Pond, PA, Pocono International Raceway *Black Sabbath, Three Dog Night, Emerson, Lake & Palmer, The Faces, J. Geils Band, Badfinger, Cactus, Edgar Winter, Bull Angus, Mother Night, Savoy Brown, Groundhogs, Claire Hamill & Ramatam*

7/10/1972 Greensboro, NC, Coliseum *Eagles, Black Oak Arkansas*

7/11/1972 Rochester, NY, War Memorial *Edgar Winter, Heads, Hands & Feet*

7/11/1972 Pittsburgh, PA, Three Rivers Stadium *Alice Cooper, Uriah Heep, John Kay*

7/12/1972 Wildwood, NJ, Wildwood Convention Hall

7/13/1972 Syracuse, NY, War Memorial

7/15/1972 Asbury Park, NJ, Convention Hall (2 shows 7:30 pm & 10:00 pm)

7/17/1972 Akron, OH, Rubber Bowl *Black Sabbath, Edgar Winter, Ramatam (Groundhogs cancelled)*

8/22/1972 New York, NY, Gaelic Park *Ramatam, Edgar Winter*

8/24/1972 Kansas City, MO, Municipal Auditorium *ZZ Top, Ramatam*

8/25/1972 Tulsa City, OK, Assembly Center *ZZ Top*

8/28/1972 San Antonio, TX, Municipal Auditorium *Malo, Ramatam*

9/3/1972 San Diego, CA, Community Concourse *Boz Scaggs, Slade*

9/4/1972 Long Beach, CA, Arena *Boz Scaggs*

9/8/1972 Berkeley, CA, Community Theatre

9/9/1972 Santa Clara, CA, Fairgrounds *Elvin Bishop*

9/12/1972 Chicago, IL, Arie Crown *Slade*

9/15/1972 Philadelphia, PA, Spectrum *J. Geils Band, Slade*

9/17/1972 Boston, MA, Music Hall *Slade*

10/27/1972 Waltham, ENG, Forest Tech

10/29/1972 London, ENG, Coliseum *Frampton's Camel*

10/31/1972 Manchester, ENG, Free Trade Hall *Frampton's Camel*

11/1/1972 Newcastle, ENG, Odeon

11/2/1972 Glasgow, SCT, Green's Playhouse

11/3/1972 Liverpool, ENG, Top Rank

11/5/1972 Bristol, ENG, Top Rank

11/6/1972 Birmingham, ENG, Town Hall

11/7/1972 Sheffield, ENG, City Hall

11/14/1972 Nuremberg, DEU, Messehalle

11/15/1972 Boeblingen, DEU, Sporthalle

11/17/1972 Berlin, DEU, Sportpalast

11/27/1972 Dusseldorf, DEU, Rheinhalle

11/29/1972 Ludwigshafen, DEU, Friedrich-Ebert-Halle

11/30/1972 Hamburg, DEU, Musikhalle

12/1/1972 Frankfurt, DEU, Festhalle

12/2/1972 Munich, DEU, Circus Krone

12/3/1972 New York, NY, Academy of Music *Aerosmith, Edgar Winter*

12/8/1972 Shreveport, LA

12/9/1972 Chattanooga, TN, Memorial Auditorium *Roxy Music*

12/10/1972 Charleston, W. VA, Civic Center *Flash, Roxy Music*

12/12/1972 Detroit, MI, Cobo Arena *J. Geils Band (no show), Roxy Music, Night Crawler*

12/13/1972 Louisville, KY

12/14/1972 Atlanta, GA

12/15/1972 Miami, FL, Sportatorium *J. Geils Band*

12/16/1972 Orlando, FL, Orlando Sports Stadium *J. Geils Band*

12/17/1972 Tampa, FL, Curtis Hixon Hall *J. Geils Band, Marc Benno*

12/31/1972 Toronto, ON, Maple Leaf Gardens *Sha Na Na, April Wine, Lighthouse, Grin*

1973

3/23/1973 Chicago, IL, International Amphitheatre

3/24/1973 Kansas City, MO, Municipal Auditorium *Black Oak Arkansas*

3/25/1973 Tempe, AZ, Big Surf *Foghat, Boz Scaggs*

3/27/1973 Denver, CO, Coliseum *Foghat, Boz Scaggs*

3/28/1973 Albuquerque, NM, Civic Auditorium *Foghat*

3/29/1973 Oklahoma City, OK, Fairgrounds Arena *Foghat, Jo Jo Gunne*

3/30/1973 Dallas, TX

3/31/1973 Houston, TX

4/1/1973 Corpus Christi, TX, Memorial Coliseum

4/4/1973 Lincoln, NE, Pershing Munich Auditorium *Foghat*

4/5/1973 Macomb, IL, Western Illinois University

4/6/1973 Knoxville, TN, Coliseum *Foghat, Gentle Giant*

4/6/1973 Bloomington, IN, Indiana University

4/7/1973 Roanoke, VA, Civic Center *Foghat, Gentle Giant*

4/8/1973 Hampton Roads, VA, Coliseum *Foghat, Gentle Giant*

4/10/1973 Boston, MA, Music Hall *Foghat*

4/11/1973 Hershey, PA

4/11/1973 Syracuse, NY

4/12/1973 Rochester, NY, War Memorial *Spooky Tooth, Tranquility*

4/13/1973 Buffalo, NY, Memorial Auditorium *Spooky Tooth, Tranquility*

4/14/1973 Cincinnati, OH, Cincinnati Gardens *Gentle Giant, Edgar Winter Band*

4/15/1973 Baltimore, MD, Civic Center *Gentle Giant, Edgar Winter Band*

5/X/1973 Sacramento, CA, Convention Center

5/3/1973 Los Angeles, CA, Forum *Barbara Mauritz (singer for Lamb)*

5/4/1973 Los Angeles, CA, Forum *Barbara Mauritz (singer for Lamb)*

5/5/1973 San Francisco, SF, Winterland *Slade, Steely Dan*

5/6/1973 San Francisco, SF, Winterland *Slade, Steely Dan*

5/12/1973 Osaka, JPN, Koseinenkin Kaikan

5/14/1973 Nagoya, JPN, Nagoyashi Kokaido

5/15/1973 Tokyo, JPN, Koseinenkin Kaikan

5/16/1973 Tokyo, JPN

5/19/1973 Honolulu, HI, H.I.C. Arena

5/22/1973 Des Moines, IA, Veterans Memorial Auditorium

5/23/1973 Detroit, MI, Cobo Hall

5/24/1973 Detroit, MI, Cobo Hall

5/25/1973 Philadelphia, PA, Spectrum *Black Oak Arkansas, Spooky Tooth*

5/26/1973 Cleveland, OH, Public Hall *Black Oak Arkansas*

5/29/1973 New York, NY, Madison Square Garden *Black Oak Arkansas*

6/16/1973 Boblingen, DEU, Sporthalle

6/18/1973 Munich, DEU, Circus Krone

6/19/1973 Offenbach, DEU, Stadthalle

6/20/1973 Offenbach, DEU, Stadthalle

6/22/1973 Mannheim, DEU, Eisstadion

6/24/1973 Hamburg, DEU, Erst-Nerck-Halle

7/6/1973 Hartford, CT, Dillon Stadium *J. Geils Band, Frampton's Camel*

7/7/1973 Greensboro, NC, Coliseum *J. Geils Band, Frampton's Camel*

7/8/1973 Chester, WV, Waterford Park *J. Geils Band, Black Oak Arkansas, Frampton's Camel*

7/12/1973 Toronto, ON, Varsity Stadium *Leslie West Wild West Show, Fludd*

7/14/1973 Asbury Park, NJ, Convention Hall

7/15/1973 Columbia, MD, Merriweather Post Pavilion

7/20/1973 Madison, WI, Dane County Coliseum *Frampton's Camel*

7/21/1973 Milwaukee, WI (Summerfest)

7/22/1973 St. Louis, MO, Kiel Auditorium *Leslie West's Wild West Show, Bachman-Turner Overdrive*

7/23/1973 St. Petersburg, FL

7/24/1973 Charlotte, NC, Coliseum

7/25/1973 Memphis, TN, Mid-South Coliseum *T. Rex, Hydra*

7/26/1973 New Orleans, LA, Municipal Coliseum

7/28/1973 Savannah, GA, Coliseum

7/29/1973 Birmingham, AL, Rickwood Field

7/30/1973 Jacksonville, FL, Coliseum

10/24/1973 Glasgow, SCT, Apollo Centre *Heavy Metal Kids*

10/27/1973 London, ENG, Edmonton Sundown *Heavy Metal Kids*

10/28/1973 London, ENG, Edmonton Sundown *Heavy Metal Kids*

10/30/1973 Manchester, ENG, Hard Rock *Heavy Metal Kids*

10/31/1973 Birmingham, ENG, Odeon *Heavy Metal Kids*

11/15/1973 Los Angeles, CA, Forum *Foghat, James Montgomery Band*

11/16/1973 San Diego, CA, Sports Arena *Foghat, Maggie Bell*

11/17/1973 San Jose, CA, Santa Clara County Fairgrounds *Foghat*

11/18/1973 Bakersfield, CA *Foghat*

11/19/1973 Fresno, CA, Selland Arena *Foghat, Electric Light Orchestra*

11/21/1973 Salt Lake City, UT, Salt Palace *Foghat*

11/22/1973 Salt Lake City, UT, Salt Palace (original date) *Foghat, James Montgomery Band*

11/23/1973 Portland. OR, Paramount Theater

11/24/1973 Seattle, WA, Paramount Theater

11/27/1973 Denver, CO, Coliseum

11/28/1973 Omaha, NE, Civic Auditorium

11/29/1973 Tulsa, OK, Assembly Center

11/30/1973 Ft. Worth, TX, Tarrant County Convention Center *Foghat*

12/2/1973 San Antonio, TX, Municipal Auditorium *Foghat, John Martyn*

12/3/1973 Houston, TX, Sam Houston Coliseum *Foghat*

12/6/1973 Dayton, OH, Hara Arena

12/7/1973 Ann Arbor, MI, University of Michigan

12/8/1973 Indianapolis, IN, Fairgrounds Coliseum *Frampton's Camel, Ronnie Montrose*

12/9/1973 Chicago, IL, International Amphitheater *Frampton's Camel*

1974

2/15/1974 Orlando, FL *Spooky Tooth*

2/16/1974 Miami, FL *Spooky Tooth*

2/17/1974 Tampa, FL, Curtis Hixon *Spooky Tooth, Montrose*

2/19/1974 Mobile, AL *Spooky Tooth*

2/19/1974 New Haven, CT

2/21/1974 Hampton, VA, Coliseum *Spooky Tooth*

2/22/1974 Richmond, VA, University of Richmond, Robins Center *Spooky Tooth*

2/24/1974 Baltimore, MD, Civic Center *Spooky Tooth*

2/25/1974 Toledo, OH, Sports Arena

2/26/1974 Toledo, OH *Spooky Tooth*

2/27/1974 St. Louis, MO, Kiel Auditorium *Spooky Tooth*

3/1/1974 Terre Haute, IN *Spooky Tooth, Montrose*

3/3/1974 Knoxville, TN *Spooky Tooth, Montrose*

3/4/1974 Chattanooga, TN, Municipal Auditorium *Spooky Tooth, Montrose*

3/6/1974 Uniondale, NY, Nassau Coliseum *Spooky Tooth, Montrose*

3/8/1974 Hershey, PA, Hersheypark Arena *Spooky Tooth, Montrose*

3/9/1974 Binghampton, NY, Convention Center *Spooky Tooth, Montrose*

3/11/1974 Boston, MA, Music Hall *Spooky Tooth, Montrose*

3/13/1974 Buffalo, NY, Memorial Auditorium *Spooky Tooth, Montrose*

3/14/1974 Flint, MI, I.M.A. Auditorium *Spooky Tooth, Montrose*

3/17/1974 Columbia, SC, University of South Carolina *Spooky Tooth, Montrose*

3/18/1974 Atlanta, GA, The Omni *Spooky Tooth, Montrose*

3/22/1974 Memphis, TN, Ellis Auditorium North Hall *Spooky Tooth, Montrose*

5/18/1974 Charlton, ENG, Charlton Athletic Field *Who, Lou Reed, Bad Company, Lindisfarne, Dave Mason, Maggie Bell*

6/6/1974 London, ENG, Rainbow Theatre

7/6/1974 Buxton, ENG, Booth Farm (Buxton Festival) *Faces, Chapman/Whitney, Strider, Trapeze, Badger, Blue*

9/20/1974 Bracknell, ENG, Sports Centre

9/21/1974 Essex, ENG, Southend-On-Sea, The Kursaal

9/27/1974 Eppelheim, DEU, Rhein-Neckar-Halle *Electric Light Orchestra, Black Oak Arkansas, Chapman + Whitney*

9/28/1974 Dortmund, DEU, Westfallenhalle *Rory Gallagher, Electric Light Orchestra, Black Oak Arkansas, Chapman + Whitney, Johnny Rivers Boogie Band, Peter Frampton, Bo Hansson, Geordie*

10/15/1974 Munich, DEU

10/31/1974 Birmingham, ENG, Odeon *McGuinness Flint*

11/1/1974 Portsmouth, ENG, Guildhall *McGuinness Flint*

11/2/1974 Oxford, ENG, Polytechnic *McGuinness Flint*

11/3/1974 Bristol, ENG, Hippodrome *McGuinness Flint*

11/4/1974 Plymouth, ENG, Guildhall *McGuinness Flint*

11/5/1974 Bournemouth, ENG, Winter Gardens *McGuinness Flint*

11/7/1974 Sheffield, ENG, City Hall *McGuinness Flint*

11/8/1974 Leeds, ENG, Leeds University *McGuinness Flint*

11/9/1974 East Ham, ENG, Granada *McGuinness Flint*

11/10/1974 Croydon, ENG, Fairfield Hall *McGuinness Flint*

11/11/1974 Swansea, ENG, Top Rank *McGuinness Flint*

11/14/1974 London, ENG, Hammersmith Odeon (cancelled) *McGuinness Flint*

11/15/1974 London, ENG, Hammersmith Odeon *McGuinness Flint*

11/17/1974 Glasgow, SCT, Apollo *McGuinness Flint*

11/18/1974 Newcastle, ENG, Odeon *McGuinness Flint*

11/19/1974 Preston, ENG, Guildhall *McGuinness Flint*

11/20/1974 Manchester, ENG, Free Trade Hall *McGuinness Flint*

11/21/1974 Cardiff, WLS, Capitol *McGuinness Flint*

11/22/1974 Uxbridge, ENG, Brunei University *McGuinness Flint*

12/5/1974 Cologne, DEU, Messehalle

12/9/1974 Paris, FRA, Olympia

12/15/1974 Boblingen, DEU, Sporthalle *Focus, Thin Lizzy*

1975

2/14/1975 Pittsburgh, PA, Civic Arena *REO Speedwagon*

2/15/1975 New York, NY, Academy of Music (2 shows)

2/16/1975 Buffalo, NY, Kleinhan's Music Hall

2/17/1975 Detroit, MI, Cobo Hall *Flash Cadillac & The Continental Kids*

2/19/1975 Atlanta, GA, Municipal Auditorium

2/21/1975 Pittsburgh, PA, Civic Arena *REO Speedwagon*

2/22/1975 Boston, MA, Orpheum Theater

2/24/1975 Chicago, IL, International Amphitheater *Montrose, Babe Ruth*

2/25/1975 Madison, WI, Dane County Coliseum *Babe Ruth, Brownsville Station*

2/28/1975 New Orleans, LA, The Warehouse

2/29/1975 St. Louis, MO, Kiel Auditorium *Montrose*

3/3/1975 San Diego, CA, Sports Arena (cancelled)

3/5/1975 Fresno, CA, Selland Arena *Robin Trower*

3/6/1975 Long Beach, CA, Arena *Journey, Iron Butterfly*

3/7/1975 San Francisco, CA, Winterland *Pavlov's Dog, Iron Butterfly*

3/8/1975 San Francisco, CA, Winterland *Pavlov's Dog, Iron Butterfly*

3/9/1975 Sacramento, CA, Community Center Exhibit Hall

3/12/1975 Charleston, WV, Civic Center *John Entwistle's Ox*

3/13/1975 Louisville, KY, Convention Hall

3/14/1975 Memphis, TN, Auditorium North Hall

3/15/1975 Philadelphia, PA, Spectrum *John Entwistle's Ox*

3/16/1975 Columbus, OH, Veterans Memorial Auditorium

3/19/1975 Dallas, TX, Memorial Auditorium *Robin Trower*

3/21/1975 San Antonio, TX, Municipal Auditorium *Robin Trower*

3/22/1975 Tulsa, OK *Robin Trower*

3/23/1975 Houston, TX, Music Hall *Robin Trower*

Drum Kit Diagrams

by Jon Cohan, with Jerry Shirley

"Bitza" drum kit circa 1961-62

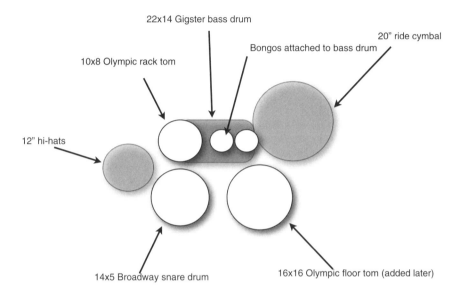

22x14 Gigster bass drum

20" ride cymbal

Bongos attached to bass drum

10x8 Olympic rack tom

12" hi-hats

14x5 Broadway snare drum

16x16 Olympic floor tom (added later)

Premier drum kit circa 1964 - Black Duroplastic finish

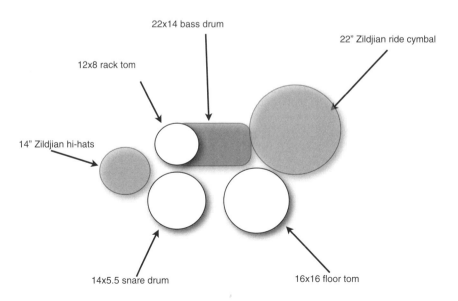

22x14 bass drum

22" Zildjian ride cymbal

12x8 rack tom

14" Zildjian hi-hats

14x5.5 snare drum

16x16 floor tom

1965 Ludwig Super Classic drum kit - Sparkling Siver Pearl

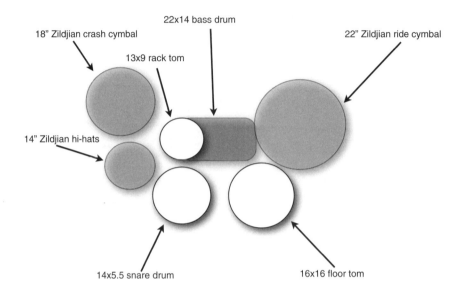

22x14 bass drum

18" Zildjian crash cymbal

22" Zildjian ride cymbal

13x9 rack tom

14" Zildjian hi-hats

14x5.5 snare drum

16x16 floor tom

1st Humble Pie kit - Ludwig Super Classic drum kit circa 1969 Sparkling Silver Pearl

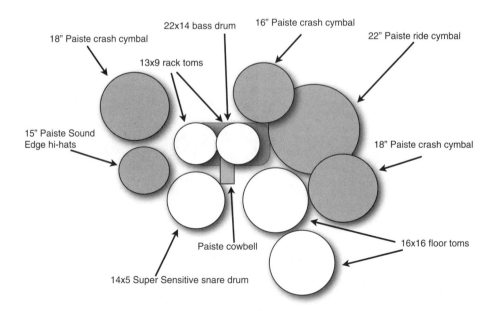

22x14 bass drum

16" Paiste crash cymbal

18" Paiste crash cymbal

22" Paiste ride cymbal

13x9 rack toms

15" Paiste Sound Edge hi-hats

18" Paiste crash cymbal

Paiste cowbell

16x16 floor toms

14x5 Super Sensitive snare drum

2nd Humble Pie kit - Ludwig drum kit 1970 - 1972
Sparkling Pink Champagne Pearl

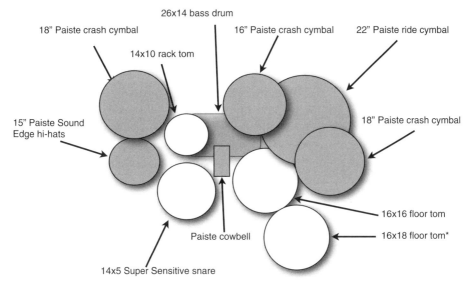

26x14 bass drum

18" Paiste crash cymbal

16" Paiste crash cymbal

22" Paiste ride cymbal

14x10 rack tom

15" Paiste Sound Edge hi-hats

18" Paiste crash cymbal

16x16 floor tom

16x18 floor tom*

Paiste cowbell

14x5 Super Sensitive snare

*Jerry says the very unusual 16" diameter x 18" deep floor tom came with the kit, which he got from the Sam Ash store in NYC.

3rd Humble Pie kit - Ludwig drum kit 1972
custom hand-painted "Rose" finish*

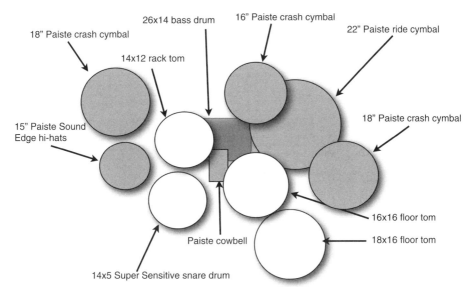

26x14 bass drum

16" Paiste crash cymbal

22" Paiste ride cymbal

18" Paiste crash cymbal

14x12 rack tom

15" Paiste Sound Edge hi-hats

18" Paiste crash cymbal

16x16 floor tom

18x16 floor tom

Paiste cowbell

14x5 Super Sensitive snare drum

Jerry says this kit was originally painted a custom "matte white by Ludwig, and I played it that way for a while. I eventually had the roses hand-painted on it in 1973/74 by a guy at Ludwig who worked in the publicity department, if I remember correctly. I think they charged me $70 for the whole paint job." In addition, Jerry used a Speed King bass drum pedal and Ludwig Ringo Starr drumsticks.

About the Author

Photo by Dr. Ben Middleton

Jerry Shirley was born February 4, 1952, in Waltham Cross, North London. At just 16, he was recruited by noted vocalist and guitarist Steve Marriott, along with Peter Frampton and Greg Ridley, to join the newly-formed Humble Pie. Shirley remained Humble Pie's drummer throughout the group's entire career. He also worked on Steve Marriott's solo projects and was a co-founder of the popular 1980s group Fastway. He is also known for his session work with Syd Barrett, B.B. King, John Entwistle, Sammy Hagar, and others. From 1988 to 1999, Shirley fronted a reformed Humble Pie in the US. During this period, he also worked as a disc jockey at WNCX in Cleveland, Ohio. Shirley returned to the UK in 1999, and in 2000, he reformed Humble Pie with original bassist Greg Ridley; mid-period former member, guitarist and vocalist Bobby Tench; and Dave "Bucket" Colwell. Recently, Shirley has performed with the Deborah Bonham Band. He resides in Cornwall, England.

About the Editor

Photo by Elizabeth Carnegie

Tim Cohan's writing career began at 14, when he wrote a teen column for the Lansing, Michigan, *State Journal*, the same newspaper he had delivered as a paperboy two years earlier. He went on to write for a variety of other newspapers and magazines before moving into advertising, marketing, and public relations, where he wrote award-winning copy for some of the world's largest companies and organizations. Cohan is also a songwriter and musician, playing guitar, bass, and keyboards. His current project is *Golden Tiger Edward*, the debut album from his musical collaborator, Wilson Quick. He lives in Ann Arbor, Michigan.

Editor's Note

When my brother, Jon, called to ask me if I wanted to take over editing this wonderful book from him (because he had decided to go back to school and wouldn't have the time to do it), I didn't have to think for more than a nanosecond before I split his ear with a near-falsetto "Yes!" As a Humble Pie fan who, back in the day, owned several of the band's LPs on the original vinyl—and as a connosieur of British rock in general—the prospect of working with *Jerry Freakin' Shirley* was a thrill beyond compare.

Imagine my delight, then, when Jerry turned out to be as nice a guy as I've ever known. And not just nice, but also incredibly enthusiastic, funny, caring, and—yes—humble. The truly remarkable thing about this book is that, before he wrote it, Jerry had never before used so much as a typewriter, much less a computer. This is a man who left school at a very young age to pursue his musical dream (which, as we know, he achieved, and then some), and who therefore didn't have a complete educational grounding in the niceties of grammar, syntax, and other aspects of the English language.

Yet, despite his own reservations about his writing skills, Jerry has written what could well be the definitive exemplar of the rock-star-memoirs genre. But it's also very different than most of its predecessors: there is nothing jaded here, no self-serving spin, no moaning about how genius is pain. Jerry's energy, honesty, and love—for the music and for the people he made it with—jump out from every page.

Tim Cohan
Ann Arbor, Michigan
July 2011

Editor's Acknowledgements

To Jerry: thank you, dear boy, for *everything*. Bless you, your heart, and your cotton socks. To the rest of the team: Jon, for bringing me on board ("Who's my buddy? Who's my pal?"); Brad, for believing in me and wanting this book to be a calling card for me; Rob, for being very, very patient; and Nicole and Linda, for making the inside and cover, respectively, real purdy. To my family, near and far, for a lifetime of love, especially my father, Leon; sister, Nicole; nephew, Charlie; and niece, Leila. To my dear departed mother, Heidi; and my Uncle George and Aunt Pearl, both of whom passed away during my work on this book. To other loved ones and friends for their support and encouragement, especially Miriam, Wilson, Rich, Liz, Jack, Sveta, and Tina. And to HMS Humble Pie and all who sailed in and with her, for the music—past, present, and future. No semicolons were harmed in the making of this book.

Index

REBEATS PUBLICATIONS
distributed by Hal Leonard Corp.

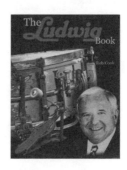

THE ROGERS BOOK
by Rob Cook
Business history,
dating guide

THE LUDWIG BOOK
by Rob Cook
Business history,
dating guide

THE MAKING OF A
DRUM COMPANY
The autobiography of
Wm. F. Ludwig II,
with Rob Cook

THE BABY DODDS
STORY
Autobiography of Baby
Dodds, as told to Larry
Gara

THE SLINGERLAND
BOOK
by Rob Cook
Business history,
dating guide

HAL BLAINE & THE
WRECKING CREW
Autobiography of Hal
Blaine, with Mr. Bonzai

GENE KRUPA, HIS
LIFE AND TIMES
biography of Gene
Krupa, by Bruce
Crowther

TRAPS, THE DRUM
WONDER
biography of
Buddy Rich,
by Mel Torme

The Insiders' Guide to Factual Filmmaking

The Insiders' Guide to Factual Filmmaking is an accessible and comprehensive 'how to' guide about the craft of making documentaries for TV, online or social media. Filmmaker Tony Stark distils a long career at the BBC and as an independent producer to explain the conceptual, visual, editorial and organizational skills needed to make impactful and stylish factual films.

Interviews with top industry professionals in the UK and US – commissioners, executive producers, filmmakers, strand editors and media lawyers – add valuable insight and authority to this book. For more experienced filmmakers *The Insiders' Guide* tells you how to get the green light for undercover investigations, how to tell film stories online and on social media, and how to budget a factual film.

This is a key text for anyone who wants to succeed in the rapidly changing, competitive freelance markets in Britain and America. It provides expert guidance to students on filmmaking courses, journalists wanting to move from print to video and non-professionals with an interest in filmmaking. Whatever the final destination of your film – and whatever the budget – *The Insiders' Guide* provides a vital roadmap.

The book's accompanying website is a 'show-me' resource for new directors: with 24 specially-shot film clips illustrating the key rules of filmic grammar and sequence shooting – together with downloadable versions of essential production forms.

Tony Stark is a documentary filmmaker, executive producer and former BBC commissioner with a 30-year career making high profile documentary films and series for broadcast television, specializing in investigative filmmaking. His films have been shown on the BBC, Channel Four, ITV, Al Jazeera, American PBS channels and many European TV channels. His programmes have been nominated for several industry awards: a BAFTA, the Foreign Press Association Media Awards, the Association for International Broadcasting and the San Francisco International Film Festival. For more information go to moonstonefilms.co.uk